WORLD HISTORY
SOCIETIES OF THE PAST

Charles Kahn

Ken Osborne

Maureen McCulloch

Norman Lee

John Einarson

PORTAGE & MAIN PRESS

First edition, 1992
Second edition, 2005

Portage & Main Press acknowledges the financial support of the Government of Canada through the Book Publishing Industry Development Program (BPIDP) for our activities.

Printed and bound in Canada by Friesens.

08 09 10 11 5 4 3 2

LIBRARY AND ARCHIVES CANADA CATALOGUING IN PUBLICATION

World history : societies of the past / Charles Kahn ... [et al.].

First ed. had title: People through the ages.
Includes bibliographical references and index.
ISBN 1-55379-045-6

1. History – Textbooks.   I. Kahn, Charles, 1945-   II. Title: People through the ages.

D21.P44 2005   909   C2005-903415-7

Editor: Leigh Hambly
Project conception and direction, first edition: Kahn and Associates
Book and cover design, second edition: Relish Design Studio Ltd.
Book and cover design, first edition: Pat Stanton
Cover illustration: David Morrow
Illustrations: David Morrow (all, except as noted); Jess Dixon (figures 1.9, 1.16)
Maps: Marcie Seidler
Photo research and acquisition: Pat Paige

ACKNOWLEDGMENTS

The publisher would like to thank the following individuals who reviewed the text and illustrations for accuracy and suitability:

Gerry Bowler, University of Manitoba; Christopher Frank, University of Manitoba; Henry Heller, University of Manitoba; David Howorth, University of Manitoba; Sid Kroker, Quaternary Consultants; William Lee, University of Manitoba; Eliakim M. Sibanda, University of Winnipeg; Vaitheespara Ravindiran, University of Manitoba; Greg Smith, University of Manitoba; Daniel Stone, University of Winnipeg; Raymond Wiest, University of Manitoba.

The publisher would also like to thank the following educators and individuals for their contributions to this project: Linda Connor, Sharon Conway, Barb Evans, Marilyn Mackay, Linda McDowell, Gary Perrett, Saira Rahman.

A special thank you to Gary Evans for his substantial contribution to this project.

PORTAGE & MAIN PRESS

100-318 McDermot Ave.
Winnipeg, MB Canada R3A 0A2
Tel: 204-987-3500
Toll free: 1-800-667-9673
Toll-free fax: 1-866-734-8477

ENVIRONMENTAL BENEFITS STATEMENT

Portage & Main Press saved the following resources by printing the pages of this book on chlorine free paper made with 30% post-consumer waste.

TREES	WATER	ENERGY	SOLID WASTE	GREENHOUSE GASES
27	9,765	19	1,254	2,353
FULLY GROWN	GALLONS	MILLION BTUs	POUNDS	POUNDS

Calculations based on research by Environmental Defense and the Paper Task Force.
Manufactured at Friesens Corporation

Mixed Sources
Product group from well-managed forests, and recycled wood or fibre
www.fsc.org Cert no. SW-COC-1271
© 1996 Forest Stewardship Council

Contents

Getting to Know Your Textbook

What Is Inside

This introduction is important. Read it for hints on how best to use the textbook. You will probably spend a lot of time looking for information in this book, so the more familiar you are with it, the more useful it will be.

Look at the cover of your book. The title, *World History: Societies of the Past*, tells you what the book is about. The figure outlines give you clues about some of the people you will be reading about. Do you recognize any of them? Do you know what period of time they are from? Write down the name of anyone you recognize. Examine the cover again at the end of the school year, and see how many more names you have come to know.

The table of contents, page 1, shows you that the book is divided into five parts and fifteen chapters. The chapter titles give you information about several societies, from the time of early peoples through to 1850. If you look at page 3, you can see a world map that shows the location of all of the societies you will learn about in this book. Each part has a world map that highlights the locations of the societies you will study in that section. You will also find timelines to give you some idea about what was going on in each society during that period. Be sure to check the map and timelines as you read each part.

Flip through the textbook, and you will see many colourful illustrations – paintings, maps, diagrams, and drawings. The visuals will help you see what was happening in each period of time. Wherever possible, the pictures are from works created by someone who was alive then. In very early times, paintings or statues that could show us what life was like are not available. Instead, an artist has created illustrations especially for this book. The artist has used historical information to prepare the illustrations to give you an idea of what things *might* have looked like during that time.

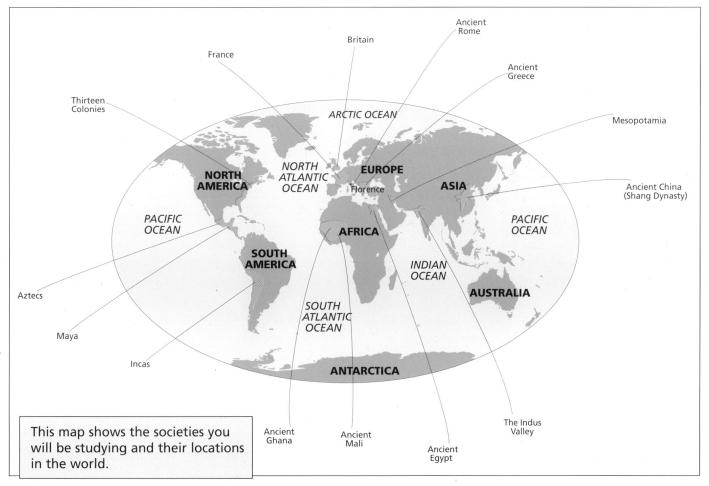

France
Britain
Ancient Rome
Ancient Greece
Thirteen Colonies
Mesopotamia
ARCTIC OCEAN
NORTH ATLANTIC OCEAN
EUROPE
Florence
ASIA
Ancient China (Shang Dynasty)
NORTH AMERICA
PACIFIC OCEAN
AFRICA
PACIFIC OCEAN
Aztecs
SOUTH AMERICA
INDIAN OCEAN
AUSTRALIA
Maya
SOUTH ATLANTIC OCEAN
Incas
ANTARCTICA
Ancient Ghana
Ancient Mali
Ancient Egypt
The Indus Valley

This map shows the societies you will be studying and their locations in the world.

It is easier to find paintings of important people of a society than it is to find pictures of the ordinary workers and poor people. Keep in mind that some of the powerful people may not have looked exactly as the paintings show them. If a king were paying you to paint his portrait or his family's picture, would you dare show any of them in an unflattering way?

Visuals make the book interesting, and while they are not always accurate, they also provide you with useful information. Examine the pictures and read the captions. They provide information that you will not find anywhere else in the textbook.

Two icons, or symbols, are used throughout the textbook. One, a starburst, alerts you to little-known historical facts about people, places, and events. For example, you can find out how North America and South America got their names.

The starburst icon looks like this:

The other icon is a symbol of Seshat, the Egyptian goddess of writing and archives. This icon appears wherever you can "be an historian." This section, which appears at the end of most chapters, shows you how to think like an historian. In Be an Historian, you can read excerpts from real letters, speeches, and articles written during the time period you have just studied.

The Seshat symbol looks like this:

The captions and information boxes often contain things that most people do not know. Now is your chance to amaze your family and friends with all your knowledge!

As you are reading the textbook, you will come across words in **bold type**. These are words and phrases that may be new to you and are explained in the Glossary.

Following the Glossary, you will find the Index. An index is an alphabetical list of the important words and ideas from the book, with page numbers beside the words. Use the Index to locate information about a particular person, place, event, or idea.

Getting Information from the Chapters

A colourful drawing runs across the top of the first two pages of each chapter. In chapter 2, "The Early Peoples," for example, you can see a mastodon at the top of the left page. In chapter 8, "Ancient Rome," a drawing of the Colosseum appears at the top of the left page. These images are important symbols of the society discussed in the chapter. In time, you will probably be able to identify each society just by looking at these drawings.

Each chapter begins with the heading, Our Study of…. This section is a preview of some of the topics you will be learning about. The list may help you recall something you already know about the society. The list may also help you make comparison to other societies you are studying in the textbook.

You will find a shaded box at the beginning of each chapter called, Questions to Think About. There are no right or wrong answers to the questions. These questions are to help you focus on certain things as you read through the chapter. The box looks like this:

Questions to Think About

+ Since we cannot travel back in time, how do we know anything for certain about what happened in the past?

+ How can we be sure that what we think we know about the past is accurate?

+ How does the past shape the ways we think about the present and the future?

+ Is it important to know about what happened in the past? Why or why not?

History is full of difficult words and names – often from other languages. The first time these kinds of words are used, they are in italics. To help you say them, the pronunciations are provided in square brackets. For example, a cluster of homes and land in a Maya town is called a *calpulli* [kahl-POO-lee]. The pronunciation is given the first time the word appears in the text.

Each topic in the chapter is organized into short sections of one page or less. The heading at the beginning of each section lets you know what you will be reading about.

Most chapters have a story or two that gives you more details about everyday people and events than you will find in the general text. Did you know that for most of history, people of your age were considered adults, and there was no such thing as teenagers? The stories will help you make comparisons between your life and life in earlier times.

Each chapter ends with a short Summary and a Connecting and Reflecting question. Try to imagine what the world would be like if the society you have just read about had never existed. How would your life be different? Spend some time making a connection between your life today and life back then.

Numbering the Years

As you begin to read this textbook, you need to pay attention to the way in which the years have been numbered. You will find that most dates are followed by the letters BCE or CE. What do these letters mean?

The calendar used by most of the Western world was developed during the time of Julius Caesar. His calendar, called the Julian calendar, was based on the time it takes the earth to revolve around the sun. This is called a *solar year*. A normal year in the Julian calendar has 365 days. Every fourth year is a Leap Year, with 366 days. Over the centuries, the Julian calendar was adapted to fit a Christian culture.

At some point, people had to decide *when* to start numbering years. The system we use was established in the 16th century. That was when Pope Gregory XIII decided to start numbering years, beginning with the year in which Jesus Christ was thought to have been born. The years before the date of Christ's birth were designated B.C. ("before Christ"). The years after Christ's birth were designated A.D., from the Latin words *anno Domini* ("in the year of the Lord"). Our calendar, a modified version of the Julian calendar, is called the Gregorian calendar (after Pope Gregory).

Some people argue that B.C. and A.D. should not be used because the letters are based on a Christian idea. As you know, many people in the world use other calendars. For example:

- Jewish religious holidays are based on an ancient Hebrew calendar. The calendar begins with the year 3761 B.C., the year in which Jews used to believe the world was created (according to the Old Testament of the Bible).

- The Islamic calendar, widely used in the Middle East, starts on January 16, 622, the day after the *Hegeira* [heh-JEER-ah], the most important event in the Muslim religion.

In recent years, more and more people have replaced B.C. and A.D. with designations that do not refer to a specific religion. These designations are BCE ("before common era") and CE ("common era"). BCE and CE are used in this textbook.

Sometimes, you will see a "c." in front of a date. This means *circa,* which is a Latin word meaning "around." For example, when you read that Muhammad was born in c. 570, it means he was born *around* 570. Often, when an actual date is not known, historians have to use clues to guess the date.

Numbering the Centuries

A century is a period of 100 years. A century can start at any time, but it always ends 100 years later. Therefore, from 1753 to 1852 is a century.

You may wonder why we call the century we are living in now the 21st century. The 21st century began in 2001, and it will end in the year 2100. This makes sense if you go back to the 1st century CE. It began in the year 1 (there was no year 0) and ended in the year 100. The 2nd century began in the year 101 and ended in the year 200. The 3rd century began in the year 201 and ended in the year 300. You can see the pattern: the name of the century is one number more than the years in that century suggest. The same system works for the centuries BCE, but in reverse. The 1st century BCE began with the year 1 BCE and ends 100 years earlier, in the year 100 BCE. In this textbook, when you read that something happened in the 17th century CE, that means it happened between 1601 and 1700. If something happened in the 18th century BCE, that means it happened between the year 1800 BCE and the year 1701 BCE.

Part 1

In chapter 1, you will read about why and how we study societies of the past. The first societies are so ancient that they might not seem to have any relation to life today. You will see that by studying what happened to people thousands of years ago, we can learn a great deal about the nature of human life. Knowledge from the past can teach us about the kinds of decisions we are facing today. These lessons include:

- *The importance of the natural environment to people and human societies* Changes in the environment had a major impact on human development. For example, following the last **Ice Age**, humans were able to move successfully into every part of the world by adapting to the environment and using it intelligently. Today, humans continue to be dependent on the natural environment and need to make decisions that will preserve it.

- *Recognizing our common roots* Scientists generally agree that all human life began in Africa. Despite any apparent differences, all humans are very closely related.

- *The contributions of many cultures to human life* Human inventions and discoveries of the past from every part of the world have contributed to the modern world. In today's world, we have even greater opportunities to learn from other cultures and from our knowledge of history.

In chapter 2, you will begin your exploration of peoples of the past. We begin by briefly discussing some different accounts of the beginnings of human life. Most of what you will read, though, is from the point of view of modern science. We call scientific accounts of early life *theories*. These theories represent the most likely interpretations scientists can make from the **evidence** that has been found. The

All dates are approximate

THE EARLY PEOPLES	2 500 000 BCE– 1 200 000 BCE	1 000 000 BCE– 700 000 BCE	250 000 BCE	100 000 BCE	40 000 BCE– 13 000 BCE	13 000 BCE– 10 000 BCE	8000 BCE
	Beginning of Paleolithic Age (Old Stone Age). *Homo habilis*, our first direct human ancestor, appears in East Africa. First use of tools made from stone. *Homo erectus*, a new human species, appears in Africa. 2 000 000 BCE Ice Age begins.	Humans begin to move from Africa to Europe and Asia. 700 000 BCE Fire is used for the first time.	*Homo sapiens* humans appear. Neanderthals appear in Europe. Humans extract ochre, a type of iron ore, from the earth and use it as paint or dye.	Cro-Magnons appear in North Africa, Europe, and Asia.	Humans move from Asia, first to North America and then to South America. 20 000 BCE Humans are making musical instruments.	Humans are painting on cave walls at Lascaux, France. End of the last Ice Age. End of Paleolithic Age and beginning of Mesolithic Age (Middle Stone Age).	End of Mesolithic Age and beginning of Neolithic Age (New Stone Age). Humans begin to domesticate animals and cultivate plants. 6000 BCE Jericho, thought to be the world's first town, has a population of about 2000.

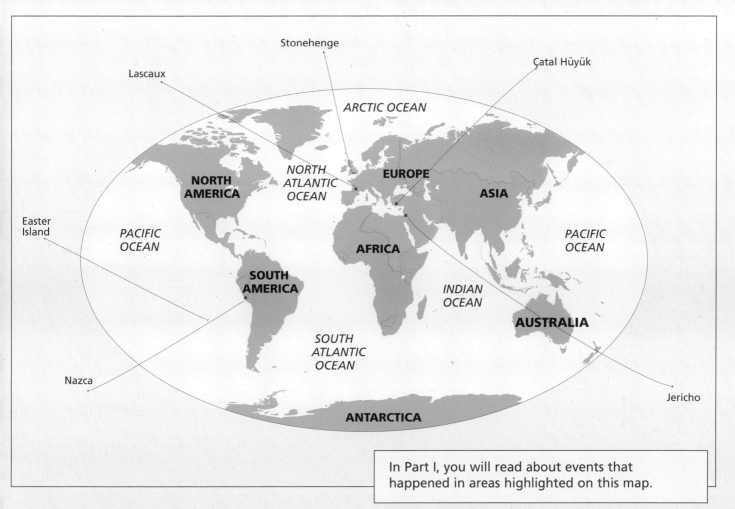

Lascaux

Stonehenge

Çatal Hüyük

ARCTIC OCEAN

NORTH
ATLANTIC
OCEAN

EUROPE

ASIA

NORTH
AMERICA

Easter
Island

PACIFIC
OCEAN

PACIFIC
OCEAN

AFRICA

SOUTH
AMERICA

INDIAN
OCEAN

AUSTRALIA

SOUTH
ATLANTIC
OCEAN

Nazca

Jericho

ANTARCTICA

In Part I, you will read about events that
happened in areas highlighted on this map.

story the scientists tell is not the final version,
however. As new discoveries are made and
new technologies are developed to interpret
evidence, theories will continue to change.

We examine how humans changed from
hunters and gatherers to an agricultural way of
life. We discuss the development of language,
the rise of permanent settlements, and the
technological achievements of these early Stone
Age societies.

5000 BCE	3500 BCE	2500 BCE	1500 BCE	1 CE	600 CE
Before 6000 BCE South American Indians are growing corn.	End of Neolithic Age.	The building of Stonehenge begins in southern England.	Beginning of Iron Age.	The statues on Easter Island are carved.	Nazca lines are made in Peru.
5000 BCE People in Mexico are gathering wild potatoes.	Beginning of Bronze Age.				
5000 BCE Surgery is being practiced.	The first systems of writing are developed in Mesopotamia.				

Why Study the History of Societies?

HISTORY

What Is History?

The past includes everything that has happened since the beginning of time. History is our knowledge of the past and involves the study of its records or sources of information. Since there are no records for most of the past, there is much we can never know for certain. Even when records do exist, they can be difficult to understand. Therefore, our knowledge of the past can never be complete.

Why Study History?

The past influences us in ways we are not even aware of. Consider some products of the past that we now take for granted.

- *Place names* The names of many towns, cities, streets, and schools refer to earlier times or people. Winnipeg and Manitoba are Aboriginal names. Other place names in Manitoba show the influences of various **cultures**: St-Pierre-Jolys (French), Gimli (Icelandic), and Komarno (Ukrainian) are some examples.

- *Personal names* Our names may reflect a family tradition or something that was in the news at the time we were born. Many of our surnames tell us about our ancestors. For example, *Johansson* means "the son of Johan." *Baker* suggests that at one time an ancestor made bread for a living.

- *Language* The alphabet we use and the ways we spell and pronounce words have all been shaped by history. Many English and French words come from ancient languages such as Greek (for example, *democracy* and *school*) and Latin (for example, *video* and *student*). Other English words come from languages such as Arabic (for example, *cheque* and *algebra*), Urdu (for example, *khaki*), and French (for example, *restaurant* and *rendezvous*). In the same way, the language of mathematics owes much to the discoveries of the Greeks (geometry), East Indians (the use of zero), and Arabs (algebra).

- *Values and beliefs* Many of our beliefs about government and about people from other parts of the world have been shaped by history. As you will learn in later chapters, Canadian ideas about freedom and **democracy** have their origins in ancient Greece, the American Revolution and French Revolution of the 18th century, and a variety of other historical developments. In addition, knowledge of history allows us to see how other people have lived. When we learn about the values and beliefs of others, we discover that our own way of life is neither the only one nor necessarily the best one. When we study alternative ways of thinking and learning, we find out how much we owe to peoples of other times and from other places.

- *Institutions* Many of Canada's institutions have their roots in history. The origins of Canada's system of parliamentary monarchy date back to when Canada was a British **colony**. Today, the reigning monarch of the United Kingdom is also the reigning monarch of Canada. In the Canadian parliament, the person who chairs the debates in the House of Commons is called the Speaker. The term goes back to medieval England – the Speaker was the person who presented parliament's views to the king or queen.

History and Memory

We need memory. It gives us a personal past. Memory helps us define who we are, where we live, and who our family and friends are. Memory helps us remember the basics of how to live, such as traffic rules, street routes, where to shop, and how to use money. Organizations also need memory. For this reason, most organizations keep records of their past activities and decisions. History is a way of preserving memory. Shared memories can help unite a group of people or an organization and provide a sense of identity.

Figure 1.1 The horns that appear on Viking helmets are one of the most often seen "false versions" of the past. There is no evidence that Viking helmets ever had horns. In fact, most historians and **archaeologists** agree that Viking warriors wore helmets made of leather. This statue is in Gimli, Manitoba.

Memory, though, can be unreliable. What we remember might not be what actually happened, or we might forget some key details. An important purpose of history is to make sure that what we remember is accurate. History both preserves and corrects memory.

At the same time, history can create a false version of the past. This can be done intentionally to instill distrust and hatred among people in the present. It may also be done because our interpretations of historical events are based on evidence, and evidence often changes.

Questions to Think About

- Since we cannot travel back in time, how do we know anything for certain about what happened in the past?

- How can we be sure that what we think we know about the past is accurate?

- How does the past shape the ways we think about the present and the future?

- Is it important to know about what happened in the past? Why or why not?

Historical Thinking

The study of history involves more than learning about what happened in the past. It includes realizing that history is a never-ending debate about why something happened, its results, and its importance. To learn history means learning to think historically; that is, understanding how historians use history to reconstruct and understand the past. When we think historically, we do the following:

- We realize that we can never know the past directly, only indirectly through the evidence that has been left behind.

- We see the past through the words and records and thoughts of the people who experienced it.

- We recognize that the past can be very different from the present.

- We accept that there is much we cannot know about the past because there are no records, or the records are incomplete or difficult to understand.

- We understand that any statement about the past is only as good as the evidence supporting it.

- We understand the differences between facts and interpretations and learn how to judge among differing interpretations.

- We understand the forces that shape people's interpretations of the past.

- We question what we read or are told about the past. For example, we might ask: Is this true? What is the evidence? What other explanations might there be?

Archives and Museums

Two places that preserve the records of the past are archives and museums.

Archives are collections of visual, written, and oral records, kept in special buildings or rooms. In Canada, the National Archives in Ottawa keeps government records and a wide variety of other records about the past. The provinces and territories and many cities and towns have their own archives, as do organizations such as churches, universities, unions, and businesses.

Archives are used for many reasons. Most people use archives to research their family history. Businesses and organizations use archives to research land claims and property titles. Historians probably use archives more than anyone else, since this is where they find much of the evidence they need to learn about and reconstruct the past.

Museums hold collections of objects such as tools, pottery, jewellery, and clothes. Some museums specialize in one aspect of the past, such as natural history, war, costume, or transportation.

Figure 1.2 Today, governments protect the past for the enjoyment and information of future generations. These employees of the Canadian Parks Service take on the roles of 19th-century inhabitants of Lower Fort Garry near Winnipeg, Manitoba. In the 19th century, Lower Fort Garry was an important fur trade centre. Museums like this are sometimes called *living museums*, because visitors "travel" back in time to see and feel what it was like to live in the past.

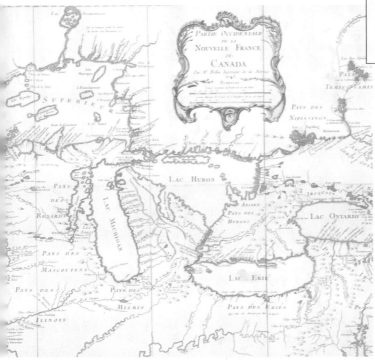

Figure 1.3 Historians and other researchers learn to think historically by deciphering and studying original documents from the past. This map, drawn in 1745, shows what people at that time thought the area around the Great Lakes looked like.

In Manitoba, the Western Canadian Aviation Museum houses the largest collection of airplanes in western Canada. The Costume Museum of Canada in Dugald, Manitoba, holds the largest collection of clothing in Canada.

Museums as we know them today were first built in the 19th century. They were created as centres of education where people came to learn about the past. They also served as research centres for scientists such as historians and archaeologists who study the past. Today's museums are more than research centres and storehouses. They showcase interesting displays and exhibitions that attract millions of visitors each year.

Figure 1.4 Museum experts build models and dioramas to bring the past to life. This reconstruction of an Algonquian camp, on display at the Manitoba Museum, enables visitors to see how people lived in the past.

History and Historians

Historians use two types of records when they investigate the past: primary sources and secondary sources. A primary source is anything that existed at the time being researched; for example, a diary or photograph. A secondary source is anything that was created afterwards, such as this textbook.

Both primary and secondary sources can be difficult to understand. They are often incomplete, biased, or inaccurate. Like eyewitnesses to an accident, sources describing the same event can contradict each other.

When historians have obtained as much information as possible from a source, they organize the information so that it tells a story or proves or disproves a theory. For example, if all the facts in this textbook were listed in random order, all the information would be here, but it would make no sense. Facts have to be organized so that they make a point.

Historians do more than describe the past, however. They try to explain it by showing why something happened and what the results of the event were. History combines description, explanation, and interpretation.

This does not mean that history is just a matter of opinion. Historians cannot ignore facts or make them up. They interpret and explain the facts based on the evidence. Historians have to be as objective as possible.

What Caused the Accident? – A Question of Interpretation

One rainy evening, a man walked to the corner store to buy some orange juice. As he was crossing the street at a sharp corner, he was hit by an oncoming car. What caused the accident?

Theory 1: The man's love of juice. He decided to go to the store that evening, rather than wait until the next day.

Theory 2: The engineer who planned the road. He should not have included such a sharp and dangerous corner.

Theory 3: The weather and the time of day. It was raining and nearly dark.

Theory 4: The man. He probably did not look both ways before crossing the street.

Theory 5: The car driver. He should have been paying extra attention when approaching a sharp corner in rain and darkness.

Theory 6: The driver's employer. The driver had just been fired from his job and was very upset.

History is a science and an art. Historians are like skilled detectives investigating a crime. They find their evidence, test it, and come up with a theory to explain what happened and what it means in ways that people find convincing. History is an art because historians use their sources to tell a story, solve a problem, or construct an explanation.

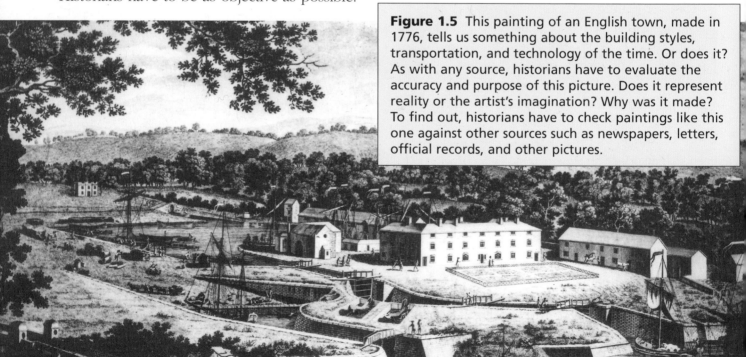

Figure 1.5 This painting of an English town, made in 1776, tells us something about the building styles, transportation, and technology of the time. Or does it? As with any source, historians have to evaluate the accuracy and purpose of this picture. Does it represent reality or the artist's imagination? Why was it made? To find out, historians have to check paintings like this one against other sources such as newspapers, letters, official records, and other pictures.

Theory 7: The driver's garage mechanic. The car had just been safety-checked, but no one had noticed that the tires were nearly bald.

Theory 8: All these factors were involved. Some were more important than others.

Theory 9: No one caused the accident. It was just one of those things – an accident.

Which theory do you favour? Why? Examine the arguments for and against each theory before reaching a decision. Perhaps you can come up with a different theory.

Historians face similar problems when they are deciding what caused some event in the past. This is also why there may be many different interpretations of the same event. Historians not only have to find out what actually happened in the past, they have to identify the causes and results of events and decide why they are important.

In other words, historians have to describe, explain, and assess.

His Story or Her Story?

Until recently, most history was written by men and was about men and their activities. This was due, in part, to historians' emphasis on government, war, and politics. These areas were dominated by men. Only women who were involved in areas of life that men considered important are remembered; for example, Jeanne d'Arc and Elizabeth I. Most women and their experiences were ignored.

Since the 1960s, the women's movement has drawn attention to this gap in history. As a result, the lives of all women, not just the lives of "famous" women, are now studied.

Historians are writing about topics such as the education of girls, women's work, marriage, women's political beliefs, childbirth, and childrearing. They are studying how historical events affected women and the roles that women played in these events. Historians are also interested in the relationships between men and women and in how people in the past saw women's place in society. Historians also investigate how different societies defined how men and women were supposed to act.

Social History

For centuries, accounts of the past were written to commemorate and praise famous people, such as warriors or rulers. Those in power used history to explain why they deserved to be in power and how they came to hold their position. In many ways, history was used as a form of **propaganda**, a way of convincing others. It was also used to make people proud of their tribe, religion, or country and to make them suspicious of others. History was used as a way of distinguishing between groups of people and often as a way of proving that one group was superior to all others.

Today, more attention is being paid to social history. Social history is the story of everyone and everything, not just of the powerful and of wars. Both women and men from all walks of life are now studied by historians. Crime, the family, marriage, food, work, and institutions such as schools are just a few of the topics investigated and written about by historians.

Figure 1.6 In this photograph, a woman is bringing food and clothing to a poor family in Winnipeg in the early 1900s. Until recently, most historians thought that activities such as this were not important enough to write about. Historians now realize that to ignore the roles of women in history is to ignore half of the past.

Oral History

Although history focuses on the written record, historians also get information by interviewing people who have personal knowledge or experience of an event. Oral history is another type of evidence, not another form of history. In societies without a written language (for example, First Nations people in Canada, African societies in Ghana and Mali), oral history was the only way in which records of the past were passed on from generation to generation.

Historians do not interview only famous people like presidents or prime ministers. Oral history is concerned with the experiences of all people. Oral historians want to know what it was like to be an immigrant factory worker, a homemaker, or a student in a particular place at a particular time.

People who have personally experienced an event have firsthand knowledge. They often remember small details unknown to others. They can bring the past to life. However, oral history has some disadvantages. People forget details, or they do not recall an event accurately. Sometimes, they may not want to tell the truth. More often, they know only one aspect of an experience.

Oral historians try to make up for these disadvantages in three ways. (1) They listen carefully to as many people as possible to get a wide range of viewpoints. (2) They ask questions to clarify the information. (3) They check their interviews against any written records that exist – such as newspaper accounts, official reports, and **autobiographies** – and point out inconsistencies.

Visual History

Historians also obtain information about daily life from visual sources: objects and representations. The objects range from things as big as a whole town or city, to particular buildings, to items of clothing. Visual representations – paintings, cartoons, maps, photographs, posters, and movies – can show how people dressed, what kinds of food they ate, how their houses were designed, and so on.

Objects and visual representations can also reveal a great deal about the ideas and beliefs of the people who created them. For example, artists may add or change details, or use light and shade and perspective, to make us see things in a certain way. When artists paint a picture or photographers take a photograph, they often do so to make a particular point, not simply to depict what they were looking at when they made their picture.

When the French artist Jacques-Louis David was commissioned to paint Napoleon's coronation as emperor of France in 1804, he had to determine what to include.

Figure 1.7 The British general, James Wolfe, was killed at the Battle of the Plains of Abraham outside Quebec City in 1759. When Benjamin West painted this picture of General Wolfe dying on the battlefield, he did not paint what actually happened. First, a group of people would not pose for an artist in the middle of a battle. Second, First Nations people did not take part in the battle. West was portraying General Wolfe as a hero. West's painting was such a success that people paid him to paint copies with them in the group surrounding the dying general. Historians have to carefully assess pictures such as this and ask: Does this image describe what actually happened? If not, what does the artist want us to think really happened?

Figure 1.8 This picture was commissioned in the 16th century by the Mogul emperor Akbar the Great for a book about the emperor's life. The scene shown here is the birth of Prince Selim, the emperor's son. Use the questions on the left to help you decide how reliable this picture is as a source of historical information.

For example, he wanted to depict the **pope**, who was present at the ceremony, sitting on a chair with his hands on his knees. At Napoleon's suggestion, he changed this to show Pope Pius VII raising one of his hands as if in blessing. In addition, he included Napoleon's mother among the spectators, although she did not attend the ceremony.

David's painting is not a true-to-life record of Napoleon's coronation. Instead, it is a statement, authorized by Napoleon himself, of how Napoleon wanted the event to be remembered.

In the same way, portraits can "flatter" their subjects by making them appear more good-looking or imposing than they really are. A particular pose or background can deliver important messages about a person's social status or character. In the 18th century, for example, English landowners sometimes had their portraits painted against the background of their mansions and lands, to show how wealthy and powerful they were.

Historians, then, have to decide whether a visual source is genuine or fake. They have to think about why it portrays something in the way that it does. To decide how realistic a picture is and how reliable it is as a source of information, they have to know why a picture was made. In effect, historians "ask" whoever produced the visual source what he or she was trying to make the viewer think and feel.

ARCHAEOLOGY

Archaeology and Archaeologists

Archaeology is the study of people who have lived before us. Archaeologists study the physical evidence, called **artifacts**, that people left behind. Artifacts give us glimpses into the lives of early humans. Tools used for hunting, gathering, and preparing food tell us much about people's technology, diet, and clothing. Human remains help us determine what people looked like and may provide evidence of their religious/spiritual ideas and practices. From animal bones, we can learn about people's diet and about the environment in which they lived. Remains of human settlements, such as postholes and firepits, provide archaeologists with information about the type and size of settlements. From carvings and wall paintings, archaeologists can determine the religious and spiritual beliefs of a society, the kind of environment the people lived in, and the animals that they killed for food and clothing.

Archaeological evidence is not always easy to interpret. New discoveries often require archaeologists to change their theories. As well, certain types of evidence can never be recovered. While bones and stone tools can remain in the earth to be rediscovered hundreds of thousands of years later, other evidence, such as spoken language, is lost forever. Historians and scientists can only guess at when language developed and what form it first took. Nevertheless, we can learn a great deal from archaeology.

How Archaeologists Work

Most archaeologists have been working the same way for decades. When a site is discovered, it is mapped and separated into small squares called a **grid**. Archaeologists then carefully excavate each square using tools such as trowels, toothbrushes, paintbrushes, dental picks, dustpans, buckets, and sieves. Each find, however small, is noted as to the soil layer in which it was found, and its location and position within the square. Archaeologists use the information to help them reconstruct the past.

Archaeologists can use several different methods to date artifacts. Since the late 1940s, one of the most common techniques used is called radiocarbon dating. In this method, the amount of radioactive carbon-14 in an object is measured to determine its approximate age. Radiocarbon atoms are found in all living matter. When an organism dies, the level of carbon-14 in it begins to drop. We know that

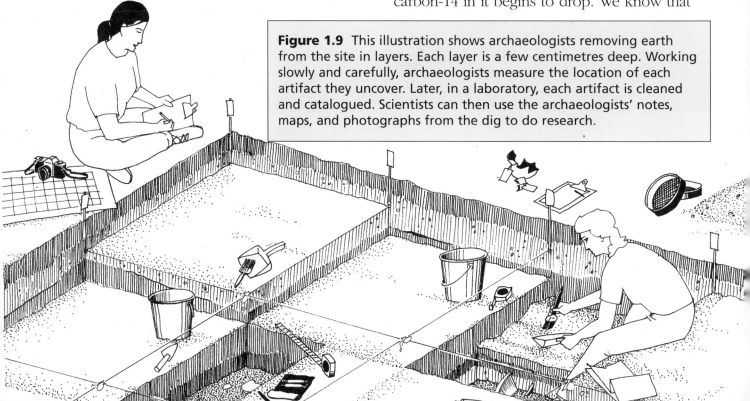

Figure 1.9 This illustration shows archaeologists removing earth from the site in layers. Each layer is a few centimetres deep. Working slowly and carefully, archaeologists measure the location of each artifact they uncover. Later, in a laboratory, each artifact is cleaned and catalogued. Scientists can then use the archaeologists' notes, maps, and photographs from the dig to do research.

radioactive carbon has a half-life of 5730 years; that is, 5730 years after an object has died, half of the carbon-14 in it has disappeared. In another 5730 years, another half of what was left disappears, and so on. Although the method is useful in dating artifacts, it has been found that levels of carbon-14 have not remained constant through the ages. As a result, some of the dates obtained by this method may not be accurate. Scientists, however, are constantly using new technologies to improve dating methods.

Archaeologists also use some of the most recent technologies to find sites and to examine artifacts. These include:

- *Aerial photography* Pictures taken from airplanes can reveal areas of ancient settlements not evident from the ground. The colour and height of plants growing over buried settlements are different from those in surrounding areas. Archaeologists can use this information to determine where they should dig. (In chapter 3, you will read about ancient roads found from imaging.)

- *DNA testing* DNA is the substance in living things that determines heredity. For example, DNA determines the colour of our eyes. Scientists obtain DNA samples from early human remains and compare them with DNA of present-day peoples. In this way, the biological relationships between humans have been traced. DNA samples indicate the common ancestry of all races.

Artifacts and the Environment

Some environments protect artifacts better than others. The Nazca Lines (see page 45), for example, are located in a desert region of Peru. In a wetter climate, they would have been erased long ago. The dry conditions in the desert have preserved them through the centuries.

Fortunately, water does not always destroy artifacts. Ancient ships have been recovered from under the sea, preserved by the cold water. By examining the cargoes the ships carried, archaeologists can learn a great deal about trade patterns and goods. Bogs have been another good source of discovery.

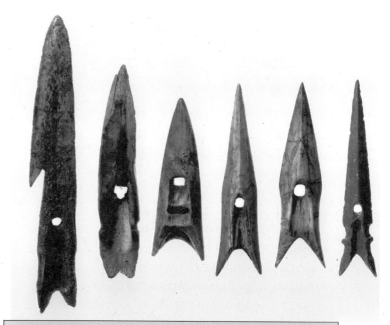

Figure 1.10 Archaeologists try to date some objects by placing them in sequence. They examine how the shape, pattern, and design of each object has changed over time. In this illustration, archaeologists have used these criteria to sequence (from left to right) how they believe Inuit spear points have developed over time.

Several well-preserved human bodies have been recovered from bogs in places like Denmark (see page 49).

The ice and cold of northern and mountainous areas are also good preservatives. In Siberia, carpets and objects made of felt, the kinds of artifacts that are usually destroyed by weather, have been recovered.

Plant materials like seeds and pollen can survive in the right environmental conditions. Seeds often survive burning, which hardens rather than destroys them. Pollen that falls into bogs has also survived for a very long time. Archaeologists can learn a lot about the plant life of ancient times from evidence like this.

While weather and the passage of time have destroyed a great deal of the past, so too have humans. Earlier explorers of ancient sites were sometimes more interested in finding treasures or bringing home souvenirs than in using what they found to add to the knowledge of human history. Cities have been built over earlier cities, burying them. Burial sites have been looted for gold and jewels. People have carried off stones from ancient buildings and monuments to use in their own construction.

SOCIETY

Society and Identity

In this textbook, we are examining the history of societies in the past. However, before we can do that, we have to know what a society is.

The term *society* is more difficult to define than it first appears to be. In Canada today, we speak of Canadian society. However, we also speak of Aboriginal society, immigrant society, French-Canadian society, and so on. Sometimes, society is used in a very specific sense to name an organization, such as the Society of Canadian Artists or the Canadian Red Cross Society. What exactly, then, is a society?

Society is the way groups of people have organized themselves to live together; for example, in bands, tribes, chiefdoms, or villages. Societies change when economic and environmental conditions change, and they can exist at various levels: locally, regionally, nationally, and internationally. Early humans lived in hunter-gatherer societies. By 7000 BCE, many humans lived in agricultural societies. Today, most people still live in agricultural societies, while some live in urban societies.

The people in a society share a number of things in common, including identity. They may identify with their country and call themselves Canadian, German, or Mexican. They might be more specific and refer to themselves as French-Canadian, Ukrainian-Canadian, or First Nations-Canadian. They might call themselves Winnipeggers, Montrealers, or Vancouverites. A person has many identities and belongs to several societies at the same time.

A society can also include clubs and professional organizations that help to identify it. In Canadian society, for instance, there is the Canadian Broadcasting Corporation and the Canadian Football League, to name two. Sometimes we even talk of "global society" or "world society," suggesting that the entire human race can be seen as one society.

For us to understand the past, we also have to know what a civilization is. A civilization has to have a central government that is responsible for organizing and maintaining a society's internal structure, such as a drainage or sewer system. Civilizations are characterized by several other criteria that you will learn about in Part 2. It is important to know, though, that a society and a civilization are not the same thing.

Studying Society

When historians study a society, they ask certain questions so that they can understand how the society works.

1. What are the society's main values? How are the values protected or enforced? Does everyone share them? What happens to people who do not share these values?

2. What is the society's belief system?

3. What do people do for leisure and recreation?

4. How does the society raise its children and ensure its survival over time?

5. How does the society get its food and most other basic needs? How do people make a living and support themselves?

6. Does the society accept or resist change? How does it respond to new ideas?

7. How does the society protect itself against enemies? What is its attitude to war and peace?

8. What is the society's attitude to the outside world? Is the society open to trade and travel?

9. What is the system of government? Who has power? How do they use their power?

10. How is the society organized? How are families structured? How are men and women treated? How are wealth and property divided?

As you study world history, ask yourself these questions to better understand how each society has evolved. You can also use the questions to compare the societies with each other and with societies today.

Figure 1.11 A society is more than just a lot of people who occupy a shared space. A society consists of people who have joined together for protection and/or to satisfy their material and non-material needs. Material needs include food, clothing, and shelter. Non-material needs may include religious and spiritual beliefs, entertainment, recreation, and the arts. A protest march or an audience to see the pope, for example, does not form a society, even though the people who are attending the event may have many things in common. Which of these pictures shows a society rather than just a crowd or gathering of people?

Government and You

Government today plays an important part in our lives. For example, the house or apartment that you live in has to meet government safety standards for such things as electrical wiring and appliances, gas pipelines, and furnaces. The foods that we eat have to meet government health standards, which are set to help protect people from disease. The labelling, packaging, and advertising of this food also have to meet government requirements.

Radio and television are licenced by government authority. The telephone companies and post office are also either operated by or regulated by government. So, too, are the water, gas, and electricity that you use. The streets and sidewalks that you travel on were built by government. The traffic laws were determined by government and are enforced by the police department, which is operated by government.

The school you attend was funded by government, unless it is a private school, and even then it is partly funded by government. Government decided that you must attend school, and the curriculum and textbooks you are using have been approved by government.

We can learn more about our government by examining other forms of it. As you read the chapters that follow, think about how the governments of past societies were organized, and compare them to governments today. Here are some key questions to ask:

- Who forms the government?

- How is the government chosen?

- What are the powers of the government?

- How are these powers limited or controlled?

- What rights do people have?
  - How are these rights protected?
  - What duties do people have?
  - How are these duties enforced?

Language

Language makes it possible to describe the world and to communicate with other people. Language also shapes how we see the world. Words such as *friend, enemy, love*, and *tree* create pictures or images in our mind. In this way, language gives us a sense of shared identity with others who speak the same language. It also divides people: those who understand each other's language and those who do not.

Culture

The word *culture* is used to describe a society's way of life. All societies hope to pass on their culture to future generations. A culture consists

Figure 1.12 These card players lived in Holland in the 1600s. A strength of this painting is that it gives us some information about styles of dress, pastimes, and, perhaps, even the relationship between men and women in Holland at that time. The picture also raises some questions. Why is everyone wearing something on their head even though they are indoors? Was it for warmth or was it fashion? What is the group actually doing? Why is the woman at the left looking away from the group and pointing at the table? A weakness of this painting is that we cannot find the answers to these questions from it. We also do not know if the artist is trying to make a point or a statement.

Figure 1.13 These are the remains of Teotihuacán [tay-oh-TEE-wah-kon] in Mexico. This picture suggests that Teotihuacán formed a civilization that had developed advanced political and social organizations and had a well-defined culture. The ruins of the city are about 1500 years old. At its height, the city may have been home to as many as 200 000 people. A city as large as Teotihuacán needed many tradespeople with special skills. The people who built, maintained, and operated the city were not **nomadic** hunters and gatherers or probably even farmers. The inhabitants would have depended on others to supply their food and other needs while they worked at specialized jobs. A city this size also needed a sophisticated form of government to make decisions, maintain law and order, and keep everything running smoothly.

of three main elements: knowledge, values, and ways of doing things. For much of history, all three elements have been closely connected with the religious and spiritual beliefs of a society. Historically, these beliefs have formed an important part of a society's culture.

Knowledge is all those things that people are expected to know about the society in which they live. Knowledge includes facts, terms and definitions, names, events, and anything else that helps people understand their world. This shared knowledge builds a sense of identity that establishes people as members of a specific culture. Canadians, for example, know that Ottawa is the capital city and that Canada has two official languages.

A culture is also built on a foundation of shared values that its members see as important. Canadians believe that they have the right to speak their minds freely. They also believe that they have the right to drive a car, own private property, read whatever they want, use a telephone, and, generally, live as they think best.

Finally, practices help make a culture distinct from other cultures. For example, Canadians drive on the right side of the road, while the British drive on the left side. Dress, food, and

other aspects of daily life also help define culture. Since countries like Canada are made up of peoples from many different parts of the world, Canadian culture reflects contributions of all these people.

In the past, a society often contained at least two cultures: the upper-class rulers and the ordinary people. Since the members of the ruling group were more powerful than those who were ruled, they were able to make their culture more or less official. Art, literature, language, and music usually reflected what the ruling class saw as important, not the interests and tastes of ordinary people. Much of the writing of past societies, therefore, has focused on the history of the upper class. Today, historians try to reflect the history of all people in society.

The Importance of Tradition

In all societies, people believe in right ways and wrong ways to do things. What is right and what is wrong are often based on tradition. For much of human history, the experiences and wisdom of elders were the main sources of tradition.

This reliance on tradition – looking to the past for guidance – was strengthened by religious and spiritual beliefs. All religions depend on tradition. They are usually based on a sacred book or on a body of customs and beliefs maintained by priests and other officials.

Societies maintain their traditions with pride. Important events are occasions for celebration and ceremony. For example, Canada Day in Canada and Bastille Day in France are national holidays, occasions when traditions are emphasized. Traditions can give people a sense of security.

Sometimes, traditions can prevent worthwhile and necessary change. In the 20th century, for instance, some people opposed women's fight to win the right to vote because they believed that this right would destroy the traditional role of women as wives and mothers.

Tradition does have its uses. We need contact with the past to remind us of our beginnings. For example, old buildings and structures are often saved and restored to commemorate important historical events. Some towns preserve old schools or farmhouses to remind people of the early years of their communities.

It can be difficult, however, to reach a balance between tradition and reform. People often disagree over whether a particular tradition is worth preserving or should be changed in favour of a new way of doing something.

Figure 1.14 Although Canadians had talked about adopting a new flag since the 1920s, Canada did not have its own official flag until 1965. When the flag debate opened in the Canadian House of Commons in June 1964, Prime Minister Lester B. Pearson wanted a flag without any association to Canada's colonial past. The leader of the opposition, John Diefenbaker, wanted a flag honouring the countries that had "founded" Canada. Canadian citizens were as divided as the politicians. Many wanted to keep the red ensign (top). The debate lasted six months. Finally, on February 15, 1965, the red and white maple leaf became the official flag of Canada.

Religious and Spiritual Beliefs

Throughout history, religion and spirituality have been important elements of society. From very early times, humans have tried to explain and control the world in which they live. Historically, most people have believed that something beyond the human world both created it and shaped it.

In this textbook, you will read about societies with different beliefs. Some believed in one god. Others worshipped many gods. Some believed spirits guided all forms of life. People were expected to follow the beliefs of their society and, in many cases, were punished if they did not. Some people were banished from the group or even put to death. These beliefs, explained and enforced by priests, elders, or other specially qualified people, were often supported by the rulers or governments of the society.

Religious and spiritual beliefs, then, helped to hold society together by contributing to a sense of shared identity and shared origins. These

Figure 1.15 This is a statue of Chacmool [CHACK-mool] a god of the Toltecs, an early people in Mexico. Note the flat surface on the figure's stomach. It was used to hold offerings that people made to the god. The statue provides us with some important, but limited, information about the Toltecs: they worshipped one or more gods, they were skilled carvers, and their art was very sophisticated. The statue also suggests (although it does not actually tell us) that the Toltecs had special priests or others to look after the offerings made to this god. At the same time, the statue raises questions: Did the Toltecs have one god or many gods? We would need to find other statues to answer that question. To establish a more complete picture of Toltec culture, researchers need to find many more kinds of artifacts from the Toltecs.

beliefs also provided a way of understanding the world. In addition, they helped shape the values of society by defining standards of right and wrong. Above all, religious and spiritual beliefs offered people a way of thinking about the meaning of life and what it meant to be a human being.

It is impossible to understand world history without taking into account the influence of religious and spiritual beliefs and of specific religions such as **Judaism, Christianity, Islam, Hinduism, Buddhism,** and **Confucianism** on world societies. In the chapters that follow, you will read about these different beliefs.

THE WORLD, CONNECTIONS, AND CITIZENSHIP

The World and You

Our lives are shaped by the world in ways that we often take for granted or do not even realize. Much of what we eat and wear is made outside Canada. A visit to any supermarket shows how much of our food comes from other countries. Most of the television programs that we watch come from elsewhere. Even the television sets that we watch these programs on were probably made in a country such as Japan.

Any letters or telephone calls that come from another country depend on an elaborate system of agreements and equipment to reach us. When we visit the doctor, he or she often uses information or medicine that has resulted from research done in, perhaps, Germany or the United States.

Many of our games originated from elsewhere: soccer and tennis in England, football in the United States, curling in Scotland. Our official languages originally came from England and France, and many of the words that we use come from the ancient languages of Greek and Latin.

Our use of clock time depends on an international agreement to use the same twenty-four-hour clock. Our calendar goes back to ancient Rome. Most of our religions have their roots in European Christianity, Arabic Islam, Eastern Mediterranean Judaism, or Buddhism and Hinduism from India. Music we listen to uses South American or African rhythms.

Whether we like it or not, we are part of the world, and the world is part of our lives.

The World's Connections

Since very early times, the different regions of the world have been connected in various ways. One example follows. You will find many others in this book.

About 1900 years ago, important parts of the world were connected through trade, which extended from the Atlantic coast of Europe to the east coast of Africa. As figure 1.17 shows, the Roman Empire encompassed much of Europe, North Africa, and the Middle East (the area from Libya east to Afghanistan, and including Egypt, Sudan, Israel, Jordan, Lebanon, Syria, Turkey, Iraq, Iran, Saudi Arabia, and the other countries of the Arabian peninsula). Other empires built and maintained roads, organized river transport, collected tolls from travellers, and, generally, enforced law and order to protect travellers from bandits.

Over time, traders and merchants began to look for new goods and customers. Chinese silk was fashionable with wealthy Romans.

Figure 1.16 This scene from a contemporary Canadian home shows the influence of the world's many cultures on our lifestyle. List at least ten items in this illustration that might have come to Canada from another country.

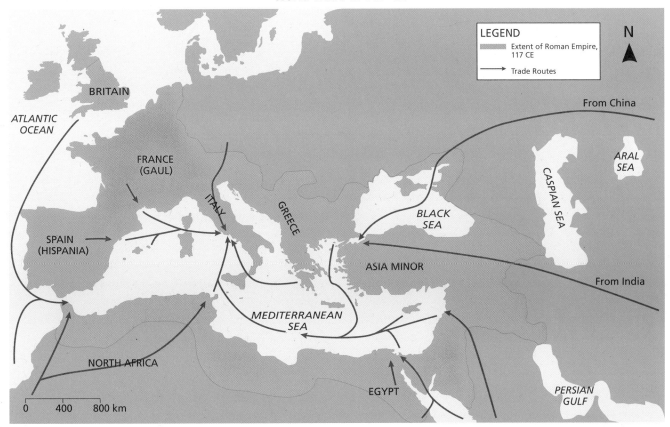

Figure 1.17 This map shows how ancient Rome was the centre of a system of world trade almost 2000 years ago. Silks and textiles were brought overland from China; spices, especially pepper, came from India and, indirectly, from the East Indies; granite, marble, wine, wheat, and some foods were imported from North Africa; marble, olives, and other foods came from Greece; gold came from south of the Sahara Desert in Africa; leather, tin, metals, wool, and natural products were brought from Britain and northern Europe. Rome also imported a wide variety of wild animals, including bears, lions, and tigers for its arena spectacles. To pay for these goods, Rome exported wine, pottery, olives, olive oil, gold, and silver.

Traders in India supplied textiles and provided pepper for rich Romans. In return, Europeans supplied glass and metals, especially gold and silver, to the merchants of Asia.

An important system of trade routes developed both overland and by sea. Chinese silk was often transported by the **Silk Road**, a network of trails and roads that crossed deserts and mountains and stretched for thousands of kilometres from China to the Mediterranean Sea. Sea routes were even more important than land routes. East Indian sailors used their knowledge of weather patterns, ocean currents, winds, the direction of waves, and other clues to cross the Indian Ocean without having to follow the coastline. By the 1st century CE, ships were regularly sailing from the Red Sea to the mouth of the Indus River in Pakistan. These ships could easily carry hundreds of tonnes of cargo and were an important part of the trading connection between east and west. Even in those early times, the world was connected.

Globalization

Today, the world is more interconnected than it has ever been. There is more trade among countries than in any previous time. Corporations do business around the world, and some of them are bigger and more powerful than many countries. International organizations such as the World Bank and the World Trade Organization have the power to tell governments what to do. The process is called **globalization**. Supporters say globalization is bringing increasing prosperity to the whole world. Opponents fear that globalization is letting rich countries and big corporations take advantage of smaller, poorer countries. They argue this is widening the gap between rich and poor and undermining the power and policies of smaller governments.

Figure 1.18 These women, from the Swan River Valley in Manitoba, are protesting for the right to vote. Until 1918, Canadian women could not vote in federal elections.

History, School, and Citizenship

Every country in the world requires its students to study history in school to learn what it means to be a **citizen**. To understand why, we need to explore two questions: (1) What is citizenship? (2) What does it mean to be a citizen?

What Is Citizenship?

Most definitions of citizenship include:

- A sense of national identity, which means seeing oneself as, for example, Canadian, German, Jamaican, or Nigerian.

- An entitlement to rights. For example, the Canadian Charter of Rights and Freedoms says that Canadian citizens are entitled to freedom of speech and religion, freedom to meet and travel, the right to vote, protection of the law, and freedom from discrimination.

- Responsibilities such as paying taxes, obeying the law, and, perhaps, serving in the military.

- The right to self-government, including the right to vote and to run for public office.

- A belief in the values written in a country's constitution or bill of rights. In Canada, this includes bilingualism, human rights, Aboriginal rights, and democracy.

- A balance of personal rights and interests with the rights of others and the good of society as a whole; for example, speaking freely but not speaking hurtfully of others.

- Respect for other citizens and of human rights generally.

- Respect for the environment.

What Does It Mean to Be a Citizen?

To be a citizen means to belong to a particular country. Everyone is a citizen of some country. When we understand what a citizen is, we can understand the idea of the **nation-state**. This is the idea that the world's people can be separated into nations, and that nations are the best and most natural way for people to live together. According to this idea, each nation has its own language, or languages, and history, and each is entitled to its own land and government, or state.

Although the concept of the nation-state implies that each nation has its own country, in reality, every country has minority groups that speak languages and have cultures different from the majority. Many nation-states try to force minorities to live like the majority. Although we see citizenship as a good thing, for many minorities it has led to, and sometimes continues to lead to, discrimination and persecution. Canada, today, is based on a belief in multicultural citizenship; Canadian citizens are free to blend their own cultures with loyalty to Canada as a nation.

National and Global Citizenship

Some people want us to think of ourselves as global citizens: loyal to the world rather than to a specific country. As these people see it, no one country can solve the majority of the world's problems. Until we see ourselves as global citizens, the economic gap between rich and poor countries will continue to widen, and concerns such as terrorism and environment will continue to grow.

A key question facing citizens today is: Can the ideas of national and global citizenship be combined, and, if so, how? Some think this can be done if countries work together to resolve global problems. Others believe that countries must give up some of their powers to the United Nations or other international organizations or even that some kind of world government be established.

The Continuing Debate About Citizenship

Identity, rights, and duties are part of citizenship, but not everyone agrees on what they are or should be. For example, does the right to free speech include the right to preach racism or some other form of prejudice? Should voting be compulsory, with citizens being fined if they do not vote, as in Australia? Does being a citizen mean supporting one's country, at any cost, or does a citizen have the right to oppose the policies of his or her country? Do citizens have the right to disobey laws they think are wrong? In a democracy, being a citizen means being able to take part in debates on these questions and others like them without fear of punishment.

History can be and has been used as a form of propaganda. In some countries, history is distorted to show the citizens that their countries are better than any other country. The leaders of these countries want their citizens to do whatever the government wants.

History can also be used to teach people to think for themselves. Through history, we can learn that there are different ways to do things. When we think historically, we can learn from the past. We can try to see the world as other people see it and to look for the reasons why things happen as they do. Learning from the past helps us understand what it means to be a citizen, how definitions of citizenship have changed, and how people have struggled to win the rights of citizenship.

Summary

History shows us what has happened in the past and how the past has affected the present. History helps us better understand ourselves and the world in which we live. It also shows us different ways of doing things and widens our range of choices.

History can be, and often has been, misused. What people think they know about the past can lead to hatred and persecution of other people. Racism, sexism, and other forms of prejudice are often based on false and inaccurate understandings of the past.

Most of what we know about the past comes from historians. Historians are more than a walking encyclopedia of past events. Historians analyze historical arguments and interpretations. We can never know everything that happened in the past, only what historians (and other scientists) can tell us about the past. Therefore, we have to know how to investigate the past. We have to learn to think historically. In most chapters, you will have the chance to Be an Historian. First, you can read a sampling of documents from that time period. Then, you can think about and discuss the documents – just like a real historian!

In a democracy, thinking historically is an important part of being a citizen. Historical knowledge and historical thinking help citizens think for themselves and make informed decisions, not just believe what they are told to believe.

As you read about societies of the past, ask yourself these questions:

- What was this society's definition of citizenship?
- What can we learn about being a citizen today from this society?

Connecting and Reflecting

Reflect on what you have learned about how to study history and why history is important to our present-day society. Use the information to explain how it helps you connect to your world *as a citizen of Canada and a citizen of the world.*

The Early Peoples

Our Study of Early Peoples

Most of this textbook deals with the last 5500 years of the world's history. In terms of your life, this is an immense amount of time. In terms of how long humans have inhabited the earth, it is only a short span.

Scientists have determined that the first humans originated in East Africa over 2.5 million years ago. These early people were small in size, lived in small groups, and were relatively defenceless. They shared the dry, grassy, sparsely treed plains with animals such as elephants, antelope, and giant baboons that were faster, larger, and fiercer than they were.

Early humans survived by physically adapting to their environment. Three important adaptations were: (1) upright posture, (2) hands that could grasp objects, and (3) a large brain. The ability to walk upright on two legs allowed humans to use their hands to make and use tools and weapons.

Scientists believe upright posture and the use of tools contributed to the growth of the human brain. As brain size increased, humans made better tools and developed language to communicate. Gradually, humans learned how to change their environment to meet their basic needs of food, shelter, and clothing.

Many different accounts have been given of the beginnings of human life. Some have been provided by spiritual leaders, some by the world's religions, and others by science. Below, we look at an example of each.

Questions to Think About

+ How did humans in very early times meet basic needs such as food, shelter, and clothing?

+ How did early humans interact with their physical environment?

+ How did early humans communicate with each other?

+ How has life changed over time?

An African View of the Origin of Life

The following story is one explanation for the appearance of humans in Africa and their movement throughout the world. It is told by the Kono people, an **indigenous** *group who live in Guinea in West Africa.*

Death, whose name was Sa, had a wife and daughter but no place to live. He created a sea of mud and built a house in the middle of it.

God, whose name was Alatangana [AL-ah-TANG-anuh], came to visit. He did not like Sa's home, because it was a dark and dirty place. Alatangana made solid earth from the sea of mud, as well as plants and animals to live on the earth. Earth was a much more cheerful place.

Sa was pleased with what Alatangana had done and invited him to meet his family. Alatangana fell in love with Sa's daughter. Sa refused to let him marry her as he did not want

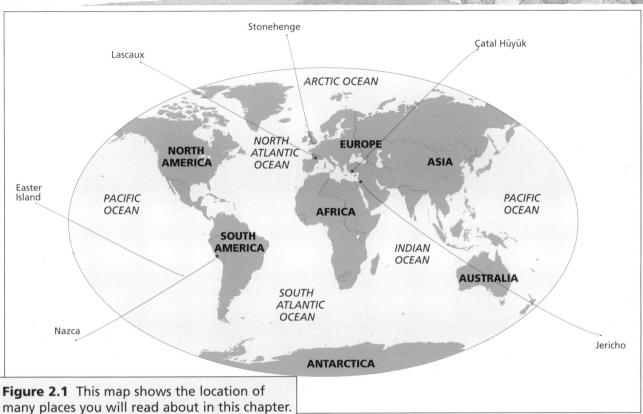

Figure 2.1 labels: Stonehenge, Lascaux, Çatal Hüyük, ARCTIC OCEAN, NORTH ATLANTIC OCEAN, EUROPE, ASIA, Easter Island, NORTH AMERICA, PACIFIC OCEAN, PACIFIC OCEAN, AFRICA, SOUTH AMERICA, INDIAN OCEAN, AUSTRALIA, SOUTH ATLANTIC OCEAN, Nazca, Jericho, ANTARCTICA

Figure 2.1 This map shows the location of many places you will read about in this chapter.

to lose her. Alatangana married Sa's daughter anyway and ran away with his bride to escape Sa's anger.

The couple had fourteen children. Each spoke a different language, and Alatangana and his wife were not able to understand them.

Alatangana pleaded with Sa for help. Sa told his son-in-law that as punishment for marrying his daughter, Alatangana would never be able to understand his children.

When Alatangana's children grew up, they moved to every corner of the earth. From these children come all the peoples of the world, speaking many different languages.

Two European Views of the Origin of Life

Creationism **Creationists** believe that all life owes its origins to divine guidance, and many also believe that humans were created in the present form by God. Some creationists believe that the earth was created in six days, as told in the account of creation in Genesis, the first book of the Bible. Others interpret the "days" as symbols of long periods of time. Current science evidence says that the earth is about 4.5 billion years old.

Evolution The scientific view of the **evolution** of life on Earth – that humans descended from a common ancestor who lived millions of years ago – is relatively recent. In the mid 1800s, Charles Darwin published *On the Origin of Species*. Several years earlier, Darwin had been on a scientific expedition to the Galapagos Islands. While there, he noted with great interest that many animal species, such as finches and tortoises, looked different on each island. He believed that each species had a common ancestor but had gradually changed over time. This was the basis of his theory of evolution through natural selection.

Figure 2.2 When the ice receded during the ice ages, the northern hemisphere of the earth probably looked similar to Arctic tundra. The lack of trees for shelter and fuel and the sparse vegetation made human survival in this kind of environment very difficult.

The Ice Ages

From about 2 000 000 to 12 000 years ago, huge sheets of ice, called glaciers, covered the northern areas of what are now Asia, Europe, and North America. These glaciers increased and decreased in size as the earth's climate cooled and warmed. The cold periods, called *ice ages* by scientists, lasted for thousands of years.

The lands just to the south of the glaciers were similar to the Canadian **tundra** – treeless plains – with extremely cold winters and short summers. Although Africa escaped the cold, the ice ages had an effect there, too. The desert areas in the north were wetter, and the tropical areas to the south were drier.

Since much of the earth's water was frozen into the huge glaciers, the water levels of the oceans were lower than they are today. Parts of the earth that are presently under water were dry land during these cold periods.

From time to time, the climate warmed and the glaciers receded. Whenever this occurred, trees and other plants grew much farther north, and animals moved into these environments. For example, hippopotamuses and rhinoceroses lived in Europe thousands of years ago. Today, hippopotamuses are found only in Africa, and rhinoceroses are found only in Africa, Asia, and the Malay Archipelago.

The ice ages had a great impact on humans. To survive, humans learned to adapt to very different conditions. Many moved as the physical environment changed, first from their original home in Africa, and eventually across the world.

The Stone Age

The period from almost 2.5 million years ago to about 5500 years ago is called the *Stone Age.* During this period, stone was the material that people most often used to make tools. The Stone Age can be divided into three distinct periods: Paleolithic, Mesolithic, and Neolithic.

Paleolithic times

During this period, humans were hunters and food gatherers. At first, they ate plant roots, nuts, berries, other vegetation that grew around them, and the meat that animals such as boars, lions, leopards, and baboons left behind after a kill. Later, humans began to hunt animals for food.

These early humans learned to make tools to help them obtain food. The first tools were very simple. Humans used pointed sticks for digging roots and sharpened pieces of rock for cutting meat and scraping animal skins. As hunting became increasingly important as a means of obtaining food, early humans began to make more sophisticated tools such as arrows, spears, knives, and harpoons.

Mesolithic times

As the earth warmed and the glaciers melted after the last ice age, vegetation and animal life began to change. To adapt to the new conditions, human ways of life also changed.

The Stone Age

Paleolithic times (Old Stone Age): from about 2.5 million to about 12 000 years ago

Mesolithic times (Middle Stone Age): from about 12 000 to about 10 000 years ago

Neolithic times (New Stone Age): from about 10 000 to about 5500 years ago

---

The most notable human adaptation began in the Middle East, in present-day countries such as Turkey, Iraq, Jordan, Israel, and Syria. While the people remained hunters and gatherers, they learned to harvest wild wheat and barley. The wheat and barley provided a reliable supply of food and enabled humans to stay in one place for long periods of time. Humans also developed tools, such as the scythe, to harvest their new food sources.

Neolithic times

The beginning of Neolithic times was marked by a very important change in the way some humans lived. In parts of the world, people began to farm. Humans became food producers rather than food gatherers. They settled in one place, grew crops, and tended animals such as sheep, goats, cattle, and pigs. With a new way of life came the need for new tools; for example, sickles for cutting grain, stones for grinding grain, pots for storing food, and looms for weaving cloth. In addition to the old technique of chipping tools from rock, humans now began to grind and polish stone to make tools.

The Development of Humans

Humans who were living at the beginning of Paleolithic times looked and behaved very differently from humans who lived during Neolithic times. Scientists have named these early humans according to stages of their physical development.

Homo habilis ("skilful human") These first humans lived in Africa. They were about 1.5 metres tall and had heavy ridges above their eyes, flat noses, large front teeth, and protruding jaws. Their brains were about half as big as the human brain is today. They lived from about 2.5 million to about 1.5 million years ago.

Homo erectus ("upright human") These humans were taller than *Homo habilis.* They had flat faces with sloping foreheads, large brow ridges over the eyes, and large jaws and big teeth. They had larger brains than *Homo habilis* and were more skilful at adapting to their

Figure 2.3 Neanderthals were the first humans known to bury their dead. When people died, they were often placed in a sleeping position and buried with food and tools to take with them to the next world. In Turkey, the remains of a Neanderthal body was found apparently covered with spring flowers. The care with which these humans were buried suggests that Neanderthals were beginning to develop ideas about life after death and the value of each human life.

environment. They improved their weapons and tools, and they learned how to use fire. These weapons and tools enabled them to live longer and to successfully reproduce. Eventually, many *Homo erectus* moved from Africa to other parts of the world. They lived from about 1.5 million to about 200 000 years ago.

Homo sapiens ("thinking human") These humans probably first appeared in Africa. There were several regional groups of *Homo sapiens* throughout the world. One European group is known as the *Neanderthals.* Neanderthals looked like modern-day humans *(Homo sapiens),* although they tended to be heavier and shorter and had pronounced brow ridges. Neanderthals were both more skilful at survival and had greater control over their environment than had earlier humans. Another group, discussed in this chapter, is known as *Cro-Magnon. Homo sapiens* have existed for about 250 000 years. Humans who lived on Earth 40 000 years ago were, physically, almost the same as humans are today.

Figure 2.4 This group of early humans is camped beside a stream, which provides them with fresh drinking water. The man in the foreground is gathering berries, while another man is using a wooden digging stick to obtain roots and leaves for food. In the background, some people are using stone blades to cut meat from an animal that may have been killed and left behind by a larger predator such as a sabre-toothed tiger, lion, or leopard.

PALEOLITHIC TIMES

Early Hunters in Africa

Lake Turkana [TUR-kan-ah] is a large lake in Kenya, East Africa. This part of Africa was home to some of the first humans. Here, archaeologists have found piles of bones (both human and animal) and collections of stones that humans used as tools. By carefully uncovering and examining these remains, scientists have started to put together the story of our earliest ancestors. In 2001, a 4-million-year-old skeleton was uncovered in the area. Although a link between it and modern-day humans has not been established, the skeleton shows the species was walking upright.

About 1.5 million years ago, the humans we call *Homo erectus* first appeared in East Africa. They lived in small groups of perhaps twenty people. Much of their food probably came from plants. They gathered nuts and berries, made stone tools, and used wooden sticks with pointed ends to dig up roots.

Sometimes, members of these groups killed animals and birds. Small animals like pigs, sheep, and monkeys, and old or sick animals would have been the easiest to kill. However, there is evidence *Homo erectus* occasionally hunted larger game. At one site in Africa, large bones were found together with stone tools. By comparing these bones with the bones of present-day animals, scientists

learned they were from giant baboons. Hunters may have surprised a troop of sleeping baboons and killed them with wooden clubs before the baboons awoke and could defend themselves.

When the food supply in one area was exhausted, humans moved on and set up a temporary camp in another location. These camps were probably erected on the sandy shores of streams that fed into Lake Turkana. The streams provided fresh water, and the trees that grew along the streams' banks sheltered the people from the hot sun. At night, the sand made a soft bed. To protect themselves from the cool night breezes, *Homo erectus* may have built shelters of stone or huts made from twigs.

Early Societies

Humans who lived in Africa 1.5 million years ago did not have a complex social organization. They probably stayed together in small or extended-family groups of three generations. Each group member – men and women, young and old – helped to gather food. Occasionally, several groups joined together to hunt or for protection. These groups must have had some means of communicating their needs to each another, but they probably "spoke" with gestures, signs, and grunts.

Early humans were becoming skilled toolmakers. Their most-used tool was the hand axe. A hand axe was a large piece of stone chipped from a large rock and shaped to fit the hand. The edges were then sharpened. The hand axe was used to cut meat, scrape bones and hides, and dig up roots.

Early humans learned how to control and use fire to keep warm, defend themselves against animals, and cook food. Fire may also have been used to drive animals into areas where they could be trapped and killed. Fires could have been started from lightning strikes. Fires were constantly looked after to keep them going for as long as possible.

The Spread of Humans

Over a period of hundreds of thousands of years, groups of early humans travelled beyond the African **savannah** into Asia and Europe. This movement may have been caused, in part, by changes in climate. Whatever the reason, as animals moved north in search of food and water, some humans followed them.

They learned to adapt to climatic conditions that were very different from the tropical conditions in their original home. Their hunting skills improved. Their weapons became more varied and sophisticated as they learned how to work flint and bone into knives, spears, and harpoons with longer, sharper blades.

While no records exist of peoples' movements in these early times, scientists have drawn conclusions based on the physical remains (skeletons, tools, and remains of camps, for example) that have been discovered.

During a cold period in the earth's past, when the ocean levels were lower than they are today, scientists believe that most of the islands in southeastern Asia (for example, Java) could be reached by land. Early humans probably made their way south across these **land bridges**. Most scientists also believe that around 40 000 years ago, people were building boats and crossing the seas, first to New Guinea and then to Australia.

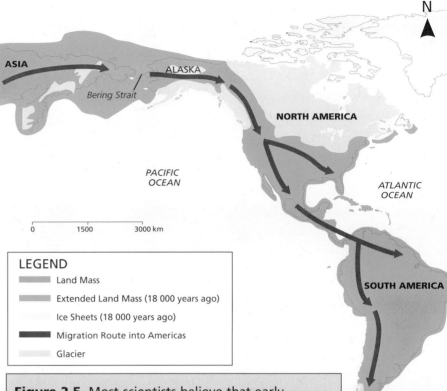

Land Bridge and Migration

LEGEND
Land Mass
Extended Land Mass (18 000 years ago)
Ice Sheets (18 000 years ago)
Migration Route into Americas
Glacier

Figure 2.5 Most scientists believe that early humans used land bridges to travel from one continent to another in search of food. To reach North America, humans crossed a land bridge, now under water, between Asia and Alaska. They then travelled south along the east side of the Rockies in what is now Alberta. When they reached the southern boundary of the glaciers, they headed east and then south to the tip of South America. This population movement took place over a period of thousands of years.

At the height of the last ice age, between 40 000 and 12 000 years ago, it is believed that some of these groups crossed into North America from Asia on a land bridge about 1000 kilometres wide. It covered what is now called the Bering Strait.

At the same time, other groups of humans probably travelled south along the west coast of Alaska and British Columbia, living on the ice-free islands and along the coast. Evidence of early settlements is being recovered from archaeological sites in British Columbia that are up to fifty metres below the current sea level.

The different areas into which humans moved had a great effect on the types of societies that they developed. Although scientists believe that all humans developed from the same ancestors, factors such as climate and isolation from other groups led to many differences among humans. These include differences in tools, beliefs, languages, and ways of life.

The Cro-Magnons

From archaeological research, we know a lot about a group of *Homo sapiens* who lived in Europe, the Middle East, Russia, and Siberia. The physical structure of some of these humans was like that of present-day Europeans. Scientists have named them *Cro-Magnons*, after the place in France where their remains were first found. These people were tall and intelligent, and they probably had a well-developed spoken language. Forty thousand years ago, Cro-Magnons were well established in many different environments – the deserts of Africa and Australia, the tropics of southeastern Asia, and the cold plains of Europe and Russia.

Figure 2.6 The man and woman in the foreground are tanning a hide, which will then be sewn into warm clothing. The man by the fire is sharpening the point of a spear that he will use to hunt game for the winter. In the background, a woman tends her baby, while a man builds a hut. Cro-Magnon huts were probably dome-shaped. In Central Europe where trees were scarce, mammoth bones were used to frame the walls, which were probably covered with hides. Bones were also used to weigh down the huts to prevent them from blowing away. In Africa and the Middle East, huts were made on a base of stones with walls of branches and twigs covered with mud.

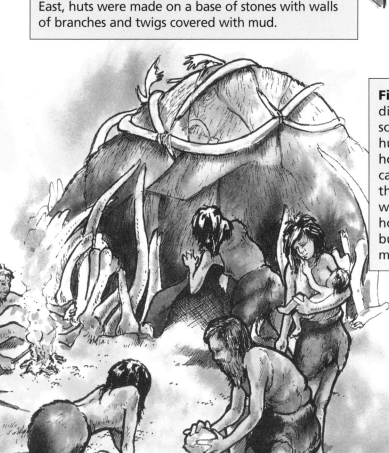

Figure 2.7 At a site in France, archaeologists discovered the carcasses of 10 000 horses. The scientists determined that a group of Cro-Magnon hunters had worked co-operatively to herd the horses to their death. One group of hunters, carrying flaming torches, chased a herd towards the nearby steep cliff. Another group of hunters waited at the bottom of the cliff and killed any horse that survived the fall. The horses were butchered at the site, and the hunters carried the meat back to their camp.

Preparing for Winter the Cro-Magnon Way

In this story, a group of Cro-Magnons prepare for winter.

Following the summer hunt, the group began their trek south. The days were becoming shorter and the nights colder. The families pushed on swiftly. Several days later, they reached the campsite where they would spend the winter.

A single glance around reminded them that they had a lot to do. Since the previous winter, two of the huts had collapsed and would have to be rebuilt. Three huts needed repairs. The exhausted travellers gathered around a hastily made fire to share the last of the fresh horse meat from the previous day's kill. Then they wrapped themselves in bearskin robes and lay down to sleep.

When Daga awoke at dawn, her mother and most of the other women were already gathered around the fire. Mammoth had been spotted nearby, and the younger men were preparing for the hunt. A good hunt today would allow the men to devote the next couple of days to repairing the camp.

Several women set off in search of animal bones they needed for making tools. Daga, her mother, and some other women began to sew skins together into parkas to replace the tattered ones from last year. Daga had her own bone needle that Boru, her grandfather, had made for her. Daga enjoyed sitting with the older women and listening to their stories as she sewed, but the work was tiring. Her fingers quickly grew sore and bruised from pushing the needle, threaded with sinew, through the thick animal hides.

The men did not return that night. Those left in camp ate an evening meal of dried reindeer meat and a handful of berries. The women then stoked the fire, and everyone curled up in their animal robes to sleep. Daga had a restless night. It was cold, and she could hear the howls of wolves somewhere beyond the firelight. Beside her, she heard Boru moaning and tossing in his sleep.

When Daga awoke at first light, she noticed Boru was gone. Her mother explained he had died during the night. Daga's eyes filled with tears. She had little time to think about her grandfather, though. There was so much to do before the men came back from the hunt.

The men returned in midafternoon, staggering under great loads of mammoth meat. That night everyone feasted. Daga ate until she felt that she would burst. Then she sat and watched as the men acted out scenes from the hunt.

The next morning the men dug a shallow pit in the centre of the camp, while the women dressed Boru's body in a fur parka newly made for this occasion. His face was daubed with red dye. The men then carefully placed his body in the grave. On it, they laid two mammoth bones, a tribute to Boru's hunting skills. Beside him in the grave, they placed a spear and a knife to help him in the hunt in the next world. Then they filled in the grave.

Cro-Magnon Homes

Most Cro-Magnons were nomadic. However, when there was enough food in a particular area to support them, they built homes that they could live in for long periods of time. In places like southwestern France, where a great number of caves can be found in soft limestone rock, they lived as cave-dwellers. They preferred to settle near streams or rivers in south-facing caves that caught the warmth of the sun. They kept fires burning for cooking and heat. The fires were built in stone hearths at the mouths of the caves to protect the entrances from wild animals such as bears and wolves. Piles of rocks at the cave entrances provided shelter from cold winds. Inside the caves, skins of animals such as deer and bison were hung on the walls to add warmth in cold weather.

Cro-Magnon Tools

Cro-Magnon hunters developed a new technique for toolmaking. They held a length of bone or antler upright on a rock and pounded the bone or antler with a hammer of stone, bone, or wood. The force of the blows caused long, narrow, blade-shaped flakes to break from the rock. They used these flakes to make a variety of tools and weapons.

In addition to the traditional hand axes, Cro-Magnons made arrows, chisels, scrapers, and knives. They fashioned spears by attaching arrowheads to long sticks. They then developed spear throwers so that they could kill animals while remaining at a safe distance from them. They invented harpoons for catching fish.

Social Organization

There was a division of labour between men and women. However, each would have been able to do tasks of the other. Because women bore children, they also reared them. This kept the women close to home but gave them time to gather plants, berries, and nuts. It is likely that they also prepared the food and made the clothing. Because of their greater physical strength, men did the hunting.

Children had their own chores – collecting firewood and hauling water. They also worked with the adults, learning the skills that they would need in later life. Boys hunted, trapped, and were taught how to make tools. Girls learned which plants could be eaten and which could be used as medicine, and they were taught how to cook and to make clothing.

The kind of social life indicated by a communal hut found in Russia was probably much more common among Cro-Magnons than it had been for earlier humans. Building a large hut from mammoth bones and hunting large animals required a great deal of co-operation. People had to work together if these projects were to be successful. Both activities also required good communication. Cro-Magnons would have had a well-developed spoken language.

Decisions had to be made and enforced as a group; for example, when and where to hunt, how to organize the settlement, and how to ration the food. Decisions were made only after everyone had voiced an opinion and general agreement had been reached. The opinions of some group members would have been treated with special respect because of their age and experience or because of their skills. But everyone was allowed an opinion. A leader usually acted only with the advice and consent of the whole group.

Figure 2.8 These Cro-Magnons are performing a ritual dance in a sacred cave. Note the artwork on the cave walls. Some scientists believe that Cro-Magnons practiced a form of hunting magic, in which they made representations of animals to ensure success in hunting. However, it is not possible to know for certain the real meaning of these drawings.

Religion, Music, and Dance

Early humans did not have a written language that we can study. Therefore, we have no clear way of knowing about their views of life. We can find some clues, however, in the drawings that they created and in their burial sites.

Cro-Magnons created the first great art. Magnificent cave and rock paintings have been discovered in southwestern France, in Spain, in the mountains of North Africa, and in South Africa. Most paintings depict animals – such as bulls, horses, stags, deer, and boars – that shared the land with these early humans. A series of human portraits was discovered in one cave in France. Other caves show the imprints of many human hands. The artists used brilliant reds and yellows, as well as black, to create these paintings. Archaeologists have also found scenes representing animals and different seasons carved on tools and weapons.

Scientists believe the cave paintings had religious meaning. Many paintings are well hidden, suggesting they were meant to be seen only by those who knew of their "secret" location.

In other parts of Europe, carved figures of women have been found. Scientists think that these figures were goddesses of the earth. The figures would have been used in fertility ceremonies. Many carvings show fine detail and a high degree of artistic skill.

Figure 2.9 This painting of a horse is in a cave at Lascaux, France. Scientists have suggested that the paintings were intended as offerings to the gods to ensure a successful hunt.

Scientists suggest that Cro-Magnons believed in an afterlife. At a burial site in Russia, bodies were found decorated with red dye, dressed in furs, and adorned with ivory beads and other jewellery. Many bodies were surrounded by weapons and animal bones.

Music was another form of art that appeared during the Cro-Magnon period. Musical instruments dated as early as 20 000 BCE have been found in Ukraine. Instruments include whistles and flutes, drums made from mammoth hides and painted with ochre, rattles made of ivory, and a pair of castanets. Ancient footprints found on the floor of a cave in France suggest that a ritual dance may have been performed there, perhaps to increase the fertility of the animals depicted on the cave walls.

The Incredible Story of Lascaux

One of the great Cro-Magnon sites is Lascaux [Lass-COE], in southwestern France. Paintings drawn deep within a cave remained undisturbed and undiscovered for about 15 000 years.

In 1940, four teenagers found an opening in the earth and decided to explore it. Once inside, they discovered they were in a very large cave. As they looked around, they found a vivid scene of wild horses, bulls, and deer "in motion" painted on the cave walls. One bull measured over six metres in length. The Hall of Bulls, as this section of the cave became known, proved to be only one of a series of connected chambers, each painted thousands of years ago with scenes of horses, bulls, rhinoceroses, and birds.

When news of the discoveries became known, the cave at Lascaux became one of the most popular tourist attractions in France. Soon, it was too popular. Exposure to the outside air and to excessive moisture damaged the paintings. Algae formed on the cave walls, and the colours in the paintings began to fade. Eventually, the French government closed the caves to the public. Today, only a limited number of people are admitted, and then only under strict conditions. Two galleries from the cave have been reproduced on-site for public view.

The Development of Spoken Language

No one knows when humans first developed spoken language. It is possible that *Homo erectus* made a range of sounds. However, it was probably not until *Homo sapiens* that language as we know it developed. Neanderthals likely had a limited language. By studying the structure of Cro-Magnon faces, scientists think that these early humans were able to produce a language that was more complex than that spoken by Neanderthals.

The development of spoken language was very important in the evolution of humans. Through language, people were able to develop and express new ideas and to develop complex working relationships. Language also provided a means for humans to teach others what they had learned, so that each new generation could build on the knowledge of the previous generation. In Cro-Magnon society, the elderly had an important place, because they had a rich store of knowledge to pass on to the young.

Once humans used language to communicate, more than just practical knowledge was passed along. Ideas about where people came from and the meaning of life were developed and shared. These kinds of ideas became the sources of legends, religion, and art.

MESOLITHIC TIMES

About 12 000 years ago, the earth began to change as the temperatures warmed. The glaciers receded far north, leaving most of Asia, Europe, and North America free of ice. The oceans increased in size as the ice caps melted. The land bridge between North America and Asia was cut off by rising water levels. Britain was separated from the rest of Europe by a channel and the North Sea. In southeastern Asia, land was submerged, creating chains of islands and isolating groups of people.

The warmer, moister climate produced lush growth in many areas. Grasslands, where herds of large game animals had grazed, gave way to forests. The herds gradually decreased in size or moved farther north. Men began to hunt smaller game (deer, beaver, ducks, and geese) that now inhabited the forests. Fishing became more common as new life – fish and shorebirds – appeared in the waters and along the shores of the warmer seas. The women gathered wild plants, grasses, and grains that grew where it had once been too cold for vegetation to grow.

In the Middle East, humans began to harvest wild grains such as wheat, rye, and barley. They added the wild grains to their diet of nuts, plants, and berries.

With a more varied, abundant, and reliable supply of food, humans no longer had to follow animals in order to survive. Life became more settled, populations increased, and people began to live longer. They produced new tools, such as sickles and grinders, to harvest grain. They invented dugout canoes, made from the trees that now grew abundantly around them, to travel by water.

Today, some societies survive mainly by hunting and gathering their food. The people live in places that are remote or where the land is not good for farming, such as the Arctic, the deserts of Africa and Australia, and the tropical forests of Africa, Asia, and South America. As in Paleolothic times, women gather the plants and berries, while men hunt and fish. Among the !Kung people of the Kalahari Desert in southwest Africa, the hunters provide only one-third to one-half as much food as the women.

NEOLITHIC TIMES

About 10 000 years ago, people no longer simply harvested the wild grains that they found around them. They began to grow their own crops from seeds that they had saved each year. They also began to tame and tend to animals. Within 5000 years, different groups of people in completely separate parts of the world had begun to practice agriculture.

With the development of farming came a more sedentary way of life. Not all groups farmed, though. In most areas of the world, people continued the hunting-and-gathering way of life. Even today, there are still hunting-and-gathering societies in the world.

Figure 2.10 A change in climate worldwide caused animal and vegetation populations to shift and provided Mesolithic peoples with new sources of food. In this picture, both a man and a woman are using sickles to harvest grain. Once they collect the grain, they will carry it back to camp in baskets woven from reeds.

A Neolithic Voyage into the Unknown

When food became scarce, groups of families often moved to new lands in search of a better life.

Following the birth of their fourth child, Fara and her husband, Belek, decided to move from the village where they had grown up. In their parents' time, the grain fields outside the village had provided enough food to feed everyone. Now, there was not enough food for all of the young families. The grain from one season's crop was gone before the next crop could be harvested.

Fara and Belek met with several other young couples to discuss their future. The plan they made was a bold one. Traders had told them of a large, uninhabited island lying some distance to the south. Perhaps the island could provide them with the space that they needed to farm and to raise their families.

About a dozen men, Belek among them, set out in small dugout canoes to scout the location. Fara, with the help of her two oldest children, struggled to carry on the work at home. All the while, Fara constantly kept an anxious eye on the sea and offered grain at the shrine of the goddess for Belek's safe return.

Just as the first crop of grain was ready to harvest, the men returned. Belek was excited about the new location. The island had land for many families, a good supply of fresh water, and pastures to graze sheep and cattle.

Fara dreaded the journey ahead. She feared for the safety of her children on the crossing, and she did not want to leave friends behind. Belek confidently assured her that life in a new land would be better for the whole family.

The preparations for the journey took several months. The men had to carve new canoes to transport the families and build boats for the cargo that they would take with them. These boats were each about nine metres long and would require eight people to row and one person to steer.

The women packed everything that they would need to begin farming on the island: grain seeds, tools, baskets, pots, and cloth, as well as food and fresh water for the families and animals during the journey. Fara also wrapped a small statue of the household goddess in fine flax cloth and carefully packed the statue in a basket. The family would need the goddess's protection on the crossing, and her presence on the island would ensure good crops.

When it was time to leave, the families loaded the boats. The whole village came to see the group off. Tearfully, Fara embraced her friends, certain that she would never see them again. Then the families climbed into the boats and set out for their new home.

Figure 2.11 Fara and her family are almost ready to leave for their new home. The animals – a cow and a bull, a male calf and a female calf, and 7 ewes and 3 rams – have been carefully selected for their size and stamina. The family has tools, utensils, containers for storage, and equipment for hunting and fishing.

Figure 2.12 To clear land, Neolithic farmers sometimes used a method called "slash and burn." This method of clearing land involves cutting down the trees and shrubs and burning them. Slash and burn is still used in many areas of the world.

Slash-and-burn farming is now considered to be harmful for the environment. When trees are removed, moisture and nutrients are lost from the soil. The land quickly loses its fertility and is vulnerable to erosion from wind and rain.

First Attempts to Control Nature

In the Middle East, the first crops that farmers grew were wheat, barley, and rye. In eastern Asia, **millet** and, later, rice became the main grain crops, while other crops such as yams and beans were also domesticated. Corn, beans, and squash were an important part of people's diets in Central America and North America. In South America, several varieties of potato were developed. In Africa, various plants such as bulrushes, millet, peanuts, and yams were domesticated.

In time, a type of wheat was developed that was easier to harvest than the wild cereals. Soon, farmers began to **irrigate**, or water, their crops. People were taking the first steps to control and change nature to suit their needs.

During this period, humans began to breed animals for specific characteristics. Farmers preferred smaller, gentler animals that were easy to manage. The earliest domesticated animals were probably dogs, sheep, and goats, followed by cattle, poultry, and pigs. These animals provided humans with food and clothing. Animals such as horses, camels, oxen, and llamas were used mainly for transportation.

The First Farmers

The Middle East was one of the places where the new agricultural way of life first appeared. However, as the population in the region increased, the land settled by farmers could no longer support all the people. Many chose to leave their homes to search for new land; others were forced out. All of these people took their farming tools with them, as well as the seeds and animals that they would need to set up their own agricultural communities. In this way, farming spread out from the Middle East in all directions. By 6500 BCE, humans were farming in the Nile Valley of Egypt, in eastern European countries near the Mediterranean Sea, and in Iran.

Farming also developed in other parts of the world. In Mexico, for example, people were growing corn about 7000 years ago. In China, where millet was an important crop, people were also farming. Over the next few thousand years, farming became a way of life in European countries around the western Mediterranean and in southeast Asia.

Not All People Farmed

The change from hunting and gathering to farming did not occur quickly, nor did it occur in all parts of the world. In much of Europe and on the plains of Asia, most people continued to hunt and gather their food for several thousand years after the development of agriculture in China and the Middle East.

On the plains and in the deserts of western North America, where mammoth and then bison roamed, some people continued to live

Before 6000 BCE, nomadic South American Indians collected wild potatoes on the central Andean plateau. The plateau stretches from Cuzco, Peru, to Lake Titicaca (located in Peru and Bolivia). Today, there are about 500 potato varieties in different colours such as red, yellow, white, and purple.

Farming 5000-10 000 Years Ago

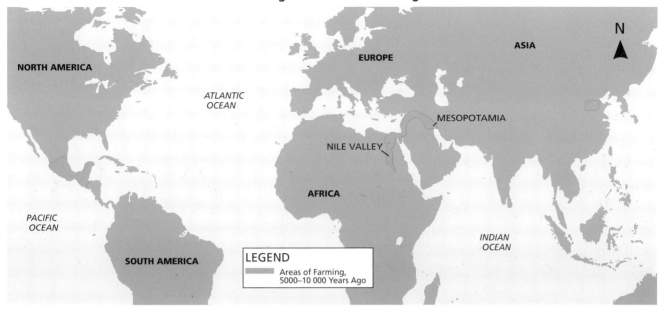

as hunters and gatherers until the 19th century. Today, the Inuit of northern North America, the Aborigines of Australia, and many African societies south of the Sahara Desert continue to hunt and gather.

Societies maintain a traditional way of life for several reasons. Some are isolated from other parts of

Figure 2.13 Farming began in different parts of the world between 5000-10 000 years ago. Some of the first farmers lived in the river valleys of the Nile River in Egypt and the Tigris and Euphrates rivers in Mesopotamia. There, the soil was fertile and the climate was moderate. Wild grains such as wheat and barley grew in abundance nearby, and sheep and goats roamed the area. The high hills surrounding the valleys provided natural barriers to the animals, enabling early settlers to control and, in time, domesticate these animals.

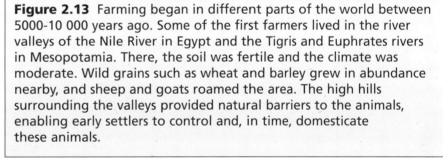

Women were the first farmers. While men were hunting, women planted and cared for the crops. It is likely, then, that women invented many of the earliest farming tools: sickles for cutting grain, husking trays for removing the tough outer coat of grains and seeds, and grinding stones for reducing the grain to flour.

the world. Some keep their original ways for as long as the environment continues to supply traditional foods, the population does not outgrow the supply of available food resources, or their land has not been claimed by others. For some, such as the Inuit, the harsh environment in which they live makes agriculture impossible.

For several societies, however, the change from hunting and gathering to farming was not a choice. As the world's population increased, people with more advanced weapons and tools simply overran hunting-and-gathering societies. In North America, for example, Aboriginal weaponry proved no match for European cannons and guns or even disease. In some cases, entire societies were wiped out by epidemics of smallpox or measles from which the Aboriginal peoples had no immunity.

Figure 2.14 In the Kalahari Desert in southern Africa, Bushmen survive by gathering and hunting their food, much as the first humans did hundreds of thousands of years ago. Because the land they occupy is arid and barren, the Bushmen have never turned to farming as a way of life.

The Rise of Permanent Settlements

To survive, hunters and gatherers must be continually on the move, following the animals on which they depend and moving to where the plants that they use are available. Farmers, however, are bound to their land. They have to tend their crops and their animals. They also need a permanent place to store their seeds and harvested crops. One major result of the growth of farming was the settlement of permanent communities. Two early communities, Jericho and Çatal Hüyük [CHAT-al HYU-yuhk], were located in the Middle East.

Jericho

Jericho, in what is now Israel, is thought to have been the world's first town. It is estimated that 10 000 years ago it covered an area of four hectares (about the size of a baseball stadium) and had a population of about 2000. It was a very large settlement for its time. Jericho also had a feature that was to become common in later towns and cities: it was surrounded by a high stone wall. This wall protected the population against wild animals and hostile neighbours. An eight-metre-high tower just inside the wall served as a lookout.

The first houses resembled the shelters built by earlier hunters in the area. Simple round huts were set on stone bases, and the twig walls and roofs were covered with clay. As farmers became established in their new way of life, they began to build more substantial and comfortable homes. These houses were rectangular in shape and furnished with simple benches for sitting and cupboards for storage. They were usually constructed of sun-dried mud bricks and often included a fireplace or an oven for cooking.

The living space of these houses varied from one room to several rooms and had storage areas for grain and seed. Some houses had a courtyard, which was used as the cooking area. In some communities, two-storey houses were common.

The Growth of Specialization and Trade

As communities developed and populations became more organized, specialization and trade increased. With a secure food supply, people could turn some of their energies from collecting food to developing a new skill, or specializing. Those who were good at working with stone would make stone tools that they then traded with someone in their community who specialized in making pottery. Specialization was the beginning of tradespeople such as bakers, blacksmiths, and masons.

Communities also began to specialize in the production of certain goods that they could trade with other communities. Products that were plentiful were traded with those that were needed. The people of Çatal Hüyük, for example, traded obsidian (a volcanic rock resembling glass), which they obtained from a volcanic mountain near their village, for flint that came from Syria. They used this flint to make high-quality blades for their tools.

Figure 2.15 This drawing shows Khirokrtia [keer-o-KEE-tia], a town in Cyprus, 7500 years ago. In the background, on the other side of a stone wall, are fields of grain. Farmers are carrying the harvested crop into town. In the right foreground, two residents are processing the grain into flour with husking trays and grinders. The interior of a dome-shaped hut shows a firepit in the middle of a single room, an oven for cooking, and a raised sleeping loft. The hole in the centre of the roof allows smoke from the fires to escape, while the other opening lets in light.

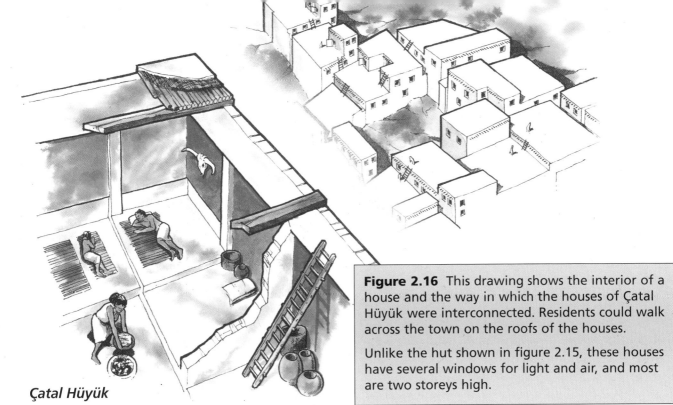

Çatal Hüyük

The remains of Çatal Hüyük, located in what is now Turkey, have been dated to about 8000 years ago. The town was built on the banks of a river and covered about thirteen hectares of land. It is estimated that as many as 6000 people lived there.

Çatal Hüyük was a farming community. Wheat and barley were cultivated on the irrigated plains outside the town. People learned how to produce berries, other fruits such as crabapples and grapes, as well as nuts. Cattle, goats, sheep, and dogs were raised. Craftspeople produced tools of obsidian, wove baskets and flax cloth, made pottery, and crafted copper ornaments. Archaeologists have discovered similar objects in other regions of the Middle East, suggesting that the residents of Çatal Hüyük traded with people in other settlements.

Houses were made of mud brick and had flat roofs. Houses were built against each other around a courtyard. There were no streets or paths in Çatal Hüyük. Instead, the residents moved about the town on the flat roofs. They entered and exited their homes through an opening in the roof. These entrances may have been designed this way as protection against wild animals or flooding.

Most homes had one large main room and a storeroom. The main room served as the sitting and eating areas during the day and sleeping area at night. Platforms made of brick and covered with mats made of rushes were built around the main room. These platforms were used for sitting during the day and sleeping on at night. The cooking area had a hearth of stone and sometimes an oven for baking. A ladder led up from the room to the door opening in the roof. Some houses had an opening for a window as well.

An important aspect of people's lives was their spiritual beliefs. In most homes, space was set aside for shrines to both life and death. Life was represented with paintings, statues, and reliefs that honoured their fertility goddess, who is often shown giving birth. Life was also represented in paintings and statues of animals: leopards, rams, and especially bulls, which were also a symbol of fertility. Death was represented in paintings of huge vultures pecking at human skeletons.

Many of these shrines served as burial places. Most people were buried in their own homes after they died. First, the body was taken outside the city walls, where it was left in the open to be picked clean by vultures. The bones were then gathered and buried under the sleeping platforms in the house.

Figure 2.16 This drawing shows the interior of a house and the way in which the houses of Çatal Hüyük were interconnected. Residents could walk across the town on the roofs of the houses.

Unlike the hut shown in figure 2.15, these houses have several windows for light and air, and most are two storeys high.

Mysteries from the Past

Several structures around the world – such as Stonehenge in Britain, the statues on Easter Island, and the Nazca Lines in Peru – have puzzled people for centuries. Scientists believe that these structures were built for spiritual or religious purposes during the Neolithic period. Since those who created the structures left no written records, their origins and purposes remain speculative.

Stonehenge

Stonehenge looms over Salisbury Plain in southern England. It is one of many structures around the world made with **megaliths** (large stones). Some ancient stone structures were built as tombs to house the dead, but Stonehenge was not.

Scientists believe that people began to build the monument over 4500 years ago. The structure was then added to and changed over a period of at least 500 years. The original Stonehenge looked very different from the Stonehenge that stands today. Over time, some of the stones have broken, some have fallen over, and others have disappeared. What remains, however, is still a mystery. Who built it? How was it built? Why was it built?

The Construction of Stonehenge

The construction of Stonehenge was a huge undertaking. The workers, likely farmers, began by drawing the circle for the outer trench. To place the trench, they used a compass that consisted of a rope made of hide attached to a wooden peg. The builders then used wooden digging sticks to dig out the trench along the circle.

The stone slabs weighed up to forty-five tonnes each and had to be cut out of solid rock some thirty kilometres away. The workers then moved each stone slab over rough terrain, placed the slab upright, and topped it with more slabs of rock. The builders had only very simple tools of wood or stone to work with. How could they have made the structure?

Figure 2.17 The drawing (top) shows what scientists think Stonehenge looked like when it was first completed. The photograph (bottom) shows what Stonehenge looks like today. By studying indentations in the earth and comparing fallen rocks with those still standing, scientists believe that Stonehenge originally consisted of an inner series of capped pillars surrounded by a closed circle of upright stones topped with horizontal slabs. Several smaller stones stood on three sides and at some distance from the circle. An entranceway on one side of the site was protected by a series of stones. Many of the missing stones may have been carted away by local builders. Wind and rain have eroded the stones that remain.

The stones were shaped with stone hammers and moved to the site by rolling them on logs. Each stone was eased off the log platform and into a deep hole dug for it. From there, the stone slab was very gradually raised to an upright position using a lever and pulley system. The final step was to place horizontal stones on the uprights.

Why did people go to all this trouble? Scientists believe that Stonehenge was the site of religious ceremonies. Some believe that it was connected to astronomy – the study of the sun, moon, and stars. Others believe it was linked to astrology, or it could have had both a scientific and spiritual purpose.

Figure 2.18 These are some of the giant stone statues on Easter Island. These statues were carved from very hard volcanic rock and moved great distances from inland rock quarries to the coast, where they look out to sea. The features of the statues are highly detailed. The eyes of some are made of white coral with pupils of red lava. Many wear headdresses made from red lava. The statues may represent the ancestors of the people who carved them. They stand between the earth and the sky and link the island inhabitants with their gods.

The Statues of Easter Island

The statues on Easter Island pose another mystery. Easter Island lies in the Pacific Ocean almost 4000 kilometres west of the South American country of Chile. Over 600 giant statues of humans are situated throughout the island. Some of the statues are as high as thirteen metres. Some have been crowned with stones weighing about twenty-seven tonnes.

The Easter Island statues were carved approximately 2000 years ago. Some seem to be guarding burial platforms. Tablets with writing on them have also been found on Easter Island, but no one has been able to translate the language on the tablets.

Nazca Lines

On a desert plateau in Peru, a series of lines and drawings cover an area of hundreds of square kilometres. These lines were made by removing stones to uncover the bare earth underneath and then piling the stones to outline a design. The most curious thing about the lines is that the images are so large that they can only be identified from the air. Scholars believe that the images were made to be seen by deities, or gods, and are, therefore, religious in nature.

Figure 2.19 The Nazca Lines cover almost 500 kilometres and include images of various birds, a spider, and geometric shapes. The drawings, like this one of a hummingbird, were made before 600 CE by the Nazca people of Peru.

Figure 2.20 This ivory carving of a woman's head was found in France. It is thought to be about 25 000 years old. The carving is quite finely detailed, indicative of the artistic skill of some early humans. From this carving and others like it, archaeologists have been able to learn something about the appearance of people who lived during this time. Scientists believe that the many carvings of women from this period represent goddesses of fertility.

Technological Developments of the Stone Age

Humans began to control their natural environment very early on. Over a period of thousands of years, they learned to use the materials in their surroundings to build more secure, comfortable lives for themselves. By the end of the Stone Age, their technological achievements included the following:

- *Making and using fire* Very early in the Paleolithic period, humans learned to produce fire by striking flints against iron ore. They also found that the friction caused by rubbing wooden sticks together eventually produced sparks. Cro-Magnons discovered other natural materials that would burn and keep the flame going. They also developed oil wick lamps. By the Neolithic era, fire was being used to shape clay pottery and to extract copper from iron ore.

oil lamp

- *Hunting tools* The first hunting tools included spears, spear throwers, bows and arrows, daggers, axes, and harpoons made of stone or of ivory from the antlers of animals. Scrapers were used for cleaning hides. By the Neolithic era, copper was being used more and more to make tools.

  As fishing became more important during Mesolithic times, humans developed nets, fishhooks, and small boats. They learned to weave baskets from reeds.

harpoons

- *Domestic tools* Stones for grinding plants, grains, and dye, and mortars and pestles for crushing seeds were developed. Humans used digging sticks and reaping tools to gather plant food. To carry their possessions from camp to camp, nomadic peoples used leather containers made from the hides of animals such as deer.

  With the beginning of farming in the Neolithic period, the range of domestic tools expanded. In some of the houses at Çatal Hüyük, cooking was done in ovens. Early farmers learned to mould clay and fire it to make containers for storing food.

- *Using metals* About 250 000 BCE, humans were extracting ochre, a type of iron ore, from the earth and using it as red or yellow paint or dye. Ochre was used in early cave paintings in what is now France. Ochre may also have been used to tan hides and protect the human skin against the sun. Bones dyed with red ochre have been found in gravesites, indicating that ochre had a role in burial rituals.

In Neolithic times, copper was extracted from iron ore to make both ornamental items like jewellery and beads and practical objects like needles and pins.

- *Medicine* Surgery was being practiced in Mesolithic times. Signs of a procedure called **trepanning**, in which part of a person's skull is removed, were found in the skeleton of a man (who seems to have survived the operation) from about 5000 BCE. This procedure was probably used to relieve epilepsy, mental illness, or severe headaches.

  In 1960, a human skull was found in Denmark with a hole drilled into a molar with a large cavity – evidence of the very early practice of dentistry. The hole may have been drilled to relieve the pressure of an abscess.

  The pain from surgical and dentistry procedures would have been eased by the use of herbal anaesthetics. Opium, alcohol, mandrake root, and coca were among the narcotics used to dull pain. One archaeologist has even suggested that the herbs for these painkillers, not grains, were the first crops grown.

- *Art and music* Cro-Magnons mixed ochre and other substances, such as charcoal, to

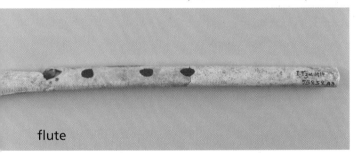

flute

create the colours they used in their paintings. The paint was sprayed on with blow tubes, or it was applied with brushes, probably consisting of horse hairs bound together. Sculptures, especially of goddesses and animals, were made from ivory and stone.

As early as 20 000 BCE, humans were making musical instruments such as flutes, drums, rattles, and castanets.

- *Housing* In farming communities from the Neolithic period, houses were built of bricks made from mud and dried in the sun. In places like Jericho, towers and high defensive walls were made of sun-dried bricks. The residents of Jericho also made walls and floors of plaster.

- *Clothing* Bone needles were used to sew together the skins and tanned hides of animals to make clothes. In the early farming communities, wool and perhaps flax (from which linen is made) were woven into materials for clothing, wall hangings, and rugs.

- *Ornamentation and jewellery* Bracelets, headdresses, and necklaces made of ivory beads and animal teeth and bones have been recovered from gravesites that date to Paleolithic times. Combs and needles carved from bone have been found.

  Copper beads were made during the Neolithic period. The people of Çatal Hüyük also had mirrors made from obsidian.

bone bracelet

Explorers of Early Times

Archaeologists (see chapter 1) are just one of many kinds of scientists who have contributed to our knowledge of very early times. Others involved in the search for our beginnings include the following:

- *Geologists* study the formation of the earth itself. They contribute to the study of early peoples by identifying the sources of the rocks used in making tools. By identifying Syria as the source of the flint used to make tools at Çatal Hüyük, for example, scholars were able to trace some ancient trade routes.

- *Paleoanthropologists* specialize in the study of early humans. Some research how humans developed physically. Others are interested in ways that humans behaved; for example, how societies governed themselves and educated their young.

- *Paleontologists* study the fossils of plants and animals to identify the vegetation, animal life, and climate that existed at a particular time in the past. By studying pollen from 10 000 years ago, for example, they can determine what kinds of crops the earliest farmers grew.

- *Biochemists* examine human tissue to determine the relationships among different groups and races of people. Biochemists helped to establish *Homo habilis* and *Homo erectus* as common ancestors of modern humans.

- *Artists*, such as sculptors, can put "flesh on the bones" of a fossilized skull, recreating the head of an early man or woman to show what the person may have looked like when alive. Painters create realistic pictures based on scientific knowledge. These pictures enable us to "see" early humans as they existed in their environment.

Frauds

The amount of material that scientists have to work with is often very slight, and the evidence can be interpreted in different ways. Scientists

Figure 2.21 Until recently, almost all facial reconstructions of early humans were done by sculptors. Today, many scientists use 3-D imaging to recreate the skull. In this photograph, pegs have been attached to the recreated skull at key points to indicate the thickness of the soft tissue, muscle, and skin to be modelled over top.

constantly question each other's conclusions. A new find can destroy a carefully developed theory about human origins.

The case of Piltdown man is a good example of why scientists use caution. In 1912, in southern England, part of a skull, a jawbone, and some teeth were found during an excavation. The remains seemed to be from a single species that was part man and part ape. If this were true, experts would have to change all their ideas about the physical development of early humans. However, many researchers were not convinced that the skull and the jawbone were from the same species.

Forty years later, when the remains of Piltdown man were dated, it was discovered that the skull was that of a man who had lived in the 13th century CE, and the jaw belonged to a modern ape. While no one is sure who arranged this hoax, or why, it was a deliberate attempt to confuse the picture of early human life.

A Consequence of Fraud

Today's scientists face new dilemmas. In 1891, a magnificent ivory carving of a man's head was discovered in Czechoslovakia at a Cro-Magnon site. Tests in 1988 indicated that the carving was 26 000 years old. Clearly, the ivory head came from a site where the art of the people was highly developed. However, no other art of this age and complexity has ever been authenticated. To accept the carving as genuine, scientists would have to change their ideas about the cultural development of people at that time. While experts agree that it would be difficult to make a modern piece appear 26 000 years old, new techniques to definitively date the object have yet to be developed.

Figure 2.22 After Piltdown man, scientists have been more careful than ever to authenticate their findings. As we see below, this discovery was well documented. In 1950, this man was found well preserved in a bog in Tollund, Denmark. He died about 2000 years ago. Burial sites such as this one give a great deal of information about the past. Because the man had a tight noose around his neck, scientists believe that he was sacrificed at a religious festival. Scientists also analyzed the contents of his stomach and found that his last meal was porridge flavoured with herbs. The herbs provided researchers with information about the plants that were growing in the area. The body was naked except for a pointed leather cap on the head and a hide belt around the man's waist.

Summary

As humans responded to their environments in unique ways, societies became more diverse. Most human societies were isolated from each other and developed different languages, different ways of organizing and governing themselves, and different ways of meeting their needs for food, shelter, and clothing. They developed their own distinctive sets of beliefs to explain the world in which they lived. These things bound together the members in each society, while it separated them from other societies with different sets of beliefs and ways of life. In North America, for example, the unique ways of the Aboriginal peoples and the European settlers have resulted in misunderstandings between the two groups that have lasted for centuries.

In today's world, societies may be becoming less diverse. Technologies such as television and Internet enable people in China and Canada to share the same experiences at the same time. Air travel continues to bring groups of people together from all over the world. Through immigration, people of many cultures live together.

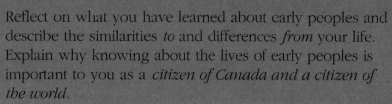

Connecting and Reflecting

Reflect on what you have learned about early peoples and describe the similarities *to* and differences *from* your life. Explain why knowing about the lives of early peoples is important to you as a *citizen of Canada and a citizen of the world*.

EARLY SOCIETIES OF MESOPOTAMIA, EGYPT, THE INDUS VALLEY, AND CHINA

Part 2

In Part 2, you will read about the complex societies that developed in several river valleys between 3500 BCE and 500 BCE. The fertile flood plains along these river valleys produced abundant crops, freeing the peoples who lived there from the constant need to search for food.

Most of the settlers were farmers. Their crops provided food for others as well as themselves, so that some people were able to choose occupations such as making tools, furniture, pottery, and clothing. Eventually, these occupations became specialized. In time, people learned engineering skills that allowed them to build basic structures such as irrigation systems and storage buildings. Later, they built magnificent temples and tombs and designed cities. As the river valley communities grew in size, many formed **city-states**.

Life in the city-states became highly organized. With so many people living together in such small areas, rules and laws had to be established to control the distribution of land, the payment of taxes, and the settlement of disputes. In time, these societies needed a means of keeping records. This led them to develop forms of written language to record laws, accounts, and decisions. Those who kept the records were called **scribes** (recorders or secretaries), and they had to spend many years training for this vocation.

With the transition from hunting and gathering societies to farming societies, systems of government began to change. In small hunting-and-gathering societies, people could make decisions through a process of discussion and consensus (general agreement).

In the larger farming societies, it was not possible for leaders to consult with everyone. They came to depend more and more on advisers to help them decide what to do, since the decisions they had to make were increasingly complicated. Codes of laws were created, and courts and judges were appointed to enforce them. Religions were developed partly as a means to help people explain and understand such things as day and night, storms, and death. Religions were also used to strengthen the power and influence of the rulers, who sometimes assumed the status of gods.

Priests, judges, clerks, advisers, and officials all worked full-time at their non-farming jobs. They had to be provided with food by others, so farmers were either persuaded or forced to give up part of their crops in the form of taxes.

When societies developed armies to protect themselves from invaders, the power of their governments and their rulers greatly increased. Strong rulers also used their armies to control their own peoples.

As the river valley societies became more organized, they became more structured. Eventually, each developed into a civilization. You may think that a society and a civilization are the same thing, but they are very different. All animals can live in a society, but only humans can create a civilization. Civilizations have all or most of the following characteristics:

- the existence of cities
- advanced division of labour based on specialized occupational groups
- social classes, including a ruling class that is exempt from work for basic subsistence

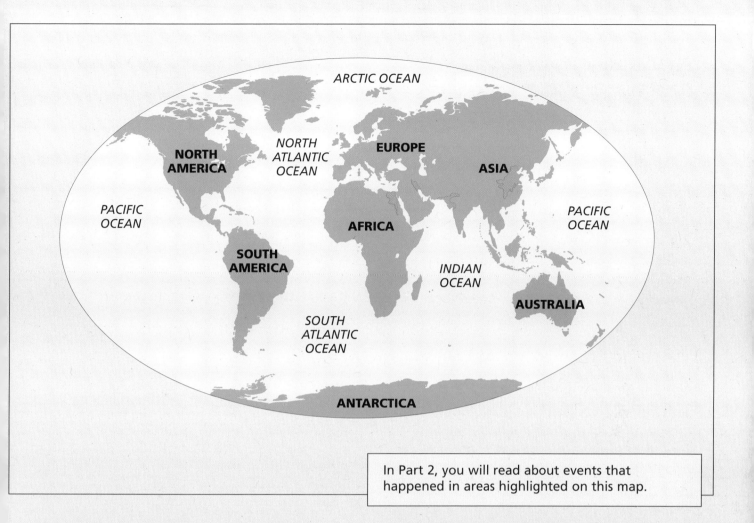

In Part 2, you will read about events that happened in areas highlighted on this map.

- an administration that can collect "social surplus" (taxes or tribute)
- public buildings not designed as dwellings but for communal purposes
- record keeping in written form

As you will see in the four chapters that follow, the river valley societies evolved into civilizations. In chapter 3, Mesopotamia, you will read about the Sumerian people who settled in the river valleys between the Tigris and Euphrates rivers. Mesopotamia is often called "the cradle of civilization." Their land, now known as Iraq, included parts of Turkey and Iran.

In chapter 4, you will read about the Egyptians. They developed a highly sophisticated society along the flood plains of the Nile River. Many of the remarkable structures that Egyptians built still exist, some 5000 years later.

The Indus Valley people are the focus of chapter 5. No one knew of their existence until about 100 years ago. They settled along the fertile banks of the Indus River and the River Riva and developed some of the most advanced cities in the world up to that time. Their land was in present-day Pakistan and northwest India.

In chapter 6, you will read about the ancient Chinese **dynasty** called the Shang. Until the 1920s, people thought this dynasty was a myth. Now, archaeologists are constantly finding out new information about these people. We do know that they had the earliest form of writing in China.

The common thread in all these societies is the rivers. As you read about them, think of all the benefits rivers provided to these ancient civilizations.

MESOPOTAMIA	c. 8500 BCE	c. 7000 BCE	c. 5000 BCE	c. 4300 BCE	c. 3300 BCE	c. 3250 BCE	c. 3000 BCE
	People are farming in the Middle East.	People begin to settle in the valley between the Tigris and Euphrates rivers in an area called Mesopotamia.	A group of people called the Sumerians begin to settle in southern Mesopotamia.	The Sumerians have established several city-states including Ur, Lagash, Kish, Nippur, and Uruk.	Sumerians develop a format of writing based on pictographs.	Sumerians are using the wheel for pottery-making and transportation.	Doctors and veterinarians are practicing medicine.

EGYPT	c. 5500 BCE	c. 4000 BCE	c. 3300 BCE	c. 3100 BCE	c. 2700 BCE	2558 BCE-2532 BCE	c. 2500 BCE
	People began to settle in permanent villages along the Nile River.	First evidence of medical treatments.	First appearance of hieroglyphics.	King Menes unites Upper Egypt and Lower Egypt.	Great Step Pyramid is built at Saqqara.	Khafre, credited with building second largest pyramid in Giza, rules.	The Sphinx is built.

THE INDUS VALLEY							c. 2600 BCE
							Evidence people have a system of writing by the time they moved into the Indus Valley. Indus Valley people settle along the Indus River and River Riva and establish several cities, including Mohenjo-Daro and Harappa. Cities have well-planned and well-made drainage and sewage systems.

CHINA	c. 5000 BCE	c. 4000 BCE			2737 BCE		
	Silk production begins.	Neolithic farmers settle near Huang Ho River.			According to legend, Chinese emperor Shen Nung discovers tea.		

Mesopotamia

c. 2760 BCE	2324 BCE	c. 1800 BCE	c. 1770 BCE	c. 760 BCE	c. 550 BCE
Sumerians begin to combine copper and tin to make bronze.	The Akkadians, led by Sargon the Great, take control of many Sumerian cities.	Babylonians move into Mesopotamia.	The Code of Hammurabi, a set of 282 laws, is created.	Assyrians invade Mesopotamia.	Persians invade Mesopotamia.

Egypt

c. 2000 BCE–1700 BCE	c. 1800 BCE	c. 1650 BCE	c. 1550 BCE	c. 1400 BCE	c. 1361 BCE	c. 1300 BCE	332 BCE
Egyptians begin to write down descriptions of medical knowledge.	Hebrews move from the Arabian Desert to Egypt.	End of pyramid-building era.	Use of term *pharaoh* begins.	Queen Hatshepsut, the best-known female pharaoh, begins her rule.	King Tukankhamen, the boy king, begins his rule.	Hebrews begin to settle in Canaan (the area between Egypt and Mesopotamia).	Alexander the Great conquers Egypt.

Indus Valley / India

c. 2000 BCE	c. 1900 BCE	c. 1500 BCE	c. 1000 BCE	c. 600 BCE	c. 567 BCE
Indus Valley people teach Chinese how to cultivate rice.	Indus society in decline. Semi-nomadic Indo-Aryans begin moving into Indus Valley.	Indo-Aryans begin to settle on farms to raise cattle and dominate the river valley.	Indo-Aryan domination of Indus Valley ends.	A new society that practices Hinduism emerges in India.	Buddha (Siddhartha Gautama), founder of Buddhism, is born.

China

1766 BCE	1027 BCE	551 BCE	c. 500 BCE	221 BCE
Beginning of the Shang dynasty. Chinese develop a form of writing using drawings called *pictographs*.	The Shang dynasty is overthrown.	Confucius, founder of Confucianism, is born.	Metal coins are invented.	Qin Shi Huang Di unifies China. All existing walls throughout the Chinese kingdom are joined together and form the Great Wall.

Mesopotamia

Our Study of Mesopotamia

Our study of Mesopotamia includes the following topics:

- Where the Sumerians Lived
- The Importance of Rivers
- Government
- Social Organization
- Cities
- Housing
- Farming
- The Development of Writing
- Education
- Religious and Spiritual Beliefs
- The Legacy of the Sumerians
- Other Societies

Questions to Think About

- How was life in the Tigris and Euphrates river valleys similar to and different from life elsewhere in very early times?

- How did Sumerians satisfy their non-material needs (e.g., entertainment, recreation, music, art, literature, religion)?

- What achievements of Sumerian society (e.g., inventions, religion, values, buildings) are considered important today?

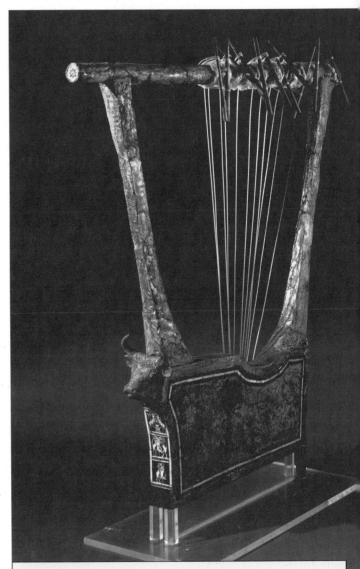

Figure 3.1 This silver lyre was found in the tomb of a Sumerian queen who was buried in about 2500 BCE. Musical instruments like lyres, harps, and oboes were often played during religious activities.

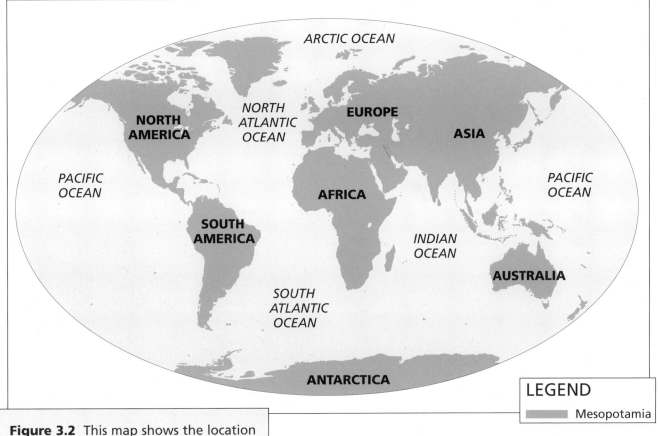

ARCTIC OCEAN

NORTH
ATLANTIC
OCEAN

EUROPE

ASIA

NORTH
AMERICA

PACIFIC
OCEAN

AFRICA

PACIFIC
OCEAN

SOUTH
AMERICA

INDIAN
OCEAN

AUSTRALIA

SOUTH
ATLANTIC
OCEAN

ANTARCTICA

LEGEND

Mesopotamia

Figure 3.2 This map shows the location
of Mesopotamia in about 3500 BCE.

People settled in permanent villages in the Middle East in very early times. There, they learned how to grow crops and to domesticate animals. By about 7000 BCE, some of these people were living in the valley between the Tigris [TI-gris] and Euphrates [yoo-FRAY-teez] rivers, located in present-day Iraq.

This valley is called *Mesopotamia* [meh-suh-puh-TAY-me-uh], which in Greek means "between the rivers."

Mesopotamia is sometimes referred to as "the cradle of civilization," because some of the first-known civilizations have been found there.

For several centuries, Mesopotamia followed a pattern of settlement and conquest. The Sumerians [soo-MAYR-ee-uhns] lived in southern Mesopotamia by about 5000 BCE. We know most about this group of people because many of their written records have survived. Their life in about 3500 BCE is the main focus of this chapter.

Other groups that occupied Mesopotamia included the Akkadians (2334 BCE-2100 BCE), Babylonians (1900 BCE-1100 BCE), Assyrians (750 BCE-605 BCE), and Persians (550 BCE-330 BCE). Each group learned things from the people who were conquered, adding to the cultural richness of the area.

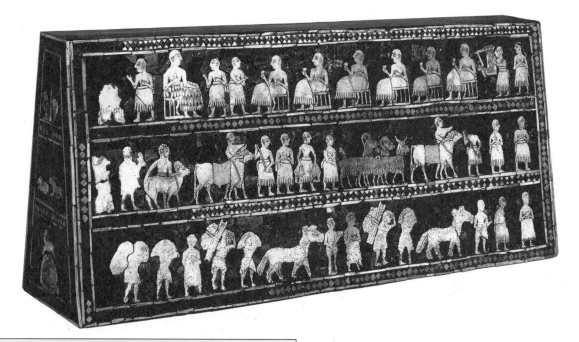

Where the Sumerians Lived

The climate and physical geography of the Middle East have changed little from ancient times. The weather in Mesopotamia was extremely hot in summer and cold in winter. Much like today, summer temperatures reached 40°C, while winter temperatures were often below 0°C. There was little rain. As a result of this climate, vegetation was sparse. Short grasses covered most of the region, and small trees and bushes grew along the riverbanks. Mesopotamia lacked many natural resources such as timber, stone, and minerals.

The Importance of Rivers

Each spring, snow in the Anatolian highlands of present-day Turkey melted, and the water flowed into the Tigris and Euphrates river valleys. Most years the valleys flooded. Some years, the runoff from the mountains was so great that the flood plains were inundated with water. Damage to homes and fields could be extensive. As flood water receded, a layer of silt and dead plants rich in nutrients covered the flood plains. In time, the flood plains became very fertile and ideal for growing crops.

Much of Mesopotamia was flat plain. Because there were no natural barriers, people from the surrounding areas could enter the territory easily. This allowed for ideas and goods to reach the area, but also made it possible for foreign armies to invade the region, a primary cause of its history of settlement and conquest.

By about 7000 BCE, most people in the world were still hunting and gathering their food. In Mesopotamia, people had begun to farm along the fertile plains. With farming, only some of the people were needed to produce enough food to feed everyone. Others could work at different occupations. Eventually, people began to specialize; for example, they became builders, traders, craftspeople, artists, priests, and government workers.

Where They Came From

The Sumerians migrated into the area between the Tigris and Euphrates rivers, probably from the Zagros Mountains in the northeast. Their language, which was unlike any other in the region, soon became the dominant tongue. Over several hundred years, with a succession of strong rulers, the Sumerians flourished and conquered many of their neighbouring city-states.

Government

Early societies were organized as villages. The villages were small, making it possible for everyone who lived there to be involved in making decisions that affected them. As villages grew in size and population, people developed more effective ways of making decisions. Some in the community were given the responsibility to keep order, provide protection, and ensure people's needs were met. This is how early governments developed.

Over time, Sumerian settlements grew into city-states. A city-state is a self-contained urban centre with its own ruler and government. A city-state is usually surrounded by a small dependent rural area, villages, or towns.

By 3000 BCE, between fifteen and twenty Sumerian city-states had been founded. Uruk was one of the most powerful – its government ruled seventy-six neighbouring villages. Other powerful city-states included Lagash, Ur, Kish, and Nippur. Conflicts between city-states were frequent, and stronger cities were able to conquer and control cities with weaker governments.

The first government leaders were probably priests. They had both religious and government responsibilities. As conflicts between city-states increased, military leaders were chosen as rulers. In time, these rulers took on the role of kings. They made and enforced the laws. They also supervised

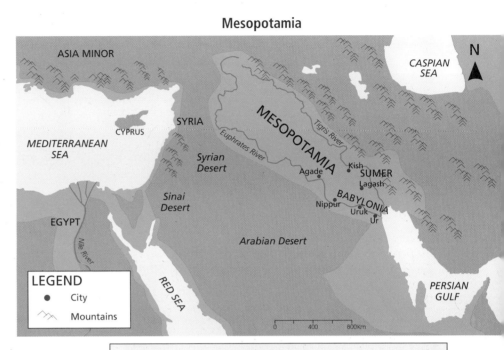

Mesopotamia

Figure 3.4 This map shows the major city-states in Mesopotamia in about 4300 BCE.

the building of major structures such as dams, temples, and canals. When rulers died, they were often replaced by relatives. A succession of rulers who are all related to a common ancestor is called a *dynasty*.

Sumerians believed that their cities had been created by **deities** (gods and goddesses). The lands and people of the cities belonged to these deities, and each king acted on behalf of the local diety. It was in this way that kings claimed to rule by "**divine right**." Sometimes a king, such as Gilgamesh, claimed to be a deity. Gilgamesh ruled the city-state of Uruk (called Erech in the Bible) around 2750 BCE. Gilgamesh was known for conquering nearby cities. His life, achievements, and a great flood are in an epic poem about his adventures. It is written on twelve clay tablets and may be the oldest written story ever found. The story of Noah in the Bible has many similarities to the **epic** of Gilgamesh. In the Bible, Noah built an ark and saved two of every kind of animal during the Great Flood.

As cities grew in size, the responsibilities of the kings grew. Additional workers were hired to collect taxes and write and enforce laws. These government workers joined the wealthy merchants and the priests as members of the upper class. Some of them had huge farms, and all of them lived comfortably.

Social Organization

Each city-state had its own king or ruler. Society consisted of upper, middle, and lower classes, and slaves.

Within families, men were the heads of the household. The father was responsible for arranging the education of his sons and the marriage of each daughter. A man could pay off debts by hiring or selling his wife or children as slaves.

Women had some rights, and some were financially independent of their husbands. When a woman married, her parents gave her a **dowry** of either money or goods to use as she wished. Many used their dowry to set up a business or buy land.

Many households had slaves. Most Sumerians treated their slaves fairly, because they realized anyone could become a slave through bad luck, debt, or by being captured in war. Some slaves were bought and sold, but many could be hired for a length of time. Slaves could own property, become traders and craftspeople, and buy their freedom.

Beer was the most popular drink in Mesopotamia. Beer was available in taverns, but people also brewed beer in their homes for their own use and to sell.

What They Ate

Sumerians ate grain, such as barley and wheat. The barley was made into flour for bread and cereal (much like porridge). Sumerians also ate vegetables such as chickpeas, lentils, beans, onions, and lettuce. They raised cattle and goats for milk, cheese, butter, and yogurt, and sheep for wool and mutton. Only the wealthy ate meat. Date palms produced dates that were eaten fresh, dried for later use, and made into syrup that was used as a sweetener.

What They Wore

The clothing worn by Sumerians varied with the seasons and signified social status. During the hot summer months, wealthy women wore colourful, long, loose-fitting gowns. Orange, yellow, green, and scarlet were popular colours. Wealthy men wore short, wide skirts similar in style to kilts and often draped a fringed shawl over one shoulder. Poor men and women wore simple knee-length tunics. During the cold winter months, everyone wore heavy clothes made of sheepskins and other animal skins, and cloaks made from wool.

Social Order

King/Ruler
|
Upper Class
(nobles, priests, important government officials, wealthy landowners, successful merchants)
|
Middle Class
(tradespeople, craftspeople, soldiers, well-to-do landowners, most government officials)
|
Lower Class
(fishermen, farmers)
|
Slaves

Figure 3.5 During the summer months, men and women dressed simply.

Life in Ur

This story shows many aspects of life in Ur, including agriculture, trade, education, division of labour, family, and religion.

Taboc was a scribe. His job was to keep written records of the barley, flax, and other crops that Sumerian farmers brought to the temple of Nanna. The Sumerians believed that the god Nanna had founded the city of Ur.

As Taboc stood on the walls that surrounded the temple, he looked out over the busy harbour and the planted fields. He could see farmers working in the fields and the trading boats, each with its single sail, near the docks. The scene filled him with pride, because he knew his contribution to the welfare of the city was important.

Thousands of people lived in Ur. Most had no need to read or write, though. Many were farmers. Others specialized as carpenters, brick makers, leather workers, basket makers, and artists. Sons – and sometimes daughters – usually took their fathers' professions, having learned about the work as children. Taboc's father had been a scribe.

Figure 3.6 This clay-baked tablet lists barley rations for 17 gardeners for one month. At his job as a scribe, Taboc kept records similar to this one.

Taboc returned to his work. He was compiling lists of what had been made and grown in Ur. One of his responsibilities was to ensure that enough food was stored to feed the population over the winter months or during a drought or war. If Taboc did his work well, no one in the city would ever starve.

Women wore makeup, such as lipstick and eyeshadow, and used perfumes and body oils. Some women wore wigs.

Both men and women wore jewellery. The poor wore jewellery made of coloured stones or shells. Wealthy women wore jewellery made of gold from India and the Middle East, and lapis lazuli from Afghanistan.

Cities

Most cities were surrounded by a moat and a high, strong wall made from sun-dried mud bricks. The gates into the cities were massive. Some were made from bronze.

Inside the gates, the city was a maze of narrow streets that led to the city centre. The city centre, called the *temenos*, was the ceremonial area and included important buildings such as temples and the king's palace. Important buildings were made from **kiln**-dried bricks, which were much longer lasting than sun-dried brick.

The closer a family lived to the city centre, the more important and the wealthier the family (or person) was.

Figure 3.7 Farmers used ploughs with bronze blades pulled by oxen to plough their fields. Note the farmer putting seeds into a funnel. In this way, the ploughing and planting were done at the same time.

Figure 3.8 On the left is a typical Sumerian house made of reeds. Some houses in what was southern Mesopotamia are still built in this way. Later, most people lived in one-room mud-brick houses. Some of the larger homes had multiple rooms (right) built around a central courtyard.

Housing

The first houses in Mesopotamia were single-room dome-shaped buildings. Later, houses were made of mud-brick and had flat roofs. Families slept on the rooftops on hot summer nights.

The wealthy lived in two-storey mansions. The rooms on the second floor ringed a private courtyard and were connected by balconies. On the main floor, large, arched doorways opened to the courtyard. Some roofs were sloped so that rainwater could be collected in containers and used for drinking and cooking. Roofs and walls were whitewashed to reflect the hot sun.

Most Sumerians, rich or poor, owned few pieces of furniture. Inside a home were storage chests, stools, a table, and reed mats for sleeping on. In winter, homes were heated by animal dung burning in metal containers called braziers.

Farming

Nobles owned large farms, which were farmed by tenants and slaves. Tenants were the common people. They worked as sharecroppers for wealthy, powerful landowners. Sumerian rulers and their advisers decided what to plant and when to plant it.

The families of the slaves and tenant farmers also worked on the farms. About half of each farmer's produce was donated to the temple and the landowner. Often, the farmers were left with barely enough food to feed their own families.

Some independent family farms operated on land owned by the local temple. Farmers who were granted permission to use these lands paid their taxes to the religious leaders in the temple.

Figure 3.9 This picture depicts the way that Sumerians lived and worked on the farmland outside their city walls. Important aspects of agriculture included irrigation and the use of simple tools.

Living the Good Life in Ur

The following story describes what it was like to live in a Sumerian city.

Taboc finished work for the day. He stamped the temple's seal on the last clay tablets and put them away in a safe place. Other workers were also preparing to leave the temple buildings. New military uniforms made of leather hung in the tanner's shop. Weavers put away their large, flat looms for the night.

Hundreds of people worked for the temple. Some tended the temple's lands and grew food for the temple workers. Others worked as servants, carpenters, weavers, scribes, and artists. Almost everyone who had a job in Ur worked inside the temple walls. During the day, the temple complex was a miniature city.

When Taboc left the temple, it was still hot outside. He walked by many mud-brick buildings on his way home. Some were eroding from the strong winds that blew across the plains. Cracks in the walls had been caused by the extreme weather – the heat of summer and the cold of winter. These buildings would soon need to be torn down and rebuilt. Even the harder, kiln-dried bricks that paved the streets needed repair.

The route home led Taboc through a maze of narrow streets and alleys. He walked by the brick houses of the poorer workers. These one-room houses were built around a shared courtyard.

How lucky he was to be rich, Taboc thought. His family's house had two storeys and twelve rooms.

As Taboc neared his neighbourhood, he heard music. He loved the sounds of the harp, but the drums and pipes were also enjoyable if they were well played. The musicians he was listening to were probably professionals hired for the evening, perhaps for a wedding party.

Taboc would have his own wedding soon. His parents had arranged his marriage, and the marriage contract was to be finalized that evening. His father would give the bride's father money, and Taboc would meet his bride-to-be for the first time.

Figure 3.10 Craftspeople such as cabinetmakers worked in the temple.

Farmers used water from the Tigris and Euphrates rivers to irrigate their fields. First, they built dams to store water. Then, they dug small channels to divert the water to where it was needed. Sumerians used ploughs to cut into the soil, allowing seeds to be buried in the soil instead of near the surface where wind could blow them away. The plough greatly increased crops production. Equipment such as wheeled carts also made farming easier and more efficient.

Figure 3.11 With few trees growing in the region, Sumerians imported lumber. In this scene, men are unloading cedar wood, probably from Lebanon.

Trade

Sumerians traded widely with their neighbours. Archaeologists have found items they made from as far away as India and Egypt. The Sumerians traded surplus grain, wool, oil, clothing, and leather goods for precious stones, ivory, metals such as tin and copper, timber, and vegetables that they themselves could not grow. They used donkeys and oxen to transport these goods on land and boats on the rivers.

The Development of Writing

Written language developed in Mesopotamia because of religion, trade, and government. For example, priests wanted to keep track of the offerings that were made to the temples as tax payments. Traders and merchants had to keep records of the items they bought and sold. As villages grew into towns and then into cities, governments needed a way to record the taxes that were collected.

As early as 3300 BCE, Sumerians were using simple pictures, called **pictographs**, to record information. Each pictograph represented an object. For example, wavy lines were used to represent water, and a star was used to represent the heavens. Since each object had its own picture, many pictographs were created. Early pictographs represented objects, but not ideas or feelings. The need for a more sophisticated recording system led to the gradual combination of pictographs to form more complex concepts. For example, the pictographs for water and mouth were combined to represent the action "to drink."

Soon, written symbols began to stand for specific sounds. These sounds were then combined to form words, just as we combine letters to form words. In this way, the Sumerians developed their own alphabet.

Each letter tapered to a point at the base, because that was the shape of the tool that was used for writing. This system of writing is called **cuneiform** [koon-EE-I-form], which comes from two Latin words that mean "wedge-shaped."

Scribes used a sharpened reed or stick called a **stylus** to write in the soft clay. The clay was shaped into tablets ten centimetres by fifteen centimetres. Writers had to work carefully and quickly while the clay was still wet.

Education

Girls and most boys did not go to school. Sons of wealthy families attended schools run by priests. Priests made good teachers because they knew what the deities wanted, and they were knowledgeable about topics such as medicine, science, and engineering.

	(1) 3300 BCE	(2) 2800 BCE	(3) 2400 BCE	(4) 1800 BCE
Heaven				
Earth				
Male				
Female				
Mountain				
Man				
Great				
King				
Plough				
Grain				
Sheep				
Ox				
Fish				
Bird				
Mouth				
Water				
To drink				

Figure 3.12 This chart shows how Sumerian writing progressed from pictographs (column 1) to symbols (column 4). The change from column 1 to column 2 is thought to have taken place when scribes turned their tablets sideways and began to write from left to right instead of from top to bottom.

The schools were located at the ziggurat [ZIG-u-RAT]. There, students studied religious stories of their people; they also learned arithmetic, reading, and writing and studied subjects that they were interested in.

For several years, students went to school for twenty-four days each month. Classes lasted from early morning until late afternoon. Before graduation, students had to write difficult exams.

Religious and Spiritual Beliefs

Sumerians worshipped approximately 3000 deities. They believed each city was founded by its own special deity who also owned and ruled it. For example, Inanna was the city-goddess of Uruk, and her father, Nanna, was the city-god of Ur.

There were also deities for all natural things, such as water, the sky, the air, the sun, and the moon. Sumerians believed that deities controlled all aspects of daily life. Inanna, who brought spring, was an important goddess. In the fall, people made human sacrifices to the goddess to ensure a good harvest. The Sumerians made shrines to honour their deities and placed the shrines in their homes, on the streets, and in the fields.

To please the deities, Sumerians built huge temple complexes. At the centre of many of these complexes were **pyramid**-like towers called *ziggurats*. Each ziggurat was built on a mound of mud brick and debris so that it towered over the city like a mountain.

Often, new temple complexes were built on the remains of old ones. In this way, temples grew higher and higher. Ziggurats also grew in size over time, as rooms and levels were added. The largest ziggurat was about sixty metres high – about the height of a twenty-storey building. It was found at Chonga Zanbil within the ancient kingdom of Elam, located in present-day Iran.

Each ziggurat was given a name; for example, "The House of the Mountain," "Bond Between Heaven and Earth," and "Mountain of the Storm." Sumerians believed that a deity lived at the top of each ziggurat. Only kings, high priests, and other important officials such as military leaders were allowed there.

Priests and priestesses attended to the needs of the many Sumerian gods and goddesses and ensured that prayers, offerings, and religious festivals were conducted properly. Singing and chanting were thought to have healing powers. Priests and priestesses studied the stars and people's dreams to predict the future, and they were frequently consulted.

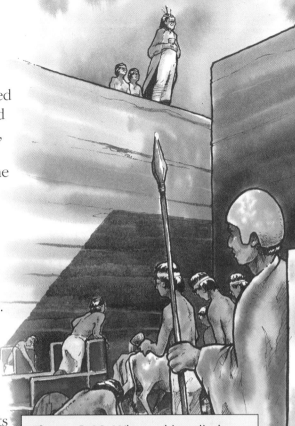

Figure 3.14 When a king died, people who worked for him and many of his possessions were buried with him. Even wagons and live oxen were included. When all the participants were properly arranged in the tomb, they were given drugs that killed them. Later, an attendant descended into the tomb to kill the animals and ensure that all the bodies were in the correct position. Then, the entire assembly was buried with the king.

Some Gods and Goddesses

Gods
*An (heaven)
*Enlil (air)
*Enki (water)
Utu (sun)
Nanna (moon)
Ninurta (south wind)

Goddesses
*Ki (earth)
Inanna (heaven, love, procreation, war)

*gods/goddess responsible for creating the universe

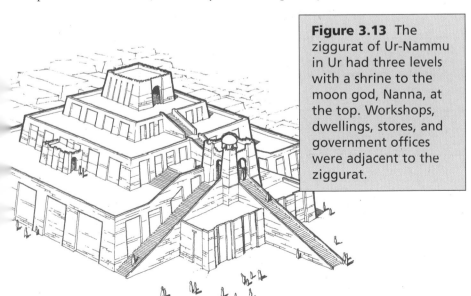

Figure 3.13 The ziggurat of Ur-Nammu in Ur had three levels with a shrine to the moon god, Nanna, at the top. Workshops, dwellings, stores, and government offices were adjacent to the ziggurat.

Figure 3.15 For entertainment, Sumerians liked to play games. Today, we would consider the game board pictured here a work of art.

Figure 3.16 The harp was a popular musical instrument.

Medicine and Magic

Both medical doctors and veterinarians practiced in Mesopotamia at least 5000 years ago. Although they relied mainly on magical chants and prayers to cure illness, they also used more practical methods such as cleansing, bandaging, and making casts. Medicines were made from natural ingredients, including snakeskins, turtle shells, and plants and spices such as myrtle, thyme, and cinnamon. Powders made from seeds, roots, and willow bark, and pear, fig, and palm trees were mixed with wine, beer, and plant oils. These plants were used for their antibiotic and antiseptic qualities.

Sumerian doctors understood the importance of cleanliness. Medical writings instructed them to wash and scrub infections. These writings also describe surgical techniques for operating on the chest and skull. Doctors performed some surgery using knives, forceps, and lancets.

The Sumerians were the first to depict medical treatment of animals. A reference to a "cattle doctor" was found on a tomb wall built between 2200 BCE and 2000 BCE. Later references describe such practices as mating a donkey and a horse to produce a mule, a discussion of a disease believed to be rabies, and explanations of various injuries.

The Arts

Evidence of musical instruments has been found on seals, terra-cotta and stone plaques, ivory carvings, and sculptures. The Sumerians used percussion, wind, and stringed instruments. Musical instruments such as lyres and harps have been recovered from the Royal Cemetery of Ur.

The site of the ancient city of Ubar in Mesopotamia was discovered using remote sensing, one of the newest tools of the archaeologist. (See chapter 1.) Remote sensing uses various methods such as radio waves, infrared waves, and radar waves to take pictures of Earth from space. These pictures can reveal patterns on the earth and for up to about two metres below the surface that cannot be seen in any other way. Ubar was located when remote sensing detected a change in texture from the surrounding area. These changes revealed patterns that looked like roads. Upon investigation, archaeologists found that the patterns were caravan roads. The patterns had formed where there were fewer rocks, more sand, and deposits of camel dung.

The Legacy of the Sumerians

In addition to a written language, the Sumerians are thought to have been among the first cultures to do the following:

- *Use the wheel for transportation* The wheel was used in Mesopotamia by about 3250 BCE. The wheel may have been first used to make pottery, much as potters use a potter's wheel today. Later, wheels were attached to ploughs, carts, and war chariots to allow easier movement. These vehicles were pulled by donkeys or oxen.

- *Improve the process of pottery making* In addition to the potter's wheel, Sumerians used a kiln — an enclosed oven for baking pottery and bricks. Because it is possible to produce very high temperatures in a kiln, the pottery and bricks are much harder and more durable than those dried by the sun.

- *Produce copper in quantities large enough to make tools and weapons* The Sumerians combined copper with tin to make bronze, which was then used to produce tools that were stronger than those made of copper alone. These superior tools allowed the Sumerians to build bigger and stronger boats and land vehicles. With improved means of transportation, Sumerians could trade with people in faraway places such as India.

- *Irrigate fields* At first, they may have simply carried water from the rivers to their fields. In time, they dug channels and canals that allowed water to flow from the rivers to the fields.

- *Study the stars* Sumerian priests calculated the best times for tilling the fields and planting and harvesting crops. They created a calendar that had two seasons: summer and winter. Their calendar, based on the phases of the moon, consisted of twelve months of thirty days.

- *Develop engineering skills* Sumerians used their knowledge of mathematics to build huge temples and complex systems of canals, dikes, and ditches. They invented a number system based on sixty, which was used by mathematicians and astronomers until the 1600s. The system is still used today for measuring angles and time.

- *Develop an efficient numbering system* Clay tablets that date to about 3000 BCE, for example, show five barrels of oil represented by the symbol for oil drawn five times. As cities grew and the need to keep track of economic activities increased, Sumerians developed a system that separated the symbol of the item from the amount. Using this method, five barrels of oil would be represented by the symbol for five and the symbol for oil. This new system was especially helpful when dealing with large quantities.

Figure 3.17 The Sumerians used war chariots long before the Romans had chariots.

Wall paintings have been difficult to find. Sumerians made their buildings from mud bricks covered with plaster, and the bricks have not been preserved well. Some wall paintings, found in places such as the temple at Tell Uqair, include pictures of leopards and other animals and humans.

As in other ancient societies, the priest-king is a frequent subject to sculpt. The royal lion hunt is a common theme in Sumerian art.

Sumerians also liked to listen to stories of their heroes, such as Gilgamesh (see page 57), and play various games, including board games.

Other Societies

The following four groups of peoples either lived close to Mesopotamia or conquered the area. All had a great influence on the region.

Akkadians

The Akkadians lived close to Mesopotamia near the Persian Gulf. By 2334 BCE, one of their leaders, Sargon the Great, controlled many Sumerian cities. The Akkadians ruled the area for only a short time. The Sumerians took back control less than 200 years later.

The Akkadians were semi-nomadic, and little is known about their history and culture before they dominated this area. Some lived near Sumerian cities, and in some places they became part of the communities. Even after they conquered the Sumerians, the Akkadians adopted much of the Sumerian culture.

Figure 3.18 This is the royal portrait head of Sargon the Great.

Their most important contribution to Mesopotamia was the introduction of the Semitic languages, which include Hebrew and Arabic. These languages became dominant in this area. The Akkadians also developed a system of roads throughout the area, and they devised a postal system.

Babylonians

The Babylonians, named after their major city of Babylon, came to power around 1900 BCE. Among the greatest contributions of the Babylonians were the Code of Hammurabi and the Hanging Gardens of Babylon. The Babylonians ruled this area until they were conquered by the Hittites who came from the area of present-day Turkey.

Figure 3.19 The Code of Hammurabi was created so that everyone would know the laws and the punishments for breaking them.

The Code of Hammurabi was named after Hammurabi (1792 BCE-1750 BCE), the greatest ruler of the first Babylonian dynasty. The Code of Hammurabi is the earliest known record of laws set forth by a government.

The code, found carved on a slab of stone, had 282 laws. For example, there were laws that covered trade, business and prices, family law, criminal law, and civil laws. Included were two innovative systems set up by Hammurabi: one for collecting taxes that were fair and another that set prices and wages for his people.

The Hanging Gardens of Babylon is described in many ancient documents as a mountain-like structure, covered in trees and other greenery. The "mountain" was actually a ziggurat that had been built for the wife of a Babylonian king, probably King Nebuchadnezzar II [NEB-uh-CHAD-nay-zar] (604 BCE-562 BCE). His wife missed the natural mountain surroundings of her homeland, it is said.

Assyrians

The Assyrians came from areas of modern-day Iran, Iraq, Syria, and Turkey. From 750 BCE-605 BCE, they were the most powerful people in the region. Their empire included Mesopotamia, its surrounding area, and Egypt. The Assyrian army was the first to be equipped with iron weapons such as swords, spears, iron-tipped arrows, and armour.

The Assyrians controlled their empire through a well-developed government administration,

Figure 3.20 The Hanging Gardens of Babylon was considered one of the Seven Wonders of the Ancient World.

supported by a military that enforced strict rules. The form of government – local rulers responsible to a central power – is still used today in many countries.

The Assyrians created the first locks and keys. Our system of keeping time was developed by them. Assyrians were the first to construct paved roads, aqueducts, and arches. Their central administration created a postal system, libraries, and zoos. Some of their buildings had plumbing and flush toilets.

Persians

The Persians, influential at different times in the history of Mesopotamian, were most powerful between 550 BCE-330 BCE. Their empire included present-day Iran and stretched from the Mediterranean Sea to India. Cyrus the Great was the first important Persian ruler to conquer neighbouring peoples. Cyrus declared the first Charter of Human Rights. In 1971, the United Nations published the charter in all of its official languages.

Like the Assyrians, the Persians had a very strong central government. However, as the Persians were much more tolerant than the Assyrians, the peoples they ruled could maintain their religions, customs, and languages. Most Persians were Zoroastrians. The founder, Zoroaster, taught that life was a struggle between good and evil. Those who had lived good lives – practiced tolerance, moderation, generosity, for example – were destined to go to a heaven.

The Persians created four large regional capital cities to help maintain control of the government. Horsemen used a well-maintained road system to courier messages between the king and his regional governors. Relay stations were located about every twenty kilometres. The Persians may have established the world's first pony express.

Summary

The Tigris and Euphrates rivers played an important role in the settlement and growth of Mesopotamia. People used the rivers as transportation routes and as the water sources for irrigation systems. Both trade and farming thrived.

Because the Sumerians, and others who settled in the region, did not have to spend their days searching for food, people had the time to specialize in other areas.

Pottery making, field irrigation, astronomy, engineering techniques, and an efficient numbering system are all legacies of Mesopotamia.

Connecting and Reflecting

Reflect on what you have learned about the Sumerians. Use the information to describe the similarities *to* and differences *from* your life *as a Canadian and as a citizen of the world.*

Be an Historian

Do you believe everything that you read in a history text? Do you ever wonder what information has been left out? When you study history, you are usually reading the results of what historians have researched and written. In this section, you will have the opportunity to do your own research and ask yourself the same kinds of questions that historians ask themselves. You will not be reading history; you will be doing history!

Historical research is very complicated. (See chapter 1.) It demands knowledge, skill, and patience. Historians have to:

- locate their evidence
- interpret what it means
- sort out what is true from what is probable and what is false

Read the excerpts below. When you are finished, answer the following questions:

- Where do these sources come from?
- Are they sources that you can trust?
- What do you know about the author? If you do not know anything, how can you find out?
- Does the author have knowledge, experience, or credentials that makes you willing to trust his or her work?
- As you try to understand the past, how important is chronology?

The Code of Hammurabi
(a selection of Hammurabi's laws)

6. If any one steal the property of a temple or of the court, he shall be put to death, and also the one who receives the stolen thing from him shall be put to death.

7. If any one buy from the son or the slave of another man, without witnesses or a contract, silver or gold, a male or female slave, an ox or a sheep, an ass or anything, or if he take it in charge, he is considered a thief and shall be put to death.

10. If any one take a male or female slave of the court, or a male or female slave of a freed man, outside the city gates, he shall be put to death.

16. If any one find runaway male or female slaves in the open country and bring them to their masters, the master of the slaves shall pay him two shekels of silver.

21. If any one break a hole into a house, he shall be put to death before that hole and be buried.

44. If any one take over a waste-lying field to make it arable, but is lazy, and does not make it arable, he shall plow the fallow field in the fourth year, harrow it and till it, and give it back to its owner, and for each ten gan ten gur of grain shall be paid.

48. If any one owe a debt for a loan, and a storm prostrates the grain, or the harvest fail, or the grain does not grow for lack of water; in that year he need not give his creditor any grain, he washes his debt-tablet in water and pays no rent for this year.

53. If any one be too lazy to keep his dam in proper condition, and does not so keep it; if then the dam break and all the fields be flooded, then shall he in whose dam the break occurred be sold for money, and the money shall replace the corn which he has caused to be ruined.

57. If a shepherd, without the permission of the owner of the field, and without the knowledge of the owner of the sheep, lets the sheep into a field to graze, then the owner of the field shall harvest his crop, and the shepherd, who had pastured his flock there without permission of the owner of the field, shall pay to the owner twenty gur of corn for every ten gan.

102. If a merchant entrust money to an agent for some investment, and the broker suffer a loss in the place to which he goes, he shall make good the capital to the merchant.

108. If a tavern-keeper does not accept corn according to gross weight in payment of drink, but takes money, and the price of the drink is less than that of the corn, she shall be convicted and thrown into the water.

117. If any one fail to meet a claim for debt, and sell himself, his wife, his son, and daughter for money or give them away to forced labour: they shall work for three years in the house of the man who bought them, or the proprietor, and in the fourth year they shall be set free.

120. If any one store corn for safe keeping in another person's house, and any harm happen to the corn in storage, or if the owner of the house open the granary and take some of the corn, or if especially he deny that the corn was stored in his house: then the owner of the corn shall claim his corn before God, and the owner of the house shall pay its owner for all of the corn that he took.

175. If a State slave or the slave of a freed man marry the daughter of a free man, and children are born, the master of the slave shall have no right to enslave the children of the free.

191. If a man, who had adopted a son and reared him, founded a household, and had children, wish to put this adopted son out, then this son shall not simply go his way. His adoptive father shall give him of his wealth one-third of a child's portion, and then he may go. He shall not give him of the field, garden, and house.

195. If a son strike his father, his hands shall be hewn off.

196. If a man put out the eye of another man, his eye shall be put out.

200. If a man knock out the teeth of his equal, his teeth shall be knocked out.

202. If any one strike the body of a man higher in rank than he, he shall receive sixty blows with an ox-whip in public.

205. If the slave of a freed man strike the body of a freed man, his ear shall be cut off.

206. If during a quarrel one man strike another and wound him, then he shall swear, "I did not injure him wittingly," and pay the physicians.

219. If a physician make a large incision in the slave of a freed man, and kill him, he shall replace the slave with another slave.

224. If a veterinary surgeon perform a serious operation on an ass or an ox, and cure it, the owner shall pay the surgeon one-sixth of a shekel as a fee.

229. If a builder build a house for some one, and does not construct it properly, and the house which he built fall in and kill its owner, then that builder shall be put to death.

235. If a shipbuilder build a boat for some one, and do not make it tight, if during that same year that boat is sent away and suffers injury, the shipbuilder shall take the boat apart and put it together tight at his own expense. The tight boat he shall give to the boat owner.

245. If any one hire oxen, and kill them by bad treatment or blows, he shall compensate the owner, oxen for oxen.

253. If any one agree with another to tend his field, give him seed, entrust a yoke of oxen to him, and bind him to cultivate the field, if he steal the corn or plants, and take them for himself, his hands shall be hewn off.

260. If any one steal a shaduf or a plough, he shall pay three shekels in money.

267. If the herdsman overlook something, and an accident happen in the stable, then the herdsman is at fault for the accident which he has caused in the stable, and he must compensate the owner for the cattle or sheep.

Egypt

Our Study of Egypt

Our study of Egypt includes the following topics:

- Where the Egyptians Lived
- The Importance of the Nile River
- Government
- Social Organization
- What They Ate
- Farming
- What They Wore
- Housing
- The Development of Writing
- Education
- The Arts
- Medicine and Magic
- Trade
- Religious and Spiritual Beliefs
- The Legacy of the Egyptians

When most people think of ancient Egypt, they think of the pyramids. These immense monuments still remain, thousands of years after they were built. They suggest the great power of the Egyptian **pharaohs** [FAIR-ohs], the kings and queens who ruled Egypt. The pyramids also testify to the sophisticated engineering skills of those who built them.

Figure 4.1 At Giza, the largest pyramid was built for the pharaoh Cheops, who was also known as Khufu; the second pyramid was built for Chefren, or Chephren, who was known as Khafre; and the third or smaller pyramid was built for Mycerinus, who was also known as Menkaure.

The ancient Egyptians settled along the banks of the Nile River in northern Africa. Their civilization lasted for almost 3000 years – from about 3100 BCE to 332 BCE. At its height, Egypt is thought to have had a population of between nine and ten million people.

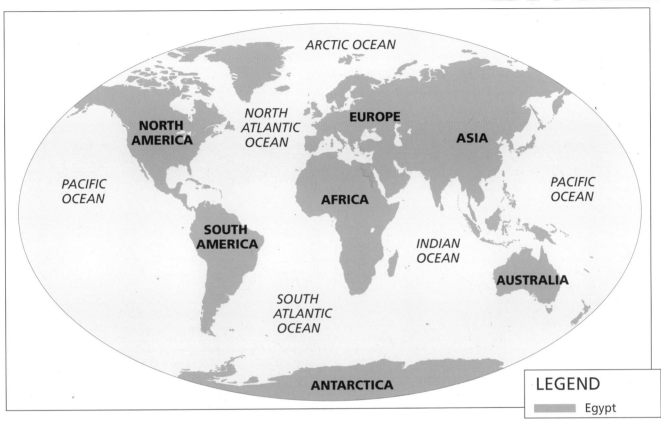

ARCTIC OCEAN

NORTH AMERICA

NORTH ATLANTIC OCEAN

EUROPE

ASIA

PACIFIC OCEAN

PACIFIC OCEAN

AFRICA

SOUTH AMERICA

INDIAN OCEAN

AUSTRALIA

SOUTH ATLANTIC OCEAN

ANTARCTICA

LEGEND

Egypt

Figure 4.3 This map shows the kingdom of Egypt in about 1500 BCE.

Figure 4.2 This limestone beast with the head of a man and the body of a lion is called the *Sphinx* [SFINGKS]. It was built about 4500 years ago in Lower Egypt. The Sphinx is believed to represent the sun god, Ra. Its face is thought to be that of Khafre [KAF-ree], a pharaoh of the 4th Dynasty who ruled from 2558 BCE– 2532 BCE. Khafre is credited with building the second largest of the three pyramids at Giza.

Questions to Think About

✦ How was life in the Nile Valley similar to and different from life elsewhere in very early times?

✦ How did Egyptians satisfy their non-material needs (e.g., entertainment, recreation, music, art, literature, religion)?

✦ What achievements of Egyptian society (e.g., inventions, religion, values, buildings) are considered important today?

Where the Egyptians Lived

The geography of ancient Egypt played a key role in the development of its society. Egypt's northern border is the Mediterranean Sea. This gave Egyptians access to the resources of the sea and to trading networks in the region. To the south, a series of **cataracts** – large, steep waterfalls – on the Nile River made travelling on the river extremely difficult. These cataracts provided protection from enemy attacks. To the west, the Libyan Desert, or Western Desert, acted as a barrier to outsiders. To the east, the Arabian Desert lay between the Nile Valley and the Red Sea, making it difficult for invaders to attack Egypt from that direction. Unlike many other peoples, such as the Babylonians, the Egyptians did not have to defend themselves constantly. They could focus more on internal matters that included governing the area fairly and ensuring peace within the country.

Two separate regions developed in the Nile Valley. The delta near the Mediterranean Sea, located in the north, was called *Lower Egypt*. This swampy and dangerous area was home to many wild animals including crocodiles and hippopotamuses. The land along the Nile River from Memphis to the First Cataract at Aswan was called *Upper Egypt*.

Figure 4.5 Water level measurements were made with a nilometer [NEYE-low-me-ter]. A nilometer had ruled horizontal lines cut into rock surfaces along the river's banks to check on the inundation levels of the Nile River. Several nilometers were located along the Nile. At Elephantine (south Egypt), the Nile starts to rise one month before it does in Memphis (north Egypt). The nilometer at Elephantine acted as a warning for what the inundation would be in a particular year.

Figure 4.4 People were living in the Nile Valley by about 5500 BCE. They settled in small villages along the fertile flood plain of the Nile River. Memphis and a few other settlements on the delta grew into large cities.

The Old Dam at Aswan was constructed and heightened three times between 1902-1933. The High Dam (Aswan Dam) was started in 1960 and finished in 1971. Lake Nasser was formed behind the dam and flooded much of what is called Nubia. The people of that region had to be relocated to other areas of Egypt, mostly around Aswan.

The Importance of the Nile River

In many ways, the story of ancient Egypt is the story of the Nile River. In Egypt, the Nile flows from south (Upper Egypt) to north (Lower Egypt) for about 1000 kilometres, connecting the entire country. Most of the river's valley is less than twenty kilometres wide. The valley is much wider at the river's mouth, where the Nile Delta, a large triangle of extremely fertile land, is located.

During ancient times, the Nile flooded its banks every year in late spring and deposited fine black silt on the land around it. The levels of flooding varied greatly from year to year. When the flood waters were too high, villages and fields were destroyed. If the flood waters were too low, crops failed and infestations of pests such as scorpions and rats occurred. When the flood waters receded, the farmers planted their crops. The farmland had to be re-surveyed each year, because the markers that allocated the size of each farmer's land were moved by the flood waters. The Egyptians were good at mathematics, especially geometry, and they developed surveying techniques that ensured measurements were accurate every year.

Government

In about 3100 BCE, Upper Egypt and Lower Egypt were united under Pharaoh Menes of Memphis. (In some writings, he is referred to as Narmer.) Menes founded the first dynasty. Under his rule, Egyptian society began to develop and advance. Historians have divided the history of unified Egypt into the Old Kingdom (2700 BCE to 2200 BCE), the Middle Kingdom (2050 BCE to 1800 BCE), and the New Kingdom (1550 BCE to 100 BCE). From

Egyptian Dynasties*

2700-2625 3rd Dynasty
2625-2500 4th Dynasty
2500-2350 5th Dynasty
2350-2170 6th Dynasty
2170-2130 7th-8th Dynasties
2130-1980 9th-10th (Herakleopolis) Dynasties
2081-1938 11th (Thebes) Dynasty
1938-1759 12th (Itj-Tawy) Dynasty
1759-1630 13th (Itj-Tawy) Dynasty
1675-1630 14th (Western Delta) Dynasty
1630-1523 15th (Avaris) ("Hyksos") Dynasty
1630-1523 16th Dynasty
1630-1539 17th (Thebes) Dynasty
1539-1292 18th (Thebes) Dynasty
1292-1190 19th (Thebes) Dynasty
1190-1075 20th (Thebes) Dynasty
1075-945 21st (Tanis) Dynasty
945-712 22nd (Bubastis) Dynasty
828-725 23rd Dynasty
724-712 24th (Sais) Dynasty
760-656 25th ("Nubian" or "Kushite") Dynasty
664-525 26th (Sais) Dynasty
525-405 27th Dynasty (Persian)
409-399 28th (Sais) Dynasty
399-380 29th (Mendes) Dynasty
381-343 30th (Sebennytos) Dynasty
343-332 31st (Persian) Dynasty

* All dates are BCE and approximate.

the formation of the Old Kingdom to the time Egypt was conquered by the Romans around 300 BCE, thirty-one dynasties ruled Egypt.

The rulers developed laws to control the behaviour of their people within the society. The Egyptian belief in justice, truth, and order made their culture more humane than many earlier cultures. For example, grain was stored in granaries to feed people in times of **famine**. Laws were adopted that protected the poor from being exploited by the rich. Most people, except slaves, were considered to be equal regardless of their wealth or social position.

Figure 4.6 This painting from a tomb wall shows a family outing on the river.

Social Organization

Around 1550 BCE, Egyptians began using the term *pharaoh* to refer to their king. The pharaohs were considered to be descendants of the gods, and most ruled with absolute power. The ruling pharaoh owned the people, livestock, and land in Egypt. A pharaoh was the religious leader of the country as well as the government head. The power of the pharaoh was passed along through family lines so that the dynasty could continue.

Below the pharaoh, the Egyptian society was divided into classes.

Hierarchy of Egyptian Society

Pharaoh
|
Vizier, Nomarchs
(governors who controlled
nomes or districts), Nobles
|
Scribes, Overseers, Teachers,
Doctors, Artists, Government administrators,
Business owners
|
Soldiers, Peasant-farmers, Farm and
household labourers, Slaves

Officials were chosen to help the pharaoh administer the country. These officials were given land. The most important officials, the **vizier** [vi-ZAIR], enforced the laws and wishes of the ruler.

We know less about the daily lives of ordinary Egyptians than we do about the ordinary members of many other ancient societies. People in the upper classes often arranged for a scribe to write information about them on their tombs.

Wealthy men were involved in business or government, and they worked outside the home. Married women ran the home and tended to the needs of the children. When a family entertained, the wife was in charge of the preparations.

Family life was important. Many pictures depict children at play; boys with bows and arrows, wrestling, and playing ball; girls playing with dolls and board games, or throwing balls.

Figure 4.7 Egyptian society was run mostly by men. Although a number of queens had great power and influence, only a few became pharaohs. The most famous female pharaoh was Queen Hatshepsut [HAT-shep-suit]. She became a ruler around 1400 BCE during the 18th dynasty. Queen Hatshepsut often dressed as a man to conform to the traditional idea of kingship. Her reign was marked by few wars, extensive trade, and good diplomatic relations with her neighbours.

The poor did not leave records about their lives – they could not write, and they could not afford to hire scribes. Even if some left writings behind, most of the settlements where they lived are now covered by modern cities.

Life was not as pleasant for poor people. Men from the lower class spent long days alongside their wives working in the fields, serving the rich, or making clothing or food.

Both men and women were considered "citizens." Both paid taxes, took part in the legal process, and helped priests with religious ceremonies.

Most women married at about age thirteen. By law, women had many of the same rights as men, such as the right to own property. Men, however, made the decisions for their families.

Figure 4.8 This woman is playing a game called *zenet* (also spelled senet). Zenet uses a chess-like board with 30 squares in 3 lines of 10 squares each. Although the rules of the game are not known, the game is played with two players.

An Unusual Day

In this story, Nefer celebrates with others as they welcome the new pharaoh to their town.

Nefer woke up just as Ra, the sun god, was starting his journey across the sky. She put on her linen tunic and sandals made from papyrus reeds and joined her family for breakfast. After a meal of bread and honey, goat cheese, and weak beer, Nefer helped her mother grind barley into flour. With the flour, they baked flatbread in the open firepit in the yard.

After the bread was baked, Nefer walked to the river to wash some clothing. She did not have to walk far to reach the water. The Inundation had peaked recently, and the river waters were still high. She kept a careful watch for crocodiles.

Later, her mother asked her to go to the market. Nefer was happy to leave her chores behind for a while. As she followed the path along the river into town, she watched herons and ducks in the reeds that grew there. Sometimes, her brother and his friends hunted the birds from a papyrus skiff.

Nefer was almost at the village when she saw a large crowd gathering beside the dock. Today, the new pharaoh was coming to visit her town. He was travelling throughout the kingdom, visiting all of his subjects. The crowd erupted into a huge cheer as a beautiful boat appeared around the bend in the river. Men were rowing in time to a drumbeat, and flags and pennants flew from the wooden mast. The hull of the boat was painted with pictures of the gods that protected the pharaoh.

The boat glided up to the dock, and some soldiers jumped ashore. A tall man wearing a red and white crown strode across the gangplank. He was followed by a beautiful, slender woman. She was wearing a white linen dress and a gold necklace. Nefer quickly realized the two visitors were the new king and queen. She joined the crowd as they bowed in respect.

Nefer followed the crowd as priests led the procession to the temple. Offerings of fruit and flowers were given to the gods. Afterwards, Nefer met some friends and they attended the feast held for the villagers. They ate roast goose, onions cooked with milk and cheese, stewed beef, and many kinds of breads and cakes, some shaped liked pyramids and some shaped like crocodiles.

Following the meal, dancers and acrobats from the pharaoh's household entertained the villagers. When darkness fell, the pharaoh and his wife returned to the royal boat. Nefer joined her family and they all walked home together. As they approached the house, Nefer's favourite cat, Miw, ran up to her with a dead mouse in her mouth. Cats were very important to Egyptians. Nefer had heard that some people even had their cats mummified when they died.

Nefer's father and brother lit a lamp and checked that the goats were safely penned for the night. Nefer and her mother brought in the washing that had been drying since morning. The night was warm, so they all moved their reed mats outside. As Nefer drifted off to sleep, she thought to herself: "What an exciting day. I can't wait to see what will happen tomorrow!"

What They Ate

Wealthy Egyptians, like wealthy Sumerians in Mesopotamia, ate a wide variety of foods. Beef, mutton, poultry, and pork were eaten. The Nile Valley produced fruits and some vegetables including pomegranates, figs, watermelons, dates, sweet melons, grapes, and cucumbers. Honey was used as a sweetener.

Poorer Egyptians seldom ate meat, although some raised ducks, geese, chickens, or rabbits. Their meals usually consisted of bread, onions, and fish. Vegetables such as lentils, peas, and chickpeas were also eaten.

The Egyptians ate a great variety of breads, usually made from barley. These included hollow rolls filled with vegetables, flatbread cakes, round crusty breads, and heavy unleavened bread. A worker might eat as many as ten bread rolls and drink as much as two jugs of beer each day. Beer was made from barley, bread crumbs, water, and fermented dates. Egyptians often gathered at taverns to drink beer and wine, much as people do today.

Figure 4.9 Farmer-peasants are winnowing harvested wheat.

Farming

Most Egyptians were farmers. They planted their crops after the Nile flood waters receded in October, and the ground was still wet and easy to work. They had to plant quickly, because the ground soon hardened in the sun.

All villagers were involved in the important task of planting. Workers used small hand hoes to break up the soil. They guided wooden ploughs that were pulled by oxen. Other workers walked behind those who were ploughing and sowed the seeds, which they carried in shoulder bags made from reeds. Sheep and cattle were then led over the planted seeds to push the seeds into the soil.

The crops were ready to harvest from mid-February to early June. At that time, scribes and officials decided how much to give to the pharaoh, the landowner, and the farmers, and how much to save as seed for the following year. The first pick of each crop was offered to the deities, such as Min, the god of fertility, as thanks for the harvest.

One important non-food crop was papyrus [puh-PIE-ruhs]. It grew in marshland and had many uses. Baskets, mats, boats, sandals, and paper were all made of papyrus.

Making Paper

The Egyptians made the world's first paper over 4000 years ago. They used papyrus plants that grew on the banks of the Nile River. The plant can grow up to a height of about 3.6 metres and has long, thin, triangular-shaped stems.

The papyrus plants were harvested and cut to the desired length. The stems were peeled, leaving only the white pith, and sliced into thin strips. These strips were soaked in water for many days. They were then placed side-by-side on flat stone plates in a lattice pattern. The strips were beaten and, because the juices form a strong glue, the strips bonded together into sheets. The strips were then placed between felt mats to absorb any water. Heavy stones were placed on top of the felt mats to squeeze out the excess water. Finally, the sheets were dried and scrubbed. They were then ready for the scribes to write on.

What They Wore

The most common clothing for women was an ankle-length sheath dress that attached at the shoulder. Women from the upper class wore dresses made from fine materials such as linen. Many also wore a beaded net dress over a close-fitting sheath dress. Some lower-class women wore more loosely fitted dresses that allowed them to work comfortably in the fields or at home.

Men wore wraparound skirts, called *shenti,* that resemble kilts. The fabric, length, fit, and decoration of each skirt depended on the man's rank and wealth. The skirts of the wealthy were usually pleated, but there were many different styles. Men seldom wore tops, and poor men and slaves wore only loincloths. As fashions changed, some men wore longer skirts over the shenti and sometimes wore short-sleeved tunics as well.

Linen was the most commonly worn fabric, probably because it is very cool. Linen is made from flax, a plant that grew easily in Egypt. Some cloth was dyed; most was not. Wool was not widely used for clothing, but some people wore it for outer garments. The skins of animals such as the gazelle and leopard were tanned and made into shoes and sandals.

Wealthy men and women wore makeup such as heavy black eyeliner called **kohl** to protect their eyes from the brightness of the sun. They also wore lipstick, and nail polish, and gold jewellery.

Housing

Most Egyptians lived in one-room houses made of mud bricks and reeds. The houses were covered with roofs made of large palm leaves. People often slept outside when it was hot.

The wealthy lived in large homes with many rooms. At the front of each home was a grand entrance. Inside were bathrooms, bedrooms, halls, a kitchen, and guest rooms. The floors were covered in mats, and the walls often had wall hangings. Many homes made from mud brick were built around courtyards, which often contained swimming pools and gardens. These homes had flat roofs where people spent their evenings in hot weather and where they often slept at night.

Middle-class and upper-class Egyptians owned wooden furniture. Many pieces of such furniture have been found in the pyramids. The wealthy slept on beds, sat on chairs or stools, stored household items in baskets and boxes, and used lamps, kitchen utensils, and pottery. Lamps were usually pottery or stone bowls with a wick and filled with oil. Torches, made of pottery, were mounted on walls.

Kitchen utensils included storage jars, bowls, pots, pans, ladles, sieves, and whisks. Clay dishes were used, and the tableware was made of bronze, silver, and gold. Many people, especially the poor, ate with their fingers. Food was cooked in clay ovens and over open fires.

Figure 4.10 The way these workers are making mud bricks is still used in Egypt today. The mud is mixed with straw and shaped into bricks using wooden moulds. The bricks are then dried in the sun. These unfired bricks were used for homes, while stone was reserved for tombs and temples. Homes of both the wealthy and the poor were made of these mud bricks.

The Development of Writing

Hieroglyphics, the Egyptian form of pictorial writing, appeared about 3300 BCE. At first, the **hieroglyphs** represented actual objects. Later, during the Middle Kingdom around 2000 BCE, the glyphs represented sounds, which, like the cuneiform sounds of the Sumerians, could be combined to form words.

There may have been up to 6000 hieroglyphs in the early stages of this form of writing. Gradually, the system was simplified into an easier cursive form of writing called **hieratic**, with about 3000 glyphs for scribes to learn.

Hieroglyphics were developed to record what was produced, taxes that had been paid, supplies required for temples, and military information. Later, scribes used hieroglyphics for letter writing and recording stories. Hieroglyphs were placed on the inner walls of temples and tombs, on pottery and slabs of limestone, and on papyrus.

Hieroglyphics were last used by Egyptian priests in the 4th century CE. The priests kept the meaning of the writing a secret, and no one was able to read the hieroglyphs for another 1500 years. Then, French soldiers serving with Napoleon found a stone slab near the Egyptian delta town of Rashid, whose ancient name was Rosetta. The stone had text written in three languages: Egyptian hieroglyphics, Coptic (an Afroasian language), and ancient Greek. Since scholars could understand Greek, it was possible to decipher the hieroglyphics by using Greek as a guide to translation.

Education

The education of Egyptian children, both girls and boys, was based on religious beliefs. Schools were located in the temples, and the priests were the teachers. The students were mainly the sons and daughters of the wealthy.

Students started school at age five and continued until they were seventeen years old. Classes began at sunrise and continued until sunset. Teachers were very strict, and students who misbehaved were beaten.

Figure 4.11 Jean-François Champollion (1790-1832), the man who deciphered the Rosetta Stone, never actually saw the stone. Although the stone had been found by French soldiers during the Napoleonic Wars (1798-1801), it was in the possession of the British. They had demanded the Rosetta Stone after defeating the French during the wars. Today, the Rosetta Stone is on display at the British Museum in London, England.

Boys were usually better educated than girls. Few women learned to read and write, so they did not become doctors, lawyers, engineers, or government workers.

The main function of the schools was to train scribes. Doctors, lawyers, engineers, and military leaders were all trained as scribes. They were responsible for recording everything from agricultural production to taxes and government records to historical events, such as victories in battle. Scribes held an honoured place in Egyptian society. Almost the only way that a poor person could move up in society was by becoming a scribe.

Most Egyptian children did not attend school. They learned the skills of their parents by being involved in their parents' work and by observation. Girls learned from their mothers, and boys learned from their fathers.

The Arts

Arts and crafts were very important in ancient Egypt. Artists and craftspeople created paintings, sculptures, weavings, and other forms of artistic expression. These illustrated the universe as they knew it.

Artists used mineral pigments to paint detailed scenes on the walls of the tombs of the pharaohs and nobles. After painting the walls, substances such as snake venom and egg whites were often mixed and painted over the colours to protect them from rain, wind, sand, and other elements. Paintbrushes were made of natural fibres, such as reeds or animal hair, and were of many different sizes.

Using Mineral Pigments to Create Colours

Blue: azurite, an ore of copper; a compound of silica, copper, and calcium

Red: iron oxide

Green: malachite

White: sandstone, calcium carbonate, calcium sulphate

Black: basalt, powdered charcoal

Yellow: yellow ochre

Dancing and music were important parts of daily life in ancient Egypt. Entertainment at official banquets and private celebrations was provided by troupes of professional singers, dancers, acrobats, and musicians. Ritual dances were performed as part of funerals and burial ceremonies. Castanets and rattles known as **sistra** were used to keep the rhythm.

Medicine and Magic

All societies develop a form of medicine, and there is evidence of Egyptian medical practices dating to about 4000 BCE. The best descriptions of their medical knowledge come from records of the time period from 2000 BCE to 1700 BCE. There is information on internal disease, skin disease, eye problems, diseases of the tongue, teeth, nose, and ears. There is also information on how to perform surgery. Records indicate that some doctors specialized in dentistry, internal medicine, and **ophthalmology** (treatment of the diseases of the eyes).

Magic played a role in medicine. Spells to keep snakes away as well as to cure or alleviate snakebites were common. Collections of charms and incantations for the protection of babies have been found as well as spells to protect against childhood diseases and dangers. People prayed to several deities, such as Isis and Hathor, to protect a mother and child during pregnancy. People also prayed to Selqet, the scorpion goddess, to banish scorpions or cure the effects of their stings.

Figure 4.12 A town named Kom Ombo, near Aswan, was a famous medical centre. People of all classes came from all over Egypt to consult with doctors about their medical conditions and with midwives about giving birth.

Trade

The Nile River was always the most important travel route in Egypt. The Egyptians traded with their neighbours to the east (present-day Lebanon, Jordan, and Syria) to obtain goods that they could not produce themselves, such as wood. With their neighbours to the south, they exchanged jewellery and cloth for wild animals, leopard skins, giraffe tails, ostrich eggs, and plants for making perfume. With the peoples of western Africa and the island of Crete, they traded for bronze, items of gold, and ceramic pottery.

Myrrh was a much sought-after trade item. The Egyptians used myrrh, a fragrant, gummy substance with a bitter taste, in medicines, perfumes, and incense. The Egyptians imported animal skins, ivory, gold, and monkeys from the kingdom of Punt. The Egyptians thought that monkeys were sacred and kept them as pets. Monkeys are often shown in Egyptian art.

To improve trade efficiency, the Egyptians built ships and boats. Boats were also soon used for a variety of other purposes including fishing, travel, and warfare. The earliest watercrafts were rafts made from papyrus. The construction of rafts and other boats using papyrus or other reeds is still carried on in parts of Africa such as Lake Chad and in South America on Lake Titicaca.

Trade goods were transported along the Nile River on huge, flat-bottomed boats. Often the

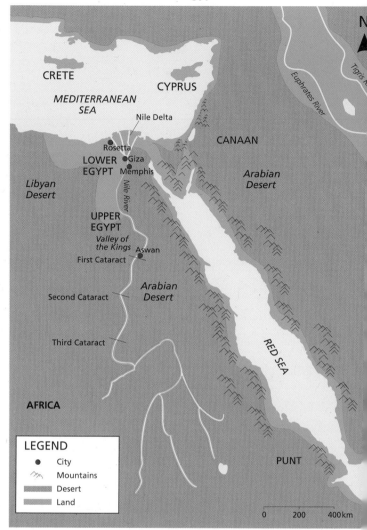

Egypt

Figure 4.14 Egyptians settled along a narrow band of land on both sides of the Nile River.

larger boats were pulled by smaller boats, which were powered by crews of rowers. Egyptian sailboats used rowers when there was no wind.

Larger boats made of wood were built to move heavy loads, such as the large blocks of stone used to build the pyramids, temples, and other structures. Cedar, imported from Lebanon, was highly prized for boat building, as it was strong and straight and lasted a long time. Other large boats, over fifty metres in length, were built for trade and for war. These ships were slightly smaller than the boats that Christopher Columbus sailed across the Atlantic Ocean.

Figure 4.13 This picture shows a Canaanite ship being unloaded in an Egyptian port about 1500 BCE. This type of ship was used for ocean travel.

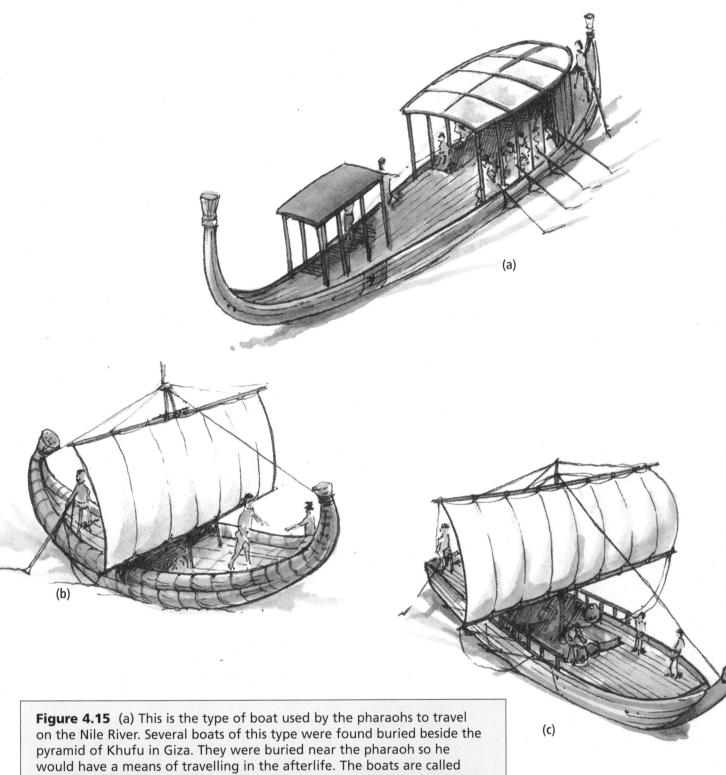

Figure 4.15 (a) This is the type of boat used by the pharaohs to travel on the Nile River. Several boats of this type were found buried beside the pyramid of Khufu in Giza. They were buried near the pharaoh so he would have a means of travelling in the afterlife. The boats are called solar boats when they have this connection to the afterlife, because they are similar to the ones used by Ra, the sun god, in his daily journey across the sky. (b) The most common type of watercraft used on the Nile was built by tying papyrus reeds into tight bundles. The papyrus reeds needed to be lashed together very tightly to be waterproof. The bundles were then tied together with the ends of the boat turning up. These craft could be propelled by a sail or were poled in shallow waters. Smaller boats used on the Nile for fishing and hunting were made of papyrus. (c) The Egyptians did not use nails to build their wooden ships. The planks of wood were tied together tightly with ropes. Tar-like substances were used to patch areas that might develop leaks. Bigger ships had large square sails, as well as oars for rowing.

Religious and Spiritual Beliefs

Like most ancient peoples, the Egyptians understood little about the natural world. They were in awe of events such as the annual flooding of the Nile River. As a result, the flooding became part of their religion.

The Egyptians had hundreds of deities. Some gods and goddesses were worshipped locally in the towns and villages, but the following four deities were important to all Egyptians:

- *Ra* was the sun god. Each day he sailed across the sky in a papyrus boat, bringing the sun with him.

- *Osiris* was the god of the underworld. The underworld was a cool, well-treed place where the souls of Egyptians went after they died. Osiris was one of the most important gods because of the importance of the afterlife to the Egyptians. Osiris was also the god who taught Egyptians how to farm. Osiris had been killed by his evil brother, Seth. Seth cut the body of Osiris into fourteen pieces and scattered them throughout the world.

The ancient Egyptians hieroglyphics did not include vowe When the names of the pharaohs, gods, and goddesses we translated into English, vowels were inserted to make the words more understandable. As a result, different authors/historians spell the words in a variety of ways. So examples of these different spellings are:

Gods

Bas	Bes		
Seth	Set		
Amun	Aman	Amen	Amon
Khnum	Khnoum		
Aten	Aton		

Goddesses

Hathor	Hathour
Tefnut	Tefnout
Nephthys	Nephtees
Sekhmet	Sakhmet

Pharaohs

Akhenaten	Akhenaton		
Ramesse	Ramses	Ramesses	
Tutankhamun	Tutankhaman	Tutankhamen	Tutankhamo

- *Isis* was the wife of Osiris. She collected the fourteen pieces of Osiris's body from all over the earth and then brought him back to life. Isis was the protector of children.

- *Anubis* was a god of the dead and the guardian of the tombs. He was often represented in pictures as a jackal. The Egyptians believed that their souls were judged by Anubis when they died. Anubis means "He Who Counts the Hearts."

Because religion was so important, priests were very powerful members of society. Some controlled vast estates. In addition to their religious functions, priests were often scribes, doctors, scientists, engineers, and astronomers.

Egyptians and the Afterlife

All Egyptians were very concerned with death and with life after death. The bodies of kings and queens were preserved and buried in huge tombs and pyramids. The walls of the tombs were painted, and the tombs were filled with

Figure 4.16 This painting shows judgment day. Anubis is weighing the dead person's heart against a feather, which represents truth. If the heart passes this test, the soul is allowed into the afterlife. If the person has not led a good life, the soul is devoured by monster-like creatures.

pottery, sculptures, jewellery, furniture, clothing, and musical instruments that they believed would be needed in the next life. Chariots have been found in some tombs, as they were in Chinese tombs.

The poor were buried in shallow graves in the desert sand. Their bodies were not preserved, although they were usually wrapped in linen or covered with straw. The bacteria that decompose bodies need moisture to survive. In the desert, the hot, dry air caused the bodies to lose moisture quickly, creating "natural" mummies. The poor were buried with items such as pots or food, so they would have these with them in the afterlife.

Because of their concern for the afterlife, the Egyptians left more items connected with funerals than did any other ancient peoples. Archaeologists have been able to recover many of these items. As a result, we know a great deal about the death rituals and beliefs of the ancient Egyptians.

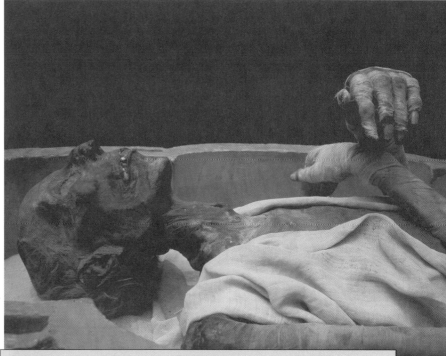

Figure 4.17 Egyptians preserved bodies for the afterlife, and priests developed **embalming**, or the preservation of corpses, to a fine art. The preserved body is called a **mummy**. The total process of preparing the mummy could take up to 70 days. The body was cleansed with oils and spices. Organs were removed and placed into containers called **canopic jars**. These jars were placed beside the **sarcophagus** in the tomb. The inside of the body was filled with sawdust and linen. A salt called **natron** was used to help the drying process. Finally, the body was wrapped in bandages that had been soaked in beeswax. The mummified body of the pharaoh Ramses II (seen here) is over 3000 years old.

Some Egyptian Deities

GODS

Amun (king of the gods)

Anubis (god of the dead)

Aten (a form of the sun god, Ra)

Bes (god of pregnant women, children, families)

Horus (god of the sky)

Khepri (god of creation)

Khnum (god of inundation)

Min (god of fertility)

Osiris (god of the underworld)

Ptah (god of craftsmen)

Ra (god of the sun)

Sobek (god of the Nile River)

Thoth (god of writing, knowledge)

GODDESSES

Bastet (protectress)

Hathor (goddess of love and joy)

Isis (goddess of magic spells)

Ma'at (goddess of truth, justice, harmony)

Nephthys (goddess of the dead)

Nut (goddess of the sky)

Sekhmet (goddess of war)

Wadjet (goddess of Lower Egypt)

Figure 4.18 The Step Pyramid at Sakkara was built for the pharaoh, Djoser (also spelled Zoser) by the architect Imhotep [im-HO-tep]. The highly regarded architect was the first to design royal tombs in the pyramid shape from hewn stone.

The Pyramids: Wonder of the Ancient and Modern World

The pyramids are the burial places for the kings, queens, and other important people in ancient Egypt. To build the pyramids, the Egyptians needed an understanding of engineering, mathematics, science, and technology that would challenge even today's best designers and planners.

Most work on the pyramids was done during the flooding of the Nile when people could not farm. It is estimated that it took 100 000 workers about twenty years to move the 2 million stone blocks used to construct a pyramid. The huge blocks were placed on flat-bottomed boats and moved on the high waters of the river to where the pyramid was being built.

The earliest stone pyramid (the Step Pyramid) was built at Sakkara (also spelled Saqqara). It was built in about 2700 BCE, south of the delta of the Nile River where stone was plentiful. About eighty pyramids were built in this area. The largest pyramid is the Great Pyramid at Giza (see page 70). The original structure was 152 metres high, and it was covered in gleaming white limestone blocks.

Technology improved as the artisans and architects designed more pyramids. To build the pyramids at Giza so high and perfectly vertical, builders began using tools such as the plumb line, mallets and chisels, and set squares. The plumb line, which is simply a weight attached to one end of a string, was used to check the vertical line of a block or wall. Wooden mallets and bronze or copper chisels were used to cut and size the blocks of stone. Chisels had to be sharpened often, because bronze and copper are soft metals. The set squares ensured that the angles and directions of the stone blocks were correct.

Pyramids were built over a period of about 1000 years, from the beginning of the Old Kingdom to halfway through the Middle Kingdom. Other famous structures in Egypt include The Sphinx and the temple of Amun, built at Karnak. As the power and wealth of the pharaohs declined, the construction of large monuments to the pharaohs declined.

Figure 4.19 This picture shows the different types of ramps the Egyptians used to build their pyramids.

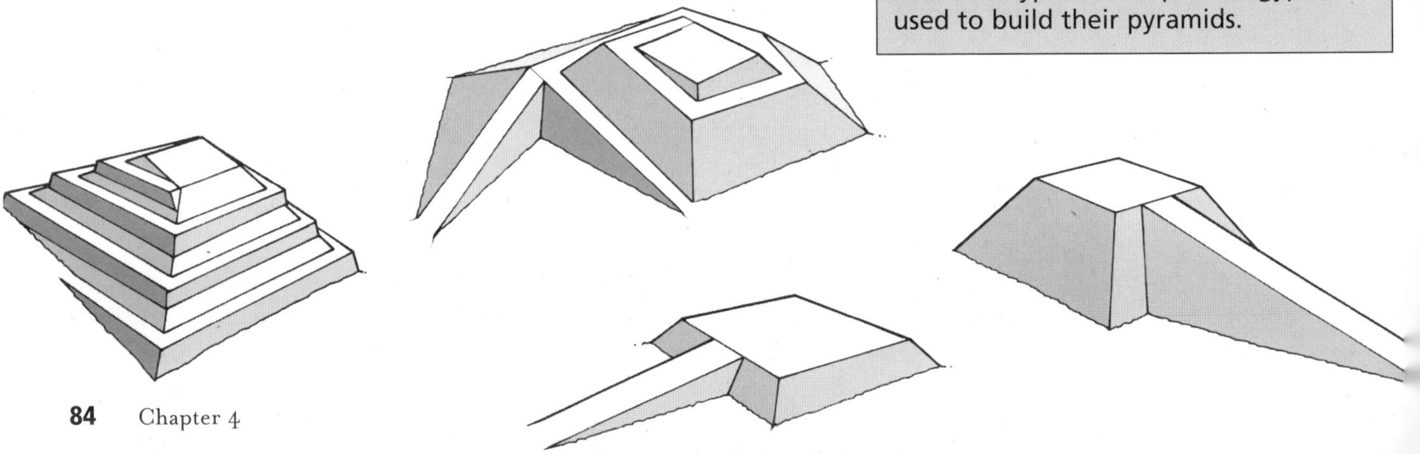

Burying a Pharaoh

This story of the preparation for burial of a pharaoh is told by a young priest. With the Egyptians' concern for the afterlife, priests had an important role in the lives of all people.

Emeni readied himself for the burial of Tutankhamen [TOOT-ank-HA-men], the young pharaoh. Emeni was nineteen years old, the same age as the dead pharaoh. Although Tutankhamen had been pharaoh for almost nine years, he had not had time to accomplish a great deal because he was so young when he became king.

Emeni went down to the sacred pool to cleanse himself, then entered the temple sanctuary, a holy place open only to priests. Emeni placed an offering of food and a sacrificed goat in front of the statue of the god Amun. Emeni chanted a special prayer for the dead pharaoh.

Emeni's studies for the priesthood had taken several years. He had learned many chants, gestures, prayers, and sacred texts, as the Egyptians had hundreds of deities. His father was a priest, and Emeni had been ready for the challenge.

Priests had many responsibilities, including performing the ceremony before the soul of a dead person could pass into the afterlife. This was especially important on this day. Tutankhamen's soul must pass into the afterlife if other Egyptian souls were to follow.

Emeni was one of a select group of priests, priestesses, and family accompanying the body to its final resting place. Many preparations had been made for the burial. The walls of the pharaoh's tomb had been covered with artwork. Baskets of food, jugs of wine, clothes, dishes, jewellery, furniture, chariots, and weapons had all been provided so that Tutankhamen had everything he needed in the afterlife.

The location of the tomb was a secret so that tomb robbers would not find it. Not even a small pyramid marked the spot in the Valley of the Kings, the place where many pharaohs were buried.

Emeni had heard that the tomb was underground and contained four rooms. The antechamber was the first and largest room. Most of the items the pharaoh needed for the afterlife were stored there. A small annex containing such items as walking sticks, crooks, and games was connected to a treasury room. Very valuable items were stored here, such as a finely crafted **alabaster** ointment container in the shape of a boat. The shrines and the pharaoh's body were placed in the last room – the burial chamber.

Emeni joined the procession that was carrying Tutankhamen's body to the solar boat. When everyone was aboard the boat, the funeral party set sail for the burial site across the river.

Figure 4.20 These are two of the items that had been placed in Tutankhamen's tomb. On the left is an ointment vase made of alabaster. The boat atop the chest is decorated with two Syrian ibex and a princess. The object on the right is an **unguent** box in the shape of a double royal **cartouche**.

Opening a 3300-Year-Old Tomb

After many years of excavation work in Egypt, British archaeologists Howard Carter and George Herbert discovered Tutankhamen's tomb in 1922. When they opened the tomb the following year, this is what Carter remembered: "At first I could see nothing. The hot air escaping from the chamber caused the candle flame to flicker. But presently, as my eyes grew accustomed to the light, details of the room within emerged slowly from the mist, strange figures of animals, statues, and gold – everywhere the glint of gold."

Tutankhamen is one of the most famous pharaohs because his tomb was discovered in good condition and with many ornate artifacts. This young pharaoh ruled from about the age

Figure 4.22 This photograph shows the antechamber of Tutankhamen's tomb. Grave robbers made it only this far, and they took only small items that were portable. This robbery took place about ten years after the pharaoh's death. The tomb then remained untouched until Howard Carter reopened it in 1923. Carter found hundreds of pieces of gold jewellery, weapons (swords, axes, spears, shields, daggers), clothing, religious items, and large statues like the ones pictured here.

Figure 4.21 Howard Carter is shown here carefully cleaning a coffin. It took him about eight years to catalogue and restore the 5398 items in the tomb of Tutankhamen who lived in about 1330 BCE. The discovery of the pharaoh's tomb stirred the interest of many people around the world. Carter often found it difficult to work with so many visitors coming to the excavation site. The popularity and importance of the site also created some conflict between the Egyptian and British governments resulting in closing the tomb area for many years.

of nine to age nineteen. His mummified body disintegrated when Howard Carter unwrapped it in 1923. The body had to be put back together by scientists so that archaeologists could study it further to learn more about the mummification process. In recent years, scientists have taken CT scans of Tutankhamen to continue research about his life.

Judaism

The Hebrews founded one of the world's major religions – Judaism. The followers of this religion are called Jews. Two other major religions, Christianity and Islam, have their origins in Judaism.

The main source of information about Judaism is the Old Testament of the Bible. The stories of the Old Testament were written over many centuries by different authors. They relate the history and ancient laws of the Hebrew people.

The Hebrews were nomadic, travelling with their animals from oasis to oasis at the edges of the Arabian Desert, east of the Nile Valley. During a drought in the mid-1800s BCE they moved to Egypt, where they thrived for a time. Eventually, they were enslaved by the Egyptians and forced to build pyramids, canals, and cities for the pharaohs.

According to the Bible, a man named Moses emerged as the leader of the Hebrews. Moses had been born in Egypt and raised by an Egyptian princess. Moses freed the Hebrews and led them out of Egypt. They settled in Canaan, an area between Egypt and Mesopotamia, between 1300 BCE and 1200 BCE. (Today it is part of modern Israel and the West Bank of Jordan.) There, they established a powerful kingdom.

Judaism is based on a belief in one just god. The concept of one god had been introduced to Egyptians for a brief period by Pharaoh Akhenaten. When the young pharaoh Tutankhamen came to power, however, he re-established the concept of many deities.

The Hebrews believed that they were a special people, chosen by their God to serve Him. In order to love their God, the Hebrews believed that they had to love their neighbours. These are further defined in the **Talmud**, which was written by **rabbis** during the time of the Roman Empire.

The Legacy of the Egyptians

The Egyptians were responsible for many inventions and advances in science and technology:

- the **shaduf** [shah-DOOF] to irrigate the fields beside the Nile River
- mummification of human bodies
- the invention of tools (levels, plumb lines, and set squares) and construction techniques such as ramps for building the pyramids
- powerful drugs such as castor oil, senna, opium, and mercury
- wooden boats
- papyrus for writing on and for the construction of boats
- sundials and water clocks to measure time
- mathematics applications, especially geometry, used in architecture and surveying techniques
- accurate twelve-month calendar of 365 days based on a knowledge of astronomy

Figure 4.23 When using an Egyptian shaduf, a container is filled with water by dipping it into the river. Then, a counterweight raises the container to the appropriate level so that the water can be emptied into the ditch.

Summary

Egyptian society revolved around the yearly flooding of the Nile River. The river was important for irrigation, food (fish), transportation, and trade. As we shall see in the Indus Valley, China, Greece, Rome, Central America, and South America, rivers and other waterways were useful to the development of many societies.

Connecting and Reflecting

Reflect on the contributions and achievements of the Egyptians. Use the information you have learned in this chapter to describe how the ancient Egyptians have influenced your life today as *a citizen of Canada and a citizen of the world.*

Be an Historian

Do you believe everything that you read in a history text? Do you ever wonder what information has been left out? When you study history, you are usually reading the results of what historians have researched and written. In this section, you will have the opportunity to do your own research and ask yourself the same kinds of questions that historians ask themselves. You will not be reading history; you will be doing history!

Historical research is very complicated. (See chapter 1.) It demands knowledge, skill, and patience. Historians have to:

- locate their evidence
- interpret what it means
- sort out what is true from what is probable and what is false

Read the excerpts below. When you are finished, answer the following questions:

- Where do these sources come from?
- Are they sources that you can trust?
- What do you know about the author? If you do not know anything, how can you find out?
- Does the author have knowledge, experience, or credentials that makes you willing to trust his or her work?
- As you try to understand the past, how important is chronology?

Herodotus, a Greek, toured Egypt in the 5th century BCE. His writings about his travels gave the first explanation of how and by whom the pyramids were built. He also wrote about areas that he had not seen himself. This is one reason why historians have to be careful about the accuracy of accounts of historical writers.

When King Cheops (also known as Khufu) succeeded to the throne of Egypt he plunged into all manner of wickedness. He closed the temples and banned the people from offering to the gods. Instead he forced them without exception to toil for him. Some were made to drag blocks of stone from the quarries to the Nile. Others received the stone blocks when they had crossed the river by boat, and dragged them to the chosen hill site. A hundred thousand men toiled constantly, being relieved every 3 months by a new contingent of labourers. It took 10 years' oppression of the people to make the causeway which would allow the passage of the blocks...to level the top of the hill and to prepare the underground chambers which Cheops (Khufu) planned to use as a burial vault...The pyramid itself took twenty years to build...

(Herodotus, Histories, Book 2: 124; Page 32, The Private Lives of the Pharaohs by Joyce Tyldesley)

We might have anticipated that the non-elite pyramid builders were fed on a diet of bread and fish, perhaps supplemented by vegetables: these, the least expensive of foods, would provide enough carbohydrates, protein and beer to fuel a workforce made hungry and thirsty by vigorous manual labour. Herodotus, ever helpful, even provides us with details of the menu offered to his pyramid-building slaves:

There is an inscription in Egyptian writing on the pyramid which records the quantity of radishes, onions and garlic eaten by the labourers who built it, and I remember very well that the interpreter who read the inscription to me said that the money spent in this way was the equivalent of 1600 talents of silver. If this is indeed a true record, what a vast sum must have been spent on iron tools used in the work, and on the feeding and clothing of the labourers, considering the length of time that the project lasted.

(Histories, Book 2: 125; Page 55, The Private Lives of the Pharaohs by Joyce Tyldesley)

Herodotus tells us exactly how he thinks that the pyramids were built:

The pyramids were built in steps; some call this technique battlement-wise, or altar-wise. After laying the stones for the base they raised the remaining blocks to their places using machines made of short wooden planks. The first machine elevated them from the ground to the top of the first step. On this there was another machine that received the block and moved it to the second step, where a third machine received the block and moved it still higher. Either they had as many machines as there were steps in the pyramid, or possibly they had a single portable machine which was transferred from layer to layer as the pyramid rose – both accounts are given, and therefore I record both. The upper portion of the pyramid was finished first, then the middle, and finally the part that was lowest and nearest to the ground.

(Histories, Book 2: 125; Page 64, The Private Lives of the Pharaohs by Joyce Tyldesley)

Unfortunately the 4th Dynasty builders remain modestly silent about their feats of river transportation and we are forced to turn to classical historian Pliny for a suggestion as to how the barges may have received their heavy cargo.

A canal was dug from the Nile River to the spot where the obelisk lay and two broad vessels, loaded with blocks of similar stone a foot (30 centimetres) square – the cargo of each amounting to double the size and consequently double the weight of the obelisks was put beneath it, the extremities of the obelisk remaining supported by the opposite sides of the canal. The blocks of stone were removed and the vessels, being thus gradually lightened, received their burden.

(Natural History, Book 36: 14; Pages 67-68, The Private Lives of the Pharaohs by Joyce Tyldesley)

Herodotus explains the fortunate circumstances of Egyptians who are living near the delta of the Nile River.

If as I before remarked, the country below Memphis, which is that where the water has receded, should progressively from the same cause continue to extend itself, the Egyptians who inhabit it might have still juster apprehensions of suffering from famine: for in that case their lands, which are never fertilized by rain, could not receive benefit from the overflowings of the river. The people who possess that district, of all mankind, and even of all the Egyptians, enjoy the fruits of the earth with the smallest labor. They have no occasion for the process nor the instruments of agriculture usual and necessary in other countries. As soon as the river has spread itself over their lands and returned to its bed, each man scatters the seed over his ground, and waits patiently for the harvest, without any other care than that of turning some swine into the fields to tread down the grain. These are at the proper season again let loose to shake the corn from the ear, which is then gathered.

(Rev. William Beloe (trans.). Herodotus, Vol. I. London: H. Colburn and R. Bentley, 1830. pp. 170-171)

The Indus Valley

Our Study of the Indus Valley

Our study of the Indus Valley includes the following topics:

- Where the Indus Valley People Lived
- What They Wore
- What They Ate
- Farming
- The Development of Writing
- Government
- Religious and Spiritual Beliefs
- The Arts
- What Happened to the Indus Valley People?
- The Indo-Aryans
- Hinduism
- Buddhism
- The Legacy of the Indus Valley

At the beginning of the 20th century, historians believed that the **urbanization** of India began after 1500 BCE. Before that date, they thought the early peoples of India lived in nomadic/pastoral societies.

In the 1920s, archaeologists began to dig several newly discovered sites in the Indus Valley of Pakistan and northwestern India. This was at about the same time that Howard Carter was excavating Tutankhamen's tomb in Egypt. What archaeologists uncovered was a large ancient urban civilization. Excavations of this civilization, called Harappan or Indus Valley, continue to this day.

Compared to the information available about the peoples of Mesopotamia and Egypt, knowledge of the people of the Indus Valley is limited. This is due, in part, to the difficulty of excavating Indus Valley sites. For example, flooding at the ancient city of Mohenjo-Daro has prevented archaeologists from digging down to the earliest layers of the site. As well, a Buddhist temple is located on top of part of the buried city. Information is not available from written sources. Although Indus Valley people had a written language, few samples have been found. Experts, therefore, have not been able to decipher the writings.

Questions to Think About

- What were the great achievements of the Indus Valley people?
- How have the Indus Valley people influenced life in India to the present day?
- What are some of the similarities between the Indus Valley societies and those described in Mesopotamia and Egypt? What are some of the differences?

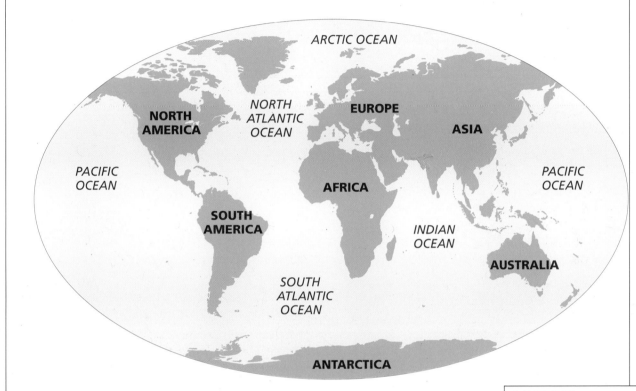

Figure 5.1 This map shows the location of Indus Valley civilization in about 2500 BCE. The Indus Valley civilization is often referred to as the Harappan civilization because Harappa was the name given to the first city discovered in the 1920s. It was probably established around 2500 BCE and lasted for nearly 1000 years, before disappearing suddenly in about 1700 BCE.

Figure 5.2 The modern-day city of Harappa is close to the ancient city of Harappa. By 2600 BCE, several large cities, including Harappa, had been established amid the small farming villages in the Indus Valley.

Where the Indus Valley People Lived

The Indus Valley included a huge area in what is now Pakistan and north-central India. It ran from the foothills of the Himalaya Mountains in the north to the Arabian Sea in the south. It included fertile farmlands along the Indus River, the Thar Desert between the Indus and Ganges rivers, and a swampy delta along the seacoast. Indus Valley society covered an area estimated to have been twice the size of the Old Kingdom of Egypt. Jungles along the fringes of the Indus Valley were home to many animals, including elephants, tigers, crocodiles, and rhinoceroses.

Temperatures were very hot and little rain fell. When snow melted in the Himalaya Mountains each spring, however, the rivers flooded and sometimes destroyed communities and villages.

Some scientists estimate the population of the Indus Valley reached 5 million. Most people lived in small farming villages near the river flood plains. By 2600 BCE, several important commercial and religious centres had been established near rivers, along the seacoast, and in agricultural regions. Mohenjo-Daro, near the Indus River, and Harappa, beside the River Riva, were the two largest cities. They were the best-planned cities in the world in this period of history. Both were also the political capitals of this region.

What They Wore

Both men and women wore bright, colourful robes. Little else is known about their style of clothing. Women wore lipstick, and their jewellery was made of gold and precious stones.

What They Ate

The diverse natural environment of the Indus Valley allowed people to grow many different crops, several of which were the same as in Mesopotamia and Egypt. People ate a varied diet that included wheat, barley, and rice. Cattle provided meat and milk. People living near rivers ate fish, molluscs, and turtles. Those settled near forested regions hunted animals

Figure 5.3 The zebu bull is a recurring theme in many of the ritual and decorative arts of the Indus Valley people.

such as wild boar. Peas, sesame, mustard, melons, and dates also were part of the people's diet. For dinner, families might have had a tasty wheat bread served with either barley or rice.

Farming

Mixed farming was the basis of the Indus Valley economy. Farmers planted their crops in irrigated fields. After the crops were harvested, the grain was taken to the nearby town where it was kept in a large central storage building. Rice, grown on the west coast, was cultivated in the Indus Valley before it was in China. The Chinese learned to cultivate rice from the Indus Valley people in about 2000 BCE. Cotton, which grows well in hot, humid climates, was grown in the Indus Valley earlier than in any of the other ancient societies.

Farmers raised two kinds of cattle, the **zebu**, an animal with a humped back, and horned, humpless cattle. Both animals provided meat and milk. Cattle dung was used as fertilizer in the fields and fuel for fires. Cattle were also used as plough animals. Water buffalo, pigs, dogs, cats, and sheep had been domesticated and were used as working animals. There is evidence that horses and camels were used for transportation, and that elephants were used as working animals. Agriculture in southern Asia today is practiced much the same as it was in the Indus Valley 4000 years ago.

Indus Valley

Figure 5.4 The Indus Valley civilization developed out of earlier agricultural societies. During the Neolithic period, farming communities were located in the mountains near Baluchistan and Afghanistan to the northwest. Farmers gradually moved onto the plains that bordered the Indus River and its tributaries and settled in small villages.

Mohenjo-Daro

Mohenjo-Daro was the largest city in the Indus Valley. At its height, it was home for as many as 40 000 people. The streets of Mohenjo-Daro, as in all Indus Valley cities, were laid out in a north-south and east-west grid pattern. Some of these streets were very wide, suggesting they must have bustled with traffic. Many people travelled around the city in carts with wooden wheels. The streets might also have been used as ceremonial routes. Small huts located at the intersection of major streets were probably guard or police stations.

The city was divided into an upper level and a lower level. Most people lived in the lower level. Government, religious, and other important buildings were located in the upper level, which researchers have called the **Citadel**. Walls and towers were found both around the Citadel and the lower part of the city. The wall around the lower mound was as high as a seven-storey building. These walls were probably built to protect the city from flooding.

The Citadel and the Great Bath

The Citadel was built on a huge platform made of brick and dirt and surrounded by brick walls and towers. One of the buildings is believed to have been a large granary, where the grain collected from the farmers in the surrounding villages was stored. The building had a loading platform for grain and ventilation in the floor to keep the grain from spoiling. This may have been a kind of state bank, where the wealth of the society was stored.

Another major building was the Great Bath. Two-storeys high, the building had a large sunken pool in the courtyard. The pool was twelve metres long, seven metres wide, and up to two-and-a-half metres deep. Broad steps on the north and south sides of the building led down to the pool.

Figure 5.5 Archaeologists believe that the Great Bath was used in religious ceremonies. Purification by water is a feature of many religions, including Hinduism, a religion widely practiced in India today. There were also a number of smaller baths in the building and several rooms where priests or workers might have lived.

Housing

Houses that were built along the city's main streets did not open onto the roads. People entered their homes through back doors that were accessible from narrow lanes running between the streets. Houses varied in size from small two-room buildings to large mansions. The different house sizes suggest there were great differences in wealth and/or different social classes in the society.

Most homes were made from standard-sized mud bricks and baked bricks. Although baked bricks were rarely used in this area of the world, the Indus Valley people built homes, wells, building platforms, and drains with them.

Figure 5.7 This photograph shows the remains of a well. Wealthy families had their own wells for drinking water and water for private baths. In poorer neighbourhoods, several families shared a well.

The ceilings in homes were high to keep the rooms cool. The floors were made from hard-packed earth covered with plaster or with clean sand. Doorways and windows had wooden or mat shutters. Many of the houses were two-storeys high, had flat roofs, and were built around a central courtyard. All windows in the house overlooked the courtyard.

Furniture was simple. People slept on reed mats and sat on low wooden stools. They stored their food in pottery containers painted in red and black designs. Statues of gods and goddesses were placed in alcoves built into the house walls.

Cleanliness was very important. All houses had indoor bathrooms with brick floors. Brick drains in the bathroom connected to covered drains that ran along the sides of the streets. These drains, which had openings to allow for inspection and cleaning, emptied into nearby rivers and streams. No other society in the world at that time took such care to keep its cities clean.

At Mohenjo-Daro, archaeologists have found several different cities built over each other. They believe that the Indus River flooded

Figure 5.6 Wooden balconies on the second floor provided shelter below from the blazing sun. This style and method of building are still common in India, as seen in this photograph.

several times, each time seriously damaging the city. Whenever this happened, the people would rebuild rather than move to a new location. The most organized and well-built city was found on the bottom layer. This may be because the builders became less able or less interested in perfection. In any case, each city that has been uncovered is greatly advanced for the period when it was built.

The Development of Writing

The appearance of writing in the Indus River Valley seems to have occurred as the society was becoming more complex. Villages were becoming larger (although cities had not yet been established), and long-distance and local trade were becoming important to the society. Writing appeared here at about the same time as in Mesopotamia, Egypt, and ancient China.

Some samples have been found at the city of Harappa. Experts have not been able to decipher the entire script. However, from a shard that was inscribed with what appears to be three plant symbols, the origins of writing can be dated to c.3300 BCE-2800 BCE. Pottery has been found with inscriptions on the bottom made before and after firing. Inscriptions have also been found on amulets. Until a translation is discovered, scholars who study ancient Indus Valley writings will continue to have various theories about the meaning of the script.

Trade

Indus Valley people were active traders. They imported copper, turquoise, and gold from surrounding areas such as Afghanistan, Iran, and southern India, perhaps by trading with hunter-gatherers who roamed these territories. Cotton may also have been exported. Trading

Figure 5.8 Indus Valley people used water routes for much of their trade.

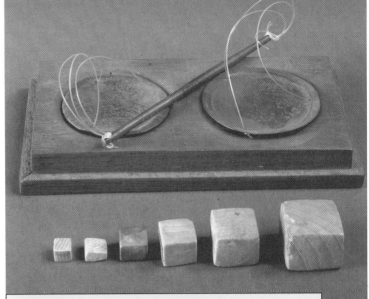

Figure 5.9 Traders and merchants used standardized weights and measures in their business transactions. The smallest weights were likely used to measure out gold or spices or for taxing goods coming into and going out of the cities. Larger weights were so heavy that they had to be hoisted with ropes. They may have been used for measuring grain.

networks connected the various regions within the Indus Valley territory. Cattle, food, cotton, lumber, and grains were likely the most common goods traded between cities.

Traders travelled overland in caravans and by sea in long, flat-bottomed boats. Traders probably sailed one-masted ships around the Arabian Sea. Heavy **monsoon** rains made travel by land difficult in the early spring. By sea, monsoon winds from the northeast in May and June aided travel to the Persian Gulf and areas around the Red Sea. Southeast winds in August made return trips easy. At other times of the year, trade ships sailed close to the coastlines.

A large dock has been excavated at the port city of Lothal on the Arabian Sea. From Lothal, goods were transported by boat to Bahrain, an island in the Persian Gulf. The people of Bahrain relayed these trade goods to Mesopotamia. A number of objects from the Indus Valley, such as seals, have been found buried with objects from Mesopotamia.

Figure 5.10 This is an artist's idea of what Mohenjo-Daro might have looked like about 4000 years ago.

Figure 5.11 Maru and his father travelled in a bullock cart, similar to the one in this photograph. Along the way, they saw several riverboats transporting goods into the city.

A Trip to the City

In this story, a young farm boy experiences life in a city for the first time.

Maru woke well before the sun was up. His father had told him that they would have to leave for the city very early, before it got too hot. Although it was not yet midsummer, it would not be long before the sun blazing down on the dusty plain would make the trip into town unbearable.

Maru had never made the trip with his father, and he was looking forward to spending a day away from the backbreaking work in the fields. After a breakfast of flatbread and dates, Maru and his father filled jugs with cold drinking water from their well. Together, they set out in the wooden cart loaded with wheat.

A few hours later, Maru saw the walls and towers of Mohenjo-Daro in the distance. As they neared the city, he was certain he had never seen anything so magnificent before in his life.

Maru's older brother, who usually accompanied their father on trips to the city, had described Mohenjo-Daro to Maru. Still, he was astounded by how wide the streets were, the crowds of people, the carts, and the animals. His father stopped briefly to greet his uncle. His uncle was a traffic guard,

which was a very important job. Not long ago, his uncle had been a construction worker at a bathhouse. His employer was impressed with his work and had him promoted to a guard. Someday, Maru knew, he would move to the city and be summoned to work on one of the government's building projects. He hoped he would be as successful as his uncle.

Maru and his father soon moved on, and the ox strained as it pulled the cart up the steep hill towards the citadel. They came to a stop outside the massive granary. An official weighed the wheat being carried in the cart and loaded it into baskets. Maru watched as men standing on a series of ledges overhead hoisted the baskets, then poured the wheat into the granary.

By the time they were finished, the sun was almost overhead. Rather than return home in the heat of the afternoon, they stopped at the home of Maru's uncle to rest. One of his girl cousins brought them water from the well located in the centre of the courtyard. Maru and his father took turns pouring the cold water over their heads in the brick bathroom inside the house. Then they sat down in the shade of the balcony with the family dog and had an afternoon nap.

Government

The Indus Valley was probably governed by a priest-king who headed a strong central government.

Cities such as Mohenjo-Daro and Harappa were built several kilometres apart, but they had remarkably similar layouts: well-constructed houses, well-laid out and well-built houses, good sanitation systems, and public baths. Building codes were strict and the workforce was large, efficient, and highly organized. Historians believe that the area was ruled by a strong central government that imposed standards on the population. To feed the large workforce, an organized distribution network must have been set up by an efficient administration of towns and cities.

One indication of a strong central government is the remarkably similar **urban planning** evident throughout the Indus Valley towns and cities. It appears that the Indus Valley people were highly disciplined and took their civic duties seriously. People kept their cities clean and co-operated with one another. Builders followed strict building codes when planning the cities and rebuilding damaged areas such as docks, warehouses, walls, and platforms. Officials used the Indus River to stay connected to people who lived along it. In this way, they were able to maintain a well-organized and efficient administration and economy over an area twice the size of Mesopotamia.

Religious and Spiritual Beliefs

The Indus Valley people had many gods and goddesses. Some statues of goddesses have elaborate headdresses and jewellery. They were probably worshipped as symbols of fertility.

Carvings on some Indus Valley **seals** show a three-faced god wearing a large headdress with horns and surrounded by animals. These animals, which include a tiger, elephant, rhinoceros, and buffalo, also appear on other seals. The three-faced god was probably a model for the later Hindu god Shiva, who was Lord of Beasts. The animals that appeared with him, and particularly the horned bull that is represented by the horns worn by the god,

Figure 5.12 This funeral urn lid indicates that some people were cremated. Several urns have been discovered at Harappa. Unlike rulers from Mesopotamia and Egypt, Indus Valley rulers were treated as common men after their deaths.

were probably also worshipped. Other images that often appear on seals include unicorns, elephants, and bulls.

When people died they were buried in wooden coffins, surrounded by pottery. This suggests that people believed in an afterlife. Ornaments such as beads and bangles adorned both male and female bodies. Jewellery made from gold, silver, and precious stones that people wore has not been found at burial sites. These items were probably passed down from generation to generation as inheritances rather than buried with the dead.

Figure 5.13 The Citadel at Mohenjo-Daro includes a very large palace-like building that may have been the home of a very important official. There is, however, no evidence that the Indus Valley people were governed by emperors who lived in huge palaces. Some homes have been found that are larger than others, but they could have been for larger families or shared by families. This statue is believed to be of a priest-king. The ruler did not live a lavish lifestyle.

The Arts

Very little art of the Indus Valley civilization has been recovered. Two statues, one portraying a priest-king and the other a native dancing girl are the most famous of the Indus Valley artworks. The Indus Valley people also produced good-quality pottery, which was often decorated with animal, bird, and plant images. Artisans produced metal ornaments and tools and ceramic toys. Archaeologists have found bowls made of bronze and silver and many beads.

Fired **steatite** beads have been found at Harappa that date to c. 2600 BCE-2200 BCE. The beads are in many of the ornaments that people wore as jewellery.

Many beautifully carved stone seals have been found with detailed figures of animals and gods. The inscriptions appear to be the names of the owners of the seals. These provide the best examples of the Indus Valley written language, but because the samples are so small, experts have not been able to decipher them. Indus Valley seals have also been found in the ruins of cities in Mesopotamia. Scientists have

Figure 5.15 The artistic flair of Indus Valley people can be seen in the many seals that have been found. Most seals are made of terra cotta and have writing and an animal on them (see above). Some seals may have been used to close jars filled with a trade good such as oil. Other seals may contain the text of important myths.

been able to use the seals to trace some of the trade routes of the Indus Valley people.

The Indus Valley people were very appreciative of arts such as dancing, music, and painting. Bronze, **terra cotta**, and stone sculptures show figures in dancing poses. Harp-like instruments have been found on an Indus Valley seal and on shell objects. Artisans also developed a new style of painting that showed animal figures in their natural environments.

What Happened to the Indus Valley People?

The Indus Valley civilization was in decline by about 1900 BCE. Many explanations have been given for the fall of the Indus Valley civilization, including the following:

• The constant flooding of the Indus River and its tributaries and planting of the same farmland year after year destroyed the quality of the land. Eventually, the farms could not produce enough food to feed everyone. As forests were cut down for fuel, the land eroded further. People began to abandon the cities in search of new land.

Figure 5.14 This squirrel was made over 2000 years ago by a technique called **glazed faience.** After it was sculpted, it was covered with an opaque coloured glaze containing a tin oxide.

- There was an upheaval in the Arabian Sea that caused an eruption of gases on land. This created a barrier that cut off the Indus River from the sea. With no outlet, the river began to flood its banks. Over many years, a lake formed and spread, eventually reaching Mohenjo-Daro. As the water encroached on homes, people had to build new structures on top of the old. In time, much of the city was under water.

- The Sarasvati, an important river system, dried up. People who lived in communities that depended on the river for drinking water and crop irrigation were forced to leave their homes and find refuge in other places. This influx strained the economies of these places and led to their decline.

- Indo-Aryans, a semi-nomadic people from the northwest, invaded the Indus Valley and destroyed the people and the culture.

No evidence exists to support the destruction of the Indus Valley civilization by the Indo-Aryans. Most scientists believe that over-expansion and changes in the river systems led to the downfall of the Indus Valley civilization. Rather than disappear, the huge territory gradually broke up into regional cultures that no longer maintained contact with each other.

The Indo-Aryans

Indo-Aryans, a semi-nomadic people from central Asia, began moving into the Indus River Valley around 1900 BCE. These people continued their semi-nomadic existence until about 1500 BCE. At that time, they began to settle on farms to raise cattle.

The Indo-Aryans did not adopt the Indus Valley culture. Within a short time, the well-organized cities, art, and language of the Indus Valley peoples had disappeared.

The Indo-Aryans spoke a language called *Sanskrit*, which shares common roots with Western languages. As people settled across northwestern India, Sanskrit became the dominant language in India.

The Indo-Aryans practiced a tribal form of government, with a chief at the head of each tribe. Their society was divided into four **castes**: (1) priests who acted as advisers to chiefs, (2) warriors and nobles, (3) merchants and farmers, and (4) labourers. Certain characteristics and skills were considered when choosing people for their position. Priests required wisdom and faith, for example, and warriors needed courage and leadership abilities. Movement between the castes was flexible.

Caste System

What we know of the Indo-Aryans comes mainly from oral religious works such as hymns, chants, and religious rites called the **Vedas** [VAY-duhs]. The Indo-Aryans worshipped a large number of deities. Hindu religion later incorporated into its beliefs some of these gods and goddesses, as well as ones from the Indus Valley civilization.

The Indo-Aryans dominated northern India until about 1000 BCE. Little is known about the events of the next 400 years, however. Around 600 BCE a new civilization appeared, based on the Hindu religion. Cities were established again, trade redeveloped, and a written language was adopted.

Sanskrit, the language spoken by the Aryan people 4000 years ago, is related to most European languages and those of Iran (Persia) and India. From the 16th century CE, Christian missionaries from Europe began to visit India. They learned some Sanskrit and noted its similarities to the languages with which they were familiar.

Here are some examples of words that show a common origin:

English	Sanskrit	Latin	French
father	pitar	pater	pere
mother	matar	mater	mere

Hinduism

Hinduism, the religion of most Indians today, is the world's third-largest religion, with almost 700 million followers. It is also one of the world's oldest religions.

Central to Hinduism is belief in **karma** and **reincarnation** (rebirth). Hindus believe that a soul is born again and again until it reaches perfection. People who are good, honest, and carry out the duties required of them are reborn on a higher level in the next life. Those who are evil, dishonest, and neglect their duties sink to a lower level in their next life. They might even be reborn in the form of an animal or insect. The level into which a person is born is determined by his or her past actions (karma).

Originally there were four main levels, or castes, in Indian society. (1) The Brahmins performed the sacred rituals and prayers. (2) The warriors and rulers were responsible for protecting kings and royalty. (3) The farmers and merchants carried out the everyday business of life – producing and selling food and other goods. (4) The Sudras performed menial work and had low status. They were forbidden even to hear the Vedas or see the sacred books of their faith, which the other castes were required to read or listen to. A large group of Indians were considered to be of such low social position that they did not

Figure 5.16 Hindus from all over India hope to make a **pilgrimage** to the sacred city of Varanasi. There, they cleanse themselves in the Ganges River.

belong to any caste. These people were called "**untouchables**" and were considered unclean.

Caste determined what work people did, whom they married, what food they could eat, whom they could touch, and their basic rights. In actuality, people's lives did not always follow these rules.

The Hindu religion has a great many deities. The major deities are Brahma [BRAH-muh], Vishnu [VISH-noo], and Shiva [SHE-vuh]. These gods can take many forms. One form of Vishnu, for example, is Krishna, a popular, handsome young god about whom there are many legends. Some deities have animal forms. Ganesha, the god of good luck, has the head of an elephant. A Hindu can worship several of these, only one, or even none. In this way, the Hindu faith is fairly open and flexible. Hindus place more importance on living a good life than on following a specific set of beliefs.

Buddhism

Buddhism [BOOD-iz-im], the world's fourth-largest religion with over 300 million followers, began in India about 500 BCE. Its founder was a man named Siddhartha Gautama. His followers called him *Buddha*, which means "the enlightened one."

Hindu Castes

Brahmins

Kshatriyas

Vaisyas

Sudras

Untouchables

Buddha was born about 567 BCE in the Himalayan foothills to a wealthy, noble family. Instead of pursuing riches, fame, or power, he followed a religious path to discover how people could be liberated from suffering and sorrow.

Buddha studied with many teachers. He was not satisfied with what he learned from them, however. One night he sat down under a fig tree and vowed to meditate there to search for the truth until he understood it. Gradually, the answer became clear, and he became the Enlightened One and a world teacher.

Buddha taught "four noble truths":

1. Life involves suffering.

2. People cause their own suffering because they are concerned only with themselves.

3. Suffering ends when people forget themselves and their desires.

4. The way to end suffering is by following the eightfold path that is learned on the path to becoming a Buddhist.

Buddhists believe that through the exercises in the eightfold path, people learn to understand themselves and discover the truth about the good life and personal liberation. Those who are successful achieve a peaceful mental state called **nirvana**.

The Legacy of the Indus Valley People

- The people were highly skilled in building and city planning. Their engineering skills as well as their studies of the tides, waves, and currents enabled them to build huge docks.

- They were among the first, if not the first, to grow cotton, which they used for making fabrics.

- Their homes had bathrooms connected to city-wide underground drains, an early form of sewage disposal called *soak pits*. People had access to clean water from deep wells.

- The decimal gradation in measuring length and mass was introduced.

Figure 5.17 Technology was not as advanced as other river valley civilizations. The Indus Valley people worked mainly in copper, rather than in bronze, which is a more durable metal. Their spears and knives were quite roughly made. In many households, stone blades were still being used.

Summary ☯

The Indus Valley civilization was based on mixed farming: grain and animals. The Indus River and its tributaries flooded frequently. The river and the environment had a tremendous effect on the Indus Valley, just as the rivers and environments did in Mesopotamia and Egypt.

The river and its tributaries and the River Riva were used for irrigation, food (fish), transportation, trade, and often for personal use, such as bathing. The Indus Valley people believed in gods and goddesses, as did the people of Mesopotamia and Egypt. The roots of two major religions, Buddhism and Hinduism, can be found in the Indus Valley.

Connecting and Reflecting

Reflect on the daily life of the people who lived in the Indus River Valley. Use the information that you have learned to describe the similarities *to* and differences *from* your life. Explain why knowing about this society is important to you *as a citizen of Canada and a citizen of the world*.

Ancient China

Our Study of Ancient China

Our study of ancient China includes the following topics:

- Where the Shang Lived
- The Importance of Rivers
- Discovering the Shang Dynasty
- Government
- Social Organization
- What They Ate
- What They Wore
- Housing
- Technology
- Religious and Spiritual Beliefs
- The Military
- The Fall of the Shang Dynasty
- The First Emperor of China and His Projects
- The Legacy of the Chinese

China is a very old civilization, although it is not as old as the civilizations in Mesopotamia. Unlike in most other places, Chinese civilization has developed *continuously* over many centuries. Their civilization has never been totally destroyed, as civilizations were in other places. Chinese civilization has continued to develop since the early days – even during times of occupation by foreigners.

Figure 6.1 The Great Wall of China is one of the Seven Wonders of the Ancient World.

The Chinese have given many inventions and discoveries to the world. They were the first to invent the wheelbarrow, paddlewheel boat, gunpowder, paper, and woodblock printing. They built a Great Wall, which is the only human-made structure that can be seen from space. When Marco Polo, a European merchant, first visited China in the 13th century CE, he was amazed at the sophisticated way of life he found there.

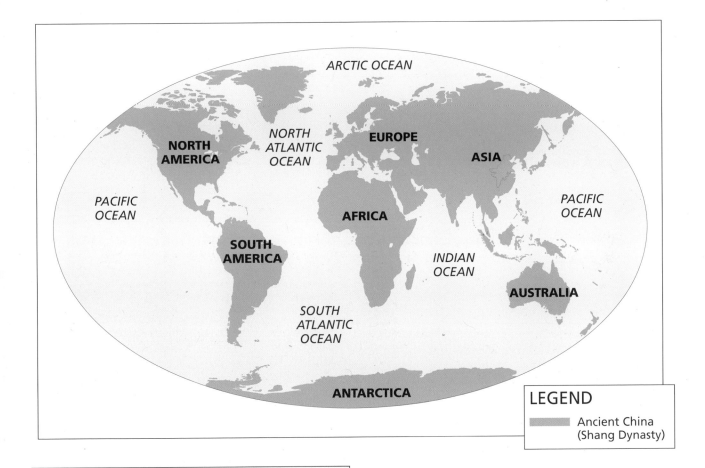

Figure 6.2 This map shows the location of the Shang dynasty.

Chinese history is usually divided into dynasties. In the first half of this chapter, we focus on the Shang dynasty [shahng DIE-nuh-stee]. When we talk about the legacy of Chinese societies in the second half of this chapter, we refer to several later dynasties (see the chart on page 105).

Questions to Think About

✦ Why did Chinese civilization develop first along the Huang Ho River?

✦ What are some of the unique characteristics of life in ancient China?

✦ Which Chinese inventions and discoveries influence our lives today?

Where The Shang Lived

China is located in Asia in an area that, in ancient times, was isolated from the rest of the world. It was cut off from India in the southwest by the Himalaya Mountains and in the west by thousands of kilometres of arid, barren plains. The sea route to the Middle East was too far away for the junks and simple sheepskin rafts the early Chinese travelled in. The Pacific Ocean ran along the eastern border. Chinese societies developed in *isolation* of, or cut off from, the rest of the world.

The Importance of Rivers

We have already seen the role that rivers played in the development of early civilizations. The Nile in Egypt, the Tigris and Euphrates in Mesopotamia and the Indus in the Indus Valley were very important in the development of those areas.

The two major rivers in China were also important. The most northern river in China is the Huang Ho [hwang huh], which means "Yellow River." Its name comes from the fine yellow silt it carries from the plains and the Gobi Desert. The other major river, located farther south, is called the Chang Jiang [chahng

Figure 6.3 The Huang Ho River deposits millions of tonnes of silt in its own bed. This results in an elevated river that, in some places, is about ten metres higher than the surrounding countryside. Sometimes the silt load is so heavy that oxygen-starved carp leap into the air.

jahng] or "Long River." This river, known as the Yangtze by westerners, cuts deep gorges through the mountains before it begins its slow run through the plains. Both rivers provided early peoples with transportation routes, water for washing and drinking, and water for irrigating crops. The earliest and most powerful societies developed along the Chang Jiang and Huang Ho. The settlements along the Chang Jiang were eventually joined to those of the Huang Ho. One of these settlements, Zhengzhou, might have been the site of the first Shang capital. During the Shang dynasty, the capital was moved several times.

Many Chinese words have several spellings in English. Here are some examples:		
Huang Ho (River)	Huanghe	Huang He
Qin Shi Huang Di	Qinshihuang	
Hsia	Xia	

Around 4000 BCE, Neolithic farmers began to settle in the northern plains of China near the Huang Ho River. The land was covered in yellow dust, called loess. The loess was very fertile when it was irrigated, which made it good soil for farming. The dust was brought into the area in two ways. (1) The loess was ground into fine particles by the glaciers and carried and then deposited on the plains by the wind. (2) The Huang Ho River, which runs through the plains, carried the dust and deposited it on the farmlands whenever the river flooded. Neolithic farmers began to grow millet and, later, rice in this soil.

The Huang Ho River provided abundant water for crops, but also subjected the people living along its banks to terrible floods. At other times, there were periods of drought, or shortages of water. The importance of the river and its unpredictability made it necessary for the Chinese to learn how to build dikes, dams, canals, and irrigation systems to control their water resources.

China in the Shang Dynasty

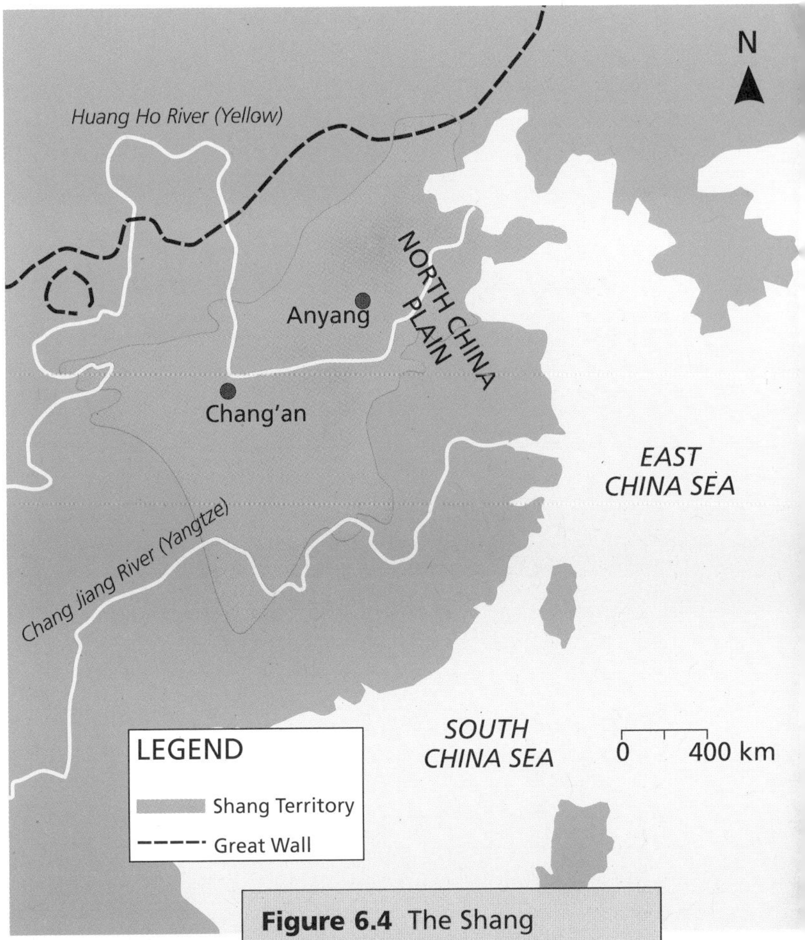

Figure 6.4 The Shang dynasty developed in the present-day province of Henan.

Unlike the Nile River, which flooded once a year, the Huang Ho could flood after heavy summer rains. In Egypt, farmers left the area and waited until the inundation was over. They would then return to plant their crops, knowing they were safe from floods until the next year. In China, unpredictable summer rains meant people were constantly on guard against flooding, and dams had to be continually maintained.

Timeline of Dynasties

Dynasty	Era
Hsia (Xia)	2000 BCE–c. 1766 BCE
Shang	**c. 1766 BCE–1027 BCE**
Chou (Zhou)	1027 BCE–256 BCE
Ch'in (Qin)	221 BCE–206 BCE During this dynasty, people from East Indian and Persian lands began to refer to the Middle Kingdom as China. This was probably a form of the name of the Ch'in Empire.
Han	206 BCE–220 CE By 220 CE, wandering nomads invaded China, and periods of unstable government followed for the next four centuries.
Three Kingdoms	220–265 Wei, Shu, Wu
Chin	265–420
Sui	581–618
T'ang	618–907
Five Dynasties	907–960
Sung (Song)	960–1280
Yuan	1280–1365
Ming	1368–1644
Ch'ing (Manchu Qing)	1644–1912

Figure 6.5 Excavations of Shang sites began in the 1920s.

Figure 6.6 The Chinese believed that the bones they were picking up in fields were from dragons, which is why they were called *dragon bones.* According to Chinese tradition, the dragon is a sacred symbol of power and lives underground. When scientists began to examine the bones, they discovered many were actually fossilized dinosaur bones.

Discovering the Shang Dynasty, c. 1766 BCE-1027 BCE

For a long time, historians and archaeologists believed the Shang people were a myth. Although Shang leaders were mentioned in early writings discovered in a tomb, no other evidence of the Shang dynasty had ever been found. That all changed at the end of the 19th century.

At that time, medicine sellers in China were selling "dragon bones." Dragon bones were often ground up and used in medicine. Farmers were constantly finding dragon bones as they ploughed their fields near the modern Chinese city of Anyang [ahn-yahng]. When Chinese scholars studied these bones, they noticed markings embedded in the bones. Upon closer examination, they realized that what appeared to be simple scratches actually resembled many 19th-century Chinese characters.

Archaeologists began to explore the area near Anyang, and, in the 1920s, they discovered thousands more bones. Near the modern-day city of Anyang, they found a settlement that they determined was the last capital city of the Shang dynasty. With the discovery of this lost settlement, they finally had proof that the Shang dynasty really had existed.

The Development of Writing

The Shang Dynasty was the earliest dynasty in China to communicate with writing. About 4500 different characters have been found, and at least 1000 of them have a connection with modern Chinese writing. Once language specialists translated the inscriptions, they found that the bones told stories of the rulers of the Shang dynasty.

How did people develop this written language? Some scholars think that ancient people needed some way to keep a record of the property they owned. Their writing may have begun with little drawings of the objects they owned. These drawings are called *pictographs*, and these little pictures eventually became characters in Chinese writing. Some of the Chinese characters today are pictographs. In later history, the written language was standardized so that all Chinese people could understand the written word, even if they spoke different dialects.

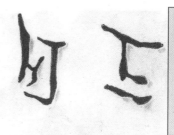

Figure 6.7 This is an early writing sample. Like many ancient societies, the Shang initially used writing as a means of keeping records.

Figure 6.8 Tortoise shell was often used for oracle scripts.

Government

The territory of the Shang was ruled by a king. All decisions were made by him. He was believed to rule by the "**mandate of Heaven**," or *divine right*, because he was a descendant of the supreme god, Shang Ti. This ancestor, along with the sun and the moon, guided all of the king's decisions. The king had great power, but he had to be responsible. If he was an irresponsible ruler, the gods would disapprove, and the nobles would withdraw their support.

The king made many of his decisions by casting oracle bones. He would write a question on a piece of ox bone or tortoise shell. A bronze pointer was heated and placed on the bone where the question was written. The bone usually cracked from the heat. The king could read the crack in four different ways: yes, no, lucky, or unlucky.

Social Organization

Shang society was rigidly divided into classes. The head of all society was the king, who was also the religious leader. The nobles, who were the warrior leaders, were below the king.

Directly below the nobles were craftspeople and merchants. The largest number of people, the farmers, made up the lowest class. Slaves were below the farmers.

Craftspeople created very fine bronze work and delicate carvings from marble or jade. They were skilled at making weapons, tools, jewellery, and pottery. Weavers made fine silk cloth that the nobles had made into lavish garments.

Merchants often used rice or **cowrie shells** to pay for goods and services. Metal coins were invented in the 5th century BCE. The first metal coins were long and thin and shaped like knives. Later, metal coins were round with a hole punched out of the middle, so the money could be strung onto a belt.

Peasant farmers grew food for all members of society and were, in turn, supposed to have the respect of those in higher classes. They were often badly treated, however. Most did not own the land they worked but rented it from noble families.

In times of war, peasant farmers became soldiers for the king. In times of peace, they had to work on the great buildings of the kingdom. Farming and construction were both difficult to do with very basic tools. It is estimated that building a new capital city required the work of 10 000 men who worked for twenty years.

Some labourers who worked on the king's buildings were probably slaves owned by noblemen and the king. Slaves were often prisoners of war, and they worked under the threat of death. Sometimes they were used as human sacrifices and were buried in a king's tomb, much as slaves were buried in the tombs of Aztec or Mesopotamia rulers. The labourers were also sometimes sacrificed and buried within the foundation of a building as it was being laid.

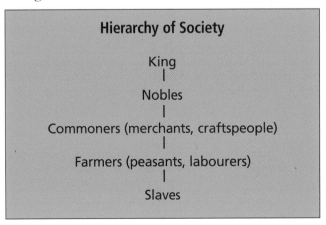

Hierarchy of Society

King
|
Nobles
|
Commoners (merchants, craftspeople)
|
Farmers (peasants, labourers)
|
Slaves

Figure 6.9 Farmers used stone ploughs, spades, and sickles to work the land.

What They Ate

The basic food of the people was millet, a kind of cereal. Barley and wheat were also grown and eaten. These crops were also grown in Egypt and Mesopotamia. The peasants grew beans and many other vegetables in their own gardens. They ate fish from the rivers and hunted animals such as deer and bears. They may have eaten as many as twenty-four kinds of meat and fish, including carp, and forty-six kinds of vegetables. They used onions and garlic to flavour their food. By the Shang dynasty, the Chinese had domesticated pigs, dogs, goats, sheep, water buffalo, and some fowl similar to chickens.

The Chinese often experienced famine, or starvation. With frequent periods of drought or flooding, it was sometimes impossible to produce food. When food was scarce, the people ate whatever they could find. Some of these foods, including different kinds of insects, became part of their regular diets.

Shang people used chopsticks for eating and for cooking. They usually boiled, steamed, or stir-fried their food.

Tea is a drink often associated with China. The earliest evidence of tea drinking found by archaeologists is from about 200 CE. The Chinese drank tea long before that, however, and there are many legends about its discovery and use. According to Chinese mythology, in 2737 BCE, the Chinese emperor Shen Nung was sitting beneath a wild tea tree, while his servant boiled drinking water. A leaf from the tree dropped into the water, and the emperor decided to try the brew that resulted. He was pleased by the taste. Tea became a favourite drink of the emperor and his people. People in India and Japan have also been drinking tea for centuries.

Tea was originally a fairly bitter drink and was used as a kind of medicine for digestive problems. Later, people began adding flavouring such as ginger or orange to the dried tea, which made tea a more pleasant drink. It was then that it became a commonly consumed beverage. One Chinese writer describes tea as "the brew that sobers one after drinking and keeps one awake." By the T'ang dynasty, tea was China's national drink. Tea became a valuable trading product, and it was an important trade item between English traders and the Chinese.

Figure 6.10 Nobles wore long elaborately decorated robes that they tied at the waist with sashes.

Peasant dress was similar in style to the clothing of the nobility, but it was made with the rougher fibres from plants such as hemp and banana leaf. Because of its warmth, wool was used as padding in outerwear and was woven into thick fabrics. Ordinary people developed styles that made it easier to work in the fields and as builders.

Men wore simple hats or kerchiefs on their heads until elaborate hairstyles became popular. Men often wore their hair in a heavy roll, with a short pigtail hanging down the back. Women's hairstyles were also elaborate. Hair was held in place with jade, bone, and ivory combs or hairpins. Women also wore necklaces and pendants made from jade and bone. Pendants were often shaped like birds such as the **phoenix** (a mythical bird) and hawk, or animals such as the tiger and elephant.

What They Wore

In the early part of the Shang dynasty, clothing was quite simple. People made clothing from animal skins in the same way people did in many other parts of the world. As people discovered that plants, animals, and silkworms supplied the flexible fibres needed to make soft wearable fabric, new types of fabrics were created. Silk production, or sericulture, became an important art and industry (see page 116).

Most men wore long, belted tunics with a jacket over top. The basic style was the same for men in all classes. The types of fabrics and the amount of decoration on the fabric indicated the social rank of the wearer. Women wore plain jackets and belted skirts over simple tunic dresses.

Silk took a long time to make and was expensive to produce. It was considered extremely precious. For this reason it was reserved for nobility. Trousers were not worn until later during the Shang dynasty.

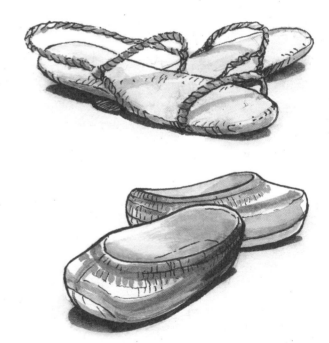

Figure 6.11 Most men wore shoes. Peasants wore straw sandals, and wealthy Chinese men wore fine cloth slippers.

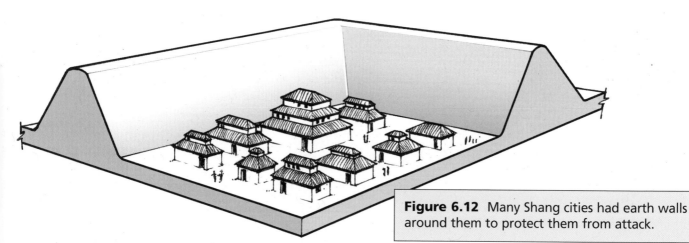

Figure 6.12 Many Shang cities had earth walls around them to protect them from attack.

Housing

The last capital of the Shang dynasty, Anyang, covered a large area along a bend of the Huang Ho River. The city was not surrounded by a defensive wall, but the river offered some protection from invasions.

Ancient Anyang was a religious, government, and industrial centre rather than a place for the common people to live. The main buildings appear to have been large palaces and temples. Packed earth was used for the foundations of the buildings. On top of the foundations, wooden pillars were used to support the walls. The walls were made of twigs, plastered with clay. Roofs were probably thatched. Most buildings were built around a central courtyard, but there were some homes arranged on parallel streets. In addition to the government section of the city, a large area was set aside for industry. Here, craftspeople worked with bronze, clay, jade, and other materials.

Most merchants and craftspeople lived outside the capital city of Anyang in mud huts. In winter, farmers lived in small villages near the city. Farmers' homes were simple one-room huts with dirt floors, mud walls, and thatched roofs. In summer, the farmers moved to their fields, where they lived in bamboo huts.

A Day on the Farm

Su and his family move to the country for the summer.

Su awoke at sunrise, just as the rooster crowed. He greeted his mother and father respectfully and sat down next to his brother to eat a bowl of rice. The family had just moved from their winter house in the village to their summer hut at the edge of their fields. The river floods had been high this year, and the waters had only recently receded. Su's father had helped to work on the dikes, which had required constant maintenance.

The nobleman who owned their land was pleased with the flood-control efforts of the villagers. They would all be rewarded with a celebration later in the summer. Su's brother would get married then along with several other couples from the village. Shortly after his marriage, his brother would leave to serve his time in the army. Su would have to do the same when he was older.

After the meal, the family knelt at the family shrine and asked Shang ti, one of the supreme gods, for blessings on their crops. Then, Su, his brother, and his parents began to clear the debris left on the fields by the flood. Later, they scattered millet seeds on the wet ground. Su led the ox back and forth over the field until the seeds were covered with mud. In another patch of land, Su planted some beans, and stopped to talk to his cousins who were planting wheat and rice in the neighbouring field.

Canals from the river would be redirected to irrigate the fields. As the crops grew, the youngest children in the village would spend the summer scaring birds away from the maturing plants.

In the evening, the family sat on their mats on the ground to eat their supper together. Su's brother had caught a carp in the river that afternoon, and they enjoyed a meal of fish and *dhofu* (tofu) flavoured with sesame seeds. Tomorrow, the overseer was coming in his horse-drawn chariot to check on the progress of the planting, and everyone needed to be ready for another hard day's work. Even before the sun disappeared for another day, everyone was sound asleep.

Technology

From Neolithic times, the Chinese used the potter's wheel to make high-quality pottery. During the Shang dynasty, artisans made elaborate chariot decorations and a variety of bronze weapons and tools – spears, knives, and axes. Beautifully decorated bronze vessels were made for the nobility and for use in religious rites.

One technique, the "lost wax" method, may have been used to make bronze urns and vases. This method involved making a mould of wax and then applying clay to it. The clay was then baked at high heat. As it was fired, the wax melted and ran out of the holes of the mould, leaving a clay mould. The clay mould was then used to form delicately decorated bronze urns.

Other craftspeople were equally skilled at working with jade, wood, and bone, and made useful tools for farmers and builders. They had cart wheels, wheelbarrows, paddlewheel boats, and sledges for transporting heavy building materials. They also used a differential windlass. A differential windlass is a system of ropes and pulleys that makes it possible for one person to lift a heavy object. Farmers had digging forks, flails, hoes, ploughs, sickles, and querns. Metal workers probably also used anvils.

Figure 6.14 Artisans began to work with bronze, and as this vessel shows, quickly developed a degree of skill and artistry that was unmatched anywhere in the world at that time.

Figure 6.15 The Shang used a hand quern, similar to the one pictured here, for grinding grain.

Figure 6.13 The windlass was used for lifting heavy objects.

Figure 6.16 This gilded bronze head was a **totem** to a Shang ruler.

A ball filled with dried tea leaves was often placed between the lips of a corpse. It was one of the many gifts to the dead in China.

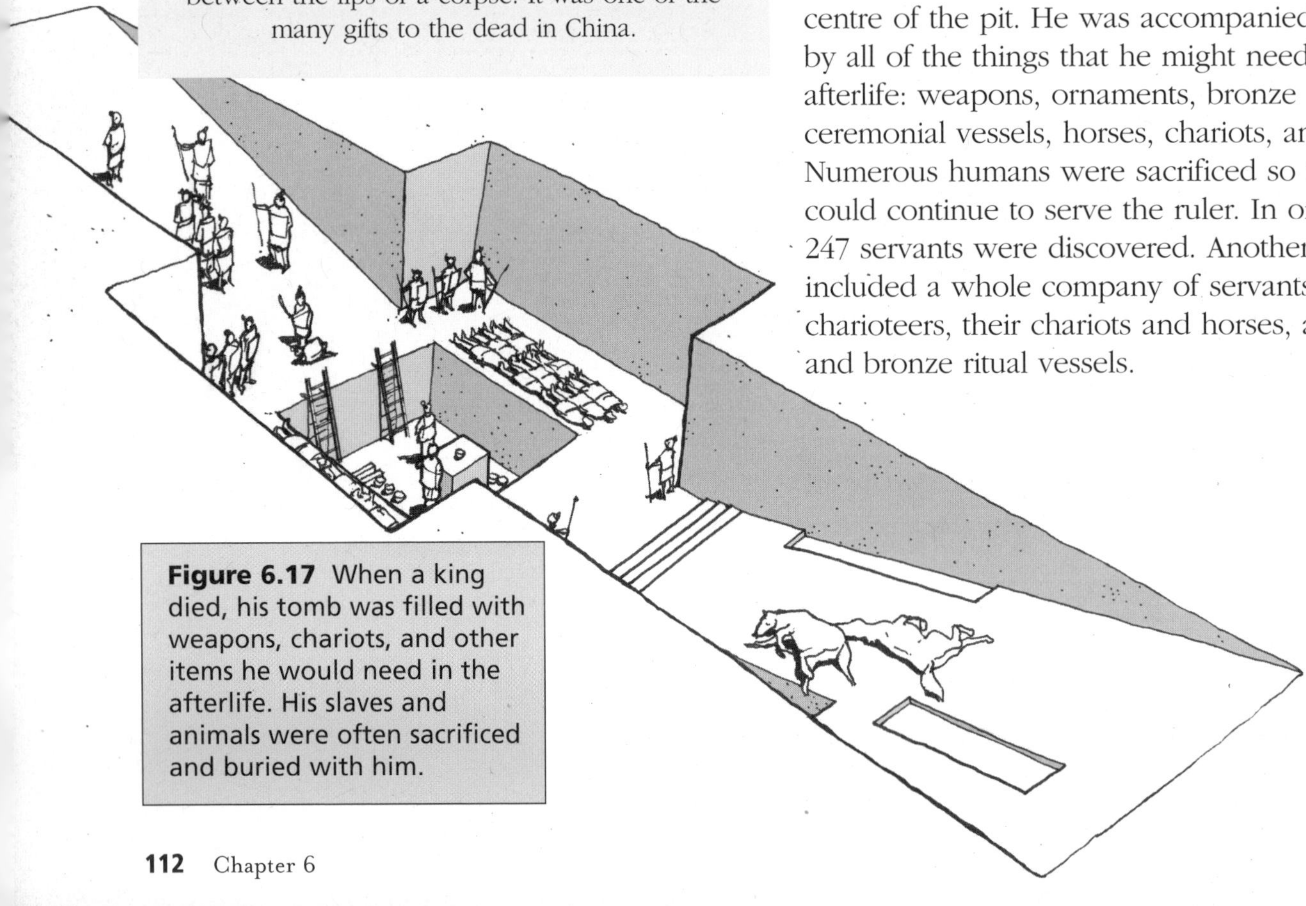

Figure 6.17 When a king died, his tomb was filled with weapons, chariots, and other items he would need in the afterlife. His slaves and animals were often sacrificed and buried with him.

Religious and Spiritual Beliefs

Most people believed in a spirit world. They worshipped many deities and believed in an afterlife. The most important god was Tien, the god of heaven. The people practiced ancestor worship. They believed in **filial piety**; younger family members were respectful of elder members of the family and the community.

The common people did not share the religion of the nobility. Instead, they worshipped various gods whom they believed controlled the earth and the crops. People consulted sorcerers (also known as a **wu**) who were either men or women. A wu provided spells to protect someone from evil spirits and could also provide the help of friendly spirits. A wu could also work magic on nature. In one ceremony, for example, the wu danced under the hot sun until he/she began to sweat. The sweat of the wu was supposed to bring about badly needed rain for the crops.

The Burial of a King

When a ruler died, a great pit was dug and ramps led down into the pit. The king's coffin was carried down the ramp and set in the centre of the pit. He was accompanied in death by all of the things that he might need in the afterlife: weapons, ornaments, bronze ceremonial vessels, horses, chariots, and dogs. Numerous humans were sacrificed so that they could continue to serve the ruler. In one tomb, 247 servants were discovered. Another tomb included a whole company of servants, five charioteers, their chariots and horses, and jade and bronze ritual vessels.

The Military

The military was often involved in battles with people who lived in neighbouring areas, especially those along the Chang Jiang River. The nobles were the warriors and led the armies. Armed with bronze axes and daggers, they rode into battle in speedy chariots with spoked wheels. They led troops of farmer-peasant soldiers who were called to serve whenever the king needed them. The foot soldiers fought at close range, using spears and knives.

Chinese military leaders were not always men. China has a history of women warriors. A noblewoman named Lady Hao, who was the third wife of the last Shang ruler, waged several military campaigns. When she died, apparently of overwork, she was buried in a large tomb, surrounded by treasures in bronze and jade.

The Fall of the Shang Dynasty

The Shang dynasty ruled for more than five centuries. Eventually, the dynasty grew weak. According to Chinese histories, the last Shang ruler had a beautiful partner named Ta Chi. Ta Chi was known for the torture she inflicted on anyone who did not show proper respect to her.

Under the cruel reign of the king and Ta Chi, people began to revolt. One group from the west, called the Zhou [joh], led the uprise against the Shang. The Zhou leaders said that the Shang ruler was not taking care of his people, so Heaven had chosen a new ruler to have the "mandate of Heaven." The last king is said to have set fire to his palace and then committed suicide.

Figure 6.18 The Shang made some weapons from bronze. Most bronze items were ceremonial. The bronze spear pictured here was found in the tomb of a military officer.

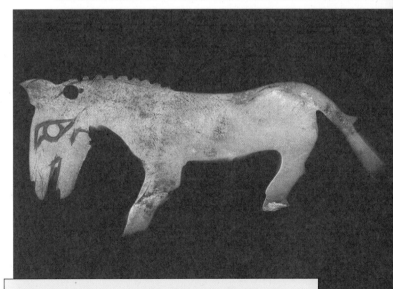

Figure 6.19 Jade, like bronze, was most often used to make ceremonial objects. This jade horse was found with other carvings in a tomb.

Figure 6.20 China's river systems flow west-east, so the canal helps travellers and traders by providing a north-south connection between several rivers. The canal may also have been built to help unify the country.

The First Emperor of China and His Projects

Of the 300 emperors of China, Qin Shi Huang Di [CHIN-shih-hwong-dee] had the greatest and longest-lasting effect on China. His dynasty ruled from 221 BCE to 206 BCE, and he became king when he was thirteen years old. By the age of thirty-eight, he had united a number of states in the area and declared himself the first emperor of a united China.

The country was large and very diverse when he set out to unify it. He set standards for writing, weights and measures, money, and the law, and all parts of the country adopted them. These changes improved communication and business within the country. To make transportation easier, he built a system of roads and canals throughout the country. People traded with countries such as Persia and India. These people called the country "China" from the name of the emperor's dynasty (Ch'in). Many of the emperor's changes worked well to unify the country, but people also feared him. He did not believe in the teachings of Confucius; he burned many books and he burned more than 400 people who believed in Confucianism. If a man disagreed with the emperor, he was killed, and so was his family.

Qin Shi Huang Di had huge projects built during his reign, including the Grand Canal, the Great Wall, and the Terra Cotta Warriors of Xi'an [Sh-ee-an]. All three have been named World Heritage sites and are favourite places for people to visit when they go to China today.

The Grand Canal

The Grand Canal is the world's longest and oldest human-made canal system. It is 1795 kilometres long and has twenty-four locks and sixty bridges. Construction of the canal started in the 5th century CE, and finished in 610 CE during the Sui dynasty. Despite the number of emperors who ruled over the construction period, it is Qin Shi Huang Di who gets the credit for building the Grand Canal. The canal runs from Hangzhou [Hang-chow], southwest of Shanghai, north to Tianjin [Ti-ent-sin] and then to Beijing [BAY-jing]. The canal goes through China's most fertile and heavily populated countryside and is still used for moving goods to and from markets.

The Great Wall

One of the few objects on Earth that can be seen from space is the Great Wall. It is one of the Seven Wonders of the Ancient World and is listed as a modern UNESCO World Heritage Site.

The Chinese say that it looks like a gigantic dragon as it winds its way across deserts, mountains, and grasslands, stretching approximately 6700 kilometres from east to west in China.

World Heritage Sites

World Heritage sites are chosen by a United Nations committee as places that should be preserved because they represent important natural or cultural heritage for the whole world. At present, there are nearly 800 sites. Canada has about 13 sites, including the cultural sites of the historic District of Quebec City and the Viking settlement at L'Anse aux Meadows in Newfoundland, and the natural site of Dinosaur Provincial Park in Alberta.

The walls are about twelve metres high, and there are hundreds of watchtowers along the Great Wall. The wall was built more than 2000 years ago, so some parts of it are in ruins or have crumbled completely.

The Great Wall was a giant defence project begun as early as the 7th century BCE. In those days, rival kings built walls around their territories. When Qin Shi Huang Di unified China in 221 BCE, all of the existing walls were joined together and new ones added to defend the country against attacks from defeated kings. It was a huge project, especially with the technology of the time. It took nearly a million people, out of a population of 5 million, to build it. Many of the workers died and are enclosed in the wall. Later dynasties strengthened or added to the wall until the Han dynasty added about 500 kilometres and completed it to its present-day length.

The Great Wall was no help when the Mongols invaded China. Some historians believe they went around one end of it. Other historians believe the Mongols came through the undefended First Gate at Shanhaiguen.

The Terra Cotta Soldiers of Xi'an

Early in 1974, Chinese farmers were trying to sink a well near the city of Xi'an when they discovered some ancient bronze weapons and pieces of terra cotta. Terra cotta is hard, reddish brown earthenware that is used for vases, statuettes, and decorations on buildings. In this case, the terra cotta was used to make statues.

At least 2000 life-size statues of soldiers have been found, and archaeologists think that there might be as many as 6000 more. They have also found life-size statues of horses, actual chariots and wagons, and lots of weapons including bows, arrows, and spears. All of these are part of the burial grounds of Qin Shi Huang Di. His ornate and richly decorated **mausoleum** is nearby, and all of the other underground pits are full of statues of people and animals to go to the next world with him. The whole burial ground employed as many as 720 000 workers and took about thirty-nine years to build. Many labourers died here during the building of the tomb. It is said that many were also killed when the project was finished, so that they would not be able to come back to rob the tomb.

Figure 6.21 When Qin Shi Huang Di died, thousands of soldiers made from terra cotta were buried with him. Each soldier is unique and may have been modelled on an actual soldier.

Figure 6.22 Bronze horses have been found in Qin Shi Huang Di's tomb alongside chariots. Many of the horses are harnessed in gold and silver.

The Legacy of the Chinese

The long, continuous history of China has provided the world with many interesting things. These range from the religious philosophy of Confucianism, to trade goods such as porcelain and the development of block printing. The Great Wall and Grand Canal, like the pyramids of Egypt and the Maya temples, are wonders of the ancient world.

Silk

Silk production, or *sericulture,* originated in China as early as about 5000 BCE. For centuries, only the ruler and his close family were permitted to wear silk. In time, other members of society began to wear tunics of silk. Silk was also eventually used for the strings of musical instruments, fishing line, bowstring, and to make paper. Silk remained so highly valued that during the Han dynasty (206 BCE-220 CE) it was worth as much as gold.

By 1000 BCE, silk had become a much sought-after item outside of China. By then, silk was so important to the Chinese economy that anyone who revealed the secrets of sericulture was punished by death.

How Silk Is Made

Silk is made from the secretions – liquid excreted from inside the body – of the *Bombyx mori* (silkworm moth). An egg is produced and when it hatches, the worm emerges. It eats a steady diet of mulberry leaves for around thirty-five days, during which time it increases its weight 10 000 times.

Once the worm is full grown, it starts to spin its cocoon to prepare for the next stage in its development. In the same way as any other moth, the worm forces a liquid out of tiny holes in its body and wraps itself in a cocoon. The liquid that is excreted from the worm hardens when it is exposed to air, and it turns into a very strong, smooth, shiny fibre. The dormant worm, enclosed inside the cocoon, is killed when the cocoon is heated to a certain temperature. Once the worm is dead, the cocoon is softened by soaking it in warm water. The fibre end is found, and the cocoon is unwound carefully. The thread that emerges from one silkworm can be up to 3000 metres long.

The Silk Road(s)

The name *silk road* reminds us of the importance of the silk trade. The name refers to the route taken by traders going to and from China (and India) to trade for silk and many other products. Most trips were overland in caravans of camels, but some traders transported products such as porcelain by ship. Either method of travel was difficult, and many people died trying to make the trip. Travellers faced storms, robbers, famine, dying animals, and hostile rulers along the silk roads. Why did traders do it? If they were successful, they could make 100, or even 1000, times what they spent to buy the goods in China.

The silk roads have been used since the 2nd century BCE, but the route was only named about a hundred years ago. When Europeans

Figure 6.23 This woman is unwinding the fibres from several cocoons to make silk thread.

found out about the products from the East, many merchants began to see opportunities to make money. Wealthy people were willing to pay high prices for the fashionable products. In the early 1700s, the king of Poland, Augustus the Strong, offered to exchange a whole battalion of soldiers for a roomful of porcelain dishes. The king was an unsuccessful military leader, but he was a lover of fine porcelain.

The ancient Greek name for China was *Seres*, the Greek word for "made of silk." Sericulture is the term used to describe the process of raising and caring for silkworms for the production of silk.

Confucius

Confucius was a Chinese philosopher. He was a great scholar and thinker who lived in northern China from about 551 BCE-479 BCE. There are many stories about his life, and it is often hard to know which ones are true.

Most historians agree that Confucius grew up in poverty. He became an administrator in the government when he was a young man, and he eventually became justice minister. At the age of fifty, he gave up his political career. He spent the next twelve years travelling around China seeking the best "way" to live. He developed a philosophy for living and tried to convince some of the Chinese rulers to follow his ideas. He was unsuccessful, and, at age sixty, he returned to his home to teach.

Confucius does not refer much to God or spiritual matters. Some people say that Confucianism is more a philosophy of life than a religion. Confucius lived in a time when there was great confusion. He knew that the Chinese people and their rulers had lived in peace with each other in early times, and he claimed that the people of his day could do the same. Confucius wanted people to follow the old ways and act properly towards one another. He emphasized personal and government morality, justice, and sincerity. Rather than do what pleases you, he preached, you should do what is right and what is best for most people.

Confucius used the family as a basis for an ideal government. He was in favour of strong family loyalty, ancestor worship, and respect for elders. Husbands were to be respected by their wives, but husbands also had to treat their wives well. Older brothers were to be respected by younger brothers.

Confucius supported the idea of a powerful emperor, but he wanted to limit the emperor's power. People were encouraged to be honest and to believe that change was possible. If a ruler was not acting properly, he would lose the "mandate of Heaven," and people could overthrow him. Many rulers did not appreciate his ideas, and he was not very welcome in some parts of China.

After Confucius died, his ideas became very popular, and many people started to follow his teachings. His descendants have been honoured over the centuries, and there are many temples dedicated to him.

Figure 6.24 Confucius expressed what we now call the "Golden Rule" – do unto others what you would want to have done to you.

Paper and Printing

The Chinese inventions of paper and printing enabled them to keep records of the property they owned and to communicate ideas.

Before the invention of paper, the Chinese wrote important messages in pictographs or characters of Chinese writing on precious silk cloth. Eventually, it was decided that old rags, hemp, and tree bark could be made into paper. Starch was added to make the paper stronger, and gelatin, made from lichens, formed a coating for the paper. By the Han dynasty, paper was commonly used. By the 9th century CE, paper had replaced the Egyptian papyrus.

Printing from woodblocks was probably invented in the 7th century CE. Two earlier printing techniques had preceded block printing. Between the 4th and 7th centuries CE, the Chinese had stamped patterns on silk cloth, and they had made rubbings on stone carvings. They adapted these ideas to woodblock printing. They used pear or jujube wood and cut the wood to the size of two book pages. They then smoothed and softened the wood by covering it with paste. The information to be printed was written on a thin sheet of paper the same size as the woodblocks. This was spread over the woodblocks and rubbed so that the ink was transferred to the wood. A woodcutter carved around the written characters so that the characters stood out from the base of the wood. The printer brushed ink on the characters and then pressed blank sheets of paper onto them to make prints. At first, the government did not print any official documents, but in 953 CE the government printed the important writings of Confucius. From that time on, printing was used as a way of getting information to many people.

Porcelain

Chinese porcelain [POUR-suh-lihn] was highly valued in medieval Europe. It is white, very delicate, and translucent (lets the light through). Good porcelain makes a bell sound if tapped. The Chinese had been making fine pottery since very early times, but they only discovered

Figure 6.25 Many Ming vases have images inside them. To see the paintings of fish, insects, and animals inside bowls and vases, the vessels have to be filled with water.

a method for making porcelain during the T'ang dynasty (618 CE-907 CE). They found that adding a mineral called **feldspar** to the clay made a much better product. At first, they just applied the feldspar as a glaze, but later they found that it worked better if they added the feldspar to the clay before they shaped the pots. When they did this and fired the pots at a very high temperature, they got a very strong and beautiful product. Porcelain is now made into expensive dishes (called *china)*, and into industrial products such as electrical insulators.

Gunpowder and Fireworks

Gunpowder was invented at about the same time as woodblock printing. The Chinese originally used gunpowder for entertainment. By the 7th century CE, they had learned to combine potassium nitrate with charcoal and sulphur to make an explosive. At first, they used gunpowder to make fireworks displays. The Chinese did not use it for war until about the 11th century CE. Europeans only became aware of the invention around the 1300s.

Footbinding

Footbinding for women is one Chinese custom that other countries did not imitate. It is a disfiguring process that only applied to girls of a wealthy class. Footbinding is a custom of tightly binding strips of linen around the feet of very young girls so that their feet would not grow large. The binding caused the feet to become crescent-shaped (called lotus-shape). Tiny, bound feet were considered a sign of female beauty and reminded women that they were not free.

The custom began in the Sung Dynasty (960 CE-1280 CE) and became popular by the 12th century CE. Mothers began binding their daughters' feet when they were about three years old. The first toe was often broken and the feet bound more and more tightly. The goal was to have feet shorter than ten centimetres. Women with bound feet were not able to walk well or do much physical work. Footbinding was more popular in the north than in the south of China. Women and men in southern China had to do a lot of work in wet rice fields, so bound feet were not practical.

Figure 6.26 The process of footbinding was very painful, feet became infected, and toes sometimes rotted and fell off. There was no way to restore a woman's foot to a natural shape after footbinding.

Summary

Our study of ancient societies has included the Tigris, Euphrates, Nile, Indus, and now the Huang Ho and the Chang Jiang rivers. These rivers played an instrumental role in the development of the different societies.

In China, as in other ancient societies studied, the rivers were used as transportation routes, as a means of irrigation, and for personal use. The legacy of Chinese societies includes many inventions, such as gunpowder and paper, which are still used today. It also includes engineering feats such as the building of the Grand Canal and the Great Wall.

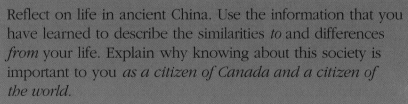

Connecting and Reflecting

Reflect on life in ancient China. Use the information that you have learned to describe the similarities *to* and differences *from* your life. Explain why knowing about this society is important to you *as a citizen of Canada and a citizen of the world.*

Part 3

In Part 3, you will read about societies in the Mediterranean region and look at 1000 years of history, from about 500 BCE to 500 CE. Ancient Greece and ancient Rome were sophisticated civilizations with written languages, complex religions, organized governments, and highly developed arts and crafts. The peoples of both Greece and Rome traded with peoples from distant lands and obtained goods that they could not produce for themselves, such as silk.

We know a great deal about Greek and Roman civilizations because written records of daily life, society, culture, art, and architecture have survived throughout the ages. The work of researchers and archaeologists and the accounts of philosophers and teachers such as Plato have also helped us to know about ancient Greece and Rome.

In chapter 7, you will read about the sophisticated societies in ancient Greece, from about 1100 BCE to 31 BCE. The focus of our study of Greece is the height of ancient Greek civilization with the growth of city-states, Athenian democracy, life in Sparta, and citizenship and identity. The contributions made by the people of Greece include many things we still recognize today. The Olympic games originated in Greece, for example.

In chapter 8, you will explore the rise and fall of the Roman Empire. At its height, the Roman Empire ruled over 50 million people throughout Europe, from North Africa to Britain. Julius Caesar is one of the best-known dictators of Rome. He was murdered in 44 BCE, but he left behind many accounts of life in Rome during his lifetime. The Roman military was one of the most organized in the world. All men were expected to serve in the army, which successfully conquered new lands.

The contributions of the Greeks and Romans to architecture, art, and literature are all still relevant today. Building techniques developed by the Romans are still used in construction.

GREECE & ROME	c. 1200 BCE	c. 1100 BCE	1000 BCE	776 BCE	753 BCE	c. 750 BCE	c. 600 BCE
	Trojan War begins.	Mycenaean society collapses.	Latins move into Italian peninsula and settle in villages.	The first Olympic games takes place in Greece.	City of Rome is founded.	City of Pompeii is founded.	Etruscans capture Rome.

	270 BCE	241 BCE	146 BCE	73 BCE	44 BCE	31 BCE	27 BCE
	Romans conquer all of Italian peninsula.	Rome defeats Carthage. Twenty years later, in 221 BCE, Hannibal begins his march on Rome. In 202 BCE, Hannibal is defeated.	Rome begins conquests of Greece and Asia Minor.	Slave revolt, led by Spartacus, threatens Rome.	End of Roman Republic. Julius Caesar is assassinated.	Roman armies conquer the Greek Kingdom of Egypt.	Caesar Augustus becomes the first emperor of Rome. Latin literature flourishes.

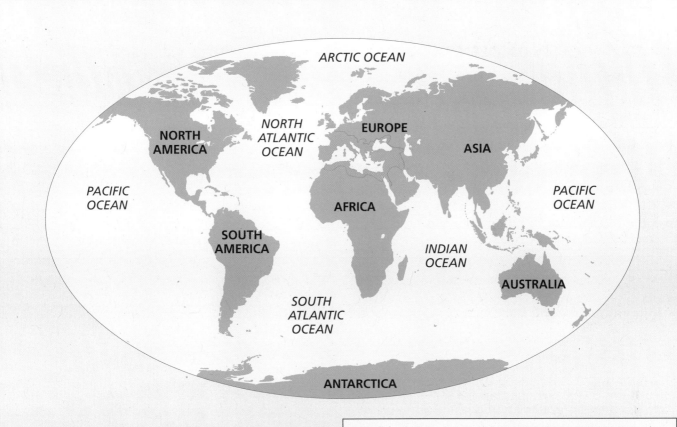

In Part 3, you will read about events that happened in areas highlighted on this map.

In the modern cities of Rome and Athens, many ancient buildings and sculptures remain. Ruins from ancient Roman structures, such as aqueducts, can still be seen throughout Europe.

Both ancient Greece and ancient Rome fit our definition of civilization. Each had the following: cities, a division of labour that included specialized occupations, well-defined social classes, an administration that collected taxes, government buildings, and ways of keeping written records.

509 BCE	490 BCE	431 BCE	399 BCE	c. 385 BCE	359 BCE	331 BCE	312 BCE
Roman Republic established. Nine years later, in 500 BCE, the Latins overthrow the Etruscans.	Persian wars begin when Persia invades Greece.	The Peloponnesian War between Athens and Sparta begins (lasts until 404 BCE).	Socrates is put to death in Athens.	Plato opens his school in the Academy at Athens.	Philip, king of Macedonia, attacks Greece.	Alexander the Great conquers Persia and declares himself king of Persia.	First highways and aqueducts are built in Roman Empire.

c. 3 BCE	79 CE	180 CE	313 CE	c. 395 CE	410 CE	476 CE
Jesus Christ is born.	Mount Vesuvius erupts and buries the city of Pompeii.	Height of the Roman Empire.	Christianity is officially accepted in Rome.	Roman Empire is officially divided into eastern and western sections.	Visigoths destroy Rome.	The Western Roman Empire ends and is divided into several small kingdoms.

Ancient Greece

Our Study of Ancient Greece

Our study of ancient Greece includes the following topics:

- Mycenae
- Stories and Storytelling
- The Growth of City-States
- The Importance of City-States
- Citizenship and Identity
- Life in Sparta
- Spartan Schooling
- Life in Athens
- An Economy Based on Slavery
- Athenian Democracy
- Socrates
- Everyday Life
- The Gymnasium
- The Greek Family
- The Olympic Games
- The Persian Empire
- The Peloponnesian War
- The Citizen as Soldier
- Greek Historians
- The Decline of the City-States
- The Legacy of Greek Society

Figure 7.1 In 480 BCE, Persians destroyed two temples to the goddess Athena, patroness of Athens. About 40 years later, the Parthenon was built to replace the temples. Over the centuries, the Parthenon was used as both a Christian church and a Turkish mosque. Later, the building became a storage facility for gunpowder. Much of the interior was destroyed in the 1600s when the gunpowder exploded.

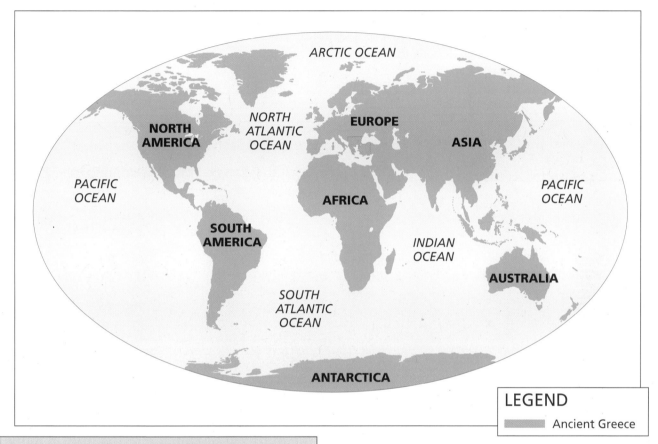

ARCTIC OCEAN

NORTH
AMERICA

NORTH
ATLANTIC
OCEAN

EUROPE

ASIA

PACIFIC
OCEAN

AFRICA

PACIFIC
OCEAN

SOUTH
AMERICA

INDIAN
OCEAN

SOUTH
ATLANTIC
OCEAN

AUSTRALIA

ANTARCTICA

LEGEND

Ancient Greece

Figure 7.2 This map shows the location of ancient Greece in 500 BCE.

This chapter looks at over 1000 years of history. It begins with the collapse of the Mycenaean [mi-see-NEE-uhn] civilization in approximately 1100 BCE and ends with the conquest of the Greek kingdom of Egypt by Roman armies in 31 BCE. As this is a long period of time, we will focus on only a small part of the history of ancient Greece.

Questions to Think About

✦ How did the ancient Greeks meet their basic survival needs (food, shelter, and clothing)?

✦ How was life for the ancient Greeks different from life for people living in very early times?

✦ How was life in ancient Greece affected by (a) the natural environment, (b) religion and mythology, (c) philosophy, and (d) contacts with other peoples?

✦ How have we been influenced by the ancient Greeks?

Mycenae

Mycenae [mi-SEE-nee] was the capital of a rich civilization in Greece that flourished from about 1600 BCE to 1100 BCE. Mycenae was ruled by powerful kings. Its wealth came from agriculture, trade, and piracy, for Mycenaean ships sailed all over the eastern Mediterranean, from Italy to Asia Minor (present-day Turkey). Trade brought Mycenae goods and riches from distant places and may also have been the cause of a long war between the Mycenaeans and the people of Troy, a city in Asia Minor. This war, called the Trojan War, took place in about 1200 BCE.

The wealth and power of the rulers of Mycenae were based on a system of slaves, farmers, craftspeople, and tradespeople. The work of Mycenaean craftspeople was of very high quality.

By about 1100 BCE, Mycenaean civilization had collapsed. Its settlements were abandoned, its buildings burned, and its treasures taken away. Historians are not sure what caused the collapse.

One theory is that economic division between rich and poor led to revolt and civil war. Another theory is that Mycenae was destroyed by the Dorians, warlike invaders from the north, who were looking for land and treasure. Alternatively, some historians believe the Dorians moved into Mycenaean territory after Myceanae collapsed, for reasons that today we do not understand. We know that the Dorians used iron. Their weapons were much stronger than those of the Mycenaeans, who used only bronze.

Following the collapse of Mycenae, the Dorians began the long, slow process of building a new society based on their own traditions and values.

Achilles [AH-kill-eez] was one of the heroes of the Trojan War. According to one well-known story about Achilles, his mother wanted him to be invincible in battles when he was older. To make him invincible, she dunked her son in the River Styx, and she held on to him by his heel. As a result, Achilles' heel did not get wet and was the only part of his body that remained vulnerable. During the Trojan War, Achilles was killed by Paris who shot him in the heel with a poisoned arrow.

Stories and Storytelling

Legend and myth were important parts of Greek life. The Greeks used stories to explain their world and their place in it. Their stories provided both a common religion and a common history. These stories were recited aloud by professional storytellers.

Greek storytellers often presented their stories in the form of songs or poetry. In this way, they developed a set of memories that all Greeks could share.

The two stories that particularly linked all the Greeks and gave them a sense of common identity were the *Iliad* [ILL-ee-ad] and the *Odyssey* [AH-diss-see], attributed to the poet Homer. The *Iliad* tells part of the story of the Trojan War. The *Odyssey* describes the journeys of Odysseus, one of the heroes of the Trojan

Figure 7.3 This is an artist's reconstruction of Mycenae. From its location on a hill, the people could see enemies approach from all directions. The dominant structure (background, centre) is the king's palace.

A Sudden End to a Long War

Part of the following story of the Trojan War is told in the Iliad.

Helen was thought to be the most beautiful woman in the ancient world. She was the wife of Menelaus [men-uh-LAY-us], the king of Sparta, a Greek city-state.

One day, Paris, a prince of the city of Troy (located in present-day Turkey), visited the home of Helen and Menelaus. Although Paris was a guest in their home, he seized Helen when Menelaus was away. Then, with the help of Aphrodite [af-ruh-DIE-tee], the goddess of love, Paris took Helen home with him to Troy.

When Menelaus found his wife gone, he called on all the chieftains of Greece to help him get her back. Since they had previously sworn an oath of loyalty to him as their king, they responded to his call. Soon, a thousand Greek ships sailed across the Aegean Sea to attack the city of Troy.

The Greeks thought that they would easily defeat the Trojans. However, they did not anticipate the ferocity of the Trojan warriors. The battles were long and savage, and many died on both sides. One problem was that the deities took sides in the battles, and neither side could achieve victory.

After almost ten years of war, many heroes on both sides were dead. Paris, the man who started the war, was one of those killed. Nonetheless, Troy seemed as strong as ever. The Greeks realized that they would never win the war unless they entered the city and caught the Trojans by surprise.

Odysseus [oh-DIH-see-us], king of the island of Ithaca, came up with the solution. He had a huge wooden horse built with a hollow interior large enough to conceal a small force of men. One night the Greeks left the horse, with a number of their men inside it, outside the walls of Troy. The rest of the Greeks boarded their ships and sailed just over the horizon so that the Trojans could not see them.

When the Trojans awoke the next day, they found the horse. Believing that the Greeks had finally given up and sailed home, the Trojans opened their gates and came out to inspect the horse.

At this point, Sinon [SEE-non], whom Odysseus had purposely left behind, approached the Trojans from his hiding place in some nearby woods. The Greeks, he said, had given up the war because Pallas Athena [PAL-us ah-THEE-nah], the goddess of war, was angry with them. He also told the Trojans that the Greeks had built the wooden horse as an offering to Pallas Athena and had left him, Sinon, to be sacrificed. The Trojans believed Sinon's story. They took down the city gate and dragged the immense horse into the city.

That night, when all the Trojans were peacefully asleep, the Greek soldiers climbed from the horse. Those hiding at sea quietly returned to Troy. They set the city on fire, destroying it and killing almost all the Trojans.

War, as he returned home after the war. Today, most historians believe that Homer was not the only author of these poems. Rather, he wrote down the words to the long song-poems that had been recited by different storytellers for many, many years. Whatever their origin, both the *Iliad* and the *Odyssey* became a central part of Greek culture. They are still regarded as among the greatest and most important poems in any language.

Figure 7.4 The Greeks were able to hide a small army of men in the wooden horse.

Ancient Greece

LEGEND
- • City
- ⌃⌃ Mountains

0   200   400 km

Figure 7.5 Geography helped shape ancient Greece. Fertile land was scarce. Proximity to the sea and to natural harbours led the people in some communities to turn to trade and travel instead of farming. Because of these factors, some Greek city-states established colonies along the coasts of Spain, Italy, North Africa, Turkey, and the Black Sea.

Where They Lived

The Dorian warriors from the north settled in southern Greece. The Ionians, descendants of the Mycenaeans, settled in Athens and on the central islands of the Aegean Sea. These peoples organized themselves into households that competed with each other for wealth, fame, and status. However, they also grouped together into tribes or clans, led by kings.

Gradually, these peoples began to farm the land and establish permanent settlements. The land supplied them with food and with pasture for their sheep, goats, and pigs. Land was inherited from previous generations and passed on to future generations. By 700 BCE, however, some land was sold for private profit.

The Growth of City-States

As groups of households settled under various kings, separate city-states developed. This process was helped by the geography of Greece. Mountains and valleys run across the country, making travel and communication between city-states difficult. The tribes developed local loyalties, and people began to see themselves as natives of Athens, Sparta, Corinth, and so on.

At the same time, the people of all these city-states had much in common. They spoke the same language, worshipped the same deities, and believed in the same myths and legends. They shared many of the same values, especially those emphasizing bravery, courage, endurance, and the ability to overcome fear. They called themselves *Hellenes* [Hell-EENS].

The Importance of City-States

The Greek word for city-state is *polis*, which is the origin of our word *politics*. For Greeks, their polis was their country. They were proud of its history, they sacrificed to its deities, their men served in its government and army, and they paid taxes to it. They enjoyed its festivals and ceremonies. At the same time, the polis ensured law and justice. It protected property and made life safe and secure.

A polis usually included an urban centre and the rural territory surrounding it. Farmers, craftspeople, and their families often lived within a polis. Those who did not usually lived within walking distance. With its clubs, gymnasiums, and other meeting places, the polis was the centre of Greek social life.

By today's standards, the polis was small, although Athens and Sparta were both quite

Our word *ostracism* comes from the Greek word *ostrakon*, which means a fragment of a pot. Greeks exiled unpopular citizens from the polis by holding an assembly where citizens debated whether or not someone should be exiled. A person who voted "yes" wrote the victim's name on a fragment of pottery and handed it in for counting. Some of these fragments still exist.

large. An average polis had 2000 to 10 000 residents and covered from fifty to eight hundred square kilometres of land. The Greeks saw this small size as a definite advantage. The philosopher Plato, for example, thought the ideal polis should have 5000 citizens. When combined with non-citizens, such as women and children and foreign-born workers, this amounted to about 20 000-25 000 people, and even more when slaves were included. Plato believed that people who lived in a polis any larger than this would lose their sense of community and put their private interests ahead of the common good.

Aristotle [AHR-is-tot-uhl], another famous Greek philosopher, thought that no state should be so big that all its citizens could not recognize each other and participate fully in the life of the polis.

Sparta and Athens are the only city-states about which we know a great deal. Each represented a very different set of values. Sparta stood for a political system in which the state controlled every aspect of people's lives and in which people gave up their personal freedom to work for the good of the state. Athens claimed to stand for greater democracy and individual freedom, although, people with unpopular opinions and people who were thought to be a threat to the polis could be punished (see page 130).

Citizenship and Identity

The polis carefully controlled who was allowed to be a citizen, and in every polis, citizens were in the minority. In Athens, for example, only men could be full citizens. There were some other basic criteria:

- Both parents had to be children of citizens.

- Men had to be free, independent, and financially secure.

- Men had to have reached the age of maturity, usually in their twenties.

The polis gave people their sense of identity. One of the worst punishments to inflict on a citizen was to sentence him to exile thereby separating him from his fellow-citizens and his homeland. Citizens were obliged to support their polis in many ways. They had to serve in its army or navy. They were also supposed to take a direct role in its government. Most citizens considered this to be their right. It was not something that they did because they had to, but because they wanted to.

Three other groups of people lived in Greek society: women, foreigners, and slaves. Women could not be citizens. Foreigners or outsiders who were not slaves could rarely become citizens.

Slaves could not be citizens. Slaves worked the land, did household chores, acted as personal servants and bodyguards, and sometimes taught. Public or "state" slaves were used for public works and as police officers. Often, slaves were prisoners of war or the children of prisoners.

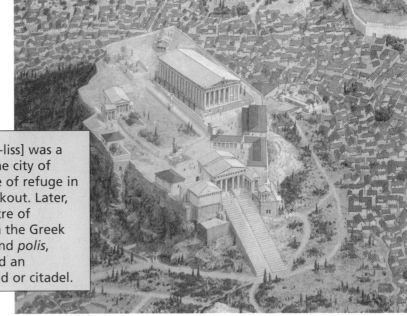

Figure 7.6 The Acropolis [uh-CROP-uh-liss] was a large, fortified rock formation above the city of Athens. It was originally built as a place of refuge in times of attack and also served as a lookout. Later, the Acropolis became the religious centre of Athens. The word *acropolis* comes from the Greek words *akros*, which means "highest," and *polis*, which means "city." Most city-states had an acropolis – a fortified natural stronghold or citadel.

Learning to Be Tough

In Sparta, a young man had to pass a test of endurance before he could become a citizen.

Leonidas was cold and hungry. It was the middle of a wintry night, and the ground was covered with frost. Leonidas had on only a thin robe for protection, and he had had nothing to eat or drink for almost twenty-four hours.

Leonidas and his classmates had been sent out into the countryside for several days to see if they could survive on their own. As a Spartan, he knew that this experience was an important part of his education. If he passed this test, he would prove that he could endure cold, thirst, and hunger, and he would be accepted by the elders as a good soldier and, therefore, as a good citizen.

All the local farmers and householders were watching their chickens, animals, and stocks of food closely – they had been alerted that the boys were in their area. Leonidas and his classmates had been told that they were not allowed to steal, but there was no other way to survive. He knew that the elders really meant that it was all right to steal if you were in true need and did not get caught.

Leonidas and his classmates knew the story of the Spartan boy who stole a fox and hid it under his cloak. When adults stopped to question the boy, he allowed the fox to tear open his stomach rather than admit to stealing it.

Leonidas understood the message in the story, but he was desperate to find a chicken, some eggs, or some bread. Whatever he found, he would have to eat raw. It was too dangerous to try to light a fire, despite the intense cold.

This survival course was the toughest part of Leonidas's education so far. It was harder than when, at the age of six, he had been sent to a boarding school that was run like a military barracks. There, he had learned how to fight and how to put up with starvation, punishment, and other forms of hardship. He learned that he was to speak only when an adult spoke to him first. He had been punished many times for speaking out of turn. He had also learned to read and write, although most of his school time was spent running, jumping, wrestling, throwing the discus and javelin, and taking part in unarmed combat.

All of this was preparation for life as a soldier-citizen. First, however, Leonidas had to pass the endurance test. He had heard that life was very different in other city-states, where boys and girls had much more freedom. But Leonidas was proud to be a Spartan. Life in other city-states sounded soft to him. He was looking forward to the day when he would be a full adult citizen. Right now, though, he had to find something to eat.

Life in Sparta

Sparta was a military society. Everything was devoted to the survival of the state. Every man was, first and foremost, a soldier. The most important values of Sparta were duty, loyalty, and obedience.

The Spartan system of government was organized for the protection of the state. No private activity was possible without the permission of the authorities. All aspects of life were subject to official supervision. To control outside influences, foreign travel was outlawed, and foreigners were allowed into Sparta only when absolutely necessary. Sparta did not welcome change, which it saw as dangerous and impossible to control.

As in other city-states, all power was in the hands of the citizens. Only free, independent

> ### Greek Alphabet
>
> The Greek alphabet has 24 letters. The English word *alphabet* comes from the first two letters of the Greek alphabet: *alpha* and *beta*.

adult men could be citizens. Women were valued as mothers. Unlike women from other city-states, Spartan women did not have to remain at home. They socialized with men in public places and exercised in the gymnasiums. Some women even received military training.

Besides citizens and women, two other groups of people lived in Sparta: slaves and craftspeople. Slaves, known as **helots** [HELL-ets], worked the land to provide the food that the citizens needed to stay alive. Most slaves were the descendants of conquered peoples. They did not belong to individual masters but to the state, and they were assigned to particular areas

Figure 7.7 In this illustration, Spartan warriors are exercising in the *dromos*, or racecourse.

Mothers had to bring up their children in certain ways. All songs and stories had to develop loyalty to Sparta and instill a willingness to serve the state. Diet, play, and exercise were to make children fit and tough.

At the age of six, boys were handed over to the state for more organized training and education. This training and education continued until they turned thirty. Only then could a Spartan man become a full citizen.

Girls, like boys, had to be healthy, strong, and fit. They learned to read, write, and dance. They took part in a demanding program of physical exercise, including running, wrestling, and discus and javelin throwing.

Figure 7.8 A Spartan soldier served his city-state for 24 years. One reason why Sparta was such a military society was to ensure that any slave revolt would be quickly suppressed.

of land as farmers and farm labourers. The craftspeople made products required by the citizens, such as weapons, wine, and leather goods. Spartan citizens were not allowed to make these for themselves since they had to be in constant readiness to fight. Few merchants or traders lived in Sparta. The city-state did not approve of trade. It tried to produce all that it needed so it would never have to depend on others.

Spartan Schooling

The security and prosperity of Sparta depended on the loyalty of its citizens. Since loyalty could not be left to chance, citizens had to be carefully trained and educated.

The goals of education were duty, obedience, and toughness. The ideal Spartan endured hardship, lived simply, kept fit and strong, served the state, obeyed orders, and was prepared to die if necessary. To this day, we still speak of Spartan discipline or Spartan conditions when we mean that things are kept deliberately tough and simple.

Government officials examined newborn babies to make sure they were fit and strong. Babies who passed this first inspection were handed back to their mothers. If there was any doubt, their parents left the baby on a mountainside to die. Whoever rescued the child could raise it as their slave.

Ancient Greece **129**

Life in Athens

While Spartans avoided change, Athenians welcomed it. Athens encouraged individual choice and freedom, within certain limits. Their different philosophies and ways of dealing with life's problems, and their economic and military powers, made Athens and Sparta rivals.

The main difference between Athens and Sparta was their attitude to individual freedom. In Athens, a citizen had freedom as long as he served in the army or navy and in government. Beyond these obligations, he was free to do as he pleased.

Another important difference was in education. Athenians received a well-rounded education that developed the mind as well as the body. Many Athenian boys attended school from ages seven to eighteen. At age twenty, they might continue their education with private tutors, although only the wealthy could afford to do this. Athenian schools were privately run, but they were supervised by the government.

Another difference was in their attitude to foreigners. Athens prided itself on its openness to foreigners, although they were not usually allowed to become citizens. Athens welcomed trade and travel.

An Economy Based on Slavery

Slaves worked in the factories of Athens, which were really small workshops, as well as on farms and in citizens' homes. Slaves also served as doctors, teachers, nurses, and musicians.

Although slaves were expensive, most citizens hoped to own one or two. Slaves did the unpleasant jobs and provided specialized services. The philosopher Aristotle called slaves "living tools" and argued that some people were fit only to be slaves.

Most Athenian slaves were treated fairly and could earn their freedom. They had no legal rights, but if they were mistreated, they could appeal to the government against their owners. The slaves who worked in the silver mines, usually in chains and under harsh supervision, lived miserable lives, however.

Figure 7.9 Many people regarded Socrates as the wisest man in Athens. Socrates was not impressed by such flattery. He responded: "The only thing I know is that I know nothing."

Athenian Democracy

Every Athenian citizen was entitled to attend the Assembly, which met regularly. The Assembly decided all important proposals. The ability to influence the Assembly with skilful speeches was important for politicians.

For some important decisions, a minimum attendance (**quorum**) of 6000 citizens was needed. For the sake of efficiency, the Assembly elected an executive committee of 500 Athenians to act in its name. Subcommittees of fifty citizens looked after much of the city-state's business.

Socrates

Socrates [SAW-kruh-teez] (469 BCE-399 BCE) was an Athenian who devoted his life to philosophy. He lived simply, owned few possessions, walked barefoot in all weather, and wore old clothes. He was well-known at the gymnasium and on the streets of Athens, and he was always eager to discuss life with his fellow-

Freedom!

In this story, we learn of one way a slave in Athens won her freedom.

Today was Olympia's first day as a free woman. She was eighteen years old and had been a slave since the age of six. When the Athenians conquered the city-state of Melos [MEE-loss], they had killed all the men and taken the women and children as slaves. However, Olympia was not badly treated. She and her mother were bought by a wealthy Athenian family and made part of the household staff. Olympia and her mother did most of the cooking, all the housework, many of the outdoor jobs, and washed the clothes.

Olympia was the one who went to the public fountain for water. She carried a large earthenware pot to the fountain, filled it with water, and, balancing the pot on her head, carried it back to her owner's household. Wealthy Athenian women stayed indoors. Only slaves and women who could not afford slaves left their houses to do shopping and other chores.

Her mistress did not seem to mind staying home. Like all upper-class women, she deliberately kept her skin pale to show the world that she did not have to work. Sometimes, she even painted her face white to emphasize this.

Yesterday, her mistress had given Olympia her freedom as a reward for saving the life of the mistress's young son. The boy had fallen against the charcoal brazier (a metal container) used for cooking, and his clothes caught fire. Luckily, Olympia was right there and quickly smothered the flames.

Figure 7.10 Olympia always looked forward to her walk to the central water fountain. These trips gave domestic servants, like the women in this painting, a chance to meet friends and enjoy the liveliness of the city.

Shortly afterwards, the family made a sacrifice to thank the deities and, at the same time, freed Olympia. Olympia found it a bit frightening to be free. She would no longer receive her meals, clothing, and lodging from the family. Instead, she would have to find a new place to live and a job. Women could work as spinners, weavers, cooks, nurses, and farm workers. Such jobs, however, did not bring in much money or bring much real independence.

Olympia would miss the family that she had lived with for most of her life. She was certain of one thing, though. She would not miss having to obey orders all the time. She knew that it was better to be free than to be a slave.

citizens. He was especially interested in finding out what it meant to live a truly good life.

Socrates challenged the opinions of everyone. Many of those he challenged were angered by being made to look foolish in front of the crowds of young men who often followed Socrates. His refusal to take anything for granted – including the politicians and the gods – made him a threat to Athenian democracy. Moreover, some of his followers were well-known enemies of Athenian democracy.

In 399 BCE, he was put on trial for corrupting the young and dishonouring the gods. Found guilty, by a jury of citizens, Socrates was given a chance to name a suitable punishment. He

suggested that he be given a pension for life. The jury, thinking Socrates was making fun of them, sentenced him to death.

His friends offered to help him escape from prison, but Socrates accepted his sentence. He said that living away from Athens would be worse than a death sentence. He also said that citizens had to obey the law even when the law was wrong. Surrounded by his grieving supporters, he calmly drank the poison, called *hemlock,* that the executioner had prepared for him. Hemlock, a poisonous plant that causes paralysis and death, was administered in Greece as a form of capital punishment.

Everyday Life

Most Greeks organized their day by the amount of natural light available. Unless they were slaves or workers, men spent most of their waking hours outdoors. They got up at sunrise, and their day usually ended at sunset when they went to bed, unless there was a party or a festival. Like people in other societies, the Greeks believed a deity controlled day and night. *Helios* [HE-lee-ahs], god of the sun, arose from the sea each morning. Helios rode across the sky and returned to the sea at dusk, prepared to rise again the next day.

The city-state helped the Greeks meet their basic needs. It also provided recreation and entertainment in the form of athletic contests, plays, and religious festivals. Religion helped the Greeks make sense of the world around them by explaining events as the actions of the gods, while philosophers were able to explain some things more scientifically and logically.

Housing

The great public buildings were made of stone, and most houses were built of sun-baked clay. Homes opened to a central courtyard rather than to the street. Most houses were small and consisted of only a few rooms. Each home had an entrance that opened into the father's quarters. Male visitors were not allowed in rooms where women and children spent most of their time. Women had their own rooms.

Craftspeople lived where they worked, and whole streets were taken over by particular trades, such as sandal makers or leather workers.

Houses had little furniture and few ornaments. Each home contained a small altar dedicated to the god or goddess of the house, couches, a table or two, and backless stools instead of chairs. Linens and a few personal possessions were stored in wooden chests. Some people had beds, although many slept on the floor. Houses had no central heating and windows had shutters instead of glass. Homes could be cold in the winter; the only sources of heat were the braziers in which charcoal was burned.

Figure 7.11 Some Greek homes and palaces had what we consider modern-day comforts, such as indoor plumbing and drainage systems.

Farming

Even in the city-states, up to 90 percent of the people lived by farming. Their year followed a regular routine, divided not by months but by seasons. The major events were harvesting grain in May, grapes in September, olives in November, and ploughing and sowing the fields in October and November.

They grew wheat to make flour for bread. Barley grew well because it was suited to Greece's dry climate and poor soil. Wealthy Greeks regarded barley as a food for animals, slaves, and the poor.

A typical farm was very small by our standards. It had a fruit and vegetable garden, some chickens and pigs, grapevines, a few olive trees, and barley growing among the trees. The soil was thin, and rocks showed through in many places. Sometimes, the rocks were gathered into piles and used as sacred markers. A farm might also have some beehives; the Greeks used honey as we use sugar.

Our word *history* comes from the Greek word *historia*, which originally meant "research" or "inquiry" and came to mean "knowledge."

Cattle were a rare luxury, and only the rich owned horses. Oxen were used for hard farm work, such as ploughing. They were stronger and less expensive than horses. When oxen died, their hides were turned into leather. People ate their meat, and used sinew for twine and fat for candle tallow. Herders looked after flocks of sheep and goats on the mountainsides.

For hauling and carrying, farmers used oxen, mules, and donkeys. Most of the farm work was done by human labour, and most farmers owned one or two slaves to help them with the work. As they do today, women took an active part in the farm work. Farm wives could not afford to stay indoors as did the women from wealthy families in the cities.

Farmers produced many materials used by city artisans and craftspeople. These materials included leather, wood, flax to make linen, and horns and bone for glue.

What They Ate

In ancient Greece, breakfast was very light, usually a drink of water and perhaps some fruit, if it was in season, or a small piece of bread. Lunch was also a light meal. Once again, the beverage was water. Lunch included bread and fruit or vegetables. The most widely eaten vegetables were lentils, peas, beans, onions, and garlic, while the most common kinds of fruit were grapes, apples, figs, dates, and melons. Nuts, olives, and eggs were also popular. The main meal was eaten in the evening and usually included wine mixed with water and some kind of broth. In areas near the sea, such as Athens, people ate fish.

Meat was reserved for special occasions and was often from animals that had been sacrificed in religious ceremonies. Cheese made from the milk of sheep or goats was also common. By our standards, the Greeks ate very simply. Many of the staple foods that we take for granted were unknown to the Greeks, including rice, potatoes, sugar, pasta, tea, coffee, bananas, and many other fruits and vegetables.

Men of wealth hunted deer and other animals for sport. Poorer people used snares and slings to hunt small birds and rabbits for meat for their families.

What They Wore

Most men and women wore a rectangle of cloth arranged around the body as a tunic or robe and fastened at the shoulder. It was called the *chiton* [KIE-ton]. A man's chiton was shorter than a woman's.

If underwear was worn at all, it was simply another piece of cloth arranged around the body. In cold weather, the Greeks wore cloaks. The only kind of footwear was leather sandals, although many people would also go barefoot.

Figure 7.12 Both men and women wore loose tunics called a *chiton*. Younger men often wore a short tunic.

Alexandros and School

As this story shows, the school Alexandros attended in Athens was very different from the school Leonidas attended in Sparta.

Alexandros awoke at dawn. One of the family slaves brought him a bowl of water and a cloth, and Alexandros washed his face and hands. After breakfast he went to school.

The teacher had spent the last year reading the *Iliad* and the *Odyssey* with Alexandros, explaining their meaning and testing him from time to time. Today, Alexandros would have to stand in front of the other students and recite at least 500 lines of the poems.

Alexandros had to remember the poems word for word, since few people had their own copies of the stories. His teacher told him that this was the way things had always been. His father said that it was the duty of all Greeks to learn the poetry of Homer.

On the whole, Alexandros enjoyed going to school. He knew that it was important to read and write. He liked reading Homer and other poets; however, he wished his teacher had more patience.

Even though his teacher was a slave, he was allowed to shout at Alexandros and even to beat him occasionally. Whenever Alexandros complained to his father, his father took the side of his teacher, saying that it was good for boys to learn discipline.

Alexandros was learning to play the lyre (a small harp) and to sing. He would have liked to play the flute, but his music teacher said that he should not play instruments that needed blowing. They distorted the face, said his teacher, and ruined the appearance of the player. They were fit only for slaves and women. Nonetheless, Alexandros, in secret, had tried playing a flute.

What Alexandros enjoyed most about school was going to the gymnasium. There he was taught by specially trained teachers, and he got the chance to play and exercise with other boys. He excelled at running and jumping contests and was learning to throw the javelin and the discus.

At the gymnasium, Alexandros also listened to the conversations of the men who came to watch the boys exercise. Sometimes the boys were invited to join the conversations, although they usually listened rather than spoke. When in the presence of adults, children were supposed to speak only when spoken to.

Alexandros often talked with Philippa, his younger sister, about his studies. Like other Greek girls, she did not attend school. Instead, she stayed at home where she learned housekeeping skills and took lessons from a private tutor.

Figure 7.13 Most Greek city-states had at least one gymnasium. We now use the word to mean a place for physical exercise, but to the Greeks a gymnasium had many functions.

The Gymnasium

The gymnasium was a men's social club, an educational centre, and a place to meet for conversation. In Greece and Germany today, the word *gymnasium* means an academic high school.

Many citizens spent part of their day at the gymnasium, either exercising or watching others do so. They might, for instance, watch a wrestling match, offering advice to the wrestlers, arguing about who would win, and discussing technique. After this, they might join another group and discuss current problems they were having with their slaves or political issues that had come up in the Athenian Assembly. Eventually, they went home for a meal or, perhaps, visited a friend.

The Greek Family

Many Greek households included parents and children, sometimes grandparents and other relatives, and slaves. The house and property belonged to the family, and it was the family's duty to pass this property on to the next generation.

The family was the smallest self-sufficient unit in Greek society. The family had two main goals. One was to produce children, so that the family would not die out. The other was to preserve and, if possible, to increase the family's property.

Marriages were usually carefully arranged. Neither the bride nor the groom had much say in the choice of a partner. Their parents looked for a match that would bring fame, credit, and possibly wealth to the family.

A wife was expected to obey her husband. We do not know to what extent husbands discussed things with their wives before deciding what to do. We do know from trial records, plays, speeches, and the writings of philosophers that the husband was expected to make the final decisions.

Wealthy men spent most of their spare time with other men at the gymnasium, talking with friends, or perhaps walking around the city. They spent little time at home.

Wealthy women stayed at home almost all the time. They supervised the slaves and servants, maintained supplies of food and drink, saw that everything was clean, and looked after their children. For relaxation, they wove cloth or sewed clothing. They were not supposed to leave the house, except on certain religious festivals. Women were responsible for

Figure 7.14 This young boy is carrying fishing nets. In city-states such as Athens, all was not work for the young. When boys were not attending school, they sometimes went fishing.

the private affairs of the household, while men took responsibility for the affairs of public life, such as government, the law, and war.

Among poorer Greeks, both husbands and wives had to work. They worked together on farms or in the city at some kind of trade. Legally, however, husbands still held all the power.

Women had more freedoms in Sparta than in any other city-state. They could inherit property and were also expected to participate in a full program of physical exercise along with males. Although Spartan men and women usually married at age eighteen, they were not allowed to live together permanently until the groom was thirty. Marriage was not allowed to interfere with a man's responsibility to serve as a soldier.

Some Greek Gods and Goddesses

Gods

Zeus [ZOOSE] Most powerful of the deities and ruler of Mount Olympus, the home of the deities

Poseidon [po-SIE-done] God of the sea and of earthquakes

Hades [HAY-deez] God of the underworld

Apollo [uh-PAW-low] God of the sun and of truth, reason, prophecy, music, intelligence, and poetry

Hermes [HER-meez] Messenger of the deities, and protector of orators, writers, traders, and travellers

Dionysus [die-oh-NIE-suss] God of wine and fertility

Ares [AR-eez] God of war

Hephaestus [hih-FESS-tiss] God of fire and industry

Goddesses

Hera [HEH-rah] Wife of Zeus, and the protectress of marriage, children, and the home

Athena [ah-THEEN-ah] Goddess of wisdom and the protectress in war of those who believed in her

Artemis [AR-teh-mis] Goddess of hunting and protectress of women, cities, and young animals

Aphrodite [af-roh-DIE-tee] Goddess of love and beauty

Demeter [dih-ME-ter] Goddess of agriculture and fertility

Religious and Spiritual Beliefs

Most Greeks believed in gods and goddesses. Each city had its own special deities, as did each family. However, the Greeks were not particularly concerned about what people believed, as long as they acted properly, for example, by attending ceremonies and by making sacrifices.

In many ways, the Greeks thought of their gods and goddesses as people – at times happy, at other times sad, sometimes quarrelsome, and sometimes angry. Even though the deities had human moods, they were far more powerful than humans. They could travel with incredible speed and take on different appearances, and they were very strong. They were superhuman.

The Greeks believed the deities were responsible for what happened to people, both good and bad. Sometimes the deities punished people, sometimes they rewarded them, and sometimes they tricked them.

A person might have one deity as an enemy and another deity as a friend. Therefore, it was important to honour the deities. This meant making proper sacrifices to them, usually of meat and wine. It also meant holding the proper ceremonies and festivals.

For a few women, religion was the one aspect of Greek society that offered them equality with men and gave them some influence and power. There were some religious festivals that only women could attend. Some temples had women priestesses, and seers who predicted the future. Of course, some of the deities, such as Athena, were women.

Figure 7.15 This reconstruction of Athens shows a religious procession through the Agora [AG-uh-ruh], or marketplace. The Agora was the religious, political, business, and social centre of Athens. The Acropolis, atop the hill on the left, contained the city's religious buildings. In 450 BCE, Athens had a population of about 300 000, about two-thirds of whom lived in the countryside outside the city itself.

Figure 7.16 This man is consulting an oracle (a priestess who predicted the future). Greeks often consulted an oracle for advice.

Religious Festivals

Each city-state held religious festivals throughout the year. The Greeks did not divide the week into workdays and weekends. They organized their calendar around festivals and feast days, which were usually connected with the deities. The important festivals were public holidays. There was at least one major festival, usually lasting two or three days, every month. One Athenian orator joked that there was only one day a year when there was not a festival of some kind.

Festivals marked significant events in each city's history. Festivals also helped the Greeks obtain the support of the deities. These occasions brought people together in a common activity and provided an opportunity for fun and relaxation. Contests in athletics, music, public speaking, and drama often drew large numbers of spectators. Free food and drink were usually provided.

Soothsayers and Oracles

Soothsayers and oracles were the Greek equivalent of fortunetellers. When Greeks wanted advice, they often consulted a soothsayer – more than one if they could afford it. On military expeditions, armies usually brought along soothsayers to advise the commanders. Sometimes, soothsayers examined the intestines or livers of sacrificed animals for signs from the deities. Other times, they interpreted signs in the world around them. Soothsayers often used birds, for example, to predict the future. The kind of bird, whether it was sitting or flying, the direction in which it was flying, the noise it made, and its colour were important signs.

Greeks also visited shrines and holy places to seek the advice of oracles. Oracles spoke through priests and priestesses. The advice given by an oracle, however, was often interpreted in different ways and could be misunderstood. The oracle at Delphi, for example, told a king that he would one day destroy a great empire. Acting on this advice, the king went to war against the Persian Empire. The great empire he destroyed was not Persia but, in defeat, his own kingdom.

Sacrifices

When the Greeks wanted advice from the deities, needed the support of the deities, or wanted to avoid the deities' anger, they offered sacrifices. Detailed rules and traditions controlled these sacrifices. Some deities demanded a certain kind of animal or one of a particular colour. Others demanded an offering of food or wine. The food usually consisted of fruit and special cakes.

When an animal was sacrificed, the custom was to bring it to an altar outside the temple. Some of the animal's hair was burned in the fire and offered to the deity. The priests then killed the animal, making sure that its blood went onto the altar. The dead animal was then skinned and its meat cooked. The deity was offered the thighbones wrapped in fat, while the rest of the meat was eaten by the priests and those taking part in the sacrifice. There were also offerings of water, wine, and olive oil. These offerings were called *libations* [lie-BAY-shuns].

Figure 7.17 The festival of Dionysus, the god of wine and fertility, was celebrated with music and song.

The Olympic Games

All Greek city-states took part in various kinds of sports ceremonies. The most important were the Olympic games, which began in 776 BCE. The games were held every four years at Olympia and were a combination of athletic contest and religious ceremony. Even people who were at war were supposed to stop fighting to attend the games.

The main events included running, jumping, and wrestling events, javelin and discus throwing, and horse and chariot racing. The most violent event was the *pankratium* [pan-KRAY-she-um], a combination of wrestling and

According to legend, the marathon race is the exact distance between the Greek cities of Marathon and Athens. In fact, the distance of the modern-day marathon, 42.2 kilometres, was determined at the 1908 Olympic games in London, England. The race started at Windsor Castle and ended at White City Stadium – a distance of 42,195 metres.

boxing in which anything was allowed except biting, gouging the eyes, and breaking the fingers. The pankratium could be a fight to the death.

Figure 7.18 The Olympic games began with a five-day religious festival in honour of Zeus. In this picture, two athletes are formally sacrificing a pig in the hope that it will bring them luck at the games.

The Olympic Dream

In this story, we attend the Olympic games held about 2000 years ago.

Demetrios was glad that he had been born in the city-state of Elis. Olympia, the site of the Olympic games, was within the boundaries of Elis, and Demetrios was able to attend the games easily. He was lucky. Many thousands of spectators had to travel hundreds of kilometres across rough and often dangerous country to attend the games.

The opening ceremonies on the first day had been fascinating. Bulls, pigs, cakes, and wine had been given as sacrifices to Zeus. People from all over Greece were there. After the sacrifices, all the competitors swore an oath that they were properly qualified to take part: they were Greek, free-born, and would honour all the rules of the games. They were also all men. Women were not allowed to compete in the games.

On the first day, Demetrios had time to wander around the stalls that had been set up by all those hoping to make some money from the spectators. There were fortunetellers, letter writers, storytellers, poets, painters, sculptors, singers, and musicians. It was noisy, colourful, and exciting as people moved along the walkways between the stalls. Everywhere, buyers were bargaining with sellers.

Athletic events interested Demetrios the most. The chariot races were the most exciting and certainly the most dangerous. Horses charged around the track with the chariot drivers trying to cut each other off and manoeuvring for position. Because of the curved course, most of the chariots travelled closely bunched together, and victory seemed to go to the drivers with the strongest nerves. Spills and pile-ups were common. In one race, two drivers had been thrown out of their chariots and killed.

Demetrios's favourite events were the running contests. Demetrios was a good runner, and he dreamed of entering the Olympic games himself one day. The next games would be in four years time, and he hoped to be able to compete then. But his best chance would be at the games after that, when he was twenty.

To win at the games was very difficult. Only the best athletes competed, and many of them trained and competed full time. Demetrios knew that he would have to train long and hard, but he had already learned some useful tips just from watching the runners. Demetrios hoped that he would be among them someday.

The Greeks dated events from the first Olympiad in 776 BCE. When a Greek writer says the Battle of Salamis took place in the seventy-fifth Olympiad, for example, we know that the year is 480 BCE (74 x 4 = 296 and 776-296 = 480). Each city-state had its own dating system, but the dates of the Olympiads provided a common framework.

The Arts

For the Greeks, literature, especially poetry and drama, helped to explain the past and the present, as well as the meaning of life. Literature, often accompanied by music, also served as entertainment. Greeks listened to poetry and attended dramas just as today we read books, watch television, and go to movies. Many Greeks could recite poetry at length. Both tragedies and comedies were first performed in Athens in the 6th century BCE. They were often part of religious festivals, especially the feast of Dionysus.

In tragedy, the deities presented the heroes of legend with problems that the heroes were unable to overcome. However, the characters' struggles with their problems presented the audience with gripping stories that raised important questions about life. Tragedies led the Greeks to think about their relationships with the deities and about other issues of life, such as love, duty, obedience, and pride.

Comedies were also very popular. Comedy writers made fun of the personalities of their own time, and sometimes of the deities themselves. In addition, they commented on contemporary issues such as the status of women, the relationship between husbands and wives, and the influence of philosophers.

Music was important. There were songs for childbirth, marriage, death, harvesting, drinking, and curing disease. The main musical instruments were the lyre and the flute.

Figure 7.19 Greek theatres were built in the open air and seated thousands of spectators, who sat around the circular stage. Greek plays had casts of no more than three actors, who each played several parts. A group of 12 actors, called a *chorus*, commented on the play's action through dance, song, and poetry.

Although many Greeks could read and write, very few owned anything written. Greeks wrote on papyrus sheets just like the Egyptians, and the sheets were pasted together to make a long roll. This roll was then wrapped around two wooden rods. A reader had to unroll the "book" to read it. Most Greeks preferred to talk and listen, rather than to read and write. Plato claimed that writing was bad, because it stopped people from thinking and remembering.

Figure 7.20 This actor of tragedy is in costume and is carrying his mask. Actors wore thick-soled boots to increase their stature. In front of their faces they held masks depicting the characters they were portraying. These masks had speaking tubes to increase the volume of the actors' voices. This actor is playing the part of a king.

Persian Empire in 490 BCE

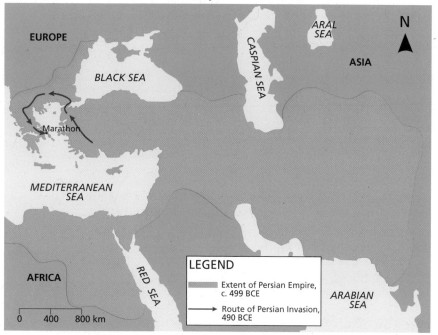

Figure 7.21 This map shows the extent of the Persian Empire in 490 BCE.

The Persian Empire

Persia ruled some Greek cities in Asia Minor, and many Greeks feared that Persia wanted to add all of the Greek city-states to its empire. They saw the Persian system of government, in which a king held supreme power, as a danger to their idea of self-governing citizenship.

The Persian Empire stretched from North Africa through Egypt and the Middle East all the way to northern India. The heartland of the empire was located in present-day Iran and Iraq. Its huge armies included soldiers from India, Africa, the Middle East, and southeastern Europe, all with their own distinctive weapons and clothing. The basis of the army was the Ten Thousand Immortals, a body of highly trained, hand-picked Iranian troops. They were called the Immortals because whenever any of them were wounded or killed, others were recruited so that there would always be ten thousand of them.

The Persian Empire was widely admired for its achievements in astronomy, mathematics, medicine, art, and architecture. Its kings allowed the many different peoples to keep their cultures but expected them to pay taxes and to recognize royal authority.

Royal officials, called the King's Eyes and the King's Ears, travelled the empire to ensure royal commands were followed. The different parts of the Empire were joined by a system of roads, a code of laws, and a common system of money.

In 499 BCE, some Greek cities in Asia Minor rebelled against Persian rule, and Athens agreed to help them. In turn, Darius, the king of Persia, vowed to crush Athens. He even appointed a slave whose job it was to say to him every day: "Lord, remember the Athenians." Darius invaded Greece in 490 BCE, but he was defeated at Marathon.

Darius's successor, Xerxes [zerk-sees], led a new invasion in 480 BCE. He destroyed Athens, but he was defeated by the Greeks. The Greeks were more certain than ever that their way of life was superior to all others.

The Peloponnesian War

After defeating the Persians, Athens formed a league of city-states to defend Greece from future attacks. Instead of being an alliance of equals, this league quickly became a way for Athens to control the rest of Greece. Some city-states, led by Sparta, began to resist what they saw as Athenian greed and ambition. They wanted to run their own affairs. Sparta, in particular, saw the growing power of Athens as a threat to its own position.

In 431 BCE, a group of city-states led by Sparta declared war on Athens. The war, named after the southern Greek peninsula of Peloponnese, lasted for almost thirty years. In general terms, the Athenian navy controlled the seas around Greece, while Sparta was more powerful on land. The turning point came when Sparta built a navy and defeated the Athenian fleet. Without a navy to protect it and to bring in food and supplies, Athens surrendered in 404 BCE.

Figure 7.22 Although Darius I is probably best known for his defeat at Marathon, he did much to improve the lives of the Persians. He organized a postal system, built highways, encouraged trade, and was respectful of other religions.

This might explain why slaves, foreigners, and women could not be citizens. Slaves and foreigners could not be trusted to fight for a city they did not belong to, and women were needed to raise the children who would become the soldiers of the future. Some slaves, however, did serve in the army or navy as a way of earning their freedom.

Everyone – citizens and non-citizens alike – was affected by the fighting. For the losing side, defeat could mean death, exile, or enslavement. Aristophanes [air-uh-STOF-uh-nees], an Athenian playwright, even wrote a play about wives who went on strike by refusing to have anything to do with their husbands until they gave up war.

Although Athens lost the war and suffered more than any other city-state, the real losers were all the city-states. The war created divisions among citizens and among city-states, cost enormous amounts of money (Sparta, for example, had turned to the old Greek enemy, Persia, for financial help), and caused a lot of destruction. The city-states were so weakened and divided that they were unable to resist Philip, king of Macedonia, who began attacking them from the north in 359 BCE.

The Citizen as Soldier

Every citizen between the ages of eighteen and sixty had to fight for his polis when required. Citizens had to provide their own equipment, such as helmets, shields, swords, spears, and armour. Citizens who could not afford this equipment served as rowers in the navy's warships. Most citizens fought in several wars during their lifetime. In the 4th and 5th centuries BCE, for example, Athens and other city-states were at war two years out of every three.

Figure 7.23 Each citizen served as a *hoplite* (from *hoplon*, the Greek word for "shield"). Hoplites fought in closely packed rows, which formed a phalanx, as shown here. The task of the phalanx was to smash into the enemy army without losing formation. Each soldier depended on the shield of his neighbour to his right for protection. Historians believe this had important consequences for citizenship. Men who depended on each other in time of battle would form a strong sense of identity as members of their polis.

Figure 7.24 This Roman mosaic shows Alexander the Great (on the left) leading his army against the forces of King Darius III of Persia (on the right) at the Battle of Issus in 333 BCE.

Greek Historians

Two Athenian writers were among the very first to write factual history: Herodotus [her-ROD-oh-tiss] and Thucydides [thuh-SID-ih-deez]. Both lived during the 5th century BCE.

Herodotus (c. 484 BCE-425 BCE) travelled a great deal in the eastern Mediterranean (read some of his writings about Egypt on pages 88-89) and around the Black Sea. He wrote a history of the wars between Greece and Persia that took place over one hundred years before Alexander the Great conquered the Persian Empire. Herodotus loved a good story. He was especially concerned about *why* events took place. Today, he is known as the father of history.

Thucydides (c. 460 BCE-400 BCE) was an Athenian general. He fought in and wrote about the Peloponnesian War between Athens and Sparta, which he saw as the most important event in history. Like Herodotus, he told a complete and interesting story. Thucydides is important because he did not just list events, but explained why they occurred and why they were important.

The Decline of the City-States

By the middle of the 4th century BCE, the Greek city-states were exhausted by years of fighting and divided by distrust. They were an easy target for Philip, king of Macedonia, in northern Greece. By the time he died in 336 BCE, Philip had defeated Athens, controlled many of the other city-states, and organized the rest into an alliance to fight Persia.

Philip was succeeded by Alexander, his twenty-year-old son. Alexander, like his father, was determined to punish the Persians for having invaded Greece many years earlier, while also expanding his own power.

Alexander had studied with the Greek philosopher Aristotle. He loved Greek art, poetry, philosophy, and science. He modelled himself on the heroes of the *Iliad* and *Odyssey*. He did not see war as a regrettable necessity, but as the greatest adventure possible. To this day, some people see Alexander as a hero; others see him as a conqueror.

By 331 BCE, Alexander had conquered Asia Minor and Egypt, defeated the Persian army, occupied all of Persia's territory, and declared himself king of Persia. He then moved into northern India and turned back only when his soldiers refused to go any farther. By this time, Alexander was fighting in lands that were unknown to Greek geographers.

Alexander's success astonished everyone. No one had ever moved so quickly and fought so successfully. In less than ten years, he had made himself ruler of a vast empire, and many people considered him a god. Today, he is often referred to as Alexander the Great.

Alexander died of fever in 323 BCE at Babylon (in present-day Iraq). He was thirty-three years old. His generals divided his huge empire among themselves. Alexander's successors built new towns and cities patterned after Greek cities. The cities were usually populated by Greek immigrants and became centres of Greek language and culture. In this way, many aspects of the Greek way of life survived the break-up of Alexander's empire.

Hippocrates (c. 460 BCE-377 BCE) was the father of medicine. He founded a school that emphasized the value of observation and the careful interpretation of symptoms. Members of his school conducted experiments that convinced them diseases resulted from natural and not supernatural causes. People, at that time, believed that epilepsy was caused by supernatural causes until Hippocrates and his school members observed that the disease has a natural cause just as other diseases have. Hippocrates set a high standard of professional ethics that, to this day, doctors swear an oath to uphold.

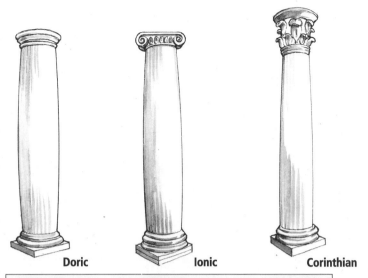

Doric   **Ionic**   **Corinthian**

Figure 7.25 These columns show the three Greek architectural traditions. Doric, developed on the mainland, is the oldest, simplest, and sturdiest. Ionic, developed in Ionia and on some Greek islands, is taller and more slender than the Doric column. Ionic columns can be identified by the ornamental scrolls at the top. Corinthian can be identified by the stylized leaves. They were first used only for the interior of buildings.

The Legacy of Greek Society

The Roman conquest of Greece and Asia Minor in 146 BCE ensured the survival of Greek culture. The Romans admired Greek learning and literature. The Romans also adopted many of the Greek gods and goddesses, although they changed their names. A Roman poet, Horace, wrote that although Greece was conquered, it took Rome captive.

Here are some things given to us by the Greeks:

- *Olympic games*
- *Styles of classical architecture* Doric, Ionic, and Corinthian columns and other aspects of Greek architecture are still used in the design of modern buildings.

- *Themes of tragedy and comedy* These serve as the basis for many plays performed in theatres today.

- *Language* Many words, such as *gymnasium, democracy, government, philosophy, history,* and *politics* are used every day.

- *Ideas* The ways we study history, philosophy, and medicine; the idea of democracy; some of the music we listen to have their roots in ancient Greece.

Summary ꝅ

Greek ideas and institutions greatly impacted Europe and parts of Asia. The Greek influence on Europe spread to many parts of the world where Europeans settled, such as Australia and North America. Europeans, in particular, looked to Greece as one of the places where European civilizations began. Even today, our lives are influenced by ancient Greece, including our buildings, theatre, values, ideas, and even our language.

Connecting and Reflecting

Reflect on the daily life in Greece. Use the information you have learned to describe the similarities *to* and differences *from* your life. Explain why knowing about this society is important to you *as a citizen of Canada and a citizen of the world.*

Be an Historian

Do you believe everything that you read in a history text? Do you ever wonder what information has been left out? When you study history, you are usually reading the results of what historians have researched and written. In this section, you will have the opportunity to do your own research and ask yourself the same kinds of questions that historians ask themselves. You will not be reading history; you will be doing history!

Historical research is very complicated. (See chapter 1.) It demands knowledge, skill, and patience. Historians have to:

- locate their evidence

- interpret what it means

- sort out what is true from what is probable and what is false

Read the excerpts below. When you are finished, answer the following questions:

- Where do these sources come from?

- Are they sources that you can trust?

- What do you know about the author? If you do not know anything, how can you find out?

- Does the author have knowledge, experience, or credentials that makes you willing to trust his or her work?

- As you try to understand the past, how important is chronology?

A Greek Historian at Work

I do not think readers will have trouble accepting my findings. My evidence is better than that of the poets who exaggerate to make a point, and that of storytellers who are more interested in pleasing their readers than in telling the truth, and who describe events that happened so long ago that they can neither be proved or disproved nor their evidence checked.

I have quoted some speeches that were given before and during the war that is the subject of my history. I found it difficult to recall the exact words used in the speeches, even when I heard them personally. My informants had the same problem. My solution has been to stick as closely as possible to the sense of the speeches in order to say what in my opinion seemed most likely in any particular situation.

Regarding the events of the war, I have made it a rule never to use the first story I heard, or to describe what I thought might have happened. Either I was personally present at the events I describe, or I heard about then from eye-witnesses whose stories I have checked as thoroughly as I know how. Even so, it was often difficult to establish the facts. Eye-witnesses did not always agree. Sometimes they did not remember things very clearly. Sometimes they were biassed in favour of one side or another.

Some readers might find my history dull because I have not made it dramatic or exciting. I will be satisfied if those who want to know what happened find it useful. Human nature being what it is, the events I have described are likely to be repeated in the future. I have not written this history in order to be a sensation today, but to be useful for ever.

(Adapted from Thucydides, History of the Peloponnesian War, I. 22)

Pericles Describes Athens in 431 BCE

Our system of government does not copy others. Others see us as a model. We are a democracy because power is shared by all citizens, not held by a minority. All citizens are treated the same under the law. If a man has some special quality, we recognize it. All citizens can serve Athens, whether rich or poor. We let our neighbours live in their own way and don't get upset if we don't like what they do. In our private lives we are tolerant and free. In our public lives we respect the law. We obey those we have placed in positions of authority and we obey the laws, especially those laws that protect the weak.

We also know how to enjoy ourselves. We have frequent games and sacrifices. Our homes are places of beauty and help us relax. We enjoy all kinds of goods, including those from other lands.

Our city is open to everyone. We welcome visitors. We do not see them as spies. We rely on our own courage and do nor fear others. Unlike the Spartans, we do not raise our children to be soldiers, but we are just as strong and brave as they are.... We do not spend our time worrying about unknown dangers that might happen in the future, but when they happen we are as well-prepared for them as anyone.

Our love of beauty and of intellectual achievement does not make us soft. We see wealth as something to be used properly, not as something to be proud of. Nor are we ashamed of being poor; only of not trying to do something about it. Even those citizens who are most wrapped up in their private affairs take an interest in government and public life. We are the only people who believe that a man who takes no interest in government is not harmless, but useless. In our system of government we make decisions only after full discussion by the citizens. More than any other people, we think before we act. Other people are brave out of ignorance but when they stop to think, they become afraid. We understand clearly the pleasures and pains of life but this does not stop us from doing what we think is right.

We are unique in treating other people well, not because we expect something in return, but because we think it is the right thing to do. We make friends with other people by what we do for them, not what they do for us. Our city is the teacher of all Greece. We Athenian citizens are exceptional in the way we live. For proof, just look at the power we have and how we are respected by other cities. We do not need Homer or any of the poets to sing our praises. All land and seas are open to us and everyone can see the good we do for our friends and the suffering we inflict on our enemies.

(Adapted from Pericles' "Funeral Oration" in Thucydides, History of the Peloponnesian War, 11, 37ff.)

Spartan Women

These sayings of Spartan women were written down by the historian Plutarch who lived from about 50 CE to 120 CE:

A mother had sent her five sons to war. Now she stood on the outskirts of the polis waiting anxiously to find out the results of the battle. When someone came by, she asked him how things had gone, and was told that her five sons had been killed. She replied, "Miserable slave, that's not what I asked you. I asked how our polis was doing." When she was told that it was winning, she said, "Then I gladly accept the death of my sons."

When a woman from Ionia was showing off a beautiful and valuable tapestry she had made, a Spartan woman showed off her four sons and said they were the kind of thing a good woman ought to produce.

A Spartan mother handed her son his shield and said, "Son, either come back carrying this or on it."

A Spartan mother saw her son approaching and asked him how the battle had gone. When he told her that all the men had been killed, she threw a rock at him, saying "And did they send you to bring us the bad news."

A mother was burying her son who had been killed in battle and someone passing by said, "You unfortunate woman, what a sacrifice." The mother answered, "No. I am doubly blessed. I gave birth to him so that he might die for his polis and that is what has happened."

A Spartan woman was being put up for sale and was asked if she had any special skills. She said, "To be trustworthy."

A soldier who had been wounded in battle and could not walk upright was crawling on all fours, ashamed at being laughed at. But his mother told him, "Son, is it not better to take pride in your courage than to fear being laughed at by fools?"

Ancient Rome

Our Study of Ancient Rome

Our study of ancient Rome includes the following topics:

- The Beginnings of the Empire
- Roman Law
- The Roman Army
- Slavery
- The Circus Maximus
- Public Baths
- The Forum
- Building Methods
- Queen Boudicca
- Roman Roads
- Jesus Christ and the Birth of Christianity
- The Byzantine Empire
- The Germanic Barbarians
- The Decline of the Western Roman Empire

During the reign of Emperor Augustus, over 50 million people lived under Roman rule, law, and organization. Later, Christianity became the official religion of the empire and spread throughout Europe.

Many Roman achievements are still used today. Roman law and government have influenced the ideals and practices of many peoples. Some words in the English language – such as *graduate, audio,* and *salary* – are derived from Latin, the Roman language.

Questions to Think About

- ✦ What were the unique characteristics of Roman life?
- ✦ What Roman achievements influence our lives today?

Where the Romans Came From

The precise origin of the city of Rome is not known, although historians believe people were living there around 1000 BCE. At that time, a group of people, later known as the *Latins,* moved into central Italy from the north.

The Etruscans [ee-TRUSS-kins] lived to the north of the Latins. Keenly interested in science and the arts, the Etruscans' culture was greatly influenced by the Greeks. For example, the Etruscans used arches in the construction of their buildings and encouraged people to learn to write.

Around 600 BCE, the Etruscans captured the Latin city of Rome and turned it into a prosperous trading centre. Their advanced farming techniques, such as draining marshes for fertile farmland, enabled them to provide enough food for the city's growing population. As well, their strong army protected them from hostile neighbours who desired their land.

In about 500 BCE, the Latins overthrew the Etruscans. Attacks from neighbouring peoples

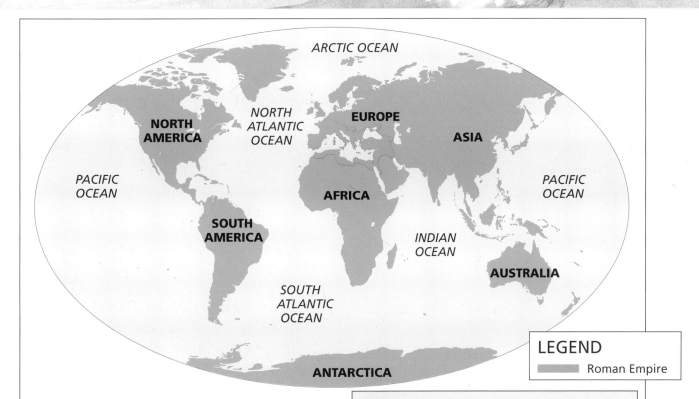

LEGEND

Roman Empire

Figure 8.1 This map shows the Roman Empire and some of the places mentioned in this chapter.

drew Rome into wars, which eventually resulted in the expansion of Roman territory. Over the next 400 years, this small community along the Tiber River grew into an empire.

In this chapter, we will be studying primarily the Western Roman Empire from about 44 BCE to its decline in the 3rd century CE.

According to a famous legend, Rome was founded in about 753 BCE by two brothers, Romulus [ROM-yoo-luss] and Remus [RE-muss]. Romulus and Remus were the twin sons of Mars, the god of war, and a Latin princess. The twins were taken from the princess, because she had broken a promise to have no children. The babies, who were abandoned on the banks of the Tiber River, were raised first by a wolf, then by a shepherd. As adults, Romulus and Remus decided to build a city along the Tiber. After a dispute over who would rule the city, Romulus killed Remus and became the ruler of the city that bears his name. This story was told by the Roman historian Livy, who gathered many myths and folk tales of the Roman people.

Figure 8.2 In this painting, Romulus and Remus are rescued by a shepherd from the banks of the Tiber River.

Where They Lived

At its peak, the Roman Empire stretched from northern Africa to Britain and from the Middle East to Portugal. The Romans not only conquered and controlled this vast territory, but managed its lands and peoples effectively.

The Tiber River provided the Romans with fertile lands for farming, a transportation route, and a strategic location in case of invasion. Their major community was about twenty kilometres from the mouth of the river. This community, located at the top of a hill (now called Palatine Hill), became the city of Rome, the heart of the Roman Empire.

Government

When the Latins overthrew the Etruscans in 500 BCE, they created a system of authority that would prevent one person from dominating government. Government, they believed, must represent the interests of the people. However, people did not include everyone. The wealthy class, called *patricians* [pa-TRISH-ens], thought that they alone should be responsible for government. They created a legislative, or law-making, body called the *senate* to represent their class. The Roman senate was comprised of 300 patricians appointed for life.

Above the senate was the executive: two consuls elected by voting citizens for one-year terms to prevent them from becoming too powerful. Ordinary citizens, called *plebeians* [pleh-BEE-uns], and slaves could not hold public office. Many senators used their power in government to benefit themselves and their families.

Praetors [PRY-tors] served as judges and were also elected annually by voting citizens.

In 494 BCE, the plebeians demanded a voice in the government. They created their own legislative assembly, called the *concilium plebis* [con-SIL-ee-um PLEH-bis], or gathering of the plebeians, and chose **tribunes** [TRI-buhns] to protect their rights and interests. The tribunes attended senate discussions. Although prevented from voting against senate decisions, tribunes had the power to reject the decrees of the senate and to initiate laws. In this way, they safeguarded the interests of the plebeians, and the Roman republic became more democratic.

These and other gains by the plebeians forced the patricians to share their power. While wealthy families maintained power in the senate, these families were frequently plebeians rather than patricians.

Citizens did not have political parties to choose from; they voted for individuals on the basis of loyalties and family ties. In later years, two political parties did emerge: *Populares* [pop-you-LAR-es], who sought changes to Roman society such as extending citizenship to conquered peoples, and *Optimates* [op-ti-MAT-es], who sought to preserve Roman traditions. Citizens still tended to vote for those they knew or from whom they received benefits.

By 133 BCE, the huge gap between the rich and the poor threw Rome into civil conflict. The poor had lost all faith in the government. Several men held almost complete power at different times, and Rome had become a dictatorship.

REPUBLIC
500 BCE – 133 BCE

Executive

Praetors   Senate

Patricians

Tribunes

Plebeians

Slaves

ROMAN EMPIRE
27 BCE – 476 CE

Emperor

Senate

Ordinary People

Slaves

The Beginnings of the Empire

The most successful dictator was Julius Caesar. After his assassination in 44 BCE, Caesar's grandnephew, Octavius, came to power. In 27 BCE, he became the first emperor (from the word *imperator,* meaning "victorious general") of Rome with the title **Augustus**, which means "the majestic." From that point until its decline in the 5th century CE, the Roman Empire was governed by emperors.

Most emperors, such as Caligula and Nero, were tyrants who abused power. Marcus Aurelius, who ruled from 161 CE to 180 CE, was a more moderate emperor. Caesar Augustus earned the respect of the people for his scholarly manner (he authored several influential essays on virtue overruling passion) and his administrative experience.

Figure 8.3 When Julius Caesar was unable to obtain an extension of his command of the army, he marched on Rome with his soldiers. He found little opposition and seized control of the government with surprising ease. The senators who opposed him fled to Greece, and Caesar eventually declared himself dictator of Rome. This gave him absolute power over all aspects of life. However, he always kept the needs of the people in mind.

Figure 8.4 As emperor, Caesar Augustus headed the government and was commander-in-chief of the army and chief priest. However, instead of calling himself emperor, he referred to himself as princeps, which means, "first citizen."

The Death of Julius Caesar

Julius Caesar pondered the words of the soothsayer: "Beware the Ides of March." He wondered why he should fear the 15th of March. He knew he had made enemies. Many senators objected to his reforms, resented that he was dictator for life, and envied his popular appeal. They did not like that he had granted citizenship to people in Rome's colonies, such as in France (Gaul) and Britain. They fought against his move to reduce the power of the senate. Caesar's enemies believed that he wanted to be a king.

Like many senators, Julius Caesar was a noble from a patrician family. Unlike many others, Caesar had earned his reputation as a leader on the battlefield. His armies had pushed the boundaries of the empire through France, and Caesar himself conducted campaigns in Britain. Caesar's soldiers were fiercely loyal to their leader. Before he became ruler, his successes had made him a hero to ordinary Romans who basked in the glory that he brought to Rome.

In only five years, Julius Caesar had tackled many of Rome's problems. He created jobs (often by giving the unemployed land in Rome's new colonies in Spain), reduced food prices, and tried to improve the tax system. The masses loved him.

On March 15, 44 BCE, Caesar entered the senate. Despite the words of the soothsayer days earlier, he was confident of his power. Although he knew many who were jealous of him, he saw a number of familiar faces among the men approaching him. One was his friend Brutus. As the senators surrounded him, Caesar quickly saw hatred, not friendship, in their eyes. Suddenly, the men around him drew their knives. One by one, each plunged his knife into Caesar. As he reeled about in anguish, Caesar saw Brutus among the assassins. As Brutus's knife pierced his body, Caesar cried out: "et tu, Bruté?" (Latin for "And you, Brutus?"), then he fell to the senate floor.

Roman Law

Early Roman laws were not written down. They were based on religious beliefs and were interpreted or changed by priests. This created problems, because people often did not know the laws they were accused of breaking. By 450 BCE, Roman laws had been written down on twelve bronze tablets. These became known as the Twelve Tables.

Romans came to value knowledge of the law. Young patrician men were expected to study the law and be able to plead a case in court. Eventually, Augustus established professional schools to teach law, and the profession of law developed. Lawsuits between individuals were heard before juries of fifty to sixty men from the upper class. No one was allowed to sue a person of higher status, and women were not allowed to take cases to court.

Under Roman law, many crimes, including murder, robbery, kidnapping, tomb robbing, and adultery, were punishable by death. Usually, citizens were allowed to go into exile to avoid the death penalty. Minor punishments included public flogging or the severing of a hand.

City-States

Figure 8.6 This map shows the Roman city-states.

After the collapse of the Western Roman Empire, Roman civil law remained popular throughout all the territories. It eventually became the basis of law throughout much of the Western world, except for English-speaking countries such as Great Britain and Canada. These countries base their laws on English common law or precedent (earlier decisions and cases).

The Roman Army

The army was central to Roman life. Initially, every adult male citizen served in the army without pay and supplied his own weapons. As Roman territory expanded, conquered peoples and allies of Rome were also expected to provide men for the Roman army.

At its height, the Roman army was the most organized military force in the world. It was made up of legions, each of which contained 6000 men with a commander appointed from

Figure 8.5 When fighting, Roman legions used an effective defensive technique. Troops made a "turtle" by holding their shields in front of them and over their heads to form a solid wall that deflected arrows.

the senate. **Centurions** [SEN-chur-ee-uns], the only full-time officers, were the backbone of the army. Discipline was very important, and those who disobeyed orders were severely punished.

Roman legions were used to conquer new lands and to maintain Roman territories. Auxiliary troops were drawn from the provinces of the empire to assist the legions by acting as scouts or as cavalry. These troops were not allowed to serve in their own homelands. In return for serving a turn of duty, these men were granted citizenship. As well as soldiers, each legion required doctors, priests, veterinarians for the horses, cooks, engineers, weapons makers, trumpeters, and standard bearers who marched unarmed with the **legionnaries**.

Figure 8.7 It took Hannibal and his army 15 difficult days to cross the Alps.

Hannibal's Expedition

Carthage, located in the present-day African country of Tunisia, faced war with Rome.

Hannibal remembered the moment well. As the Roman forces were brutally crushing the Carthaginians [kar-thah-JIN-ee-uhns] in 241 BCE, his father, the commander of the Carthaginian forces, had made young Hannibal vow to hate Rome forever. Now, twenty years later, it was Hannibal who commanded the Carthaginian army, and Carthage was once again at war with Rome.

As he sat with his generals, Hannibal faced a major decision. Since the end of the last war, Rome had built the strongest navy in the Mediterranean. There was no way to defeat Rome by sea. A naval attack on Italy would be a disaster.

After much discussion, Hannibal spoke. "As I see it, our best strategy is an overland attack on Rome from the north. If we can surprise the Romans in their own territory, we can defeat them."

It was a daring plan with many risks, not the least of which was the arduous journey required. Hannibal recalled his vow. Now was his chance to avenge his father's defeat.

Hannibal had great confidence. Within a month, he and his forces reached the Alps. To this point, both the men and the elephants that were part of the Carthaginian army had moved with great speed. Now, however, Hannibal watched in horror as dozens of elephants fell to their deaths on the slippery slopes of the mountains. Soldiers, too, fell to their deaths. In the end, Hannibal lost almost half his men and all but one elephant.

Marching south, the Carthaginian soldiers defeated all who opposed them and pressed onwards to the outskirts of Rome. Here Hannibal's forces paused, hoping that their threatening presence would force the Roman leaders to negotiate a settlement to the conflict. Despite all his skills as a military strategist, Hannibal knew that without reinforcements and supplies he stood little chance of conquering Rome.

For fifteen years, Hannibal and his troops remained within reach of Rome. They won many battles against the Roman forces but were unable to defeat them completely. Their hopes of victory were finally dashed when news arrived that the Romans had launched a naval assault on Carthage.

Dispirited, Hannibal turned his forces around and returned home to defend Carthage. In 202 BCE, Hannibal and his men were defeated at Zama, outside Carthage. One of the greatest marches in military history to that time had all been for nothing. In the end, Carthage, not Rome, was defeated.

Social Organization

Roman society was divided into distinct social classes. Wealthy citizens, the patricians, dominated the government and the economic life of the city. They formed only about one-tenth of Rome's population. Many owned large estates outside the city. To become a member of this class, a Roman had to be born into it.

Ordinary citizens, the plebeians, included tradespeople, small farmers, and labourers. At first, they had little power in society, but some became very rich and powerful. During the years of the Roman Republic (500 BCE-133 BCE), plebeians gradually acquired the same rights as the patricians (see page 148). Eventually the two classes merged.

Slaves were at the bottom of Roman society. They did not have citizenship and had no rights unless they were set free.

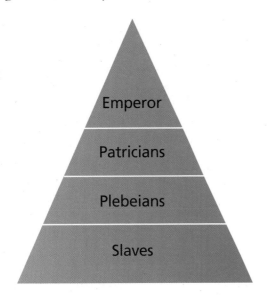

Roman citizenship was initially granted to freeborn men of some rank or wealth (patricians) who lived in the city of Rome. Citizenship was also granted to those who displayed remarkable courage in battle. Eventually, citizenship was extended to more ordinary members of Roman society (plebeians). Citizens could participate in choosing government representatives, were protected by Roman laws, had to serve in the military, and were required to pay taxes.

In time, in order to tax them, citizenship was extended to wealthy or powerful non-Romans,

Figure 8.8 Some women worked in small shops; most took care of the home.

or *peregrines* [PEAR-uh-grins], who lived in conquered lands. Roman citizenship was also granted to foreign leaders and to foreign soldiers as a reward for military service to the empire. By the 3rd century BCE, citizenship had been granted to every freeborn person living under Roman rule (including all colonies). By then, the privilege of being a Roman citizen meant far less than it once had, since Roman law, government, and custom extended to everyone throughout the empire.

Every five years, the government undertook a **census** to determine the number of citizens and their wealth for taxation purposes and for assessing military strength. Those who refused to answer the censor's questions could lose their possessions and freedom.

As in Greek society, women were not allowed citizenship. Women were regarded as inferior to men, although Roman women were treated with greater respect than were Greek women. A woman's rights depended on her social class and, therefore, varied greatly. The Roman writer Cicero wrote: "Our ancestors, in their wisdom, considered all women, because of their innate weakness, should be under the control of guardians."

Historical documents reveal that there were far more influential women in Roman society than in Greek society, and they had more rights. Roman women could own or inherit property. They could not take part in government, although some exercised considerable influence through their husbands and, especially, through their sons.

Some girls were allowed to attend elementary school; however, the education of most girls took place at home where they were taught spinning, weaving, and household skills. Boys learned to follow in their fathers' footsteps; girls were taught the skills of their mothers – managing the household, raising children, supervising domestic slaves, and looking after the entertainment and comfort of guests in the home. As in most societies, women from poor families had to work. Contrary to popular belief, some women were gladiators.

Marriages were generally arranged between families when children were infants. Girls were expected to marry and start a family during their late teenage years.

The father was head of the family and given the name *paterfamilias* [pay-ter-feh-MILL-ee-uhs], unless the grandfather lived in the house. In those instances, as the oldest living father, the grandfather was paterfamilias and ruled over the family. Decisions of the paterfamilias could not be challenged. Besides membership in their family, Romans also belonged to a wider extended family of relatives spanning several generations known as **gens** [JENZ]. Often the gens that a Roman belonged to gave him or her status.

Slavery

Wealthy Romans had a lot of leisure time, because slaves did much of the work. At one time, almost half the people of the city of Rome were slaves. In fact, the luxurious lifestyle of the rich totally depended on slave labour. No people in recorded history have ever owned more slaves than did the Romans. Few plebeians owned slaves. Purchasing a slave cost roughly four times the average annual income of an ordinary Roman.

Slaves did a variety of jobs. Most worked in homes as domestic servants, and some were highly skilled tradespeople such as cobblers (shoemakers) or metal smiths. Greek slaves were especially valued as doctors, tutors, and musicians.

The treatment of slaves varied. Some were treated like family members; others were abused. The threat of being sent to work in the countryside or in the harsh conditions of the mines was an effective way of controlling slaves.

Slaves could be set free by their masters, or, if they had enough money, slaves could purchase freedom for themselves or for their children. Slaves who obtained their freedom could become citizens.

Figure 8.9 In 73 BCE, a slave revolt, led by a runaway slave named Spartacus, threatened Rome. Spartacus led about 100 000 slaves against six legions (36 000 men) of Roman troops. When Spartacus was finally defeated two years later, the Romans severely punished the rebels. Six thousand slaves were crucified (nailed to crosses) as a warning to others. These slaves were left to rot all along the Appian [A-pee-uhn] Way, the main road into Rome. There were no more major rebellions.

What They Ate

The wealthy enjoyed many of the benefits of Roman conquests. Exotic foods were imported from the far corners of the vast empire. In contrast, ordinary Roman citizens had a simple diet. The basic foods of all Romans consisted of bread, dairy products, fruits, vegetables, and fish. Ordinary Romans did not eat meat very often. They usually ate a porridge-like dish made from boiled chickpeas, cabbage leaves, sage, garlic, and sometimes cheese. They drank water or wine sweetened with honey. On special occasions, hot water was added to the wine to make a drink called *mulsum*. Bread was made with honey, olive oil, and stone-ground flour.

The Romans liked their food highly spiced and flavoured. They used a variety of herbs imported from the East. Black pepper, garlic, rue, and mint were popular seasonings. It was said that if you smelled of garlic you were from the lower class. A favourite sauce for foods was *liquamen*, made from fish entrails. The sauce was to disguise the taste of the food, because it usually was not fresh. Many Romans suffered from dietary diseases due to poor nutrition or spoiled food.

The Romans had no forks. They used knives and spoons for eating, but they also used their fingers. Between courses, they might wash their fingers in bowls of scented water. Belching was considered polite, and spitting on the floor was acceptable. Wealthy Romans lay on reclining couches when they ate to show off the fact that they had slaves to serve them and the time to indulge in lengthy meals.

At the peak of the Roman Empire, the inhabitants of Rome consumed some 8000 tons of grain per week. In the summer months, large ships from North Africa arrived daily with loads of grain (navigating the Mediterranean Sea in winter was more hazardous). The port of Ostia housed huge grain storage facilities.

Figure 8.10 Roman clothing was similar to the clothes worn by the Greeks.

What They Wore

Until the 2nd century BCE, all Romans wore togas. Tunics then became popular for both men and women. Women wore **stolas** [STO-lahs] overtop their tunic. Men wore an outer garment called a *toga* [TOE-ga]. A Roman male who was not a citizen, women, slaves, and foreigners were forbidden from wearing the toga.

At the age of fourteen, young Roman men became citizens. They were summoned to the Forum with their families. There, they received an all-white toga, or **togas virilis** [TOE-ga ver-EYE-lis], which was the sign of adulthood and citizenship.

Eventually, different styles of the toga came to represent age, profession, social rank, and even a specific occasion. For example, the toga of a high priest had a reddish-purple band. When Romans were in mourning, they wore a dark-coloured toga. At some time during the empire, emperors began wearing purple togas.

A Young Roman's Day

In this story, we spend a typical day with a young Roman schoolboy from a wealthy family.

Marcus Cornelius got up just after sunrise. A slave brought him a bowl of water, and Marcus rinsed his hands and mouth. Marcus put on his leather sandals and a tunic.

Marcus came from a well-to-do family. In Rome, they lived in a seven-room house and owned five slaves. They also owned a *villa,* or large estate, in the countryside outside Rome where close to twenty slaves worked their land.

At breakfast, Marcus paid his respects to his father, the head of the household. Slaves served the light morning meal of wheat pancake biscuits dipped in honey. Marcus ate quickly and left for school accompanied by a slave who carried Marcus's wooden writing tablet.

Marcus's teacher was a Greek scholar known as a **pedagogue** [PED-uh-gog]. From his teacher, Marcus learned Greek language and literature, as well as Latin grammar, astronomy, geography, and history. Young Roman boys were educated to become good public speakers, called *orators*. His favourite subject was geography. Someday, he hoped to travel and see more of the empire.

Mauritia [MOR-it-ee-ah], Marcus's younger sister, stayed at home. In the morning, a Greek slave tutored her in reading, writing, and arithmetic. Each afternoon, her mother showed her how to take care of a household. Mauritia's mother often thought about how, when she was young, girls were not allowed to be educated. "How lucky you are," she often said to Mauritia.

Marcus stayed at school for much of the day. After a light lunch, he studied poetry and philosophy.

After school, Marcus and his friends and their slaves went to the baths. There, they played knucklebones, a popular game played with dice. Late in the afternoon, Marcus returned home for *cena* [CAY-nah], the most important meal of the day. The family ate their meal reclining on couches around the table. The slaves served mutton, fish, cabbage, mushrooms, and fruit for dessert. After sunset, the family was served a lighter meal before going to bed.

Every night, Marcus thanked the deities for his good life. He was grateful he had been born into a wealthy family. Many poorer families lived in tiny apartments and had little more to eat than the free bread, wine, and olive oil distributed by the government.

Housing

The comfort and size of a home was determined by the owner's wealth. The poor lived in simple dwellings, often in large multi-storey apartment blocks known as *insulae.* These were originally built of wood and, increasingly after the 1st century CE, of brick-faced concrete.

Apartments were usually built cheaply and often had cracked walls and leaky roofs. Each apartment had one room. There was no plumbing or running water and only one window with no panes of glass. Furnishings were sparse: a wood-frame bed and straw mattress, a table and stools, and, perhaps, a cupboard for storage. The height of the apartment buildings often prevented sunlight from reaching the narrow streets below. After the collapse of several insulae, a law was passed forbidding apartments to be more than six storeys high.

Wealthier Romans sometimes lived on the ground floors of these apartment blocks. A few of the very rich lived in detached homes, sometimes built on one level. In these homes, a number of rooms were built around a central courtyard, or **atrium**. All windows faced the courtyard. The two main rooms were the living room and the dining room. There might also be a small room with shrines to the family's deities (see figure 8.24).

Figure 8.11 Cooking fires were forbidden in these apartment buildings, because they were a fire hazard. Instead, residents bought their meals from one of the many fast-food shops in the marketplace.

World Trade in 117 CE

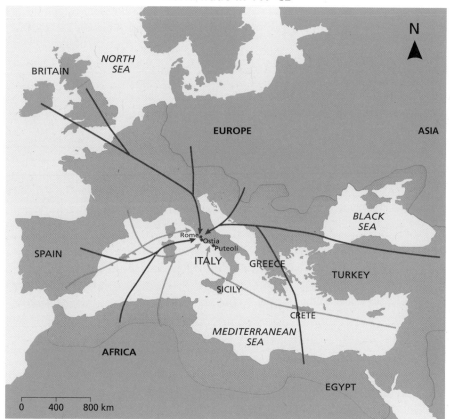

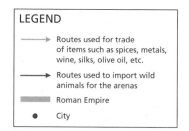

LEGEND

→ Routes used for trade of items such as spices, metals, wine, silks, olive oil, etc.

→ Routes used to import wild animals for the arenas

Roman Empire

● City

0   400   800 km

Figure 8.12 This map shows some of the trade routes and centres for various products.

Trade

Although farming was the basis of the Roman economy, trade became increasingly important as the empire expanded. As a result, Rome became a major trading centre.

Wines were made in the Campania region of southern Italy. In later years, wine was also made in France and Spain and brought to Rome. Wine was imported as a thick syrup in large pottery jars. Later, it was watered down for daily use. Glass products and liquamen came from Pompeii, cloth and dyes from the city of Aquileia on the Gulf of Venice, bricks for building from Modena in northern Italy. Apricots came from Armenia and dates were imported from North Africa.

Beyond the fertile lands banking the Tiber River, the landscape of Italy was quite rugged. Roman expansion was motivated not only by a desire to conquer but also by the need for more farming land. Romans were

Figure 8.13 These boats were built to transport goods on small rivers or canals within France, a Roman province. Canals were not common in Italy. Ships from the far corners of the empire and beyond unloaded exotic foods, materials, and crafts, first at the port of Puteoli [pew-TEE-uh-lee] on the Bay of Naples and later at the Roman ports of Ostia [AH-stee-uh] and Genoa [JEN-o-ah]. Huge warehouses held quantities of these goods. The elaborate network of roads throughout the empire also fostered the import and export of goods.

able to use much of the land that became the Roman Empire for farming, which, in turn, provided food for the Roman people.

By the 1st century CE, Roman traders were venturing east as far as Afghanistan, India, and China where they traded with the Kushan and Tamil peoples for cinnamon, pepper, and ginger, all valued spices back in Rome. They also brought back gold, glass, and pottery. Glass was transported as ingots, which artisans in Rome then melted down to make jewellery. From the Chinese came silk. Papyrus was imported from Egypt and was used as paper to write on. From the west, the Romans imported steel. In addition to goods, trade allowed for the exchange of ideas. Eastern design, art, and literature influenced Roman culture. In turn, Roman innovations in industry and construction were adopted by other cultures.

Because Rome produced few exports, the imported goods were paid for by taxes that Rome extracted from its provinces. Eventually these taxes became too heavy a burden for many people, and the gap between the rich and the poor widened. By 50 BCE, some of the poor were selling themselves as slaves or rebelling against the abuses of the wealthy.

As the city of Rome grew, so did its industries. Among the first industries were pottery and bronze works. Later industries included metal works such as iron (iron ore was imported from the northeast), jewellery, woollen works, and the building trades.

Farming

Farmers used the fertile land around Rome to produce cereal grains, vegetables, and grapes.

Each day, farm products were sold in Rome's marketplaces. Along with their produce, farmers sold milk, cheese, and meat from their goats and sheep. Rome also exported many of its farm products, especially wine. Many other products were imported. For example, grapes came from farms in France. Olives came from Spain and northern Africa. Egypt provided vast amounts of wheat. Cattle were imported from Britain.

Large farm estates each had a manager and a housekeeper, who were both slaves. They operated the farm and supervised the slave labourers. Some small landowners could afford to own slaves who did much of their farm work.

Pompeii

The bustling trade centre of Pompeii [pom-PAY] is perhaps the second most famous ancient Roman city. Its origins date to about 750 BCE, when it began as a Greek settlement. In 79 CE, Mount Vesuvius [vuh-SOO-vee-uhs], located about twelve kilometres from Pompeii, erupted. The catastrophe occurred so quickly that many of approximately 10 000 people living in Pompeii had no chance to escape. They were simply buried where they were, under six metres of volcanic ash and debris. The city was not rebuilt.

Pompeii was not rediscovered until the 18th century. At that time, archaeologists began excavating the site. They were amazed to find households virtually intact. Pets and people were found curled up in terror. Tools and utensils were found where they had last been placed. Coins were still on restaurant counters. Entire streets, not just buildings, were preserved. Pompeii became a window into Roman life almost 2000 years ago.

Figure 8.14 This photograph is of a dog – a victim of the Pompeii disaster.

The Circus Maximus

While the Greeks enjoyed participating in sports, the Romans were more inclined to be spectators. They went to the Colosseum [koll-uh-SEE-uhm] to watch gladiators compete against other gladiators or wild animals.

The **Circus** Maximus, which is a Latin term meaning a huge circle, was the setting for the great Roman chariot races.

Admission was free to all, and spectators bet on the outcome. The huge crowds cheered as twelve chariots raced around the oval for seven laps at breakneck speeds. The charioteers tried to edge each other out; some chariots spilled across the track, and their riders were trampled beneath the stampede of horses. Each spill drove the crowd wilder with excitement. The winner of each race received a wreath and money and could return the next day to race again.

The Circus Maximus held about 200 000 people. With crowds this large, the lives of

Figure 8.15 This model of Rome shows how large the city was at its height, about 350 CE. The Circus Maximus (the oval structure in the upper left) and the Colosseum (the round building) can be clearly seen. Many of the public baths can also be identified by the water in them.

spectators were often in danger. As fans jostled one another for a better view, people were sometimes trampled to death.

Kill or Be Killed

Romans were great fans of spectator sports such as gladiator fights.

"Martius [MAR-tee-us]! Martius! Martius!" The 50 000 fans at the Colosseum repeated his name over and over, as if chanting for one of their deities. Martius heard them as he sat on a wooden bench in a small room underneath the public seats. "They are eager for you today," Preticus [PREH-tih-cuss] said to him.

"It's not me they want, my friend," Martius replied to his fellow gladiator. "It's blood!"

Martius was the most popular and skilled gladiator in Rome. People came from all around just to see him do battle. They would roar in approval as he killed a foe. They knew that Martius would always give them a good show.

Like most gladiators, Martius was a slave. His function was to amuse the spectators. He had been taught to kill or, if defeated, to die with dignity. He had been given the Roman-sounding name Martius to replace his Gallic name.

There was usually no freedom for the victor. The gladiator who survived lived to fight another day. Although some gladiators were granted their freedom after many victories, they often missed the

cheers of the crowd and signed on again. Martius had won seventeen contests against both gladiators and wild animals. Still, he knew that one day he would probably be killed.

At the sound of his name, tremendous applause shook the arena. Martius entered the ring, faced the crowd, and bowed. The chanting became louder and louder. When his opponent entered the ring, Martius recognized him immediately, despite the helmet. It was his friend, Preticus. Both men knew what was expected of them.

Martius readied his sword and shield. Preticus carried a three-pronged spear and a mesh net. The two gladiators attacked each other viciously. Preticus threw his net over Martius, who became entangled in it and fell on his back. Preticus thrust his spear towards his opponent, but Martius rolled to one side. As he rolled, Martius thrust his sword into his friend's ribs. Preticus cried out in anguish.

Like the trained gladiator he was, Preticus turned to the crowd. But there was no pity for him, and the chant "Death! Death!" rose from the huge arena. Martius faced the crowd and then turned to his defenceless opponent. As the crowd cheered wildly, he said: "One day, my friend, it will be my turn."

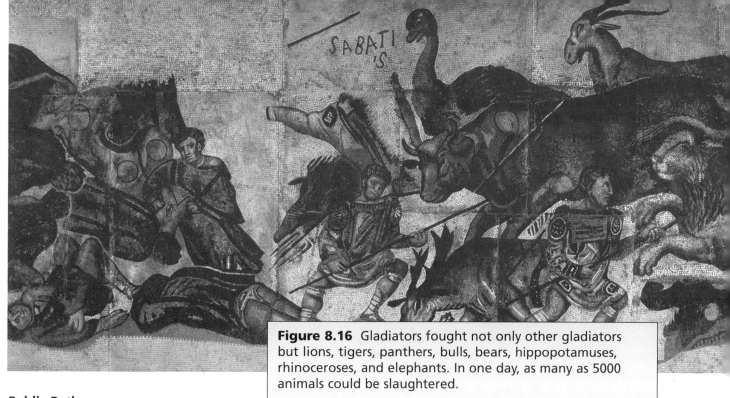

SABATI IS

Figure 8.16 Gladiators fought not only other gladiators but lions, tigers, panthers, bulls, bears, hippopotamuses, rhinoceroses, and elephants. In one day, as many as 5000 animals could be slaughtered.

Public Baths

Romans considered bathing a social event. They spent vast sums of money on an elaborate system of public baths in both Rome and its colonies. These baths were magnificent buildings that functioned as community centres. The baths had separate bathing areas for men and women, gymnasiums, rooms for meetings and discussion, galleries of artworks, gardens, libraries, and reading rooms.

At the baths, bathing was done in stages. A bather might first enter a cold bath or *frigidarium*, then a lukewarm bath, and, finally, a hot bath known as a *calidarium*. Sometimes the baths were taken in the reverse order. Romans scrubbed themselves with bronze brushes with metal teeth. Those who could afford it had massages.

Figure 8.17 Roman baths were elaborate structures that served many functions, including places for socializing and relaxing. The baths were built wherever the Romans set up colonies.

The Forum

Despite controlling vast rural areas throughout their empire, Romans regarded cities as the height of civilization. A city meant a sense of community. No city was greater or more noble than Rome. At the centre of Rome on the oldest street in the city, Via Sacra, was the **Forum** – an open area surrounded by government buildings, law courts, and entertainment facilities. From the early hours of the day, the Forum was crowded with people. Business deals were negotiated there, and vendors set up stalls to sell their goods. The Forum was also the place for meetings, celebrations, and sessions of the senate. Statues of Roman gods and goddesses such as Jupiter and Juno adorned the Forum, and the achievements of emperors were commemorated in stone such as marble.

While the Forum had many beautiful buildings, Rome was a dirty, crowded, smelly, noisy city filled with beggars, slaves, and the poor. The city became so congested with people that Julius Caesar forbade the use of carts during the day to allow people to travel about more easily. Carts carrying goods in from the country rolled over the streets all night long, creating a constant clatter on the cobblestone roads. As the city grew in size, shops and businesses expanded beyond the Via Sacra to streets radiating out from the Forum (as most streets did). Eventually more marketplaces were established in other parts of the city including the *Subura* [SUB-ur-ah], east of the Forum, where most of the poor resided.

Building Methods

The Greeks had used stone to construct their important buildings. Although it was a durable material, stone was difficult to move and to chisel into the correct shapes. The Romans preferred using bricks and mortar. They were also the first people to develop concrete. These materials were lighter and easier to handle than stone and could be mass-produced quickly and

Figure 8.18 This is how the Forum probably looked during the time of Emperor Augustus.

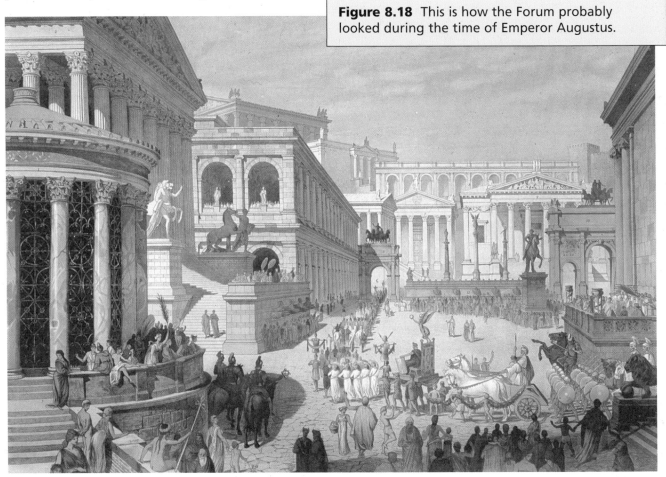

cheaply. The materials needed to manufacture them were plentiful throughout the countryside. However, the Romans also appreciated the beauty of stone and often covered brick walls with smooth slabs of marble.

The Romans learned much from Greek architecture, and they used that knowledge to develop new building designs. By using arches, vaults, domes, and strong new building materials, they were able to build immense enclosed spaces. In addition to their many roads and bridges, they built huge stadiums, marketplaces, temples, and apartment buildings. Many of their aqueducts, built to transport water to cities, remain in use today.

Figure 8.19 The Pont du Gard is an aqueduct that was built by the Romans in the 1st century BCE over the Gard River in southern France. Where deep valleys had to be crossed, multiple pipelines rather than aqueducts carried the water to the towns. Rome had a constant supply of water, which was brought to the city by a system of aqueducts from as far as 50 kilometres away. The Roman sewage system provided the city (but not individual homes) with a degree of sanitation that was unheard of in most parts of the world at that time. Cities in northern and western Europe did not develop a comparable level of public sanitation until modern times.

The Arts

By the 7th century BCE, the Romans had adopted the Etruscan alphabet. This alphabet was derived from the Greeks and from the Phoenicians [foe-NEE-shuns], who lived in what is now Lebanon in the Middle East. The Roman version of this alphabet was used for the Latin language. Modern Spanish, French, Italian, and Portuguese have all developed from Latin. Although English is a Germanic language, its alphabet is based on the Latin alphabet, and many English words are derived from Latin.

Medicine, law, and the sciences all use Latin words, and Latin is still used by the Roman Catholic Church. Latin was the language of scholarly pursuits during the Middle Ages, the Renaissance, and the Reformation to some extent. (Those periods of time followed the decline of the Roman Empire and are examined in chapters 11, 12, and 13.)

During the time of Emperor Augustus (27 BCE-14 CE), Latin literature, especially poetry, flourished. Much of Latin literature was influenced by Greek literature. This golden age of Latin literature was made possible by the patronage of wealthy Romans and, later, of the emperors themselves. Among the famous writers of this time were Cicero [SIH-suh-roe], Virgil [VER-jill], Ovid [AH-vid], and Livy [LIH-vee]. The famous general and leader, Julius Caesar, wrote a fascinating account of his military exploits in France. His exploits are still read today. The Roman historian Tacitus [TAS-i-tuhs] wrote about the Germanic tribesmen on the outskirts of the empire in his best-known work, *Germania.*

Theatre was a popular form of entertainment. Theatres were designed in the shape of the letter D. Awnings protected people from the sun as they sat on the stone seats. Audiences would often spend an entire day watching comedies, dramas, and mimes. Music recitals and poetry readings were held in smaller, covered theatres called *odeums.* Admission to all these forms of entertainment was free.

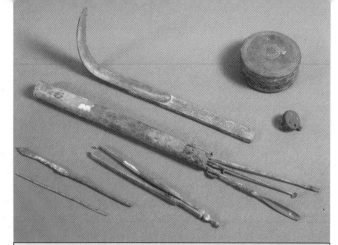

Figure 8.20 Some medical instruments have changed very little since ancient Rome. These scalpels, hooks, and forceps were used by Roman doctors.

Medicine and Magic

Many Romans died at a young age as a result of war, childbirth, or disease. As the Roman Empire grew and people travelled, new diseases such as malaria, typhus, and smallpox were brought into the city. Even with good public sanitation, the risk of infection from polluted water, spoiled food, insects, and animals was great.

During the early years of the empire, the Greeks were the chief source of medical knowledge in Rome. Roman doctors were not required to study professionally or to pass examinations. They received their education by observing those who were already practicing.

Most medicines were based on herbs, salts, and the magic spells of priests. Animal dung, gladiators' blood, and human fat were also used. The more exotic the remedy, the more Romans trusted it. The poor had little or no access to doctors, and they relied solely on local remedies and superstitions. Often, these remedies were prescribed by women healers and were more effective than the remedies of the male doctors.

Emperor Hadrian [HAY-dree-uhn], who ruled from 117 CE-138 CE, feared that Scottish tribes might attack Roman territory in Britain. In 122 CE, he ordered the construction of a wall that, when completed six years later, stretched from the Irish Sea to the North Sea. The wall was 117 kilometres in length, 3 metres wide, and 6 metres tall. A small fort for 30 to 50 soldiers was built every 1.5 kilometres.

Queen Boudicca

Boudicca [boo-DICK-ah] was the wife of Prasutagus [pra-SOOT-ah-gus], king of the Iceni [eye-SEE-neye]. The Iceni lived in East Anglia, located in northeast Britain. When Prasutagus died, in about 60 CE, he willed half of his kingdom to the Roman Empire and half to Boudicca and their two daughters. Boudicca assumed the crown as Queen of Iceni. Roman law did not allow for women to receive such an inheritance, however. Paulinus [PAW-lie-nuhs], the Roman governor in East Anglia, proceeded to take over the entire kingdom. The Iceni chieftains had their family estates taken away. Many were enslaved.

Fiercely independent and strong, Boudicca joined Iceni forces with another tribe, the Trinovantes. Together, they defeated an entire division of Roman soldiers and conquered the

Figure 8.21 Queen Boudicca was angered by the suffering of the people of Iceni when the tyrannical Roman Emperor Nero enforced heavy taxes, conscription, and other indignities on the empire. Her decision to fight the Romans came when her husband, Prasutagus, died, and the Romans took over her kingdom.

Roman colony of Camulodunum (now Colchester). They burned the temple dedicated to Claudius [CLAW-dee-uhs], the Roman emperor who had completed the conquest of Britain over fifteen years earlier. To Britons, the temple was a symbol of their slavery to the Romans.

Under Boudicca's leadership, the British forces marched on London (Londinium), sacking it and killing its Roman population and supporters. Boudicca then turned her army on Verulamium (St. Albans). In all, some 70 000 people were killed.

Finally, Paulinus assembled a force of 10 000 Roman troops in the south of Britain and attacked Boudicca's forces, slaughtering the rebellious Britons. Rather than be taken prisoners, Boudicca and her daughters poisoned themselves. Despite her valiant efforts, Roman rule of Britain continued for another 300 years.

Figure 8.23 This photograph shows a section of the Appian Way, the oldest and best known of the Roman roads.

Figure 8.22 Hadrian's Wall was successful in protecting Roman lands until it was abandoned around 409 CE. Parts of the wall can still be seen today.

Roman Roads

The expression "All roads lead to Rome" was certainly true. Roads linked Rome to its outposts throughout Europe. Markers along the way indicated the distance to Rome or other major towns. Amazingly, many Roman roads, such as the famous Appian Way, form the basis of roads still used today.

The roads were originally built to move troops and supplies as quickly and efficiently as possible. Therefore, great care was taken in their construction. The path for a new roadway was first surveyed to ensure that the roadway would be flat. A trench was dug and filled with large stones and earth. Above that, workers laid broken stones and pebbles to fill in-between the larger stones. This was all packed down to form a foundation, which was covered with a final surface of gravel or large stones. The top layer of paving stones was rounded to allow water to drain to the sides into drainage ditches, which prevented the road from cracking.

Pax Romana

The Roman Empire could not have lasted for such a long time without a strong administration. Beginning with Augustus, the empire entered an era of relative stability and prosperity. From 27 BCE to about 180 CE, Roman military strength and Roman law helped to hold vast territories as far away as Britain.

During this period, the conquered peoples found Roman rule quite generous. They were granted many of the same rights as Roman citizens. They enjoyed a large measure of independence, including control over their local governments. They also benefitted from Roman public works projects such as the building of roads, bridges, and aqueducts. Farming methods were improved, and trade and commerce increased. This era is called *Pax Romana*, or the peace of Rome.

Figure 8.24 Some homes had miniature shrines like this one, which was made to look like a Roman temple. The family's special deity is in the centre. The other two figures are household deities.

Religious and Spiritual Beliefs

The Romans worshipped many gods and goddesses. Each deity played some role in nature. Because they admired the Greeks, the early Romans identified the Greek deities with similar deities of their own but changed the names. For example, the Greek god Zeus, king of the deities, was renamed Jupiter. The Greek goddess Hera, queen of the dieties, was renamed Juno. Mars was the most important Roman deity. He represented the two greatest Roman concerns: war and agriculture.

In addition, each family had its own deities. These included the god or goddess of the home and the spirits of the family's ancestors. These deities were worshipped within the home, which they were responsible for protecting. At each meal, some food was offered to the family's deities.

The Romans sought to please whichever deity was the protector of the task before them. Before planting crops or waging war, for example, they sought the good will of Mars by offering animal sacrifices to him.

From the Etruscans, the Romans borrowed the practice of consulting soothsayers. Soothsayers were believed to be able to predict future events by studying such things as the

Some Roman Deities

Gods

Jupiter: King of the deities

Neptune: God of the sea

Pluto: God of the underworld

Mars: God of war and agriculture

Apollo: God of the sun and good health

Mercury: Jupiter's messenger

Vulcan: God of fire

Bacchus: God of wine

Goddesses

Juno: Queen of the deities

Vesta: Goddess of the hearth, the symbol of the home

Minerva: Goddess of wisdom, the arts, and defensive war

Venus: Goddess of love and beauty

Diana: Goddess of the hunt and moon

Ceres: Goddess of corn

entrails of animals or the flight of birds (see page 137).

In the time of the empire, the emperors served as chief priests. When they died, they assumed the status of deities. The Romans did not initially tolerate Christianity, because Christians accepted only one god as the true God. In later years, the Romans tolerated many of the religions under their rule, including Christianity and Judaism. Such tolerance helped to maintain peace in the empire. Many other religions, especially Oriental and Middle Eastern religious beliefs, also influenced the Roman religion.

In the Roman Catholic tradition, the pope is considered the highest church authority on Earth. The pope lives in the Vatican, a city-state, located in the centre of Rome. The Vatican is the administrative headquarters of the Roman Catholic Church. The Vatican is considered a separate country and has its own governance and police force.

It is thought that Roman Emperor Constantine saw a vision of a cross before the Battle of Milvian in 312 CE. Written on the cross were these words: "By this sign, you will conquer." Constantine was victorious in the battle, and in 313 he officially allowed Christians to practice their religion.

Jesus Christ and the Birth of Christianity

Under Emperor Augustus, Rome gained control of Judea in what is now Israel. This land was the home of the **Hebrew** religion and the Jews who practiced it. Jews were monotheists, believing in only one God. They resisted Roman rule with its many deities and refused to change their beliefs. As a result, the Romans treated Jews harshly.

In what historians now believe to be about 3 BCE, a Jew named Jesus of Nazareth was born. Although educated to become a Jewish religious leader, called a *rabbi,* Jesus instead travelled widely. He preached that God was offering all people forgiveness, love, and justice. The followers of Jesus, called **disciples**, believed he was the son of God and was sent to bring people close to God. They called him *Christ,* from a Greek word that means "the anointed one." His gospel was called *Christianity.*

Many Romans and Jews opposed the spread of Christianity. To them, Jesus and those who followed him posed a threat to peace and order. Jesus and his followers were willing to disobey the emperor and the Jewish leaders for their own beliefs. They rejected sacrifices and the Roman worship of idols. In response, the Romans arrested Jesus, crucified him on a cross, and left him to die.

The death of Jesus, however, did not stop the spread of Christianity. His followers believed that Jesus came back to life and then returned to heaven, and they began to worship him. They spread his teachings, and many people came to believe that Jesus was the son of God.

Jesus Christ became a martyr for Christians, because he had died for his beliefs. One of his disciples, Paul, travelled and wrote extensively. The story of Jesus, along with the writings of Paul, became the basis of the New Testament of the Bible.

Throughout the Roman Empire, groups of Christians formed. They built churches and adopted the cross as their symbol. Christianity eventually reached Rome when, it is believed, Peter, another of Christ's disciples, arrived and helped build the first Christian church.

For many years, Christians were persecuted by the Romans. Their resistance to these actions only helped to further the cause of Christianity. In time, some Romans began to admire Christians for their strength of faith, and they, too, embraced Christianity.

Emperor Constantine [KON-stuhn-teen] became a Christian on his deathbed in 337 CE. Near the end of the 4th century CE, Emperor Theodosius proclaimed Christianity the official religion of the Roman Empire. As a result, Rome became the centre of Christianity in western Europe. The church became the Roman Catholic Church and the Bishop of Rome became the pope. In eastern Europe, the city of Constantinople became the centre of the church, which was called the Orthodox Church.

In 134-135 CE, Emperor Hadrian decided to build a temple to Jupiter on the site of the Holy Temple in Jerusalem. The Jews protested, and, in the uprising that followed, the Romans killed an estimated 500 000 Jews. Judaism was declared illegal, and many Jews fled to other parts of the Middle East such as Syria.

Figure 8.25 Many churches were built in the Roman Empire after Christianity became the official religion in 313 CE. This one near Ravenna was built about 549 CE.

Byzantine Empire, c. 330 CE

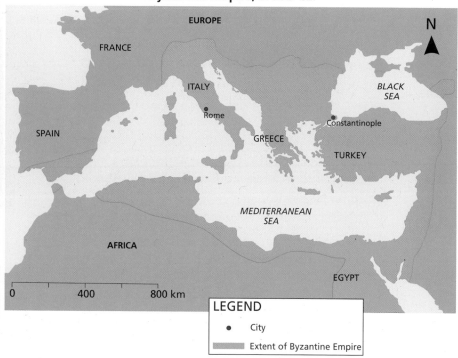

LEGEND

● City

▬ Extent of Byzantine Empire

Figure 8.26 This map shows the extent of the Byzantine Empire.

The Byzantine Empire

The Roman Empire had controlled the lands around Greece, southeastern Europe, and Turkey since before the time of Christ. Despite Roman rule, Greek culture was more dominant in these lands than was Roman culture. As a result, a unique civilization developed. It was called Byzantine [BIH-zuhn-teen] after the prominent Greek city of Byzantium [bih-ZAN-tee-uhm].

By the time of Emperor Constantine, the Roman Empire was in decline. In 330 CE, Constantine moved his residence from Rome to Byzantium in the less-troubled

Figure 8.27 These Byzantine women learned to weave, embroider, and care for the home. Some women from wealthy families were educated by private tutors and entered professions such as medicine. Mosaics from this period often show scenes from everyday life.

eastern part of the Roman Empire. He enlarged the city, and renamed it *Constantinople*. By 395 CE, the Roman Empire was officially split into two parts. The Western Empire was centred in Rome, while the Eastern Empire was centred in Constantinople.

The Byzantine (Eastern Roman) Empire lasted one thousand years longer than did the Roman Empire. It withstood attacks by both Germanic and Muslim peoples. Its influence was felt throughout the eastern Mediterranean world and as far north as Russia.

The Byzantine religion, Orthodox Christianity, is still a distinct form of Christianity. It continued to use the Greek language for its services long after the Roman Catholic Church adopted Latin in the 4th century CE. It still refuses to accept the pope as the head of its church.

The Byzantines learned a great deal from the people with whom they traded. Their scientific development and their arts were unmatched for centuries. While their libraries preserved the manuscripts of the Greek philosophers and poets, their buildings reflected the Eastern taste for colour and character in design. Domes adorned their large, ornate structures.

Byzantine design made great use of **mosaics** (as in figure 8.27). Mosaics were created using small pieces of coloured glass or stone arranged into patterns or pictures on walls, floors, and ceilings. Byzantine clothing was also influenced by trade. Wealthy Byzantines wore fine silks and other rich fabrics imported from Asia. All these features of Byzantine culture eventually found their way to western Europe through the Byzantine's extensive trading system.

Emperor Justinian

The Byzantine Empire reached its peak under the rule of Emperor Justinian from 527 CE to 565 CE. Justinian was so dedicated to building and maintaining his empire that he was called "the emperor who never slept." Justinian's dream was to reunite the Roman Empire. He spent many years fighting against the Germanic tribes who were trying to take over Roman territory. Although he succeeded in increasing Byzantine lands, he failed to reunite the old empire.

Justinian made Constantinople a city of great beauty. He commissioned architects to design elaborate and ornate public buildings such as the massive Hagia Sophia, or Church of Holy Wisdom. He also undertook to have Roman civil laws written down in a single document, referred to as the Justinian Code. The document became an important influence on the evolution of law in the Western world because of its emphasis on equity and justice rather than merely on punishment.

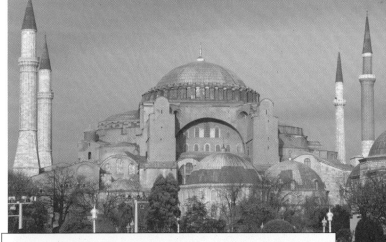

Figure 8.29 The Hagia Sophia was built between 532 CE and 537 CE. Soon after, an earthquake destroyed the dome. The new dome was replaced in 563 CE. When the Ottoman Turks conquered Byzantine in 1453 CE, they allowed Christians to continue practicing in all their churches except the Hagia Sophia. Because of its great beauty, they converted it into a mosque.

Constantinople

As the centre of a thriving international trade network, Constantinople became home to Greeks, Turks, Armenians, Persians, Jews, Slavs, Arabs, and Italians. The city was at the crossroads between East and West.

Trade brought the riches of the East to the many craftspeople of the city. They created beautiful products in gold, silver, silk, and glass, which were then sold throughout Europe. Through their dealings with traders from the Italian city of Venice, Byzantine cultural influences spread to western Europe.

Constantinople combined practical Roman planning with the beauty of Eastern architecture. It contained a forum, public baths, and ceremonial columns and arches, as well as the elaborate palaces of wealthy traders and expansive churches filled with the finest mosaics.

Constantinople resisted conquest until 1453 CE when the Ottoman Turks (see page 237), led by twenty-one-year-old *sultan* (Arabic for ruler) Mehmet II, captured it following a two-month siege. With the fall of Constantinople, the Byzantine Empire ended.

Following the capture of the city by the Ottoman Turks, Constantinople was renamed *Stamboul*. In 1930, the name was again changed officially to Istanbul, a Greek word meaning "at or to the city." Today, Istanbul is Turkey's largest city.

Figure 8.28 The site on which Constantinople was built was chosen for its defensive strengths. The city was surrounded by water on three sides and protected by 20 kilometres of thick stone wall on the fourth side.

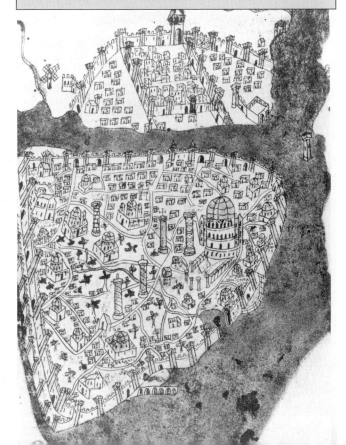

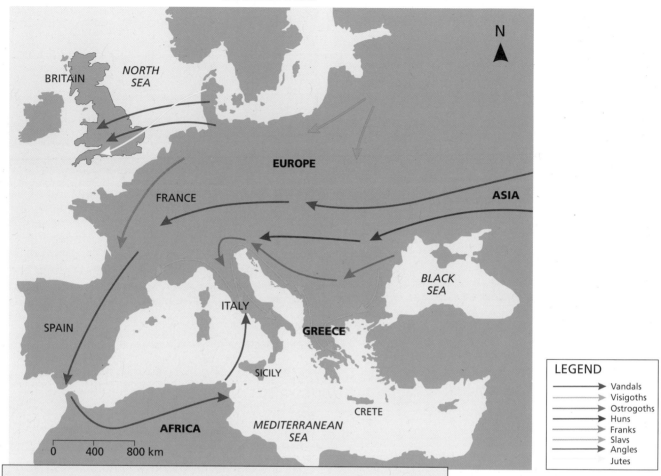

Barbarian Tribes

LEGEND

— Vandals
— Visigoths
— Ostrogoths
— Huns
— Franks
— Slavs
— Angles
Jutes

Figure 8.30 This map shows some of the routes the barbarian tribes travelled during the 3rd and 4th centuries CE.

The Germanic Barbarians

Various tribes lived on the frontiers of the Roman Empire north of the Danube River and east of the Rhine River. The Romans called these peoples "Germanic barbarians." Although the barbarians were from many different tribes such as the Vandals, Visigoths, and Ostrogoths, they had much in common.

They were semi-nomadic herdsmen who resided in forested areas beyond the fertile plains of central Europe. Even as the Roman Empire was accepting Christianity, these barbarians remained pagans.

They worshipped many dieties such as their chief god, Wotan; Tiw, the god of war; Thor, god of thunder; and Freya, goddess of fertility. Some of our days of the week are named after these gods and goddesses (Tiw for Tuesday, Wotan for Wednesday, Thor for Thursday, and Freya for Friday).

The barbarian tribes were not ruled by emperors, and they did not have written laws. Important decisions were reached only after a *moot*, or tribal council, was called and a vote of all freemen taken. Even without written laws, the barbarians maintained a strict code of conduct based on loyalty to one's family and warlord, the local chieftain.

If a family member was robbed, all of the family's relatives demanded payment, called a *wergeld*, from the robber. Any robber who refused to pay was killed. Loyalty to one's lord included making sure that he was safe. If the lord was killed, the family was responsible for avenging his death. Like the Romans, the Germanic barbarians were fiercely warlike and valued strength and courage in battle.

By the 3rd century CE, the Germanic barbarians began moving into Roman territory. They crossed the North Sea from the Jutland Peninsula (Denmark) to Britain where their tribal assemblies became the forerunner of English parliamentary government. These Anglo-Saxon tribesmen would rule much of Britain for the next 600 years. Around the same time, the Vandals travelled through Spain to North Africa, crossing the Mediterranean Sea to Rome and back.

In the late 4th century CE, the ferocious Huns swept into Europe from central Asia near the Caspian Sea. More brutal than the Germanic barbarians, the Huns struck fear into both the barbarians and Romans, who briefly united against this common enemy. At Châlons in France, a combined force of Romans, Franks, Goths, and Burgundians managed to rout Attila and forced him to turn back towards Italy. When Attila and his men arrived outside of Rome, they were met by Pope Leo who asked that they spare the city. Believing the pope to have supernatural powers, Attila agreed and returned to what is now Hungary.

Figure 8.32 The Huns, led by Attila (meaning "Little Daddy"), had little regard for life or architecture and destroyed everything in their path. The Romans believed these Asian warriors were sent by God to punish them, and gave Attila the name "the scourge of God."

Figure 8.31 A small group of Vandals and other barbarians crossed the Pyrenees Mountains in Spain looking for new land.

Figure 8.33 In 410 CE, Visigoths attacked Rome, pillaging and destroying the once great city.

The Decline of the Western Roman Empire

During the 1st and 2nd centuries CE, various hostile tribes, such as the Visigoths, Ostrogoths, Lombards, and Vandals, had moved within the borders of the Roman Empire throughout Europe. At first, the Romans were able to hold these peoples back. As the number of tribes increased, however, Rome was forced to allow these peoples to live within the empire's borders. Soon these tribes were moving deeper into Roman-held territory and were threatening Rome itself.

By the 3rd century CE, the Roman Empire was in decline. There are several reasons:

- The Roman army was no longer made up of dedicated civilians doing their civic duty. Soldiers were now professionals out for their own gain. Many were not even Romans.

- Rome was hard-pressed to keep all the lands it had conquered. At one time, legions could be rushed to a trouble spot. Now, distances were too great to permit this.

Some historians claim that many Romans suffered from lead poisoning. The lead entered their bodies from wine, lead water pipes, cooking utensils, and cosmetics. Lead poisoning can cause constipation, loss of appetite, blindness, mental disorders, and sterility.

- Those people who lived on unfertile land outside the empire coveted the good farmland of the Romans.

- People throughout the empire increasingly resented paying taxes to maintain a large army and to support a government that was not providing the services they needed. Businesses went bankrupt. Farms were abandoned. The gap between the wealthy and ordinary Romans had become enormous. While the rich got richer on the spoils of the empire, the poor became poorer.

- The traditional Roman ideals of service, dedication, courage, and civic pride were no longer practiced by all.

- Emperors were abusing their power, and many were murdered. During the period from 235 CE to 284 CE, Rome had twenty-three emperors. Clearly, the empire lacked any consistent administration.

The Eastern Empire held off most of the intruders, but the Western Empire could not. In 476 CE, Germanic invaders proclaimed their leader Odoacer [oh-doh-AY-sir] to be emperor of Rome. The Western Roman Empire lay in ruins.

The Legacy of Roman Society

Rome has influenced western society through its laws, government, buildings, roads, aqueducts, and language. Latin literature and Roman mythology have strongly influenced the literature of later peoples, notably during the Renaissance (1300 CE to 1500 CE). Such modern languages as French, Italian, Portuguese, Romanian, and Spanish are based on Latin, and many English words are derived from Latin. Latin words are also used in medicine and law. Words in medicine include: *hepatitis, hemoglobin, medulla oblongata, cardiac*. Some legal terms include: *pro bono publico* (work for free) and *caveat emptor* (Let the buyer beware!).

The Romans' admiration of Greek culture also helped to preserve the greatness of that civilization for future generations. When the Western Empire collapsed, Greek culture was preserved in the Eastern Empire. As a result, Greek mythology, philosophy, sculpture, and architecture survived and were adopted by other cultures in places like Asia Minor and by Arabs in the Middle East.

Despite the breakup of the Roman Empire into various kingdoms, the Roman Catholic religion, centred in Rome, remained a unifying force for the next 1000 years in western Europe. The first half of this period, often called the "Dark Ages," was a hostile and dangerous time for the people of western Europe. During this time, the learning and achievements of Roman civilization seemed to disappear. As time went on, however, a new social order developed, which again brought security, stability, government, and a consistent law to people's lives.

Figure 8.34 Gerasa (also spelled Jerash), Jordan, was a Greek-Roman settlement. The Corinthian columns that line the main street are testament to the Romans' admiration for Greek architecture.

Summary

Roman society was based on the conquests of other lands, such as southeastern Europe and Turkey. The Romans absorbed many of the customs and traditions of the peoples they conquered.

The Tiber River played a key role in the development of ancient Rome and the Roman Empire. The fertile lands around the river allowed for the growth of settlements such as Rome, which became the centre of the Roman Empire. The river was also an important transportation route.

The Tiber was as important to Rome as rivers were in the settlements of Mesopotamia, Egypt, the Indus Valley, and China.

Connecting and Reflecting

Reflect on what you have learned about the daily life of Rome. Think about the similarities *to* and differences *from* your life. Explain why knowing about this society is important to you *as a citizen of Canada and a citizen of the world*.

Be an Historian

Do you believe everything that you read in a history text? Do you ever wonder what information has been left out? When you study history, you are usually reading the results of what historians have researched and written. In this section, you will have the opportunity to do your own research and ask yourself the same kinds of questions that historians ask themselves. You will not be reading history; you will be doing history!

Historical research is very complicated. (See chapter 1.) It demands knowledge, skill, and patience. Historians have to:

- locate their evidence
- interpret what it means
- sort out what is true from what is probable and what is false

Read the excerpts below. When you are finished, answer the following questions:

- Where do these sources come from?
- Are they sources that you can trust?
- What do you know about the author? If you do not know anything, how can you find out?
- Does the author have knowledge, experience, or credentials that makes you willing to trust his or her work?
- As you try to understand the past, how important is chronology?

Pliny Writes to Emperor Trajan (100 CE)

A major fire occurred in Nicomedia and destroyed private houses and two public buildings. The fire spread because of the strong winds but also because the citizens stood around and just watched the fire without trying to do anything to control it. There was not a single fire engine or even a bucket available. I have given orders to put this right. Sire, would you agree that I should create a fire company of about 150 men? I will be sure to recruit suitable people who will not abuse their position. Moreover, it will be easy to keep an eye on the activities of such a small group.

Emperor Trajan Replies to Pliny

Your province of Bithynia, and especially city states like Nicomedia, are full of suspicious and unreliable characters. However good their aims, fire companies and other such associations easily become secret societies. It is best to provide fire fighting equipment and encourage home-owners to use it, and to force spectators to help fight fires when they occur.

(Pliny the Younger Letters, Book X. Adapted from W.S. Davis, Readings in Ancient History, Boston: Allyn & Bacon, 1912, pp. 213-214.)

Roman Technology

The Greeks are famous for city-building because they chose beautiful locations with good land and access to good harbours. The Romans took care of things the Greeks ignored, such as roads, aqueducts, and sewers. They built roads throughout the countryside, cutting through hills and filling in valleys, so that carts carry as much as ships. Some of the sewers, built with arched roofs of tightly fitting stones, are big enough to drive a wagon through. Aqueducts bring so much water into the cities that they are like rivers. Almost every house is connected to the water supply. The ancient Romans paid little attention to making Rome beautiful because they concentrated on more basic things. Their successors, however, did think about beauty and today Rome contains many fine buildings.

(Strabo. Geography, Book V. Adapted from W.S. Davis, Readings in Ancient History, Boston: Allyn & Bacon, 1912, pp.213-214.)

A British Chief Describes the Roman Empire

A British chief named Calgacus is reported to have spoken these words to his people who were preparing to fight the Roman army: "Whenever I think about this war and our own position, I believe that this will be the beginning of our freedom. Our people have finally united. We have never been slaves. We have nowhere else to flee. Even the sea cannot protect us since it is controlled by the Roman navy.... Until now our remoteness has protected us but now all of Britain has been opened up. Beyond us, there is nothing except water and rocks. There are no more people to help us. There are only the Romans. We have tried to escape their oppression by submitting to them. But they plunder the world, and now that there is no more land for them to conquer, they are roaming the seas. If they see a rich country; they are greedy. If they see a poor country, they want power. Neither east nor west has satisfied them. Alone of all peoples, the Romans take over rich and poor nations with equal passion. They steal, kill, destroy, and then call it "empire." They turn nations into deserts and say they have established peace."

(Tacitus. Agricola. Adapted from Jo Ann Shelton (trans.), As the Romans Did. London: Oxford University Press, 1988, p.288.)

Roman Medicine

Strains and bruises are treated with dried boar's manure. People collect it in the springtime and leave it to dry. This treatment also works for chariot drivers who have been run over or dragged or suffered some other injury, even if the manure is spread on while still fresh. Some people think it's better to boil the manure in vinegar. They also think that if it is made into a powder and mixed in a drink it will heal ruptures and sprains. People say the Emperor Nero used to take this kind of drink because he wanted to show the professional riders that he was a real chariot driver.

(Pliny the Elder. Natural History. Adapted from Jo Ann Shelton (trans.), As the Romans Did. (London: Oxford University Press, 1988, p.288.)

Pliny Writes to Tacitus, a Roman Historian

On the 24th of August, about one in the afternoon, my mother desired [my uncle] to observe a cloud which appeared of a very unusual size and shape…it shot up to a great height in the form of a very tall trunk, which spread itself out at the top into a sort of branches…it appeared sometimes bright and sometimes dark and spotted, according as it was either more or less impregnated with earth and cinders. This phenomenon seemed to a man of such learning and research as my uncle extraordinary and worth further looking into. He ordered a light vessel to be got ready, and gave me leave, if I liked, to accompany him. I said I had rather go on with my work; and it so happened, he had himself given me something to write out. As he was coming out of the house, he received a note from Rectina, the wife of Bassus, who was in the utmost alarm at the imminent danger which threatened her; for her villa lying at the foot of Mount Vesuvius, there was no way of escape but by sea; she earnestly entreated him therefore to come to her assistance….He ordered the galleys to be put to sea, and went himself on board with an intention of assisting not only Rectina, but the several other towns which lay thickly strewn along that beautiful coast. Hastening then to the place from whence others fled with the utmost terror, he steered his course direct to the point of danger, and with so much calmness and presence of mind as to be able to make and dictate his observations upon the motion and all the phenomena of that dreadful scene…. [His uncle went ashore and visited a friend for several hours. They decided to leave when the shower of stone and ashes began to fill the rooms.]…They went out then, having pillows tied upon their heads with napkins; and this was their whole defence against the storm of stones that fell round them. …They thought proper to go farther down upon the shore to see if they might safely put out to sea, but found the waves still running extremely high, and boisterous. There my uncle, laying himself down upon a sail-cloth, which was spread for him, called twice for some cold water, which he drank, when immediately the flames, preceded by a strong whiff of sulphur, dispersed the rest of the party, and obliged him to rise. He raised himself up with the assistance of two of his servants, and instantly fell down dead; suffocated, as I conjecture, by some gross and noxious vapour, having always had a weak throat, which was often inflamed. As soon as it was light again, which was not till the third day after this melancholy accident, his body was found entire, and without any marks of violence upon it, in the dress in which he fell, and looking more like a man asleep than dead…You will pick out of this narrative whatever is most important: for a letter is one thing, a history another; it is one thing writing to a friend, another thing writing to the public.

Part 4

In Part 4, you will look at several societies that thrived from about 500 CE to 1400 CE. The peoples in ancient Ghana and Mali will be studied along with the Maya, Aztecs, and Incas who lived in Central America, Mexico, and South America. You will also look at the transition to modern society, which was happening in Europe at the same time. This period is called the Middle Ages.

Few written records were preserved or have been found from Africa or the Americas. As a result, we know much less about peoples who lived in Africa and the Americas than we do of peoples from ancient Greece and Rome. Evidence of highly evolved civilizations in Central America and South America, for example, was destroyed by European conquerors such as Pizarro. The Spaniards' main interest in the region was accumulating wealth, especially gold, not understanding its people.

Most of what we know about Africa, Mexico, Central America, and South America comes from the work of archaeologists and researchers who examine artifacts and interpret information, and from stories told by people such as al-Bakri.

The period from about 476 CE to 1450 CE is referred to as the Middle Ages, because it is between ancient and modern times. As you read about the Middle Ages, you will learn that many changes took place in people's lives during this period. The first 500 years of the Middle Ages were full of turmoil, because no single leader emerged in Europe. The order and control of the old Roman Empire no longer existed. Gradually, different parts of Europe came under the control of powerful leaders who ruled as kings and queens. The territories they ruled became the foundations of countries such as England, France, Portugal, and Spain.

In chapter 9, you will look at ancient Ghana and Mali. Both kingdoms became very wealthy from their roles in the gold trade. Trade also helped both kingdoms establish ties with the Arab world and introduced the peoples to the Islamic faith. These civilizations in western Africa were not located in areas that now bear their names. Boundaries changed after colonization, but upon independence their peoples took the names as a remembrance of the past.

In chapter 10, you will learn about three ancient civilizations that once occupied parts of what are now Central America, Mexico, and South America. The Maya, Aztecs, and Incas were great builders, and many of their constructions continue to inspire awe for their size and complexity. The peoples, more than any others you will study in this textbook, were not immune to the diseases their conquerors brought with them from Europe. After the Spaniards arrived, millions became sick and died. Many others were massacred.

In chapter 11, you will return to Europe and look at societies in the process of becoming nations. At first, several small kingdoms were established throughout Europe, and a new form of social organization, called **feudalism**, developed. Feudalism gave rise to castles and knights. Feudalism also created a well-defined social hierarchy that was extremely harsh for the millions of people living as peasants and **serfs**. In this chapter, you will learn of some of the conflicts that occurred between nations as they fought for power. You will also

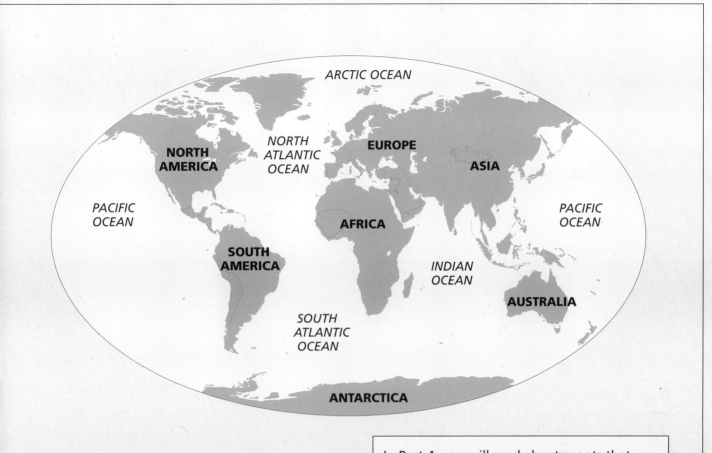

ARCTIC OCEAN

NORTH
AMERICA

NORTH
ATLANTIC
OCEAN

EUROPE

ASIA

PACIFIC
OCEAN

AFRICA

PACIFIC
OCEAN

SOUTH
AMERICA

INDIAN
OCEAN

SOUTH
ATLANTIC
OCEAN

AUSTRALIA

ANTARCTICA

In Part 4, you will read about events that happened in areas highlighted on this map.

read about the crusades, which were a series of wars between Christians and Muslims.

In this chapter, you will also find mention of the Holy Roman Empire. This empire was created during the Middle Ages, with the crowning of Charlemagne as Holy Roman emperor in 800 CE. The empire was an attempt to re-create the Western Roman Empire with the pope as the spiritual leader. Initially, the Holy Roman Empire consisted mainly of Germanic states. At its peak in the 12th century, the empire comprised most of the territory of modern-day Germany, Austria, Switzerland, eastern France, Belgium, the Netherlands,

western Poland, the Czech Republic, and Italy. As nations emerged across Europe and became more powerful, the empire declined in size and in importance. In 1806, the empire was formally dissolved.

The societies you study in this part fit our definition of civilization. Each had most or all of the following characteristics: cities, a division of labour that included specialized occupations, well-defined social classes, an administration that collected taxes, government buildings, and ways of keeping written records.

ANCIENT GHANA AND MALI	**c. 400 CE**		**c. 1000**		**c. 1200**		
	Ancient Ghana is the most powerful kingdom in West Africa. Traders start to use camels instead of horses and oxen to cross the Sahara Desert.		Kumbi-Saleh, the largest city in ancient Ghana, has a population of between 15 000 and 30 000 people. Al-Bakri, a Moorish geographer, uses the accounts of others who have travelled to Africa to write about ancient Ghana.		Ancient Ghana can no longer sustain an economy based on agriculture. The kingdom of Mali takes over the gold mines to the south of Ghana and overtakes a weakened Ghana.		

MAYA, AZTECS, AND INCAS	**c. 2600 BCE**	**300 CE-900 CE**	**c. 500-1500**	**c. 1224**	**1325**	**1424**	**1430**
	Maya settle in Mexico and Central America.	Mayan culture at peak. Farmers are growing several vegetables including corn, beans, squash, tomatoes, pumpkins, sweet potatoes. Maya have a writing system of about 800 hieroglyphs.	Chimu live in northern Peru.	Maya abandon Chichén Itzá.	Aztecs begin to build the city of Tenochtitlán.	Aztec Empire begins.	Inca Empire begins.

THE MIDDLE AGES	**570 CE**	**711**	**800**	**c. 1000**	**1066**	**1095**	**1192**
	Muhammad, messenger of Islam, is born.	Tariq ibn Ziyad defeats the Visigoths and sets up a Muslim state in Spain.	Charlemagne is crowned emperor of the Romans, or Holy Roman Emperor. The Vikings begin to look for new lands throughout Europe.	Leif Eriksson journeys along northeastern coast of North America.	William the Conqueror, from Normandy, France, invades England. Twenty years later, he takes the first census.	The First Crusade begins (and lasts until 1099).	Saladin and Richard the Lionhearted negotiate a resolution allowing Christians a safe passage to Jerusalem.

1312		c. 1324	c. 1330	c. 1400
Mansa Musa begins his reign in Mali.		Mansa Musa, the king of Mali, leaves on a *Hajj*. His generosity to lands he visits on his pilgrimage becomes legendary.	Architectural styles begin to change due to the designs by an architect who Mansa Musa brought back from Eygpt.	The Portuguese arrive in ancient Mali and overtake the kingdom.

1492	1493	1519	1521	1527	1532	1572
Columbus arrives in the Americas.	Topa Inca dies.	Spaniards arrive in Aztec Empire.	Cortés conquers and destroys Tenochtitlán and the Aztecs.	Civil war breaks out across Inca Empire.	Pizarro conquers the Incas.	Spaniards captured last Inca stronghold and kill Tupa Amaru, the last emperor of the Incas.

1212	1215	c. 1200	1279	1431	1453	1480
Almost 30 000 French and German children join a crusade to the holy lands to fight the Muslims.	King John I of England agrees to the demands in Magna Carta.	Genghis Khan rules the largest empire the world has ever known.	Kublai Khan is emperor of China.	Jeanne D'Arc (born 1412) is burned at the stake.	Fall of Constantinople, capital of Eastern Roman Empire.	Russian army, led by Ivan the Great, forces the Mongols to withdraw from Russia.

Ancient Ghana and Mali

Our Study of Ancient Ghana and Mali

Our study of ancient Ghana and Mali includes the following topics:

- Where They Lived
- The Importance of the Niger River
- Housing
- Country Life
- Trade
- What They Wore
- Government
- Religious and Spiritual Beliefs
- Farming
- The Arts
- The Legacies of Ghana and Mali

Present-day Ghana is located by the Atlantic Ocean hundreds of kilometres southwest of ancient Ghana (see figure 9.2). Ancient Ghana was a landlocked kingdom on the western edge of the Sahara Desert. Most of ancient Mali lay to the west of present-day Mali. Part of ancient Mali hugged the coast of the Atlantic Ocean (see figure 9.2). Today, Mali is a landlocked country. As well, the peoples who live in Ghana and Mali today are different peoples from those of the earlier kingdoms of Ghana and Mali.

Questions to Think About

- ✦ How did each of these people meet their basic needs?
- ✦ What factors influenced the development of each civilization?
- ✦ Which achievements of each civilization have survived?
- ✦ Why did these civilizations remain unknown outside of Africa for so long?

In this chapter, we look at the empires of Ghana and Mali in western Africa. These societies were far removed from other areas of civilization, separated by oceans, deserts, and jungle. Ghana was at its height from 400 CE to 1200 CE; Mali was at its peak between 1200 CE and 1400 CE.

In their time, these highly developed societies were renowned in North Africa and areas around the eastern Mediterranean. Few Europeans, however, had knowledge of ancient Ghana and Mali and most other kingdoms on the African continent until the 19th century. For that reason, Africa was often referred to as "the dark continent."

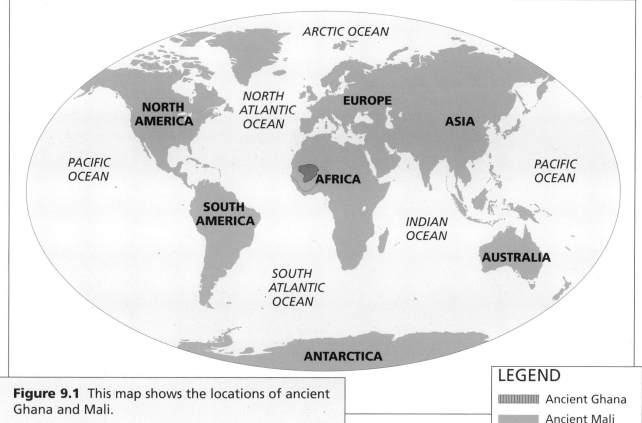

Figure 9.1 This map shows the locations of ancient Ghana and Mali.

LEGEND

▦ Ancient Ghana

▬ Ancient Mali

Modern-day Ghana was called the Gold Coast until 1957. Mali was known as French Sudan until 1960. When the two countries won their independence from the European colonizing powers of Britain and France, their peoples adopted the names of the ancient kingdoms of Ghana and Mali as a tribute to western Africa's past.

The peoples of these kingdoms did not have a written language. Our information comes from oral histories passed down from one generation to the next by bards, or **griots**, from artifacts, and from the writings of people who were in contact with them directly or indirectly, such as al-Bakri, an Arab geographer. Accounts of life in ancient Ghana and Mali were written in Arabic by Arab scholars who visited the kingdoms to trade. Accounts were also written by those within the societies who had converted to Islam and learned to read and write Arabic.

We know that the peoples of Ghana and Mali produced an abundant supply of food. Both societies had strong rulers and complex systems of government and religion. They established trade routes and developed economic and cultural ties with distant civilizations (such as Egypt, Arabia, and Palestine). They constructed impressive towns and cities, places of worship, and schools. The Mali kingdom had an Islamic university.

Although the people of ancient Ghana and Mali were similar in many ways, their societies were also very different. In this chapter, we will first look at what they had in common, then we will look at the uniqueness of each society.

Present-Day and Ancient Ghana and Mali

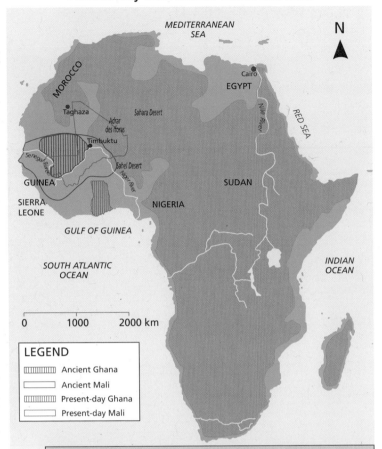

Figure 9.2 This map shows the locations of ancient Ghana and Mali and their present-day locations.

The geographical locations of ancient Ghana and Mali, between the Sahara Desert to the north and the tropical forest area to the south, enabled the kingdoms to control the trade that flowed between the two areas. The taxes collected on this trade made both kingdoms rich and powerful.

Where They Lived

The kingdoms of Ghana and Mali developed in the savannah region of western Africa. The savannah is a hot area of grassland, dotted with trees and shrubs. It is bordered on the north by the vast, arid expanse of sand and rock that is the world's largest desert, the Sahara. To the south of the savannah lies an area of tropical forests. One of Africa's great rivers, the Niger, flows through present-day Mali. Mali was the larger of the two kingdoms and located on more fertile land than Ghana.

Rainfall was plentiful in the central part of the western African savannah. There, inhabitants cultivated several food crops. In the north, near

the desert where the climate was much drier, animals such as sheep, camels, horses, donkeys, and cattle grazed. The animals provided a means of transportation. They were also used to produce meat and dairy products and hides for clothing, which the people often traded. People who lived near the rivers and lakes of western Africa made their living by fishing.

The Importance of the Niger River

The Niger River was to West Africa what the Nile River was to northeast Africa. The river served as a transportation route to trade centres in locations such as Sudan. The Niger flooded every year, leaving behind fertile soil suitable for agriculture.

The Niger River was formed by the joining of two rivers that flowed from opposite directions. The upper Niger meandered north from the hills of Guinea and Sierra Leone. The lower Niger flowed south from the Sahara mountains of Adrar des Iforas.

Housing

Village houses were made of sun-dried mud or stone and **acacia** wood. People used their houses for little more than sleeping and storing food, because the climate was so hot. Most activities took place outside. Furnishings and personal belongings in most households consisted of one sleeping mat per person, some rugs, and a stool. Some families owned a wooden or woven storage chest, but this was not common.

Farmers and their families usually lived in small villages. Their houses were round and made of mud with thatched or straw roofs.

Country Life

The residents of each village generally belonged to the same extended family, or clan. The women cooked, ate, worked, and entertained together, while the men hunted together. The land around the villages was farmed co-operatively, with everyone working together to produce food for the whole village. The villagers were required to send part of their produce as a tax to the king.

Villagers were not influenced by other societies to the extent that townspeople were. For the most part, country people met few foreigners. They followed the traditional ways, spoke their native languages, worshipped their deities, and, as their ancestors had done, passed on knowledge through their stories.

What They Wore

Ordinary people wore gold jewellery and cloth that had strands of golden thread woven into it. The hot climate of the area made wearing a lot of clothing unnecessary. Farmers wore cotton breeches, tunics, and sandals. Women wrapped their heads and draped themselves in cloth.

Figure 9.4 Africans refer to the Niger River as "Great River."

Figure 9.3 With trees so scarce, most inhabitants used other materials to build their houses: mud, which hardens in the hot sun, for walls; straw or thatch for the roof. These materials, and the absence of windows, helped keep the house interiors cool during the day. Many towns in Ghana and Mali have not changed much from when ancient Ghana and Mali were powerful kingdoms.

Figure 9.5 The Grande Mosque in western Africa was built in 1905. It is constructed of mud, the most readily available and abundant material. Mud is also effective in insulating the interior of the mosque from the heat outside.

A market has been set up in front of the mosque. Many of the people in the picture are wearing loose-fitting robes. Women and men in ancient Ghana and Mali likely dressed the same. The light colours protect them from the intense heat of the sun by reflecting the rays.

Religious and Spiritual Beliefs

Two religions co-existed in ancient Ghana and Mali. The traditional religion of the people of western Africa was based on their close ties with the land. West Africans respected their ancestors and considered that their ancestors, the first settlers, had made a bargain with the spirits of the land to ensure good crops. By maintaining contact with these spirits, the people of western Africa could also maintain contact with the spirits of the land. The living honoured the dead by acting decently.

The Soninke of Ghana believed that one supreme god created the world and gave order to all things in the universe. The great god left lesser deities in charge of running things; for example, animals, trees, rocks, birds, air, the sun, and the moon each had a spirit.

As trade developed, the people of Ghana established ties with the Arab world. They were introduced to Islam, the religion of most Arabs and of the other peoples of northern Africa. Some became Muslim, although most ordinary people continued to follow the traditional religion, as there was no official religion in Ghana.

In the kingdom of Mali, the king and the upper-class people belonged to the Islamic faith. Ordinary people continued to follow the traditional religion, because they had religious freedom granted by Mansa Musa (see page 189).

To study the **Quran**, the sacred book of their new religion, the Islamic people of western Africa had to learn to read Arabic. As Muslims, they were also expected to make a pilgrimage to the holy city of Mecca. Their conversion strengthened their ties to the Arab world of northern Africa.

Trade

The trade networks that made Ghana and Mali wealthy were far-reaching. The routes extended from the shores of Mediterranean Africa, southeast through the Sahara Desert and the savannah south of the desert, to the tropical forests in the southern part of western Africa. Trade involved many different peoples, goods, and methods of transport. A variety of goods were exchanged, but gold and salt were the most important **commodities**. The routes were well patrolled by soldiers to ensure the safety of the travellers.

Salt has always been an important commodity. There are many different kinds of salt, and they have many different uses. For example, some are eaten with food and some have medicinal purposes. In Ghana and Mali, all merchants and traders were well aware of these differences. Salt was scarce in the savannah and tropical forests of western African, but it was plentiful in the Sahara. In exchange for salt from the north, people of the south had a precious commodity – gold. Western Africa was so rich in gold that it was often collected from the riverbeds when the water was low.

Salt was the main item traded by the Berbers, although they also traded dates that they collected from the palm trees in desert oases. The nomadic Berbers travelled in camel **caravans**, the safest way of crossing the desert. Camels are sure-footed in the desert sands and capable of travelling for long periods without water. Until the 4th century CE, traders had used oxen and then horse-drawn chariots to cross the desert, often with disastrous consequences. The introduction of camel caravans allowed for expansion of trade routes.

Muslim traders from countries north of the Sahara also crossed the desert in caravans. They brought goods such as silk, copper, swords, horses, pots, and Venetian beads. In Mali, where the king and many of his officials were Muslims, Arabic books were also a major trade item.

When the caravans from the north arrived in the trading centres of Ghana and Mali, the

Figure 9.6 African traders used this bronze figurine as a counterweight on their scales when weighing gold or salt.

goods that had not been traded were transferred onto donkeys for the journey south. Donkeys are sturdy, sure-footed animals in rugged and mountainous areas, and they are capable of carrying heavy loads.

When the caravans reached the towns of the savannah south of the desert, they paid a tax to the government on the goods that they were carrying. When Ghana controlled the trade route between north and south, taxes were collected for each load that passed through its territory. Salt was such a valued commodity that it was taxed both coming into and going out of the kingdom. Gold was not taxed, but the king confiscated all large pieces. (It was reported that one gold nugget owned by the king of Ghana was so large he could tether his horse to it.) The traders kept the gold dust.

People of the south offered trade goods such as gold, hides and skins, ivory, ostrich feathers, and **kola** nuts. Many Muslim traders also bought slaves in the south. When traders travelled north, they transferred their goods from donkeys to camels in Ghana and Mali.

GHANA

The Rise of Ghana

Ghana was the most powerful society in western Africa from about 400 CE to 1200 CE. One reason for its rise to power was the introduction of iron-working from the Middle East. With iron tools, farming became more efficient. The people who lived there, a Mande-speaking group called the Soninke, or Sarakulle, could settle in one location instead of being constantly on the move in search of food. Iron was also used to make weapons that were highly effective against Ghana's enemies. The people of Ghana were able to, therefore, defend and expand their territory.

Another reason for Ghana's rise to power was its geographical location. Although there were no gold mines within the kingdom, Ghana controlled the routes between the gold mines in the southern forests and people in North Africa who wanted the gold. Ghana played the role of "middleman" for several hundred years.

The First Historians

Before the Soninke had a written language, the griots were the historians. The griots were similar to ancient Greek bards like Homer. The griots combined history, music, poetry, dance, and drama to entertain and teach the Ghanaians about their past. Every village and clan had a griot who kept mental records of all important events such as coronations, victories, and defeats. In more modern times, these oral histories have been written down.

Al-Bakri was a Moorish nobleman and scholar who lived in Cordova, Spain, during the 11th century. He visited the continent of Africa through the eyes of others. He compiled records, documents, and interviews with hundreds of people who had actually visited Ghana. Only two of his geographical books survive, and *The Book of Routes and Kingdoms* is incomplete. For many years, al-Bakri's texts were the only sources of information that historians had about Ghana. Research is being done to either confirm or challenge what al-Bakri had to say.

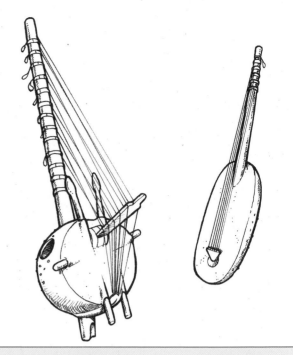

Figure 9.7 Griots remain important figures in West African societies. As in the past, some are ambassadors in the royal courts, and some are mediators. Some specialize as genealogists and historians. Many are musicians and singers. Stringed instruments, like the two pictured here, were played by many of the griots.

Farming

The major crops grown in Ghana were millet, **sorghum**, cotton, **groundnuts**, rice, cow peas, okra, pumpkins, watermelons, kola nuts, and sesame seeds. Men and women divided the various chores. The men hunted and did most of the farming. The women were responsible for harvesting and processing the food for storage and for market. For example, women made a spread from shea nuts, or butternuts. During the harvest season, the men had time to build houses; make bows, arrows, and spears; and repair or make axes, hoes, and scythes. Men also spent a month in the military on border patrol to guard against enemy invasions.

Town Life

Life in the towns was very different from life in the country. Towns were centres of trade, government, religion, and learning. The people of western Africa mingled with the Berbers of the Sahara Desert and traders, mostly Muslims, from the countries of northern Africa. Constant exposure to Arab culture and to Islam brought many changes in the traditional culture of western Africa.

The capital of Ghana, Kumbi-Saleh, had a population of between 15 000 and 30 000. In the 11th century, the Spanish Muslim geographer al-Bakri wrote that Kumbi-Saleh had really been two towns. The Muslim town housed the religious leaders and teachers, as well as Berber and Arab merchants and traders who were in Ghana on business. It had a dozen mosques. Wells around the town provided clean drinking water, and vegetable gardens provided much of the food.

The other town, ten kilometres away, was where the king and his court resided. The king's palace was an elaborate structure with glass windows and paintings and sculpture. The residents of Kumbi-Saleh lived in comfortable houses of stone and wood between the Muslim town and the royal town.

A Unique Trading Arrangement

During the time that Ghana was the most powerful kingdom in West Africa, the gold traders of the south had a unique system of exchange. The traders did not want to reveal the location of their supplies of gold. To ensure this did not happen, they refused to meet directly with the Muslim traders who wanted

the gold. Instead, the Muslims left their trade goods at an arranged spot, withdrew some distance away, and beat a drum.

The gold traders approached the goods and examined them, then left a payment of gold and backed off. The Muslim traders returned and, if they thought the payment was fair, they took the gold and left the goods. If they thought that not enough gold had been offered, they left the gold where it was and retreated once again. The gold traders then returned and added more gold. This process continued until a deal was struck.

Figure 9.8 Salt caravans like this still travel the trade routes of Africa.

Camel caravans were vital in the trade across the Sahara, and camel caravans are still used today in some areas of the Sahara Desert. Camels, with their ability to go for several days without water or food, are ideally suited to desert travel. They can close their nostrils for protection against blowing sand. Their bodies, able to adapt to wide ranges in temperature, can withstand the heat of the desert during the day and the cold temperatures at night. The feet of a camel consist of broad, flat pads, which allow them to carry heavy loads without sinking into the sand.

The camel driver in this drawing is wearing a white robe. White reflects the sun, which helps to protect him from the heat. His head is covered with a long scarf that he can pull up to cover his face to shield him from sandstorms and the blazing sun.

Figure 9.9 This modern-day photograph gives an idea of how the gold was mined. While miners would not have had electric lights, they did have candles and torches that they brought under the ground.

Government

The king of Ghana ruled from the capital, Kumbi-Saleh. The king had great personal power, but he also relied on government officials to run the affairs of Ghana. Although the king followed the traditional religion, many of his officials were Muslims, who were chosen for their ability to read and write. They kept the government records, collected taxes, administered the courts, and managed the king's lands and the capital itself. Not much is known about the role of women in the government. A wife of a king was politically powerful, and, some scholars suggest, the lineage of the king was traced through the mother.

The outlying regions of the kingdom were loosely controlled by the king. Local chiefs (local kings) usually remained in charge of their own villages (much like city-states). They sent the king produce from their land, and they provided soldiers for the king's army. In return, the king protected them against outside invaders. To ensure that the chiefs remained loyal to him, the king required that each send a son to his court, whom the king would then hold hostage.

At the height of Ghana's power, the empire was a bit larger than the size of Manitoba and included several million people. To be able to protect and defend such a large area and population, the king needed a loyal and well-trained army. Al-Bakri reported that the king had as many as 200 000 soldiers at his command, at least 40 000 armed with bows and arrows. This military strength ensured the king had control of a wide area including the trade routes through the kingdom. As a result, trade flourished and Ghana prospered.

The Arts

The Soninke people loved stories and poetry, especially those about family. Mande proverbs often have a family theme; for example, kings may come and go, but the family endures.

The blacksmiths were highly regarded as well as feared because they were thought to be powerful magicians and surrounded in mysticism. Blacksmiths took ore and with fire, an element associated with magic, turned the ore into tools people could use. The blacksmiths were the most highly respected artisans in this society.

The Decline of Ghana

Around the end of the 11th century, Ghana's power began to decline. Historians believe this happened for a couple of reasons. First, environmental changes caused the Sahara Desert to encroach on farming land. By 1200 CE, Ghana could no longer sustain an economy based on agriculture. Second, around this time the king of Mali took over the gold mines in the south.

MALI

The Rise of Mali

When the king of Mali took over the mines, he blocked gold and agricultural exports from the south. As Ghana's power weakened, Mali, which was one of the areas under Ghana's control, grew in strength. For about 200 years, from 1200 CE to 1400 CE, Mali was the dominant kingdom in western Africa. At its peak, the king of Mali controlled an area even greater than had the rulers of Ghana.

Town Life

Mali had several important towns, including Timbuktu, Jenne, and Niani, the capital. Each town had markets, mosques, and fine houses. Timbuktu had a university and was a centre of both education and culture.

Most townspeople lived comfortably in houses made of clay brick. Candles were used as lighting in some houses, a luxury lacking in

Figure 9.11 The people of ancient Ghana and Mali grew cotton, which they used to make clothing. As this photograph shows, cotton remains an important crop today.

European homes of the same period. Many people had slaves and servants to help them with their housework. The number of slaves and servants reflected a family's social status.

Farming

The farmers burned the savannahs to make room to grow grains, cotton, **calabashes**, peanuts, and other farm products. The harvest took place in November and December just before the rains came. During the rainy period, the farmers spent time as soldiers just as the Ghanaian farmers had done.

Figure 9.10 The technique used to make mud bricks has remained the same for centuries.

Government

The government of Mali was organized in much the same way as the government of Ghana. Unlike the kings of Ghana, however, most rulers of Mali were Muslim. They continued to tolerate and support the traditional religion of the African people. To the rural people of Mali, their ruler represented the spirit of their land and of their ancestors. To show their respect in his presence, they dressed in their oldest clothing, bowed to the ground, and covered themselves with dust.

Mali (like Ghana) was divided into provinces. The provinces had governors, called *ferbas*, who managed the daily operations of these areas. Each town in Mali had inspectors called *mochrifs*, as well as royal tax collectors at every marketplace.

The Arts

Artisans were important, because people believed their work to be a gift from the gods. According to a Mande myth, the universe was created when Maa Ngala said the right words. However, the world was left unfinished so that humankind could complete it. Certain people were chosen and given the gift of "creating." The weavers of Mali, like the blacksmiths of Ghana, were thought to have magical powers. Other important artisans were leather workers, woodworkers, and public entertainers.

The Mande-speaking Mandinka people were the founders of Mali. They played a variety of musical instruments, depending on the occasion. The *tabala*, a drum, was played at royal ceremonial occasions; the *guimbris*, a two-stringed guitar, was played to announce the arrival of the king. The three-stringed *bolon* was played during war, but a *kora*, a twenty-seven-string harp, was played for pleasure.

Figure 9.12 This illustration shows what Timbuktu looked liked in about 1825. The city probably looked similar to this in 1200 but with more hustle and bustle. Timbuktu was the trade and cultural centre of ancient Mali. Trade caravans from north and south arrived almost every day. In addition, the university was attended by students from all over the eastern Mediterranean.

Figure 9.13 These men are playing a 27-stringed instrument called a *kora*. In Mali, the kora was played for pleasure.

Figure 9.14 Shortly after Mansa Musa returned from his pilgrimage, new styles of building – flat roofs and fired brick walls – began to appear in Mali.

Mansa Musa

Mansa Musa (Mansa means "king" or "sultan," and Musa is Arabic for "Moses") was one of the great kings of Mali. During his reign (1312 CE-1337 CE), Mali was peaceful and prosperous. Trade and learning flourished, and the kingdom of Mali became famous throughout western Africa, North Africa, and Mediterranean Europe. The empire the king governed, an area as large as all of Europe, was second in size only to that governed by Genghis Khan in Asia.

As a devout Muslim, Mansa Musa's ambition was to make a **Hajj**, or pilgrimage, to the holy city of Mecca (in what is now Saudi Arabia). The preparations for his journey took two years. The people of Mali gave goods to their king, which he sold for gold to pay for his trip. When Mansa Musa finally set off on his pilgrimage in about 1324, he was outfitted in

splendour. His caravan consisted of 100 camels, each carrying about 140 kilograms of gold; 60 000 men from Mali; and 500 slaves, each carrying a golden staff.

Along his route, Mansa Musa impressed the rulers of the regions through which he passed with his generosity, wealth, and intelligence. He gave them gifts and established many mosques. In the Egyptian city of Cairo, he dispensed so much gold that it lost much of its value for several years. Some accounts suggest, in fact, that the king spent so much gold that he had to borrow money to return home.

Mansa Musa brought an Egyptian architect back to Mali to design and build new mosques. The king also encouraged Arab and Muslim scholars to come to Mali. By the time Mansa Musa died in 1337 CE, Mali had become an important centre of religion and learning.

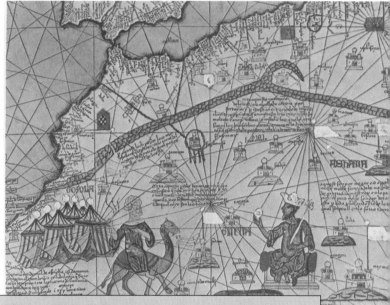

Figure 9.15 This map was drawn in Spain in 1375. It shows Mansa Musa, the king of Mali, holding a gold nugget in his hand. A Berber is riding towards him on a camel.

Tents like those shown at the bottom left of the map were the traditional housing of the nomadic Berbers. The small buildings pictured across the map are mosques. The person who drew the map had probably heard stories from travellers, but had likely never been to Africa – he has shown the Sahara as a built-up area, rather than as the vast, largely empty space that it was and largely remains.

Life as a Trader

In this story, Nadu travels with his father to Taghaza, the main salt centre in western Africa.

Just north of Timbuktu, one of the camels went lame. The caravan stopped while its cargo was loaded on the spare camel. Thirteen-year-old Nadu, travelling with his father for the first time, waited impatiently for the caravan to begin moving again. He was eager to continue the trek into the great Sahara Desert.

Nadu lived in Timbuktu, Mali, with his family. Located near the Niger River just south of the Sahara, Timbuktu was a rest stop for merchants and traders. Caravans carrying salt from the north and returning with gold and slaves from the forests to the south passed through year-round. Every trader entering or leaving Mali had to pay a tax in the form of gold. This tax on trade had made Mali a very wealthy kingdom. Nadu knew this because his father, Ahmadu, was a tax collector. Nadu was proud that his father had such an important job.

Nadu liked the exciting life of a trading town. Each caravan brought news of distant peoples and places. The streets bustled with foreigners – light-skinned Berbers from the Sahara in their flowing robes, Arab scholars from the Mediterranean, Susu traders from the Atlantic coast, and slavers from the south with their slaves all mingled with the dark-skinned people of Mali.

Many years before, Nadu's family had become Muslims. Nadu had learned to read the Quran and speak Arabic almost as well as he spoke his native tongue of Mande. He loved to listen to the stories of the travellers as they recounted their adventures along the trade routes. They vividly described far-off places that Nadu dreamed of visiting one day.

On this journey, Nadu and his father were heading north into the Sahara to Taghaza [tah-GAZ-ah], a town where salt was mined. His father occasionally travelled with caravans, partly to check on the safety of the trade routes and partly to trade on his own.

The travellers encountered many hardships during the ten-day trip to Taghaza. The days were very hot, and often the wind whipped stinging sand in their faces – yet they did not stop. At night. the desert sand cooled quickly, and the travellers had to huddle together for warmth. Only once did they see water – a small pool trapped by the rocks at a small oasis. This was the only oasis they would pass by on their entire journey. The caravan came to a halt, and the travellers topped up every container with fresh water. Nadu was always careful to stay close to the others. He knew that travellers who wandered away were often never seen again. Despite the hardships, Nadu loved the vast open space of the desert, the companionship of the caravan, and the excitement of the journey.

At last, the caravan reached Taghaza. It was a bleak place with no shade and many flies. Only slaves and their Berber masters lived here. They lived in houses built from blocks of salt with roofs made of camel skins, and they ate camel meat, dates, and millet. Nadu watched the slaves as they toiled under the blazing sun, cutting thick slabs from the salt beds. His father and the other merchants carried out their business. Then they started the journey south towards home. Ahmadu praised his son for the way that he was enduring the hardships in the desert. Nadu decided that despite the difficulties, he, too, would choose the life of a trader.

Figure 9.16 Salt workers "mine" salt today much as they did 1000 years ago.

These workers "mine" salt by using long poles to pry large slabs loose from the desert sand. The work is physically demanding – the salt slabs are heavy, as the effort of the miner in the middle of the picture show The miners work in the heat of the desert with no protection from the sun.

For centuries, salt has been used to preserve food an flavour it. Most important, salt is essential to the proper functioning of the human body. When people perspire, as they do in very hot climates like that in western Africa, their bodies lose salt, which must be replaced with more salt.

The Legacies of Ancient Ghana and Mali

The civilizations of western Africa equalled or surpassed those in many other parts of the world. However, their achievements were not known until many years after their civilizations had disappeared. Much of the African continent south of the Sahara remained unknown or ignored for centuries. For Europeans, the Sahara Desert was a great obstacle to the exploration of southern and western Africa, and so they lacked firsthand knowledge of the area.

Some of the achievements of these ancient African peoples include the following:

- They built towns and cities that were centres of trade, religion, government, and education. They constructed impressive buildings. In Mali, Mansa Musa employed an Egyptian architect, who brought new styles of building, such as flat roofs and fired bricks, to western Africa.

- They established trade routes that connected North Africa, West Africa, and countries around the Mediterranean Sea, and brought valuable new products (honey, tools, metal and leather goods, horses, and special cloth called *chigguyiya*) to them. Salt was made available to the people living to the south of the Sahara.

- The kingdom of Mali became one of the chief centres of Islamic scholarship in the world. Islam became a force uniting people of northern and western Africa.

- Through the mastery of iron-working, the Ghanaians crafted better tools, which helped to increase farming production. Iron also produced stronger weapons, which gave their warriors an advantage over their enemies who used weapons of wood, bone, or stone.

Summary

Until the beginning of the 20th century, written forms of the languages of western Africa did not exist. Because the people had no written accounts of their history, many outsiders assumed that these societies had no history.

In 1400 CE, most Europeans still believed the world did not extend beyond Europe. Those who had travelled or knew of someone who had visited faraway places thought their culture and lifestyle were better than anywhere else. We call this way of looking at the world *ethnocentric*. One result of this viewpoint is that civilizations such as Ghana and Mali are overlooked in history books.

The people of Ghana and Mali, however, were well aware of their past. In place of writing, they had an oral tradition. The past was kept alive through stories recounted from generation to generation. In recent years, scholars have been collecting these oral accounts and using them as a source of information in studying African histories.

Scholars such as al-Bakri are also a source of knowledge about African histories. Other accounts were written by traders and others who had visited the kingdoms.

Connecting and Reflecting

Reflect on the life of people in ancient Ghana and Mali. Use the information you have learned to describe the similarities *to* and differences *from* your life. Explain why knowing about these people and these societies is important to you *as a citizen of Canada and a citizen of the world.*

Be an Historian

Do you believe everything that you read in a history text? Do you ever wonder what information has been left out? When you study history, you are usually reading the results of what historians have researched and written. In this section, you will have the opportunity to do your own research and ask yourself the same kinds of questions that historians ask themselves. You will not be reading history; you will be doing history!

Historical research is very complicated. (See chapter 1.) It demands knowledge, skill, and patience. Historians have to:

- locate their evidence

- interpret what it means

- sort out what is true from what is probable and what is false

Read the excerpts below. When you are finished, answer the following questions:

- Where do these sources come from?

- Are they sources that you can trust?

- What do you know about the author? If you do not know anything, how can you find out?

- Does the author have knowledge, experience, or credentials that makes you willing to trust his or her work?

- As you try to understand the past, how important is chronology?

Royalty in Ghana

The King adorns himself like a woman wearing necklaces round his neck and bracelets on his forearms and he puts on a high cap decorated with gold and wrapped in a turban of fine cotton. He holds an audience in a domed pavilion around which stand ten horses covered with gold-embroidered materials…and on his right are the sons of the vassal kings of his country, wearing splendid garments and their hair plaited with gold.

At the door of the pavilion are dogs of excellent pedigree. Round their necks they wear collars of gold and silver, studded with a number of balls of the same metals.

(*Al-Bakri, quoted in* Corpus of Early Arabic Source for West African History.)

Muslims in Ghana

The city of Ghana consists of two towns situated on a plain. One of these towns, which is inhabited by Muslims, is large and possesses twelve mosques in one of which they assemble for the Friday prayer. There are salaried imams and muezzins, as well as jurists and scholars. The king's town is six miles distant from this one…

The king has a palace and a number of domed dwellings all surrounded with an enclosure like a city wall. Around the king's town are domed buildings and groves and thickets where the sorcerers of these people, men in charge of the religious cult, live. In them too are their idols and the tombs of their kings.

(*From an account by geographer al-Bakri*)

Justice in Ghana: Trial By Wood

When a man is accused of denying a debt or having shed blood or some other crime, a headman takes a thin piece of wood, which is sour and bitter to taste, and pours upon it some water which he then gives to the defendant to drink. If the man vomits, his innocence is recognized and he is congratulated. If he does not vomit and the drink remains in his stomach, the accusation is accepted as justified.

(Al-Bakri in Mckissack, Patricia, Fredrick McKissack. The Royal Kingdoms of Ghana, Mali, and Songhay: Life in Medieval Africa. New York: Henry Holt and Company, 1994, pp. 33-34.)

Mansa Musa, Talking to Syrian Scholar al-Umari

So Abubakar equipped 200 ships filled with men and the same number equipped with gold, water, and provisions, enough to last them for years…they departed and a long time passed before anyone came back. Then one ship returned and we asked the captain what news they brought.

He said, "Yes, Oh Sultan, we traveled for a long time until their appeared in the open sea a river with a powerful current…the other ships went on ahead, but when they reached that place, they did not return and no more was seen of them…As for me, I went about at once and did not enter the river."

The Sultan got ready 2,000 ships, 1,000 for the men whom he took with him, and 1,000 for water and provisions. He left me to deputize for him and embarked on the Atlantic Ocean with his men. That was the last we saw of him and all those who were with him.

And so, I became king in my own right.

(Mansa Musa)

About Sundiata the Hero

He was a lad full of strength; his arms had the strength of ten and his biceps inspired fear in his companions. He had already that authorative way of speaking which belongs to those who are destined to command.

About the Villain

Since his accession to the throne of Sossa, he had defeated nine kings whose heads served him as objects in his macabre chamber. Their skins served as seats and he cut his footwear from human skin.

(From The Epic of Old Mali, recited by the griot Djeli Mamadou Kouyate and edited by D. T. Niane)

An Historian Compares Ancient Mali to Ancient Ghana

To some aspect they look the same, the gold, the way they made trade. But to the opposite of Ghana, I think Mali was really able to have more territory beyond some of the area Ghana went to, like Taghaza, the salt gulf, that was all part of the empire of Mali.

So territorial position was one of the greatest differences between Ghana and Mali. And also, the kind of ties Mali was able to make with peoples outside of Africa, is one of the great differences between the two empires…Mali was much more international than Ghana was.

(Dr. Tereba Togola, Head of Archaeology at the Institute of Human Sciences, Bamako. He is responsible for all archaeological research in Mali.)

Maya, Aztecs, and Incas

Our Study of the Maya, Aztecs, and Incas

Our study of the Maya, Aztecs, and Incas includes the following topics

- Where They Lived
- Where They Came From
- What They Ate
- What They Wore
- Housing
- Farming
- Social Organization
- Religious and Spiritual Beliefs

Who They Were

Maya society reached its peak between about 300 CE and 900 CE. The Maya lived in the jungles and mountains of Mexico and Central America. The Aztecs lived in Mexico from around 1325 CE. There, they built a great city on islands in the middle of a swampy lake where Mexico City now stands. The empire of the Incas included the rugged Andes Mountains, desert, and jungle in South America. Their empire lasted for about 100 years (from 1430 CE to 1532 CE).

Few written records of these societies remain. Some words of the Mayan language have been translated, but most of our information about these societies comes from oral history, artifacts,

Figure 10.1 Today, about 2 million Maya (top left) live in Mexico and Central America. They carry on many traditions and speak their own languages. About 1.2 million Aztecs (bottom) live in small villages around Mexico City. They speak a modern version of Nahuatl. The descendants of the Incas (top right) number about 6 million and live mainly in the mountains of Ecuador, Peru, and Bolivia. They speak the Incan language, Quechua [KEH-chu-ah].

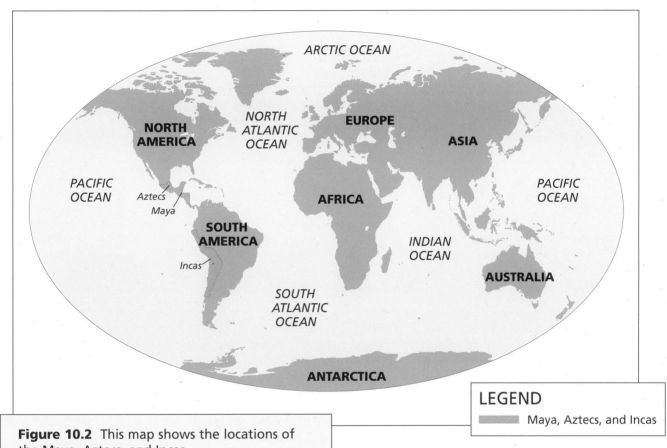

LEGEND

Maya, Aztecs, and Incas

Figure 10.2 This map shows the locations of the Maya, Aztecs, and Incas.

Questions to Think About

+ How did the Maya, Aztecs, and Incas meet their basic needs?

+ What factors influenced the development of each civilization?

+ Which achievements of each civilization have survived?

and accounts by people from elsewhere who were in contact with them. The Spaniards, who overthrew the Aztecs and Incas, wrote about both societies. We know, for example, that all of these peoples grew crops that were unknown to the rest of the world. They also had elaborate trade systems, well-organized governments, and complex religious beliefs. We will look at all of these topics in this chapter.

MAYA

Where They Lived

The Maya lived in the jungles and mountains of Belize, El Salvador, Guatemala, northwestern Honduras, and southern Mexico. The area covered about 300 000 square kilometres – about one-sixth the size of Mexico.

The Maya were an agricultural and trading people. They cleared large areas of jungle by cutting down the vegetation and burning what was left to make room for settlement. This clearing technique, known as slash and burn (see chapter 2), was called **milpa** [MILL-pah] by the Maya.

Social Organization

Maya cities were not united to form an empire. Each city was a separate state, just as they were in Greece. The city-states were connected to one another through marriage, trade, art, and by a common language, writing system, calendar, and religion. At its height, there were about sixty city-states. Each included a city, which was the administrative and religious centre for the region, and several towns and villages. Most cities were not surrounded by walls, but moats encircled some.

Maria's Pride

In this story, Maria learns some of the history of her people.

Maria was very tired by the time she reached the top of the pyramid temple at Chichén Itzá [chee-CHEN eet-SAH]. At times, she had to sit down and rest because the stairs were so steep. But each time she stopped, her aunt urged her on. Maria's aunt was determined to show her niece Chichén Itzá, a city that had been built by their Maya ancestors.

The idea for visiting the ruins came when Maria asked her aunt what seemed like a simple question: "Where did our people come from?"

Now, at the ruins, Maria's aunt smiled. "Do you know, Maria, that the Maya have lived here in Mexico for about 4000 years?"

"Were most of them poor farmers like we are?"

"Many of them were farmers, Maria, but they weren't all poor," her aunt replied quickly. "The farmers grew so much food that many other people had the time to build large temples and create works of art like the sculptures and pottery you see in museums."

From the top of the temple, Maria could see why her aunt was so excited about coming here. There was the Round Tower that the Maya had built to study the stars. There was the ball court where the Maya had played a game that was similar to basketball. Maria imagined she could hear the cheering fans. She could also see the huge Temple of the Warriors and the Temple of the Jaguar.

"What are those?" Maria asked as she pointed at a number of huge stone pillars covered with carved figures.

"Those are called **stelae** [STEE-lee]. Our ancestors used hieroglyphics, a form of picture writing, to carve their history into them. They used signs called **glyphs** [glifs] to tell their stories. Each glyph stands for a word or part of a word."

"Can you read them?" Maria asked.

"No. They are very hard to read. Even scientists cannot decipher many of the glyphs. Still, much of what we know about our people comes from the stelae and the few Mayan books that have survived."

"What happened to our people? Why are only ruins left of the cities?"

"Those are difficult questions, Maria. About 1100 years ago, the Maya stopped building cities. In fact, the people already living in cities began to leave. In a relatively short time the cities were deserted. Was there a drought that destroyed their food supply? Did the people die of some disease? Was there an earthquake or some other disaster? Did the common people rebel against the nobles and destroy the society? Archaeologists have different theories, but no one knows for sure."

Maria thought this over. Archaeology was like detective work. She liked that. Perhaps someday she would study the glyphs, find out their hidden messages, and explain why Maya society collapsed so long ago. The thought of solving this big mystery brought a smile to her face.

Maya Social System

	RIGHTS	RESPONSIBILITIES
KING ("ahau")	• collects taxes/tribute • hereditary right to govern	• wages war to get human sacrifices • creates alliances • leads religious rituals • builds public works
NOBLES ("batab") war captains, town councillors, deputies, town constables, speakers, prophets		• maintain order • oversee military
PRIESTS high-priests ("Ah Kin Mai," which means The Highest One of the Sun") priests ("Ah Kin"), executioner-priests		• perform daily ceremonies
PEASANTS		• contribute labour • contribute food • serve in army
SLAVES		

Land of the Maya

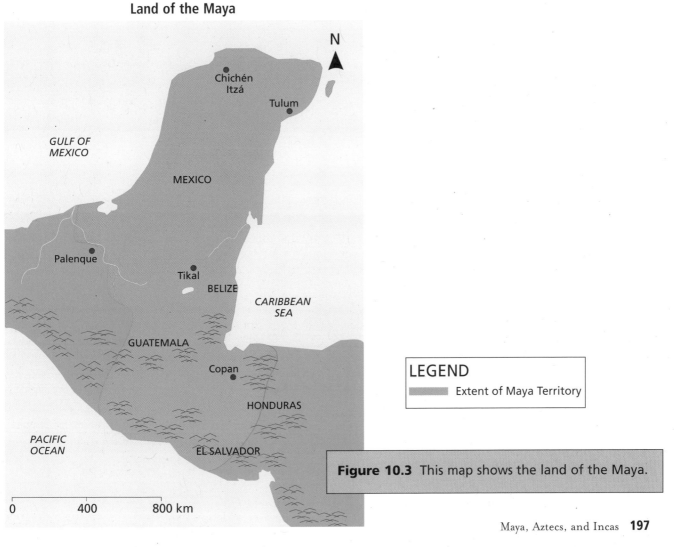

Figure 10.3 This map shows the land of the Maya.

Where the Maya Came From

The Maya originally came from the Yucatán area of Guatemala around 2600 BCE. They adopted some of the traditions of the Olmec, who were an earlier society. Little else is known about their origins.

What They Ate

Farms provided much of the food, and most of the food was grown by peasants. The main crop was corn. Corn was roasted whole, then ground up and made into either a thick soup or broth. Sometimes corn was used to make thin pancakes called *tortillas* [tor-TEE-yahs]. The Maya ate meat (deer, rabbit, turkey) and dried fish, and vegetables and fruits. Corn, beans, squash, tomatoes, chili peppers, avocados, pumpkins, cacao, and sweet potatoes were first grown by the Maya. These foods are now grown and eaten by people throughout the world.

Figure 10.4 This is an example of Maya textiles. It is made by weavers who use techniques handed down for over 1000 years.

For the Maya, money really did grow on trees. Most of the time, the Maya bartered their surplus goods for items they needed. But when they needed "money," they used cacao beans from the cacao tree. These shiny beans were valued because their filling was – and still is – used to make chocolate.

What They Wore

Most clothing was made of cotton. Cotton was ideal for the hot, humid climate of the area. The cloth was woven on a loom and coloured with dyes made from plants and insects.

The poor dressed simply. Men wore loincloths and, sometimes, sleeveless shirts or jackets. Sometimes they wore light capes knotted at one shoulder. Women wore long, loose skirts or dresses and, on occasion, shawls. Most Maya went barefoot, although some wore sandals made from animal hide or plant fibre.

The rich dressed quite lavishly. Men wore short skirts (similar in style to kilts), sandals, and richly ornamented belts. They had long capes, often made from jaguar skin, and headdresses that looked like snakes or animal heads.

Both men and women wore a lot of jewellery made largely of jade, although gold, silver, bone, wood, shells, and stone were also used. The men wore decorated necklaces, large ear plugs, headbands, and headdresses. Men of wealth wore headdresses with two folds, bracelets, and beaded necklaces.

The Maya tattooed their bodies. Both men and women filed their teeth to points and then had them inlaid with jade. Both also wore long, braided hair.

In 1562, a Spanish monk ordered the burning of Maya books called **codices**. "Because they [the books] contained nothing but superstitions and falsehoods about the devil," the monk wrote, "we burned them all, which the Indians felt most deeply and over which they showed much sorrow."

Housing

Maya rulers and priests lived near the central plaza in great stone palaces. These palaces contained large apartments. Their owners slept in beds draped with skins or cotton bedding and built into the stone walls. There were shelves for storage and separate kitchens where servants made the meals.

Merchants, craftspeople, artists, and government workers also lived in the towns. Their houses were much more modest than those of the rich. Homes were built on raised platforms to keep them cool, and free of crawling insects. Sometimes, the homes were built of stone, but most often the walls were made of a framework of poles plastered over with dried earth. The thatched roofs were steeply pitched to keep the houses cooler. Cooking was usually done in a separate building or outdoors in the shared courtyard.

A husband and wife and their unmarried children lived together in one house. Grandparents, aunts, uncles, and cousins lived in houses nearby. The entire family shared a courtyard. Each extended family kept a shrine, for religious celebrations, in the courtyard.

The division of labour between men and women was clearly defined. The men built huts and cared for the cornfields. The women prepared food, made clothing, and tended to the family's domestic needs.

The peasants' homes in the farming areas were simpler versions of the houses in town. Often, they were just one-room huts. The peasants sometimes had gardens and fruit trees. Harvested crops were kept in stone-lined underground storage areas.

Farming

Maya farmers had to work long hours to prepare their fields. They dug canals to drain swampy ground. They planted raised beds in their gardens. On hilly slopes, they retained the soil behind stone walls and made terraces to grow crops (see figure 10.24). To ensure a steady supply of water, they dammed rivers and built reservoirs for irrigation.

When planting, farmers used pointed sticks to make holes in the earth for the seeds. The Maya did not have ploughs, metal tools, horses or oxen, or wheeled vehicles to help them. They were still able to grow enough food for everyone.

Figure 10.5 Most peasants lived in one-room huts similar to the huts shown here. In this illustration, the men in the foreground are making tools. In the background, one woman is making tortillas. Another woman is weaving with a backstrap loom.

Trade

Each city was ruled by a chief, priests, and members of their families. These people, most of whom were men, appointed others to collect taxes, supervise trade with other cities, construct buildings, and fight wars. At the bottom of the social ladder were farmers, and those who hunted and fished.

Traders had an important place in Maya society. They were considered nobles and members of the ruling class. From the highlands, they traded goods such as jade, flint, and the feathers of the **quetzal** [KET-sal] bird. From the lowlands and coastal areas, they traded cotton, salt, honey, wax, fish, and cacao beans. Traders spread both ideas and goods between the city-states. The trails they travelled on by foot became roads that linked the city-states. Over water, they travelled in canoes that were often ten metres long. Trade routes covered much of Central America, including the Gulf Coast to Central Mexico, Chiapas highlands, Guatemala, El Salvador, Costa Rica, and Panama.

The Quetzal Bird

The quetzal bird (along with the snake) was the most sacred animals of the ancient Maya. The bird symbolized creation and the will of the creator to come to Earth. The ruler wore the feathers of the quetzal bird as a symbol of his power and connection to the deities.

Figure 10.6 This picture shows the Great Plaza (left) and the Acropolis (right) at Copàn, Honduras, as they might have looked in the year 750 CE. The vertical figures in the Great Plaza are stelae of Maya rulers.

Figure 10.7 On market day, the plaza bustled with people. Women came to buy fresh meat, dried fish, fruits, and vegetables to feed their families. They also bought cotton cloth and animal skins that they would later sew into clothing. Traders offered jade and precious metals for jewellery. Local craftspeople sold tools, candles, and pottery.

Town Life

Each town was built around a large plaza, just as Roman cities and towns were built around **piazzas**. The plaza was the town's religious and trading centre. Some pyramid temples rose over thirty metres above the plaza. Other stone buildings were used for government offices and the rulers' palaces.

Raised roads led from the main plaza to smaller neighbourhood plazas with their own pyramids and buildings. Many archaeologists believe these roads were raised one or two metres because the roads led to places of worship. The raised roads may also have

helped to protect worshippers from the many poisonous snakes and insects in the area. Dotted around the public squares were people's homes, which were arranged in groups around courtyards. The rich lived close to the centre of town. The poor lived farther out.

Figure 10.8 The Maya played a ball game called *tlatchtli* on courts like this one. There were several variations of the game. The object of the game shown here was to knock a solid rubber ball through a stone ring placed midway along a wall of the court. The ball could be bounced off the ground or the walls of the court. Players propelled the ball using only their bodies not their hands or feet. Whichever team won the game could claim the jewellery and clothes of the spectators. The games were taken so seriously that losers were sometimes put to death. The Maya placed large bets on each game.

The Development of Writing

To the Maya, writing was a sacred gift from the gods. Only a small, select group of people learned to read and write. These highly trained scribes believed they had been chosen to interact directly with the gods.

Maya writing was in the form of hieroglyphics. The glyphs represented words or syllables that were combined to form words and concepts about topics such as gods and goddesses, numbers, food, time periods, and places. The Maya used writing as a propaganda tool, rather than as a way of recording their history. Inscriptions dealt mainly with important events such as marriages and births in the ruling family, military campaigns, and victories of rulers.

Scribes carved glyphs into stone and wood on monuments and architecture, or they painted them on paper, plaster walls, and pottery. Glyphs were also painted on codices made of deer hide or bleached fig-tree paper that was then covered with a thin layer of plaster and folded accordion-style. Most of the codices were burned by the Spaniards in the 16th century. Four codices have survived and are important sources of information about Maya society.

Religious and Spiritual Beliefs

The Maya worshipped many deities. Two of the most important were Itzamna and Chac. The Maya believed that Itzamna created the world and invented the calendar and glyph writing. Chac was the god of rain, and rain was crucial to the Maya farmers.

Both animals and humans were sacrificed to the Maya deities. Human sacrifices included orphans, slaves, captured enemy warriors, and criminals. Sacrifices were made to ensure that the deities would be friendly towards the Maya.

The Maya believed that Chac and a number of other deities lived underground. Sometimes, people were thrown into **cenotes** to try to please these deities. If the victims survived, they would come to the surface. They would

Figure 10.9 The Maya had about 800 glyphs.

then be asked to report on what they had found out about the underworld.

The priests studied the stars and created an accurate calendar. Calendar dates and the movements of planets were important because the priests used them to determine when farmers should plant and harvest crops. Holidays and feast days were also set by the calendar. The Maya believed that disaster would strike if they did not celebrate these special days.

Some churches in Mexico and Central America are built on the ruins of Maya's pyramids. Pyramids were the religious centres.

Figure 10.10 Cenotes are formed when underground water streams erode the earth's surface bedrock and cause the ground to collapse, creating "sinkholes." Several thousand cenotes can be found in the Yucatán Peninsula in Mexico.

Figure 10.11 Stelae were carved to depict Maya gods and rulers. The glyphs on a stela [STEE-lah] described important events during a ruler's time, information about the ruler's family, and the date when the stela was carved.

Figure 10.12 Almost no ancient Maya clothes or furniture have survived the damp climate. Wall paintings like this one of prisoners (bottom) and their captors (top) show hairstyles, jewellery, musical instruments, and ceremonial dress.

The pyramids represented the mountains where gods lived, and the entrances to the pyramids were made to be similar to the caves found in the mountains. Within these "caves," the king performed rituals that linked his people with the gods.

Today, Maya religion combines many ancient customs with Catholicism. For example, the sun is linked to God the Father or Jesus Christ; the moon is linked to the Virgin Mary. Both belief systems include rituals of burning of incense, religious imagery, and pilgrimages.

Many villages still have **shamans** who pray for souls at mountain shrines or call on the gods of forests or agriculture to help their people. Crosses, an important Christian symbol, and the jaguar statue, important in classic Maya religion, often appear together to ward evil away.

The Arts

The Maya produced outstanding stone carvings, ceramics, clay figures, jewellery, and books with drawings and hieroglyphic writing. Artists were highly educated members of the elite.

Ceramics were made from ground pigment, clay, and water. The pottery was covered with slip paint and decorated with images of rituals, myths, geometric patterns, and hieroglyphs. The Maya used ceramics as tableware, currency, incense burners, musical instruments, vases, and as containers for offerings to the dead. Clay pots were also made for cooking and storing food.

The Collapse of the Maya

Maya civilization appears to have collapsed very quickly. For many years, archaeologists did not have a good explanation for this. However, improved technology has provided scientists with new information. It is believed the Maya abandoned their ceremonial centres because of famine.

We now know that by about 900 CE, several droughts had destroyed the economy of the region. The Maya also used non-sustainable agricultural practices: (1) They used slash and burn to clear the land. (2) They planted crops in the same fields year after year instead of rotating fields to allow the earth to recover.

After a while, the land surrounding the cities was not fertile enough to grow enough food to support the population. Without enough food, many people starved. Most left the large centres in search of food elsewhere.

The Valley of Mexico

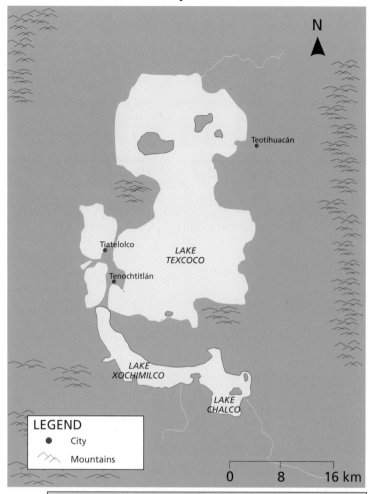

Figure 10.13 This map shows the area first settled by the Aztecs.

At some point, according to legend, Huitzilopochtli [wee-tseel-o-POCH-tlee], the god of war, told the Aztecs to search until they found an eagle sitting on a cactus eating a snake. They were to build their city where they found the eagle. The eagle was found on an island in Lake Texcoco. That is where they built Tenochtitlán. Today, the Mexican flag shows an eagle holding a snake in its talons, sitting on a cactus.

Figure 10.14 This map was drawn by the Spaniards in 1521 and shows the area where the Aztecs settled in what is now known as the Valley of Mexico. The original name of the Aztecs was Mexica [meh-SHEE-kah]. The descendants of the Aztecs still live near Mexico City. A modern form of their language, Nahuatl [nah-WAH-tl], is spoken by peoples of central Mexico. The Aztecs were preceded by Olmec, Zapotec, Teotihuacán, and Toltec civilizations.

AZTECS

Where They Lived

The Aztecs ruled an area that extended across Mexico from the Gulf of Mexico to the Pacific Ocean. The Aztecs maintained a well-trained fighting force and conquered the lands of their neighbours. Despite this, their power lasted less than a century before Cortés from Spain, in 1519, defeated them in his search for gold.

Where They Came From

The Aztecs probably arrived in the Valley of Mexico from the northwest. They had spent many years wandering from place to place, looking for somewhere to settle. Every time, they were driven away by neighbouring peoples.

Growing Up in Tenochtitlán

In this story, a young boy realizes how good his life is compared to many.

Tizoc looked up from his father's cloth stall in the Great Market. Among the thousands of people wandering through the square, he could see warriors dressed in brilliant feathers and jaguar skins. They were leading captives through the crowd. Each captive had one ear cut off. Soon their beating hearts would be ripped out as a sacrifice to Huitzilopochtli, the god of war.

Tizoc's father had taught him that the deities made the Aztecs the strongest people in the Valley of Mexico. If they were to remain powerful, it was very important to keep the deities happy. This was why human sacrifices had to be made.

Tizoc's people were both tough and clever. In less than 100 years they had converted a dirty, salty swamp into productive land. They built dams to create reservoirs. By controlling the streams that fed the lake, they had fresh water for drinking, bathing, and irrigating the farmland. They built *chinampas* [chee-NAHM-pahs] to increase the amount of land they could farm. (See figure 10.18)

The Aztecs conquered many of their neighbours. The conquered were required to pay a tribute (a kind of tax) to the Aztecs twice a year. This tribute could be paid in gold, jewels, food, or even human sacrifices to the gods.

Tizoc knew that he was lucky. Most people were unable to improve their position in Aztec society. If you were born a slave, you were likely to die a slave. Tizoc's father had been born a commoner. He had become a noble because he was a great warrior, and he had managed to become wealthy by working as a trader.

Traders lived exciting lives. They travelled great distances and brought back food, products, and ideas from faraway places. They exchanged Aztec products such as cloth, blankets, clothes, and knives, for jade, emeralds, jaguar and puma skins, and the feathers of the quetzal bird. Traders also lived dangerous lives. On their travels, they often had to defend themselves against robbers. Tizoc wasn't afraid. He was looking forward to the day his father took him on one of his trips.

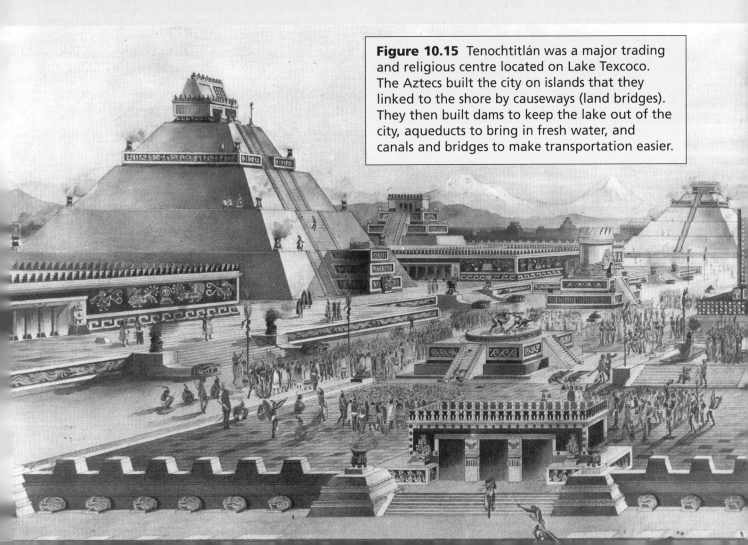

Figure 10.15 Tenochtitlán was a major trading and religious centre located on Lake Texcoco. The Aztecs built the city on islands that they linked to the shore by causeways (land bridges). They then built dams to keep the lake out of the city, aqueducts to bring in fresh water, and canals and bridges to make transportation easier.

Social Organization

Everyone belonged to a **calpulli** [kahl-POO-lee], a group of families descended from the same ancestor. Each calpulli chose its own leader to represent it in the government. The calpulli gathered its own taxes for the state and provided soldiers when they were needed. It also maintained its own temple and a school for boys to attend.

Aztec society consisted of three classes: the nobles, the common people, and the slaves. The nobles (priests, warriors, administrators) governed the state. The commoners – the merchants, farmers, and craftspeople – did the everyday work. The slaves worked the land of the nobles. Slaves were prisoners of war, criminals, or people who were forced, in hard times, to sell themselves in exchange for food and shelter. Slaves were usually treated well and could buy back their freedom. Their children were free.

The emperor was above everyone. Aztec emperors were elected (usually from the members of a royal family) and were treated like deities. Their meals were feasts, they lived in huge palaces, and they wore beautiful clothes. The emperors appointed the judges, generals, governors, and chiefs of the peoples conquered by the Aztecs. Their sons ran the different departments of the Aztec government.

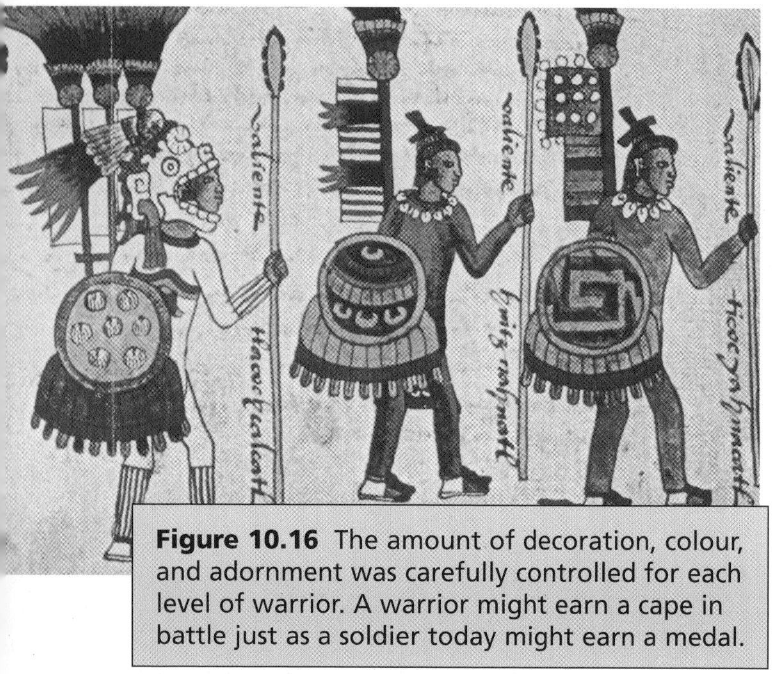

Women were valued for their ability to bear children. A woman who died in childbirth received the same honours as a warrior who died in battle. It was believed that she would become a goddess after death and help carry the sun across the sky.

Figure 10.17 An Aztec woman is teaching her 14-year-old daughter to weave using a back-strap loom. To use the loom, the weaver wraps the strap around her waist and attaches the other end of the loom to a stable object. This allows the weaver the mobility to work indoors or outside, at home or at the marketplace. This type of loom is still used in Mexico.

Aztec laws were simple and harsh. Death was the penalty for almost every crime, including stealing. Some crimes were punished by severe corporal punishment or mutilation. For example, the penalty for telling a lie was the loss of one's lips.

Figure 10.16 The amount of decoration, colour, and adornment was carefully controlled for each level of warrior. A warrior might earn a cape in battle just as a soldier today might earn a medal.

Aztec Social System

Ruler
|
Nobles (priests, army commander-in-chief warriors, administrators)
|
Commoners (merchants, farmers, craftspeople)
|
Slaves

What They Ate

The Aztecs raised turkeys and dogs, and they ate both. They also ate snakes and rats. Some people trapped ducks, hunted game in the mountains surrounding the valley, and fished. Fortunately, the Aztecs had spirulina, which they collected from the lake and swamps and made into protein-rich cakes.

Like the Maya, the Aztecs ate a lot of corn. Each morning the women made tortillas from ground corn. The Aztecs ate the tortillas in the morning and again at night with beans, chili peppers, fish, spirulina, or meat.

Most Aztec families tended their own garden and grew fruits and vegetables. All surplus produce was stored for future use. Knowing how to grow and store food was very important. Stored food could be used in times of drought. Surplus food supplies also gave some people the time to develop specific skills – for example, skills in architecture and art to design impressive buildings and to craft beautiful works of art – instead of spending all of their time farming.

In Lake Texcoco, the blue-green alga called *spirulina* (a water plant) was eaten by the Aztecs and was considered a delicacy. Since the alga is 65-75 percent protein and easy to grow and digest, some people suggest it should be harvested to help feed the world's hungry people.

Figure 10.18 Chinampas were made by placing large wicker frames in shallow parts of lakes and then piling earth on top. The roots of the plants reached down through the bottoms of the frames and attached themselves to the lake bottom.

Farming

Farming was the basis of Aztec economy and society. The Aztecs used simple hoes and digging sticks to plant crops because they did not have ploughs or the animals to pull the ploughs. Their main crops were corn, peppers, tomatoes, beans, and squash.

All available land was farmed. The Aztecs built terraced farms on the hills that surrounded them. They increased the availability of farmland by draining swamps and by creating chinampas.

The oldest known corn is about 5400 years old and was discovered in the highlands of southwestern Mexico. The cobs were only about 1.5 centimetres long and consisted of two to four rows of kernels. The Aztecs developed different varieties of corn by cross-breeding. Today, this process of altering the characteristics, or genetic makeup, of living things is called *biotechnology*.

By the time Christopher Columbus arrived in the Americas in 1492, corn was growing from Canada to the southern tip of South America. It grew as easily at sea level as it did in the mountains at 3300 metres. It grew in areas of heavy rain and in areas where little rain fell.

Housing

Most Aztecs lived in simple homes that consisted of one or two rooms and a place to cook. The walls were made of wattle (sticks interwoven with branches, twigs, or reeds) covered in mud. The roofs were made of thatched leaves from the **agave** plant. Smoke from the fires inside escaped through the loosely bound roofs. Most homes had very little furniture – low wooden benches, boxes and baskets for storing clothing and tools, and reed mats, which were used to sleep on.

As in Maya towns, the homes of an extended family shared a courtyard and garden plots. This cluster of homes and land, called a *calpulli*, was owned jointly by the family. Each individual family had enough land to produce sufficient food to feed itself.

The wealthy (important priests, military leaders, and government administrators) lived in two-storey palaces with many rooms. The palaces were made of stone or **adobe** (sun-dried brick) and had flat roofs. Often these homes were built on raised stone foundations to keep them dry in times of floods.

Education

In the most ancient societies, girls were trained in their homes from an early age for their role after marriage. With few exceptions, Aztec women married when they were about sixteen years old. A woman's status in society was dependent on the status of her husband. Some women became priestesses and served in the temples.

Women were expected to raise the children, cook, weave, and manage the household. Skill in weaving was highly prized.

Male children between the ages of twelve and fifteen attended school. At school, they learned religious songs and public speaking. They also studied history and religion. Young nobles attended temple schools. They were trained to be soldiers, priests, lawyers, and engineers.

Although women had fewer legal rights than men, they could participate in business, own property, and take legal action. A husband was supposed to respect these rights, and a woman could have much influence in the home. In fact, the word for *wife* in the Aztec language means "one who is owner of a man." If a woman was mistreated by her husband, she could divorce him.

Figure 10.19 This mask is made of turquoise and may portray the goddess of water. It shows the artistry of Aztec craftspeople. Much Aztec jewellery and many masks were made of gold and silver. The Spaniards melted most of these down and transported the precious metals back to Spain. As a result, much of Aztec artistry has been lost forever.

The cape was a very important piece of clothing. Aztec laws prescribed the length, type of fabric, amount of decoration, and the correct way of knotting a cape, and it was determined by a person's place in society. Often, the Aztecs demanded capes as a form of tribute from the peoples they conquered.

What They Wore

Only priests and warriors dressed in bright colours, furs, and headdresses made of feathers. High-ranking people wore cotton. The most colourful cotton garments had fine embroidery and were reserved for the emperor.

Common people were not allowed to wear cotton. Instead, their clothes were made from coarser materials. Their clothes were less colourful and less ornamented than the clothes of the rich.

Most clothes were made of lengths of uncut cloth. Men wore loincloths. Some also wore capes over their shoulders. These capes were similar to **serapes** [sare-RAW-pees]. Women wore long skirts and poncho-like tops.

Religious and Spiritual Beliefs

Like the Maya, the Aztecs practiced human sacrifice. Both men and women were sacrificed at certain times in almost every month of the Aztec calendar. For example, sacrifices were made at the dedication of a new temple or when a new emperor was chosen. One emperor is believed to have sacrificed as many as 20 000 people at the dedication of the main temple at Tenochtitlán. Both Aztecs and the peoples they conquered were sacrificed to the deities.

The Aztecs believed that without these human sacrifices their deities would not have the strength to carry the sun across the sky. If the sun could not rise, the Aztecs would die. Therefore, they had no choice but to offer the hearts of their sacrifices to the deities.

The New Fire Ceremony was held every fifty-two years – at the beginning of a new century on the Aztec calendar. Before the ceremony, all fires in the Aztec world were put out. All pottery and statues of deities were destroyed.

At the ceremony, someone of importance was sacrificed to the sun god. (It was a great honour to be chosen!) To begin, a fire was started on the person's chest. Priests then cut open the chest, ripped out the heart, and threw it into the fire. After the ceremony, the body was burned, and torches were lit from this fire.

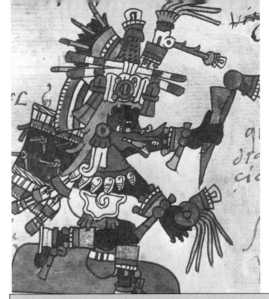

Figure 10.20 Cortés learned of the legend of Quetzalcoatl [ke-tsal-KO-atl] from neighbouring people hostile to the Aztecs. These people helped him dress and act so that the Aztecs would believe he was Quetzalcoatl.

The Legend of Quetzalcoatl

In 1521, a few hundred Spanish soldiers defeated an Aztec army of thousands. While the Spaniards had guns, cannons, steel weapons, and horses and the Aztecs did not, the Spaniards were greatly outnumbered. Some historians believe that an Aztec legend about a fair-skinned god who would come to defeat the Aztecs was responsible for their destruction.

The god, Quetzalcoatl, no longer wanted human sacrifices. This angered the other deities, and they tricked him into getting drunk. In shame, he destroyed his palace, buried his treasures, and sailed east, away from his people.

As it happened, the Spaniards came to Tenochtitlán in the year that Quetzalcoatl had said he would return. The Spanish leader, Hernán Cortés, was fair-skinned and bearded as Quetzalcoatl was said to have been. When Moctezuma, the Aztec emperor, and his advisers heard that the Spanish soldiers were advancing, they believed that the legend was coming true and that their fate was sealed.

By the time the Aztecs realized that Cortés and the other fair-skinned people were not deities, Tenochtitlán and the huge Aztec army had been destroyed.

INCAS

Where They Lived

The Incas called their empire the "Four Quarters of the World," because they believed they had conquered the whole world. At its height, the Inca Empire covered an area 4800 kilometres long and 960 kilometres wide that stretched from present-day Ecuador in the north to Chile in the south and from the Pacific Ocean to Bolivia.

The geography and climate of the empire varied greatly. In the Andes Mountains, it was hot during the day and very cold at night. In the treeless, desert coastline, the climate was hot and dry. In the jungles, it was hot and wet.

Where They Came From

Like the Maya and the Aztecs, little is known about the origins of the Incas. For many years, they were no more powerful than other peoples in the Andes. They were constantly building alliances to deal with threats from strong enemies or gain advantages over weak neighbours.

By the time Topa Inca died in 1493, the Inca Empire included a population of millions. In a span of about fifty-five years, the small city of Cuzco had expanded into the most powerful state in the Americas.

Social Organization

The Inca Empire expanded by conquering neighbouring peoples. To maintain control of so many people in such a vast area, it was a highly regimented society. The emperor, believed by the Incas to be a descendant of the sun god, maintained his power through a tight system of control. The emperor's sons were his most important advisers. Each quarter of the empire was governed by a trusted relative. Each governor appointed officials to lead smaller groups of 1000 people. The officials appointed people to rule 100 people. The smallest level of organization had officials who controlled groups of ten people.

The leaders of conquered peoples became part of the Inca government. After conquering an enemy, the Incas made sure that an Inca princess married the chief of the conquered people. They then trained some of the chief's family as administrators for the empire.

Like the Romans, the Incas built roads to make it easy to reach all parts of their empire. Commoners were not allowed to travel on the well-developed roads unless they received authorization. Sections of this road system still exist today.

Language was also used to help unite the peoples of the empire. Wherever the Incas conquered, they made people learn their language, Quechua.

The Inca Empire

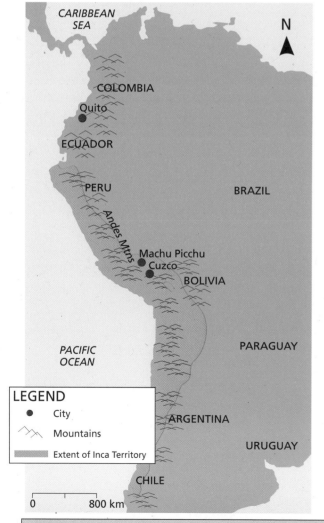

LEGEND
- ● City
- ⌃⌃⌃ Mountains
- ▬ Extent of Inca Territory

Figure 10.21 The map shows the extent of the Inca Empire.

Born Equal – Treated Unequally

In Inca society, girls did not have the same opportunities as boys.

As they worked on the terraced potato fields, Mamani talked excitedly to his sister, Doña, about the race the next day. This race was to choose runners, or *chasqui* [CHAS-kee], to carry messages to their king – Topa, the Sapa Inca.

The Incas had built 5000 kilometres of excellent roads through mountains, over rivers, and along the ocean shore. They had built rope bridges to cross the rivers and canyons. The roads were used by the chasqui, the traders, and the army to move quickly to any part of the empire.

Mamani and Doña were twins. They were fourteen years old. Soon their lives would be very different. Mamani hoped to become a chasqui. Doña would work at home. She was already learning how to plant crops and weave.

"It's time to go," Doña said as the sun sank behind the mountains. "I'll race you home."

Just beyond the last terrace, Mamani fell on some rocks. His face was twisted in pain as he pulled himself up from the ground.

"Are you all right?" Doña asked him.

"All is lost," he replied sorrowfully. "Look at my ankle. It's already starting to swell. I don't think I'll be able to run in the race tomorrow. Now I'll never be a chasqui."

Doña said nothing, but her mind was turning. "Could I race for Mamani?" she wondered as she helped her brother home.

At home, she thought more and more about the race the next day. If her brother didn't run in it, he would lose his chance to be a chasqui. She could run in the race in Mamani's place. She looked like him, and she ran just as fast. She would have to be very careful, though. Inca law prevented girls from running in these races. To disobey the law might mean death for her. Or her entire village might be forced to march thousands of kilometres because she went against the word of the Sapa Inca. How could she dare to break his law?

Doña didn't know what to do. She had been brought up to follow the rules. The laws were harsh, yet the Sapa Inca seemed fair. When people in the village fell on hard times, he provided them with food and clothing from his storehouses. Should she disobey such a fair and powerful person? For Mamani, she knew she had to.

Mamani was furious when she told him her idea. He refused to co-operate. "Please don't do it," he begged her. "It's too dangerous." But Doña would not change her mind.

The race began by the main plaza of the city of Cuzco [KOOS-koej], close to their village. A few kilometres into the race, many of the runners were having a hard time running in the thin air of the high mountains, but Doña was used to it. With less than a kilometre to go, she heard her parents call out, "Keep going, Mamani, you can do it!"

The end of the race was near. She slowed down for a moment. If she didn't finish the race, no one would notice her. If she completed it in a time that would ensure Mamani became a chasqui, the organizers might find out that she was a girl. "Well," she thought as she picked up her pace, "Even my own parents think I'm Mamani."

If you were Doña, what would you do?

Figure 10.22 Inca traders used the llama to transport goods when travelling through the Andes Mountains.

What They Ate

People who lived in mountainous areas grew corn, potatoes, and millet. Closer to the ocean, farmers grew corn, cotton, and beans. The Incas were the first people known to plant potatoes.

What They Wore

Men wore a type of sleeveless, knee-length tunic and a cloak. The tunic was made by folding a rectangular piece of cloth in half and bringing the two ends together. The sides of the material were sewn, leaving spaces for armholes. A slit was cut into the folded end so that the tunic could be put on over the head. Women wore long dresses – often two or three at the same time – and capes. Both men and women wore wide, decorated belts.

Hats were important. The type of hat that a person wore indicated his or her rank in society. The shape and colour of the hat identified the wearer's home village.

Women spun wool and cotton thread to make the colourful fabrics the Incas wore. They wove the cloth on simple backstrap looms that were similar to those used by the Aztecs. (See figure 10.17.) The cloth was then coloured with dyes made from roots, flowers, and minerals. Among the sources of these natural dyes are the flowers from the Ñuchu and **madder** plants, and **cochineal** (insects that live on cactus plants). Many of their beautiful clothes have been preserved by the cold, dry climate of the Andes, and can be seen today in museums.

Figure 10.23 People dressed in simple clothes made from cotton or wool.

Housing

The Incas were farming people, but they had large cities such as their capital, Cuzco. Cities were well planned. Streets were set up in a grid. Major streets ended at a large central plaza where the market was set up. Important religious and government buildings surrounded the market.

Most homes were simple. Incas who lived in the mountains built their houses of stone with thatched roofs. Those who lived by the ocean made their houses of adobe. Houses usually had one room. They were built around a courtyard with their doors and windows facing this open area. Their steep, thatched roofs helped to keep out the cold and rain.

Fortress walls, great temples, and large buildings were made of huge stones. The stones had to be cut carefully because the Incas did not have mortar to hold them together. It is estimated that the walls of one fortress took 20 000 Incas thirty years to complete.

Villagers from outside the city came to the markets to barter for goods. The Incas did not use money. Animal furs, baskets, pottery, cloth, and food were exchanged. These goods came from all parts of the empire.

Farming

Most Incas lived simple, but difficult, lives as farmers. Farmers sometimes kept llamas for food and wool and alpacas for wool. (Both llamas and alpacas are members of the camel family.) The sure-footed llama is a good pack animal for mountain terrain.

Figure 10.25 The man on the left is using the *taclla* [TAHK-la], or foot plough.

The Incas had crude farming tools. For planting they used a digging stick that was shaped like a chisel. The men dug up the ground with this tool. The women followed behind the men and planted the seeds.

The Incas increased the amount they could grow in their mountain areas by terracing the sides of the mountains. Dry farmland was irrigated. The Incas used stones to make a pathway for water to follow as it came out of its source. They collected large amounts of bird droppings for use as fertilizer and spread them on the fields.

Figure 10.24 Terracing, which is still used today, involves flattening small parts of the slopes. Low stone walls are built to hold the soil. The sides of a terraced mountain look like giant steps.

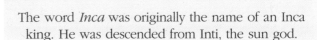

The word *Inca* was originally the name of an Inca king. He was descended from Inti, the sun god.

How the Incas Kept Records

The Inca did not have a written language. They used the *quipu* [KEE-poo] to help them remember important things.

The quipu was made of knotted strings and was about sixty to seventy centimetres wide. Each vertical coloured string represented a particular item. Knots showed the numbers of each item.

Each town had an official who gathered the information and recorded it by knotting the strings. Only the official knew what each knotted string meant. The quipu that have survived to this day are the only "documents" that the Incas left behind. Unfortunately, without "the rememberers" (the readers of the quipu), we can understand little of the meaning of the strings and the knots.

The history of the Incas was passed on by one rememberer to the next. In this way, the Incas controlled and even shaped their history. For instance, they deliberately refused to pass on the history of the peoples they conquered. As a result, we do not know much about the early history of the Incas. We know only of the creation myth they developed to explain how their nation began.

The Incas believed they came from the sun god, Inti, and his wife, Pachamama, who was goddess of the earth. Inti sent his son, Manco Capac, and daughter, Mama Ocollo, to teach people how to live. Inti's children carried a golden wedge. They placed it on the ground at the places to which they travelled. The wedge sunk into the ground at location of the city of Cuzco. Cuzco became the capital city and the place from which the Inca Empire grew.

Education

The only children who attended school were the sons of the Sapa Inca and nobles, and more gifted male children of commoners who showed intelligence and great promise in learning.

Boys who attended school were trained to be administrators for the empire. They learned the

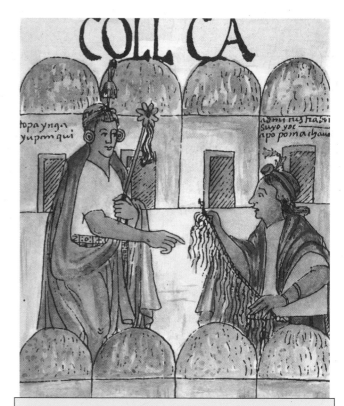

Figure 10.26 The Sapa Inca often sought information from the rememberers.

laws and geography of the country. Reading and writing were not taught because the Inca did not have a written language. However, arithmetic was important, and some boys were taught how to use the quipu. The schools were run by priests and were very strict. Children were beaten when they misbehaved.

Most children stayed at home and were expected to learn by watching their parents. Boys learned about hunting and preparing the ground for crops. They learned how to make furnishings for their homes. They were also trained to be soldiers. (Men could be called on to fight for the empire at any time.) Boys were considered to be men at the age of fourteen.

As in other ancient societies, girls learned how to cook, weave cloth, and sew clothing. The Sapa Inca and high priests chose some girls to receive an education in weaving, religion, and domestic arts. These girls also learned about various medicines and cures for ailments.

Religious and Spiritual Beliefs

Like the Maya and Aztecs, the Incas worshipped many deities. The most important were the gods and goddesses of the sun, the moon, corn, lightning, and rainbows. The Incas also worshipped the Sapa Inca because they believed he was a descendant of the sun god.

Each *ayllu* [l-yooj] (clan group) also had its own deities. These deities were given the first produce harvested from the fields. The Sapa Inca, the sun god, and other deities were also given part of the crop.

The corn-planting festival was an important religious event each year. The Incas depended on corn for food. To ensure a plentiful harvest, they had special ceremonies. The Sapa Inca himself was the first to plant the corn each season during the corn-planting festival. He used a digging stick of pure gold.

In all the villages, people worked together to plant the corn. They sang hymns to their deities as they worked. At the end of each day, people would dance and sing to the beat of small drums and the sound of reed flutes.

Medicine and Magic

The Incas lived in a warrior society. Surgeons frequently had to operate on warriors injured in battle, and so they had developed advanced medical techniques. They used instruments such as drills, saws, and chisels.

Archaeologists have found more than 10 000 skulls that had been operated on. The techniques used look similar to procedures that are used today to relieve pressure on the brain and apply prosthetics to the skull after surgery. From the conditions of the skulls, it appears that many patients survived their operations. Doctors today still use similar tools when they perform brain surgeries.

The Incas used medicines, such as the **coca leaf** and **quinine**, to reduce pain when they amputated limbs and set fractures. The resin from the balsa tree was used to stop bleeding. The Incas also used bandages, tourniquets, and forceps, and developed a technique for capping teeth.

Magic played a large part in the Incas' understanding of disease. The shaman (medicine man) used medicines and magical spells. He was well paid for his work, but he could also be held responsible if the patient died. In some city-states, when a patient died the shaman was tied to that patient and left to die in the desert.

The Arts

The Incas believed that all gold belonged to the sun god. They used gold in their buildings and artwork because they found it attractive.

The Spaniards, and other Europeans, valued gold and used it as money. When the Spanish soldiers conquered the Incas in 1532, they seized everything they could find that was made of gold and melted it all down into gold bullion. The only evidence that remains showing original artwork is found in tombs of earlier civilizations in the area, such as the Chimu.

Figure 10.27 This gold statue is from the Chimu [CHEE-moo]. The Chimu lived in northern Peru from about 500 CE to about 1500 CE.

Machu Picchu

In July 1911, an American archaeologist came across the city of Machu Picchu. It is situated in the Andes Mountains about 100 kilometres northwest of Cuzco. The Spaniards had not found Machu Picchu when they destroyed the Inca Empire 400 years earlier.

Its location, off a remote road high above a canyon, suggests that the city was a royal estate and religious retreat. It is estimated that about 1200 people lived in the city – mostly construction workers, gardeners, and others who looked after the retreat. Most of the 200 or so buildings found at the site were small houses and apartments, along with temples and storage facilities. Potatoes and corn were grown on the terraced slopes, and water from an underground stream was accessible.

Figure 10.28 Machu Picchu was probably abandoned by the time **civil war** broke out across the Inca Empire in 1527. Smallpox had already decimated much of the population, and Machu Picchu was just too expensive to maintain.

Achievements of the Maya, Aztecs, and Incas

The Maya, Aztecs, and Incas each controlled large areas of the Americas at different times. Each of these groups developed their society based on earlier civilizations.

The accomplishments of the Maya, Aztecs, and Incas were unknown to the rest of the world until long after the Spaniards had destroyed their civilizations. Unfortunately, much of their art, architecture, and culture remain a mystery.

The following are some of the areas in which the Maya, Aztecs, and Incas excelled:

- They used terraces and raised fields to increase the amount of land they could farm (see figure 10.24). They irrigated their crops and built aqueducts to transport water to their cities. In countries such as Bolivia, these centuries-old farming techniques are now being revived to increase the size of crops.

- They grew produce that was not grown anywhere else in the world at that time. For instance, more than half of the fruits and vegetables people eat today were developed by farmers in the Andes Mountains. The Incas grew 20 varieties of corn and about 500 kinds of potatoes. Other foods that were first grown in the Andes include tomatoes, squash, pumpkins, strawberries, and cocao (chocolate).

- They constructed large buildings and well-planned cities. Most were centred around a large plaza, which was the site of the market. The important temples and government buildings were located in and around the plaza. The main streets (and the canals of the Aztecs) all met at this plaza.

- They created beautiful art. They used gold, jade, feathers, obsidian, and turquoise. They decorated their temples and buildings with beautiful carvings, paintings, and statues. Pottery was as fine as any made in ancient Greece or Rome.

- The Maya and Aztecs built pyramids and palaces without using the wheel to help transport materials. They also did not have large animals like horses or oxen to pull heavy loads. Workers carried large blocks of stone in slings attached to their backs and supported by straps around their foreheads. New pyramids were often built on top of earlier ones to recycle building materials.

- Mayan writing was the most advanced in the Americas. (See the glyphs on page 202.) The glyphs were used on stelae, wall paintings, books, and pottery.

- The Maya developed a number system. It was easier to use than the systems developed by the Greeks and Romans. They used a dot to represent "1" and a bar to represent "5" so that two bars and two dots would represent "12." The system was based on units of twenty as compared to our own system, based on units of ten. The Maya used their number system to develop their calendar and to record their observations of the planets and stars from observatories.

Figure 10.29 El Carocol was the Maya observatory at Chichén Itzá. Astronomy, the study of stars, was an important science to the Maya.

Summary

The three societies studied in this chapter were highly developed and ingenious in what they were able to do. For example, the Maya grew and stored great amounts of food, which enabled some people to do things other than farm. They had time to study science, develop a system of writing, and create great works of art.

The Aztecs created aqueducts, dams, and canals to build their capital city, Tenochtitlán, on the islands in the swampy Lake Texcoco. The Incas had a strong army, and their fine system of roads helped them conquer most of their neighbours.

Historians think that the Maya, Aztecs, and Incas were as advanced as the societies of Mesopotamia, Egypt, or the Indus Valley. Their efficient growing of corn to support their large populations enabled them to focus on more than farming.

Connecting and Reflecting

Reflect on the daily life of the Maya, Aztecs, and Incas. Use the information that you have learned to describe the similarities *to* and differences *from* your life. Explain why knowing about these societies is important to you *as a citizen of Canada and a citizen of the world.*

The Middle Ages

Our Study of the Middle Ages

Our study of the Middle Ages includes the following topics:

- Becoming a Knight
- The Beginnings of Government
- Magna Carta
- Castles
- The Growth of Towns
- Guilds
- Marriage and Divorce
- Eleanor of Aquitaine
- The Black Death
- Jeanne d'Arc
- Medicine and Magic
- Religious and Spiritual Beliefs
- The Church Laws
- The Establishment of Islam
- Muslims in Europe
- Muslim Achievements
- The Crusades
- Other Peoples

In the 15th century, scholars referred to the years from about 500 CE to 1000 CE, the first part of the Middle Ages, as the *Dark Ages*. For these scholars, this period of time was "dark" because literature, art, and other cultural pursuits seemed to have declined. The scholars also knew little about this period as few written records had been kept. Today, we know that many important social and scientific developments took place throughout the Middle Ages.

Figure 11.1 Several families lived in small cottages on the estate of their lord.

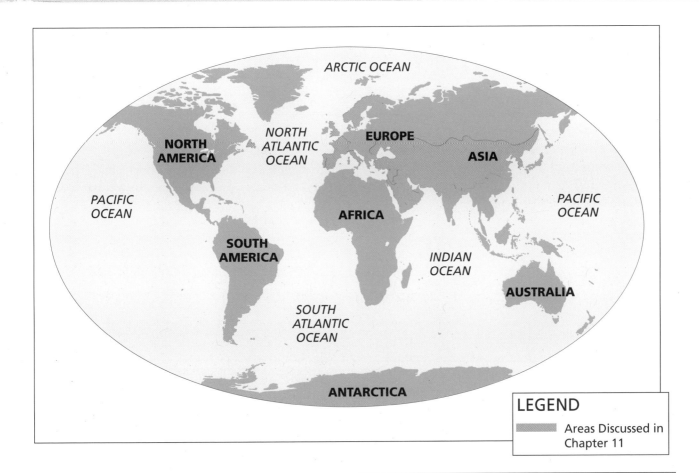

LEGEND

Areas Discussed in Chapter 11

After the Western Roman Empire ended around 476 CE, the former Roman territories were divided into many small kingdoms. A number of Germanic tribes fought one another for control of these kingdoms. Governments became more localized, with power exercised by local nobles or lords. The nobles and lords provided the king with soldiers in times of war. In return for their loyalty, the nobles received land, known as a *fief* or *feud*, from the king. This exchange led to the development of a new system of social organization called *feudalism*.

Feudalism is believed to have originated in what is now France then spread throughout western Europe.

Figure 11.2 This map shows areas of Europe, Asia, and North America mentioned in this chapter.

Questions to Think About

+ What geographic, political, and social factors shaped feudal society?

+ What was the role of religion in the Middle Ages?

Life at Different Levels of Society

The lives of the serfs remained separate from their lord and his family.

Marguerite Mancour and Françoise Huppert had never met, although they knew of each other. Marguerite had often seen Françoise ride by the fields on her beautiful horse. How different the two women were, Marguerite thought to herself, as her wooden clogs stuck in the muddy field.

Yet, in spite of their obvious differences, Marguerite and Françoise had much in common. Both women lived near the village of Limoges, France. Both were twenty-six years old and had three children. Each had been born to her position in life, and there was nothing that either could do to change her situation.

Marguerite and her husband, Guillaume Mancour, worked on the **manor** of Robert Huppert, Françoise's husband. The king had given Huppert control of a piece of land after Huppert helped the king defend his kingdom against invaders.

Marguerite and Guillaume lived on a section of this land. Guillaume worked his **selion**, a narrow strip of land that Huppert had allotted him, and shared a portion of his harvest with Huppert. He, along with all of Huppert's serfs, had to work the land Huppert kept for himself, the larger **demesne**, for three days each month. In return, Huppert allowed Guillaume to farm the plot of land and provided the Mancour family with protection and the use of a mill and common pastureland. These were Guillaume's tenant rights. Marguerite knew, however, that if Huppert ever went off to battle, Guillaume would be expected to fight with him.

She would have to take care of the home, the farm, and the children.

The Mancour's oldest child, Henri, aged twelve, already worked on the land beside his father. Nine-year-old Millette helped around the house and yard. Claude, a baby of two, was brought out to the fields to play while Marguerite, Guillaume, and Henri worked.

Marguerite had never travelled beyond Limoges. She had lived on the manor her whole life, as had her parents, her brothers, and her sisters. There were few means of transportation, and travel was very dangerous because of the threat of attack. Anyway, people needed little from beyond the local area. The community served all the needs of serfs like the Mancours. The land on the manor was fertile and provided all the food they needed.

Françoise and her husband, Robert, also had two boys and a girl. Charles, aged eleven, would take over the manor after his father died. Six-year-old Pierre was expected to become a squire on his seventh birthday. As a squire he would study to be a knight. At age five, daughter Lisette was beginning to learn how to be a lady of the manor, like her mother.

Both Françoise and Marguerite had lost two children from infections before the age of two. While few babies died in childbirth, one out of every three children died from some kind of disease such as cholera before six years of age.

Feudal System Hierarchy

King
|
Nobles/Lords
|
Knights/Squires/Pages
|
Serfs

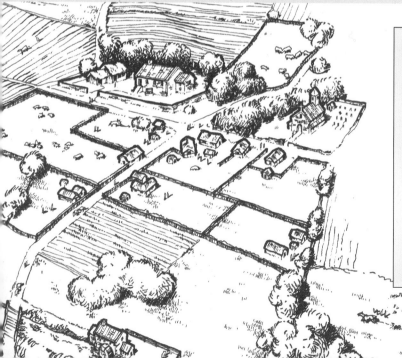

Figure 11.3 A feudal manor was divided into three sections of fields. One section was planted with winter wheat. The second was planted with spring wheat, rye, barley, and vegetables. The third section was left fallow (uncultivated). Each of the fields in these sections was then divided into long, narrow strips for cultivation. Of these strips, some were kept by the manor lord, while the serfs divided the remaining strips equally among themselves. Serfs shared a common pasture and had to co-operate with each other. As few of them could afford both a plough and enough oxen to pull it, they often worked together. They also shared the tools needed for farming, most of which were owned by the lord of the manor.

Freedom or Security?

Serfs like the Mancours were not free. They were bound to the lord of the manor – men like Robert Huppert – and had to perform a number of duties. These included working their selion and the lord's demesne and paying a tithe, or tax, in food to the lord. Many serfs objected to their lack of freedom. They resented giving up part of their crops to the lord or fighting the lord's battles. Some rebelled or ran away to become free peasants.

Since free peasants had no security or protection however, being a member of a feudal community was attractive to most. Serfs who remained loyal to their lord had the use of a piece of land, shelter, employment, enough food to eat, a church to attend and receive God's blessings, and protection from attack. It was not unusual for free peasants to volunteer to become serfs of a manor lord.

Becoming a Knight

Knights were fighters who served under nobles and lords, and they were expected to go to war whenever their king demanded it.

To become a knight, a male had to be born the son of a knight or a nobleman. When a boy was seven years old, he was sent away to train as a *page*. A page served his **apprenticeship** at a castle, waiting on both ladies and knights. Pages learned dancing, singing, courtly manners (how to act in a respectable fashion towards ladies), and were told tales of heroic deeds by great knights. Pages also polished armour and cleaned chain mail (by rubbing it in a bucket of sand).

When a page turned fourteen, he became a *squire* and apprenticed directly to a knight. A squire travelled to tournaments with his knight, carried his shield, helped him dress for the event, and provided him with water. In addition, a squire learned wrestling to develop strength. He also practiced jousting on the quintain, a dummy on a pole with a shield in one hand and either a heavy sack or a spiked iron ball in the other. For the squire, the goal was to hit the shield with a lance without being knocked off his horse by the sack or ball.

When a squire was seventeen, he could become a knight. First, though, he had to prove himself in either a real or mock battle, whether a **mêlée** or a **joust**. If he was deemed worthy to become a knight, the squire knelt before the lord or nobleman who touched him on the shoulder with his flattened sword. The new knight then gave an oath of fealty, or loyalty.

Figure 11.4 In return for his loyalty and service, a knight received a manor to administer. Most knights, though, had little interest in managing an agricultural community. They left the daily responsibilities to their bailiff (sheriff), while they devoted their time to preparing for combat.

France During the Reign of Louis IX

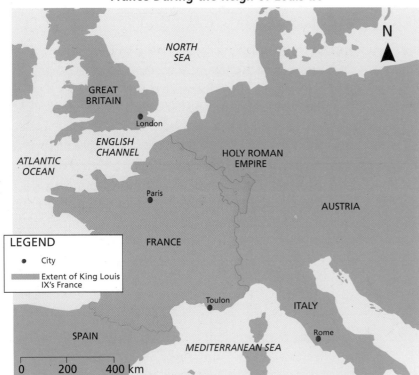

Figure 11.5 This map shows France during the reign of King Louis IX (1226-1270).

The Beginnings of Government

Feudalism was an arrangement among kings and nobles based on loyalty. Nobles swore an oath of fealty to the king. Nobles, in turn, gave out parcels of land known as *manors,* to their knights or lesser nobles, in return for fealty and a promise to fight for them when required. Feudal lords also promised their servants justice in feudal courts and protection in times of attack.

Most people in Europe lived as peasants or farmers. In western Europe, many were serfs on the estates of nobles.

Initially, feudalism created many small kingdoms throughout western Europe, each ruled by a powerful chieftain who took on the title of king. Kings were military leaders who ruled their land as hereditary monarchs. When a king died, his eldest son inherited the throne. A monarch's power came from his strength in

A form of feudal manorial system, known as the *seigneurial system,* was brought to New France (now Quebec, Canada), in the 1600s. There, habitants worked narrow plots of land administered by the seigneur or lord of the manor who ran the day-to-day affairs of the seigneurie. Habitants were expected to give part of what they grew to the seigneur and he, in turn, to the governor.

battle. Kings were often overthrown by more powerful kings or nobles. Kings relied on the loyalty of their nobles for support in time of war, and they expected their nobles to pay taxes. The noblemen, in turn, relied on their knights to provide soldiers. The system of fealty bound everyone to the king.

During Charlemagne's reign (he is also known as Charles the Great, king of the Franks, in what is now France) from 771 CE to 814 CE, the power of the king was entwined with the Christian church. Charlemagne promoted the spread of Christianity to territories his armies conquered. He also encouraged education in church-run schools. As a result of his deeds, in 800 CE, the pope in Rome crowned Charlemagne, Emperor of the Romans, or Holy Roman Emperor, defender of the faith. This action united both the politics of kings and the religious power of the pope and elevated the status of the Roman Catholic Church to proclaim kings. This unity, known as *Christendom,* lasted for over 700 years.

Through warfare and marriage, several kingdoms in Europe grew in size and power while others disappeared. In the 13th century, King Philip II and his grandson Louis IX enlarged the kingdom of France beyond the holdings of the various feudal lords. Under King Louis IX, power was centralized in Paris as the feudal nobles bowed to the king's authority. He reduced their independence and gave more power to himself. In this way, the modern-day image of a kingdom was created.

Ordinary peasants, serfs, and craftspeople had little say in the affairs of government. Even the concept of citizenship was limited as national identities were often

Many tradespeople were known in their village simply by their first name and the name of their craft; for example, Robert the Blacksmith or Robert the Smith. In time, surnames such as Carpenter, Smith/Schmidt (from Smith), Cooper (barrel-maker), Boulanger (butcher), and Miller developed from these occupations.

undefined. As towns grew in size, town officials, or **burghers**, began to exert more power over the population. In time, local councils were created with **burgesses** representing the townspeople and passing laws for the town. Burgesses were usually wealthy businessmen in the town. Serfs on manors had few rights beyond their tenant rights, and women had virtually no rights.

Figure 11.6 In 800 CE, the pope crowned Charlemagne as Holy Roman Emperor. The Holy Roman Empire was an attempt to revive the Western Roman Empire, which had been replaced by independent kingdoms in the 5th century CE. By the late Middle Ages, the emperor's powers had become mainly symbolic.

Magna Carta

In the early 1200s, English nobles accused King John I of breaking the feudal agreement that he had made with them. So angry were they with the king that they presented him with a document, called *Magna Carta* (Latin for "Great Charter"), that contained sixty-three demands. In 1215, he agreed to these demands. For example, he had to seek the consent of the barons before he raised taxes. He also agreed to return all lands that he had unlawfully seized for his own purposes. He could not imprison people without a trial (known today as the right of **habeas corpus**), and he could not deny or delay justice.

Later in English history, lawyers used Magna Carta as a means of limiting the power of kings and queens. The document is considered important to the development of democracy in England, as well as in other English-speaking countries such as Canada.

Figure 11.7 In June 1215, King John I and several English nobles met at Runnymede, a meadow by the River Thames to negotiate the document known as Magna Carta. When the king agreed to the demands put forth in the document, the barons and bishops renewed their oath of allegiance to the king. Today, four copies of the Magna Carta still exist.

Castles

Although castles remain the most visible reminder today of life in the Middle Ages, the age of castle building lasted only about three centuries. Castles were constructed for one purpose: defence. They were built on sites that offered the best defensive advantage, such as atop a hill or on a peninsula.

The first castles were known as *motte and bailey castles*. The motte was the hill on which the keep was constructed. The king or lord, his family, and the staff lived in the keep. The bailey housed the stables, storage, and barracks for the soldiers. Surrounding the motte and bailey was a wooden palisade, or fence. Because most motte and bailey castles were constructed mainly of wood, they did not offer sufficient protection and were soon replaced by stone castles.

Stone castles consisted of outer and inner curtain walls, with a tower at each corner. These castles are known as *concentric castles* because of their concentric rings of walls. A

The construction of a castle required the work of an estimated 400 stonemasons, 30 blacksmiths, 400 carriers, and 2000 labourers. It took as long as 10 years to construct a large stone castle.

gatehouse allowed passage into and out of the concentric castle and was the most heavily defended part of a castle. The castle had a drawbridge that swung upright when attackers approached, as well as a **portcullis** (a gate made of thick metal bars) and solid oak doors with drawbars behind them. Another portcullis and solid oak door were at the other end. Between them was a narrow corridor with arrow loops in the walls and a murder hole in the ceiling to drop stones or boiling oil on enemies who became trapped between the doors.

Inside the inner curtain was the inner ward, which housed the keep. The inner ward also included the Great Hall where everyone ate and socialized. Castles were cold, drafty, and damp. To make them more comfortable, tapestries were hung on walls, and fireplaces

Figure 11.8 To build a motte and bailey castle, workers first made the motte. They did this by digging a deep circular ditch and piling up the earth from the ditch into the centre. Sometimes, the motte was a natural hill, which was shaped into a usable mound and surrounded by a ditch. Mottes were between 3 and 30 metres high. When the mound was completed, its slopes were covered with an outer layer of clay. Sometimes the sides of the mound were strengthened with timber supports or stones to prevent uneven settlement and slippage of the earth. The bailey was built in the same way, but it was much larger around and lower in height.

Bailey

Keep

Motte

Moat

Trebuchet

Mangonel

were constructed in many of the apartments. Some later castles had running water: on the roof, rainwater was collected in a cistern that was connected to pipes throughout the structure. A **garderobe** was an indoor toilet connected to the cesspit below.

If a castle had a moat (a large ditch or trench), it was likely to be a dry moat surrounding the outer curtain wall. Water moats were connected to natural water bodies, but an enemy sometimes drained the moat by digging a trench to divert the water.

Attackers used elaborate weaponry and tactics to lay siege to castles; for example, siege towers, catapults like the *trebuchet* and *mangonel*, and tunnels dug under towers to erode their support. The arrival of gunpowder and cannons in Europe in the 1300s eventually made the purpose of castles obsolete.

Figure 11.9 Trebuchets and mangonels were both siege machines used to throw projectiles at or over castle walls. Both could fire objects as far as about 400 metres. The trebuchet was very accurate and could hit the same spot over and over again. The mangonel, which was the older of the two machines, was less accurate. It was, however, easier to move.

The trebuchet and mangonel fired rocks or burning objects (or vessels filled with flammable materials that created a fireball on impact) at the enemy. Sometimes partially decomposed carcasses of animals were hurled over a castle's walls. This tactic proved especially effective when food supplies inside the castle were low or rotting. When combined with the cramped living space of the defenders, poor hygiene, and infestations of vermin, the dead animals invited the spread of disease.

The Growth of Towns

Towns developed around castles and manor houses and became the centres of rural communities. Farmers sold the food they did not need in the town markets. Craftspeople such as cobblers (shoemakers) and shopkeepers who sold medicines (apothecaries) or fabric lived and worked in the towns.

Sometimes, the walls of a castle or manor house were expanded to include the various shops and homes around them. In times of conflict, people sought safety within the castle walls. The peace and prosperity of the later Middle Ages made castles and town walls less necessary. By then, towns and cities had grown beyond their walls. Often the walls were taken down, and the stones were used to construct new buildings. Walls can still be seen today in some European towns and cities such as York in northern England and throughout Italy. In London, England, several districts – for example, Bishopsgate, Aldgate, and Ludgate –

Figure 11.11 In the early Middle Ages, many towns developed within castle walls.

still bear the names of the gates to the old walled cities that were once there.

Town streets were not paved, and there were no sewers or drains. Buildings were made of wood, had plaster walls, and were usually two or three storeys. People threw their waste and garbage into the streets. Pedestrians walked with great care, since the contents of a bucket from a window above could land on them at anytime.

Most towns had some rules. For example, people had to clear the garbage in front of their houses. Families had to keep a ladder, a pole, and a tub full of water at the front of their house in case of fire.

A town of 2000 people was considered large. Cities developed from large trading towns. By the early 1300s, Paris boasted a population of about 200 000, while London's population exceeded 100 000.

Figure 11.10 Construction methods in the Middle Ages relied on the power generated by workers walking on a treadmill (see upper left).

Guilds

Today, people who work in similar trades or professions often belong to unions. Unions were created to protect workers and improve their working conditions (see page 328). The first unions, called *guilds*, were formed during the Middle Ages by craftspeople. Every craft, such as weaving, had its own guild, which set regulations for working conditions. Non-members were prevented from working in that craft.

Guilds established terms of apprenticeship, standards of quality, and prices. Failure of a business to meet these conditions could result in a fine, the loss of products, or even the loss of membership in the guild.

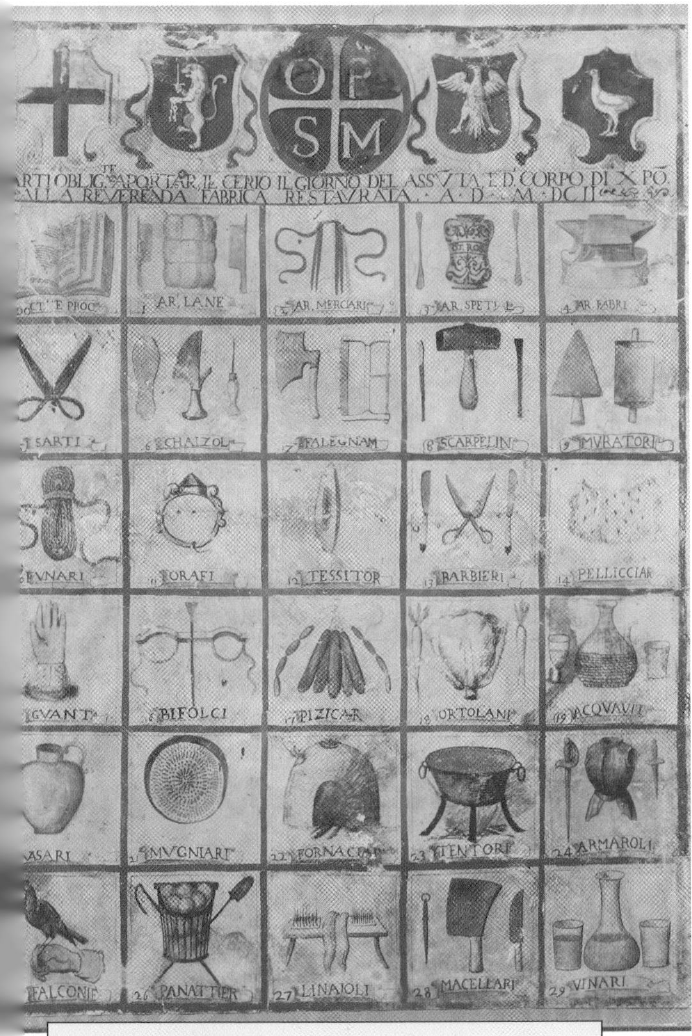

Each guild looked after its members. It helped members replace stolen tools. Guilds also provided aid to members who were ill and unable to look after themselves, as well as to members' widows with families.

Both women and men could belong to guilds. When a woman's husband died, she inherited her husband's position in the guild. In some guilds, such as the silk spinners', membership was made up mainly (sometimes solely) of women.

Figure 11.13 Both boys and girls could become apprentices. In this goldsmith shop, the young men on the left and right of the room are learning the basic skills of the trade.

Figure 11.12 Each guild had an emblem that represented its trade.

Figure 11.14 The inside of the Mancour's cottage looked like this. Most poor families lived in one-room or two-room cottages.

Life in the Homes of Rich and Poor

In this story, we learn about the foods the Mancours and Hupperts ate.

Marguerite and Guillaume Mancour's day began early. Marguerite's first task was to build a fire in the firepit in the middle of the main room of the two-room cottage. The sun was still not up as she stirred the porridge cooking over the fire. Most of the smoke from the open fireplace escaped through a hole in the thatched roof. Some smoke did linger inside, though, and rain and small animals could enter the cottage through the opening. There was only one window, and it was covered with an oiled animal skin stretched over the opening. The heat from the fire warmed the cottage.

While Marguerite was preparing breakfast, Guillaume was busy outside tending the pigs and chickens and milking the cow. When he returned to the cottage, Marguerite woke the children for breakfast. Although she was seven months pregnant, she still tended to all her duties and responsibilities.

Guillaume led his wife and children in morning prayer before Marguerite passed around bowls of porridge, goat cheese, and mugs of ale. She had been to the mill the previous week to grind some grain, so there was bread to eat as well. She had left one loaf at the manor as payment for the use of the lord's mill. The family ate at a table and sat on benches near the fire. Guillaume had made all of the furniture, including the wood-framed beds covered with straw.

Following breakfast, Marguerite, Guillaume, and Henri headed out to their field. As they walked through the village, they greeted other serfs and their families cheerfully.

Later that same day, Françoise Huppert was supervising the preparation of dinner at the manor house. Her house was not as grand as a castle, but it provided her family with comfort and safety. The Huppert's furnishings had been built by local carpenters. Tapestries, which hung on the walls and covered the windows when it was cold, helped to keep the drafty house warm.

Françoise was expecting Father André for dinner. Fresh straw was laid on the floor to absorb any spills. Trenchers (stale pieces of bread) were set out as plates. The bread absorbed the juices of the food and, at the end of the meal, was either eaten or given to the poor to eat. A knife was set to the right of each trencher. Most people ate with their hands, although a knife was often necessary to cut meat. A goblet was set beside every second plate and would be shared by two people.

When Father André arrived, dinner was served. The meal included roast rabbit, roast pheasant, turnips, carrots, peas, and prune custard. The goblets were filled with wine. It was a fine meal.

A bell sounded at sundown to signal the end of the workday. On her way home, Marguerite gathered firewood for the fireplace. Back at the cottage, she made stew for the family's evening meal. She put oatmeal, beans, and dumplings into a pot. Whole-grain bread left over from breakfast and drinks of ale completed the meal.

Noblewomen's dresses were often kept for a lifetime. Sometimes dresses were even willed to a woman's next of kin. In 1394, a wealthy Frenchman wrote a book of instructions to his fifteen-year-old daughter on how to be a proper housewife. Included in the instructions was advice for removing stains and grease spots from dresses and furs in order to preserve them for a lifetime of use. He also instructed his daughter on ways to keep her husband happy; for example, give him a good fire when he comes home each evening in winter and rid his bed of fleas in summer. As the book stated: "Some respite to husbands the weather may send but housewive's affairs have never an end."

Figure 11.15 The Huppert's home looked like this. The family lived on the second floor of the stone manor house. The first floor was used to store the produce grown on the manor. On the second floor were three rooms and a private chapel for prayer. The large fireplace was located along one wall. Huppert's wealthier neighbour lived in a home that had a fireplace in each room. The well was located just outside the door.

Marriage and Divorce

Few peasants had church weddings. Marriages were usually arranged by the couple's parents. In the early Middle Ages, two people could marry simply by telling each other: "I marry you." Usually they did this in some public place with their families and friends as witnesses. People from wealthier backgrounds had more involved marriages, often with contracts and church services.

After a church wedding, everyone went to the cemetery to pray for dead members of their families. As the couple returned home, friends threw handfuls of seeds over them and shouted: "Plenty! Plenty!" This was their way of wishing the couple a marriage blessed with many children.

Divorce was not officially allowed by the Christian church, but couples could be granted separations, and marriages could be annulled. Adultery and cruelty were acceptable reasons for seeking a church-supported separation.

Time for Fun

People liked to sing, dance, celebrate good news, listen to music, participate in sporting events, and attend plays. However, some recreational pursuits depended on a person's wealth.

For nobles, the most popular sporting activity was the tournament. Spectators watched teams of knights compete in a mêlée. Each side tried to do as much damage as possible to the opponent. The knight who remained standing or on horseback at the end of the match was the winner.

The jousting match was also popular. In this event, two knights, mounted on horses and carrying lances, charged headlong at each other in an attempt to knock the other off his horse. A tilt barrier, a long pole standing horizontally about one and a half metres from the ground, separated the two knights as they charged. In early tournaments, men were frequently wounded and sometimes killed. Later, knights wore heavy armour and used blunted weapons to avoid casualties.

Many knights travelled from one tournament to another. In addition to honour and prestige, they could win money, servants, and horses. On the other hand, losers sometimes had to forfeit everything they owned to the winner. Without a manor to oversee, these knights became known as *freelancers*. Today, the word refers to someone who independently provides a service for someone else.

Members of the nobility hunted fox, rabbit, and grouse in forests maintained for that purpose. For peasants, hunting was considered poaching, and if caught they were punished, sometimes by having a hand cut off.

Falconry was another favourite pastime of the very rich. Falcons, hawk-like birds, were trained to pursue and kill small animals or other birds such as pigeons. When falcons caught their prey, they brought it back to the falconers. Falconry was known as the sport of kings because of its popularity with the nobility.

For peasants, fairs were the most popular amusement. Jugglers, acrobats, minstrels, and musicians performed, and plays were often presented by guilds. People travelled from the neighbouring villages and manors to attend a fair. There, they saw and experienced things beyond their own manor or village.

Children of the nobility enjoyed skipping rope, and playing hoops, checkers, and chess. Children of peasants had few toys. They played games such as blindman's buff, follow the leader, and tag.

Figure 11.16 While many women of wealth painted as a pastime, few had their works displayed or preserved.

Figure 11.17 The first medieval tournaments were used to prepare knights for battle. Later, tournaments became great shows in which nobles tried to impress admirers and one another.

Figure 11.18 Travelling minstrels provided more than music; they told the news of the day in their songs. Through these songs, peasants learned of events from areas far from the manor. Some minstrels worked only for nobles, while others were hired full-time by towns. These town minstrels announced the time of day, sounded alarms, played fanfares for processions, and entertained the townsfolk.

Eleanor of Aquitaine

Eleanor of Aquitaine was born in the southern duchy of Navarre in 1122. In an era when noblewomen were expected to remain quietly behind their husbands and tend to domestic matters, Eleanor of Aquitaine charted her own course. Beautiful and intelligent, she was determined to have an interesting life. During her lifetime, Eleanor would become the queen of France and, later, the queen of England.

When she was fifteen, Eleanor inherited the duchy of Aquitaine from her father, an unusual circumstance in the Middle Ages. Soon after, she married Louis VII, king of France. Eleanor accompanied Louis on a crusade to Jerusalem, organizing a group of noblewomen she named "The Amazons" for the journey. To Eleanor, the crusade was a great adventure.

In 1152, Eleanor's marriage to Louis was annulled, and she returned to Aquitaine. There, at about the age of thirty, Eleanor married Henry Plantagenet. He was ten years younger and became the king of England in 1154. One of their sons, Richard the Lionhearted, played a major role in the crusades and was king of England from 1189-1199. When Eleanor's marriage to Henry ended in 1176, he had her confined to the Tower of London. She lived there and in other fortified buildings until Henry died in 1191. Eleanor died in 1204.

The word *holiday* comes from "holy day." In addition to Sundays, the Christian church had close to 100 holy days throughout the year. On these days, peasants did not have to work. Instead, they took part in religious or traditional ceremonies. Often they dressed up, danced, and feasted. At Christmas, the lord of the manor hosted a great feast with music and dancing for all his serfs. Not all holidays were welcomed by the poor, however, since many were not paid for days they did not work.

Figure 11.19 Eleanor of Aquitaine often witnessed the coarse way in which women were treated by noblemen, and she determined to change their attitudes towards women. She established a "Court of Love" to rule on knights' behaviour and to encourage greater respect for women.

Figure 11.20 The Black Death killed so many people that burial parties like this were quite common.

The Black Death

The **Black Death** was a deadly epidemic that wiped out about one-third of the population of Europe, about 20 million people, during the mid-1300s. Often called the Great Plague, it was caused by bacteria that passed into the human population when fleas, carrying infected blood from rats, bit people. The rats came from Asia onboard cargo ships.

In Europe, the plague began in Italy. It spread quickly in the crowded, dirty towns and cities. Townsfolk who sought refuge in the country spread the disease to rural areas. There was no known cure, although several remedies, including placing toads on the red welts of those stricken with the disease, were suggested. Many people believed the illness to be a punishment from God. They thought they could rid the world of the plague by showing God they could punish themselves. Using scourges, whips with nails in them, these *flagellants* paraded through the streets whipping themselves. The church later put a stop to the practice but not before many died from self-inflicted wounds. Some people blamed Jews for causing the plague. Several synagogues were destroyed, and a number of innocent Jews were murdered.

Pope Clement VI left his court in Avignon, France, for an estate called Chateau-neuf ("new castle"), on the River Rhone. He is said to have sat by a great fireplace in his manor house, praying that the fire and smoke would drive away the disease. Perhaps this strategy worked, because Clement survived the plague.

Eventually, the plague died out, although it reappeared periodically over the next three centuries. Improvements in sanitary conditions and the use of drugs helped to end the threat.

Jeanne d'Arc

Jeanne d'Arc (Joan of Arc) was born in 1412. Her parents were humble peasants. When she was only a teenager, Jeanne claimed that she heard the voices of St. Michael, St. Catherine, and St. Marguerite speaking to her. They told her that the future of France rested with her. At the time, France and England were at war.

Jeanne told this story to the man who would soon be King Charles VII of France. Despite her lack of military experience, Charles gave Jeanne the command of a force of French troops. Clad in shining armour and riding a white horse, Jeanne was an inspiring figure. The French troops rallied behind her, and they captured the cities of Orleans and Rheims.

Figure 11.21 Jeanne d'Arc, in her armour, rallied the French troops. In 1920, the Roman Catholic Church declared Jeanne a saint.

Unfortunately for France, Jeanne was captured. She was delivered into the hands of the English, who accused her of being a witch and burned her at the stake in 1431. Her death rallied the French, who eventually drove the English from French soil.

Medicine and Magic

Almost everyone lived in unsanitary conditions, was malnourished, had few medicines, and dealt with death constantly. No wonder those who lived beyond age forty-five were considered old. Life expectancy of a nobleman or a king was little better than that of the serfs and peasants who tilled the land.

Both people and animals were especially susceptible to diseases spread by body lice and fleas. They caused skin irritations that sometimes became serious infections. At times, epidemics of diseases such as typhus, cholera, smallpox, and influenza broke out. The causes of these diseases were not understood.

Doctors lived in cities and were available only to the wealthy. Surgical operations were rare. Although medical knowledge in the Islamic world was fairly advanced at this time, European doctors knew little about human anatomy and even less about the causes of diseases. Village healers – monks, nuns, or other local women – were often more effective than doctors at curing illness. These healers relied on magic and herbal remedies.

Midwives were, perhaps, even more important than doctors. Nuns and monks also played crucial roles in caring for the sick. Many medical discoveries were made at clinics and infirmaries established at monasteries.

Figure 11.22 This picture of a medieval hospital is from a book by Avicenna, a Muslim doctor. The book was written in Arabic in the 11th century. It was translated into Latin in the 12th century and became the standard textbook in European medical schools during the Middle Ages.

Religious and Spiritual Beliefs

The parish priest exerted great influence in the community. He was the spiritual link between the people and God.

Life for most peasants had few rewards. Violence, fire, and disease were constant threats. Religion offered a sense of purpose to people's lives. It gave them hope for a better life after their existence on Earth had passed.

Most people believed that their actions in life determined the destination of their souls in the afterlife. Attending mass regularly, showing charity towards others, and participating in the **sacraments** and church rituals were essential to earning God's graces and securing a place in heaven.

Each parish provided its priest with a plot of land, known as a *glebe*, for revenue. Those living in the parish took turns working this land. As well, parishioners had to pay a tithe to the church – one-tenth of their earnings, either in goods or produce. Priests also charged small fees for services such as weddings, baptisms, and burials.

While Christianity was clearly important, people also believed in magic, spirits, and witches. They observed the superstitions that they learned from their parents. The Roman Catholic Church sought to incorporate common pagan beliefs in order to appeal to the peasant population. For example, they established December 25th as the celebration of the birth

Most people could not understand church services, which were conducted in Latin, a language few could speak or write. Churches and cathedrals depicted biblical scenes and stories on their walls and in the stained-glass windows to educate the faithful in church beliefs.

of Jesus Christ. The date corresponds to the traditional end of the harvest and the beginning of the winter solstice pagan celebration. (Today, most historians believe Jesus was born in the spring.)

Monks

Young men had few career choices. Sons of peasants received part of their fathers' land, which they farmed for the rest of their lives. The sons (and sometimes daughters) of craftspeople usually apprenticed in their fathers' crafts. Sons of nobles and knights might consider careers as knights, scholars, or the clergy.

One option was open to young men from all walks of life: becoming a monk. Monks devoted their lives to God and the church, and they served the community. They also enjoyed the intellectual stimulation of books and of well-educated people.

Far from being places of seclusion, monasteries provided medical care for the sick, accommodation for travellers, and were centres of learning. Because monks were among the very few who could read or write, they taught the children of nobles and knights. Monks also wrote poems and music, translated and hand-copied books including the Bible, and recorded important events.

Nuns

Young girls had fewer career options than boys. Life as a nun was one of the only alternatives to a life of domestic work. Some noblewomen became nuns to avoid marriage or to develop talents in art, music, medicine, or teaching.

Nuns, like monks, lived simple lives of devotion and hard work. They served God and cared for orphans, the sick, and the homeless.

Figure 11.23 The children in this painting are taking writing lessons at a school run by monks.

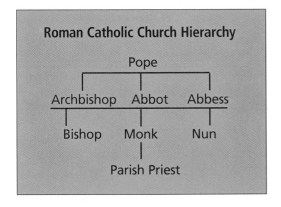

Roman Catholic Church Hierarchy

Pope

Archbishop — Abbot — Abbess

Bishop — Monk — Nun

Parish Priest

The first hospitals in Europe evolved from convents and abbeys. Today, many hospitals throughout the world are operated by orders of nuns.

Women were not allowed to become priests, but many noblewomen became **abbesses**. An abbess could rule over many manors and, therefore, rule over many serfs. Abbesses often exercised great power over lands, people, and even defence forces.

Church Laws

The church punished people who did not believe in or follow church practices or beliefs. The worst punishment was **excommunication** (banishment from the church). The neighbours of those excommunicated could not associate with them. The excommunicated could not go to confession or attend mass. They could not take communion or have their children baptized. Perhaps worst of all, they could not have the final religious rites when they died or be buried in holy ground. This meant that their souls spent eternity in hell rather than in heaven.

Law and Justice, Medieval Style

Punishment in the Middle Ages fit the crime.

Robert Huppert was summoned to settle a dispute between Guillaume Mancour and Jean Valotte. Guillaume had accused Jean of stealing two chickens. Jean denied the charge.

As lord of the manor, Huppert listened to both sides of the story. Jean had been found guilty of both stealing and poaching several times in the past. In each case, his family had been ordered to make up for the losses Jean had caused others. However, Jean's family had often failed to do this. This fact was important to Huppert's decision.

Two of the most common ways to settle a dispute were by **compurgation** and by ordeal. If compurgation was used (from the word **compurgator** meaning "to swear an oath before God"), eleven people would swear an oath for the accused's innocence. However, if the accuser produced eleven compurgators of higher rank or standing, then the accused was pronounced guilty. Huppert decided Jean's trial should be one of ordeal.

Three of the most common kinds of ordeal were by fire, by water, and by combat (often practiced by nobility, leading to the development of the duel).

Huppert told Jean that he must submit to ordeal by fire. An iron bar from a fire that had been burning all morning was placed in Jean's right hand. In tremendous pain, Jean stumbled five metres to the steps of the church and dropped the bar. His wife wrapped his aching hand in a cloth and led him home.

Ten days later, Huppert, his steward, and Father André arrived at Jean's cottage to inspect the wound. The hand was infected. "This man is guilty of theft. It is God's sign," announced Huppert. As Father André issued a hasty blessing, the steward's sword came down swiftly on Jean's wrist, severing his hand.

Figure 11.24 Some people were placed in the pillory as a punishment for wrongdoing. They were sometimes left in this structure for several days. This practice continued to be used well into the 1600s.

Spread of Islamic Faith, 900 CE

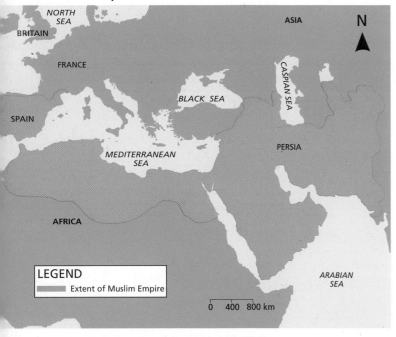

LEGEND
Extent of Muslim Empire

0   400 800 km

Figure 11.25 Muslim armies spread the Islamic faith by overtaking other peoples. This map shows the extent of the Muslim empire by about 900 CE.

The Islamic faith is based on The Five Pillars (duties):

Shahadah: declaration of faith in one God and Muhammad as God's final messenger

Salah: prayer five times a day

Sawm: fasting during the month of Ramadan

Zakah: giving 2.5 % of one's wealth to those in need each year

Hajj: pilgrimage to the city of Mecca

The Establishment of Islam

As Christianity grew in western Europe, the establishment of Islam was evident in other parts of the world.

Islam, with about 1.3 billion followers, is the second-largest religion in the world today. Islam is based on teachings of God that began at the time of Adam and Eve and ended with Muhammad. Muhammad was born in about 570 in Mecca, a city in present-day Saudi Arabia. As Muhammad grew up, he became troubled that Arabs worshipped many deities and spirits. Often, he retreated to a cave near Mecca to meditate. On one such occasion, Muhammad saw the angel Gabriel.

According to Muhammad, Gabriel told him that there was only one god. God was all-knowing and all-powerful. God decided the fate of all people, and good people who believed in God would be rewarded. God's teachings were called *Islam*, which means

"submitting to God." Believers in Islam call themselves *Muslims*, or "those who submit to God." Muslims (as well as Arab Christians and Jews) call God by the name *Allah*, which means, literally, "The God."

Muhammad was persecuted in Mecca for preaching the words of God. In 622, Muhammad and his followers fled to the city of Medina (now in Saudi Arabia). Soon Muhammad and his followers dominated the city. Muhammad's journey from Mecca to Medina is known as the *hijrah* and marks the start of the Islamic calendar.

In 630, two years before he died, Muhammad returned to Mecca with his followers and overtook it. Today, Mecca continues to be the holy city for Muslims worldwide.

Muhammad was the last prophet chosen by God to spread the message that there was only one god. That and other messages that Muhammad received from God during his twenty-three years of prophethood were memorized, recorded, and compiled into a book called the *Quran*. For Muslims, the verses of the Quran are the final word in matters of faith and practice. The Quran is to Muslims what the Bible is to Christians. Muslims believe that the prophets of the Bible were sent by God before the prophet Muhammad was sent. These include Abraham, Noah, Moses, and Jesus.

All Muslims are supposed to pray five times a day, facing in the direction of Mecca. When they pray, Muslims kneel, bow, and recite verses from the Quran. They touch their foreheads to the ground, signifying their submission to God. Muslims are expected to make a pilgrimage, known as the *Hajj,* to the holy city of Mecca at least once in their lives.

Muslim women had more rights than Medieval European women. According to the Quran, they could inherit property and could take part in business.

Muslims in Europe

In 711, a North African Muslim Berber general named Tariq ibn Ziyad crossed the Strait of Gibraltar (named Jabal al-Tarik or Tariq's mountain) into Spain. With a combined force of Arabs and Berbers, he defeated the Visigoths (a tribe of Germanic barbarians) and set up a Muslim state in Spain. Muslim rule in Spain lasted 700 years. The Arab and Berber Muslims, known as the **Moors**, built a centre for learning in Cordova. For several centuries, this centre attracted scholars from all parts of Europe to study Muslim science, medicine, architecture, literature, as well as the works of the Greeks preserved by Muslim academics.

From Spain, Muslim armies pressed farther into Europe, but their advance was stopped at Tours, France, by Charles "The Hammer" Martel, leader of the Franks, in 732. Three years later, Muslim forces were defeated at Avignon, ending their attempts to conquer western Europe.

In eastern Europe, Constantinople resisted Muslim attempts to capture the great city. In 1071, Asia Minor (Turkey) fell under Muslim rule when the Seljuk Turks took it over. By the mid 1300s, the Ottoman Turks, successors to the Seljuks, had bypassed Constantinople to take control of the Balkans, the land around

At its peak around 1000 CE, the city of Cordova, Spain, boasted schools, libraries, a university, paved streets with street lights, 3000 mosques, over 80 000 shops or businesses, and several ornate gardens. It was regarded as one of the most beautiful cities in Europe. Many buildings were decorated in *arabesque,* a calligraphic-like design characteristic of Arab art.

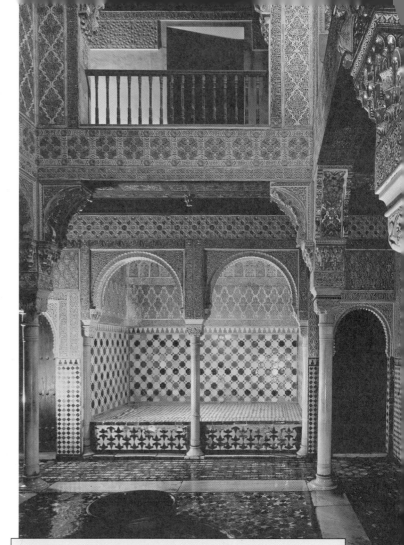

Figure 11.26 The Alhambra was built by Moors as a palace and citadel during the 13th and 14th centuries. The photograph above shows a section of the Alhambra, located in Granada, Spain.

the Black Sea, Greece, and Serbia as far north as the Danube River. In 1453, following a three-month siege, twenty-one-year-old Ottoman sultan Mehmet II and his forces did what many other Muslim leaders had failed to do – overrun Constantinople.

Under Muslim rule, the city continued to prosper as a trading centre and as a cultural bridge between Europe and Asia. Orthodox Christianity was allowed to continue although the Hagia Sophia became a mosque for Muslim worship. Christians were allowed to keep their religion because, like Muslims, they believed in one god, but they had to pay a tax, known as the **jizyah**.

Figure 11.27 By 1000 CE, Muslim doctors had set up pharmacies to dispense medicines to the sick.

Muslim Achievements

The height of the Islamic empire occurred under the rule of the Persian Abbasid dynasty centred in Baghdad (750-1055).

- Islamic doctors made many great contributions to the field of medicine. Avicenna (Ibn Sina) wrote *The Canon of Medicine*, a medical text considered so comprehensive that it was used in Europe into the 17th century.

- Al-Hazen determined that the eye receives rays of light from objects, dispelling the long-held belief that the eye emits rays. This discovery was key to the later development of eyeglasses.

- Al-Razi developed vaccinations for diseases like smallpox.

- Muslims learned and adopted the Arabic number system from Hindu traders from India.

- Muslims made many advances in mathematics, including the development of algebra and the use of x as the unknown factor.

- Muslim scientists described the eclipses of the sun and the effect of the moon on oceans.

- Islamic maps featured some of the most accurate outlines of Asia, Africa, and Europe.

- Alchemists discovered the basic building blocks of chemistry through experiments in crystallization and distillation to determine the chemical composition of objects.

- In the 12th century, Jewish physician, Moses Maimonides, who served the Abbasid ruler, wrote one of the earliest books on psychology, titled *Guide to the Perplexed*.

- Muslim scholars loved poetry, especially the writings of the Persians. The Persian poet Omar Khayyam wrote *The Rubaiyat*, which remains one of the greatest epic poems of all time. The exploits of the Abbasid ruler Harun al-Rashid became the basis of *The Arabian Nights*, including the stories of Aladdin and the lamp and Ali Baba and the forty thieves. The tales in *The Arabian Nights* were supposedly told by a slave girl, Scheherazade. To save herself from execution, she had to tell a new story every night for 1001 nights. She was always careful to leave the stories unfinished so that she could carry on the next night. In the end, she won her life.

The Crusades

Towards the end of the 11th century, Muslims were expanding farther into the Eastern Roman Empire, centred at the city of Constantinople. They eventually prevented pilgrims from reaching the Christian shrines. Christians in Europe were outraged.

When Emperor Alexis of the Byzantine Empire asked for help from his fellow Christians in the west, Pope Urban II called for a crusade to force the Muslims out of the "holy lands." Priests encouraged their parishioners to join the crusade. As a result, thousands of noblemen put on their armour and left home to follow the "will of God."

In time, the motive for joining the crusades was not purely religious. The crusades provided young men with opportunities to achieve wealth and to have an adventure at the same time. This attitude was especially true for younger sons. According to feudal laws, the oldest son of a noble inherited his father's land. Younger sons received nothing. By joining the crusade, these younger sons might return with riches that they had seized from those they conquered.

The Children's Crusade

In 1212, almost 30 000 French and German children joined a children's crusade to the holy lands to fight the Muslims. The average age of these children was only 12. Some of the young French crusaders boarded ships in Marseilles but were sold into slavery by their shipmasters. The German children set off on foot, believing that they were heading for the Mediterranean Sea. Most died before ever reaching the sea either from disease or from the difficult journey.

Several major crusades were organized between 1095 and 1300. During The First Crusade, 1095-1099, Christians captured Jerusalem and set up several kingdoms in the holy lands. The Christian hold on the territory was weak, however. Within two centuries, Muslims had driven the crusaders from the Middle East and refused Christians access to Jerusalem. In 1192, the Muslim Seljuk sultan Saladin and Richard the Lion-Hearted, king of England, negotiated a peaceful resolution allowing Christians safe passage to Jerusalem.

Figure 11.28 Pilgrimages, religious journeys to shrines or holy sites, became very popular in the 11th century. Canterbury in England and Santiago de Compostela in Spain were popular destinations for Christians, but a visit to Jerusalem was the most significant.

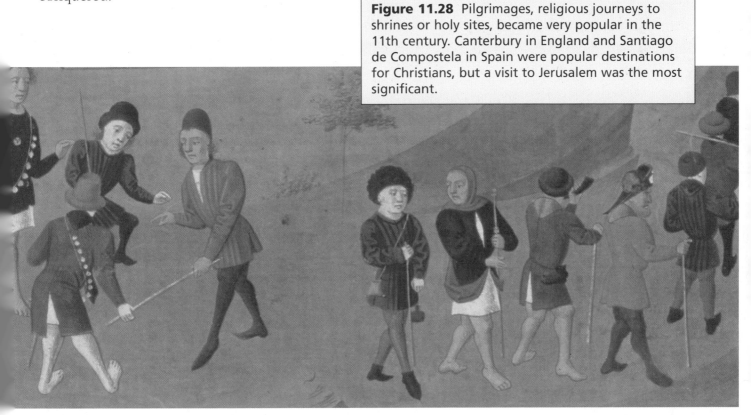

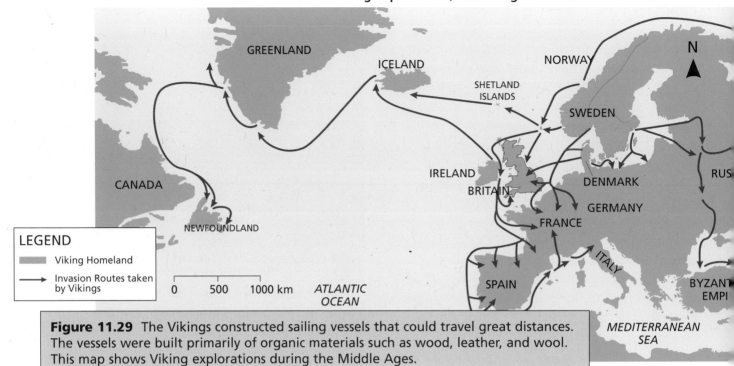

LEGEND

▭ Viking Homeland

→ Invasion Routes taken by Vikings

0   500   1000 km

ATLANTIC OCEAN

MEDITERRANEAN SEA

Figure 11.29 The Vikings constructed sailing vessels that could travel great distances. The vessels were built primarily of organic materials such as wood, leather, and wool. This map shows Viking explorations during the Middle Ages.

Other Peoples

Two other groups of people, the Vikings and the Mongols, led conquests in different parts of the world. Their inventions, traditions, and ideas were important legacies of the Middle Ages.

The Vikings

During the 800s, marauding bands of fierce warriors from what is now known as Scandinavia (Norway, Sweden, and Denmark) raided the coastal countries of Europe. Known as *Vikings,* these Northmen, or Norsemen, looted and destroyed whatever was in their path. Their conquests extended from Britain and France through the Mediterranean to Ukraine. There they ruled the city of Kiev for a time, establishing an important trade route. Although often portrayed as barbaric, Vikings were excellent shipbuilders, farmers, and iron craftsmen who also wrote of their adventures in lengthy stories.

Overcrowding and a lack of resources on their limited farmland forced Viking chieftains to set out for new lands and resources. Their long, narrow ships were manned by a row of oarsmen on each side. The Vikings became skilled sailors, and their voyages helped to open up Europe to trade in other lands.

Vikings valued strength and courage, and many eagerly engaged in war to demonstrate these qualities. The fiercest warriors, known as **berserkers**, worked themselves into a frenzy during battle in order to scare their opponents.

Figure 11.30 The Vikings were well-equipped, well-armed, and well-organized and usually prevailed over poorly equipped enemies. So fierce were the Vikings that Christian priests often led their parishioners in the prayer: "From the fury of the Northmen, good Lord deliver us."

Vikings passed on their history through a tradition of storytelling known as **sagas**. Telling these epic tales sometimes took days.

Viking Ships

The Gotstad ship, excavated in the 1960s in Norway, represents a typical Viking vessel. Shipbuilders used axes to cut and shape timbers. Vikings preferred green unseasoned timber fresh from trees – it was easier to work with and shrank very little when wet. It took about twelve trees to make a ship. Iron was used to make nails and the anchor, wool for the large sail, and leather or hemp for the rigging. The ships were steered by a rudder, which was fastened at the rear with leather. The square sail was attached to a t-shaped mast. The longship, used in battle, was long and narrow for speed. Merchant ships were wider to carry goods. In northern Europe and Scotland, shipbuilding techniques of the Vikings continued to be used centuries after the Viking attacks ceased.

Viking Exploration

In 911, the Franks granted land in the northwest of what is now France to a group of Vikings led by Rolf the Ganger (known as Rollo). This territory became known as *Normandy,* after the Norsemen who settled there. Eventually the Normans converted to Christianity. In 1017, the Danish chieftain

Figure 11.32 Viking runes, or letters, were carved into wood or chiseled into stone. The Vikings often left rune stones as tributes to warriors and family members and as markers of where they had been. For centuries, no one was able to decipher the runes.

Canute conquered England and ruled there until 1035. William the Conqueror of Normandy, a descendant of the Normans, invaded England in 1066 to claim the throne. He defeated the English who were led by King Harold at the Battle of Hastings.

Viking explorers are the first Europeans known to have set foot in North America, 500 years before Christopher Columbus. Norwegian Vikings established colonies in Iceland and Greenland in the late 900s. Around 1000 CE, Leif Eriksson, son of Eric the Red who first colonized Greenland, journeyed along the northeastern coast of North America. The coast had already been cited by a Viking sailor named Bjarni Herjolfsson. Leif established a temporary settlement at a place he called *Vinland,* thought to be located on the northern tip of Newfoundland. Leif may have travelled as far south as Nova Scotia and Massachusetts in the United States. The remnants of a Viking settlement were discovered in 1960 at L'Anse aux Meadows, Newfoundland. Archaeologists have determined that the site was inhabited for only a few years before the Vikings abandoned it because of attacks by *Skraelings,* believed to be First Nations peoples.

By the 13th century, the Vikings had established permanent settlements in Europe, accepted Christianity, and were no longer threatening European communities.

Figure 11.31 For nearly three centuries, Vikings sailed the world in search of new lands.

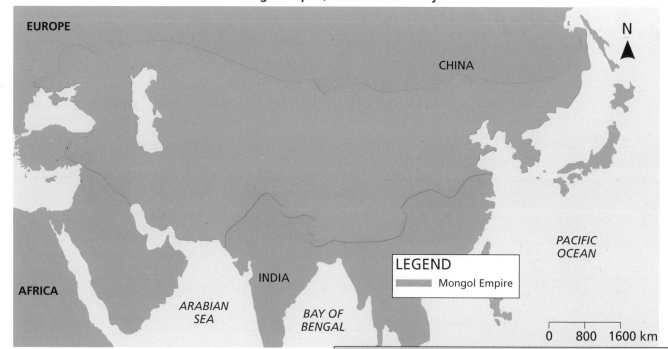

EUROPE

N

CHINA

PACIFIC
OCEAN

INDIA

AFRICA

ARABIAN
SEA

BAY OF
BENGAL

LEGEND
Mongol Empire

0   800   1600 km

The Mongols

Like the Huns (see page 169), the Mongols emerged from central Asia to threaten the people of Asia, the Middle East, and eastern Europe. Skilled horsemen, the Mongols were adept at using the stirrup to control their horses, leaving their hands free to hold weapons. A Mongol warrior's most prized possession was his horse. Boys learned to ride at age three. Mongol women could ride as well as men.

The Mongols were nomadic, and they carried their homes, tents called *yurts*, with them as they travelled. Because their land offered little in the way of sustenance, the Mongols frequently raided other tribes and communities.

Under the leadership of Genghis Khan (c. 1162-1227), the Mongols ruled over the largest empire the world had ever seen. With an empire that stretched from Korea to western Russia, the Mongols presided over a diverse group of people. They maintained authority

When Marco Polo returned to Venice, Italy, in 1295, he wrote a book *The Travels Of Marco Polo.* Christopher Columbus owned a copy of Marco Polo's book. Although he was not the first European to visit China, Marco Polo helped to bridge the distance between the two civilizations and develop important trade links.

Figure 11.33 This is a map of Mongol territories at the end of the 12th century. Mongol armies became the most efficient fighting force of their time. After defeating an enemy, Mongol soldiers left a pyramid of skulls behind as a reminder of the terror they represented.

throughout their empire by establishing a communication network that spanned their territory. They used flag signals and riders a day's ride apart, and were able to pass along information and decisions within weeks rather than months. This network required some 200 000 horses and 10 000 post-houses.

Genghis's grandsons, Hulagu, Batu, and Kublai, carried on his empire. Kublai, the most enlightened of the grandsons, served as emperor of China from 1279 to 1294. He built roads and hospitals, stored grain for times of famine, and provided for the needy. He also welcomed a young European trader, Marco Polo, into his inner court.

In Russia, Mongol rule lasted over 200 years, and it was marked by a reign of terror. Russians were forced to pay money and treasures as a tribute to their conquerors. Russians were also forbidden to trade with other nations. When some Russians attempted to overthrow Mongol rule in the late 1300s, the Mongols destroyed Moscow. Finally, in 1480, the Russian army, led by Ivan the Great, forced their Mongol overlords to withdraw from Russia in a bloodless revolution.

Figure 11.34 In 2004, archaeologists unearthed the site of Genghis Khan's palace, 240 kilometres east of the Mongolian capital of Ulan Bator. The palace was built about 1200 in a square-tent-shape attached to wooden columns. Genghis Khan's tomb is believed to be nearby, but it has not been found. To keep his grave site secret, according to legend, the burial party killed everyone who attended his funeral. Archaeologists continue to look for his tomb.

The Legacy of the Middle Ages

The following are some of the important developments and inventions from the Middle Ages:

- knowledge and goods from the East. These included Arabic numerals, printing, fabrics, carpets; spices such as salt, sugar, nutmeg, ginger, and cloves; medical innovations like inoculations and medicines; and new approaches to design and architecture including domes, concentric castle construction, and vaulted ceilings.

- the demand for spices from China and India resulted in the creation of important trade routes

- new military weapons and tactics

- the growth of towns

- establishment of guilds

- tournaments of knights as sporting events

- census taking

- spread of Christianity and Islam

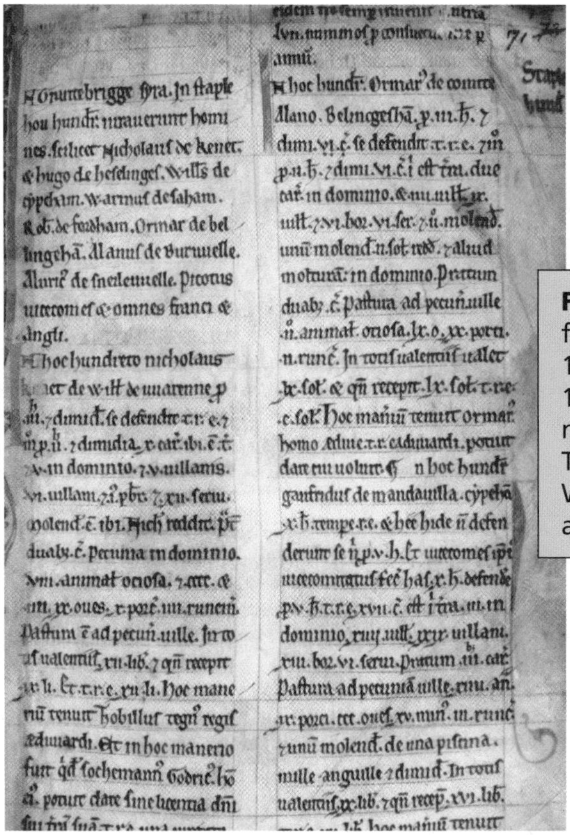

Figure 11.35 William the Conqueror, who sailed from Normandy, France, to capture England in 1066, undertook the first **census** in Britain. In 1086, officials travelled the country recording the number of people on the land and in the towns. This census, called the *Domesday Book*, allowed William to tax his subjects more efficiently. This is a page from the book.

Summary

Feudalism provided security and protection during the hostile period that followed the fall of the Western Roman Empire. Feudalism helped Europeans settle into communities and states rather than live as nomadic tribes.

However, by the late 1400s, several events caused the decline of feudal society.

- The Black Death drastically reduced the population of Western Europe. Workers in towns and on farms were now in greater demand and they, in turn, began to demand more compensation for their labour.

- The threat of attack from warring Germanic barbarian and Viking tribes declined. People no longer needed the protection that the feudal system provided.

- The importance of armoured knights on the battlefields declined as long spears (pikes) used by artillery archers and infantry became more effective.

- Contact with Asia resulted in increased trade and travel, leading to the end of European isolation. With increased trade, people in the towns and cities grew in wealth and importance. Loyalty no longer bound peasants to the manor, and peasants began to look for work in the towns and cities.

Western Europe was on the brink of a new era.

Connecting and Reflecting

Reflect on the impact of daily life, events, and changes that took place during the Middle Ages. Use the information to describe the similarities *to* and differences *from* your life. Explain why knowing about this time in history is important to you *as a citizen of Canada and a citizen of the world.*

Be an Historian

Historical research is very complicated. It demands knowledge, skill, and patience. Historians have to:

- locate their evidence
- interpret what it means
- sort out what is true from what is probable and what is false

The excerpts below are in old English and modern English.

- Do your trust the historian's interpretation? Do you understand it?
- Could you rewrite the "Modern Version" to reflect current English writing?

A Guild at Work

Hit is to be had in mynde that for a trueth of Clothmakyng to be had in this cite as foloeth, if it might be folowed, and the execucion of the same to be done schortly, or else the cite wolbe so fer past remedie to be recouered to eny welth or prosperite, hit is thought hit were good to have ij wevers and ij walkers sworn to make true serche of the wevers doing & also of the walkers & to present the trueth; and also to be chosen vj drapers to be maisters, & ouerseers of the doing of the searchers, that if some of them cannot a lesour to be at the serchyng at the dayes of the searchers, yet some of these vj maisters schall ever be ther. And by cause it were to great a besynes for the searchers to go to every mannes howse, hit is enacted at this lete to haue a howse of the gilde, or of some other mannes nyghe the drapery doore, to be ordeyned well with perches to draw over the clothes when they be thykked, and also weightes and ballaunce to wey the cloth, and when it cometh from the walkers, the walkers to bring it to the serchyng howse, and to serche it, & to se it ouer a perche, and if it be good cloth as it owght to be in brede and lengh, that the cite may have a preise by it and no sklaunder, then to sett upon hit the Olyvaunt in lede, and of the bak of the seall the lengh of the cloth, by the which men shall perceive and see it is true Coventre cloth, ffor of suerte ther is in London & opther places that sell false & untrewe made cloth, & name it Couentre cloth, the which is a gret slaunder to the cite than it deserveth by a gret partie.

Modern English Version

It is to be had in mind as a truth of cloth-making to be had in this city as follows, if it might be followed, and the execution of the same to be done shortly (= to be done quickly), or else the city will be so far past remedy to be recovered to any wealth or prosperity, it is thought it were good to have ii (two) weavers and ii (two) walkers sworn to make true search (= inspection) of the weavers' doing and also of the walkers and to present the truth; and also to be chosen vi (six) drapers to be masters and overseers of the doing of the searchers, so that if some of them cannot a leisure be (=do not have the time) to be at the searching at the days of the searchers, yet some of them will always be there. And because it is too great a business to go to every man's house, it is enacted at this leet (=gild council) to have a house of the gild, or of some other man's, near the drapery (=place where the cloth was sold) door, to be well equipped with perches (a perch was a fixed measure of about 5 metres) to draw over the cloth when it has been thickened, and also weights and a balance to weigh the cloth, and when it comes from the walkers, the walkers are to bring it to the searching house and to search it, and to see it over a perch, and if it is good cloth, as it ought to be in breadth and length, so that the city may have a praise by it and not a slander, then to set the Elephant in lead (= a lead seal with a picture of an elephant) upon it, and on the back of the seal the length of the cloth, by which men shall perceive and see it is true Coventry (= a town in England) cloth, for of surety (= it is certain) there are people in London and other places who sell false and untrue cloth, and name it Coventry cloth, which is a great slander to the city that it does not deserve by a great part.

Part 5

In Part 5, you will look at the Renaissance, the Reformation, the Age of Revolutions, and Industry and Empire, all of which occurred between about 1400 to 1850.

By the beginning of the 15th century, Europe was entering a new era. People were fascinated with anything from ancient Greece and Rome. There was increased interest in expanding trade among the peoples of Europe. Most significant, there was an increase in the exploration of faraway areas of the world.

In Europe, day-to-day life for most people did not change greatly from the later years of the Middle Ages. In chapter 12, you will learn about how people lived in Florence, Italy, which was the centre of the Renaissance in Europe. You will study the contributions of important people such as Lorenzo de' Medici, Leonardo da Vinci, and Michelangelo. You will see how the invention of the printing press made it easier and quicker for new ideas to spread.

Improved sailing technology and the compass helped to lead sailors and traders farther and farther from their European homelands. North America and South America, for example, were colonized by Europeans at this time.

Near the end of the Renaissance, a number of people began to question the authority of the Roman Catholic Church. Their questionings resulted in what is called the *Reformation*. In chapter 13, you will begin to explore how Europe became divided between Catholics and Protestants. The upheaval in established religion created deep divisions among the peoples who lived during this time, and societies were changed forever.

Several revolutions occurred after 1600. In chapter 14, you will read about four of them: the Scientific Revolution, the Enlightenment, the American Revolution, and the French Revolution. Ideas about the scientific method and modern-day government emerged from these revolutions.

Chapter 14 is divided into sections A and B. The Scientific Revolution and the Enlightenment are studied in section A. You will read about the origins of many now-common scientific ideas. Some familiar instruments, such as the microscope and the telescope, come from this period. Galileo used the telescope to map the stars in the sky. Isaac Newton invented calculus, explained the movements of the oceans' tides, and developed the bases for the laws of motion and the theory of gravity.

In section B of chapter 14, you will look at the American Revolution and the French Revolution. Great changes in societies in Europe and North America resulted from these political revolutions. For example, the American Revolution led to the creation of the

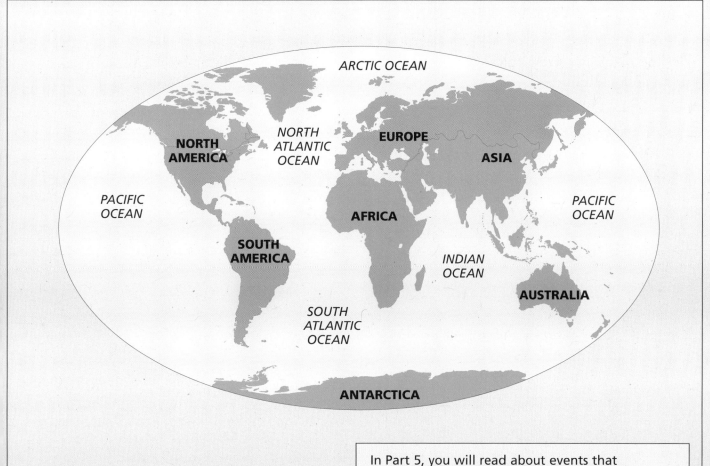

ARCTIC OCEAN

NORTH
AMERICA

NORTH
ATLANTIC
OCEAN

EUROPE

ASIA

PACIFIC
OCEAN

AFRICA

PACIFIC
OCEAN

SOUTH
AMERICA

INDIAN
OCEAN

SOUTH
ATLANTIC
OCEAN

AUSTRALIA

ANTARCTICA

In Part 5, you will read about events that
happened in areas highlighted on this map.

United States of America. In France, the French
Revolution signalled the end of royalty and
absolute rule. Even when Napoleon took
power, he continued the ideals of the
revolutionaries and made the legal system
fairer, supported education, and allowed basic
human rights.

Shaping the modern era continued with the
emergence of industry and the development of
European empires throughout the world. In
chapter 15, you will learn about two more
revolutions: the Agricultural Revolution and the
Industrial Revolution. Both changed the ways
people worked and produced food and goods.
The steam engine greatly changed every aspect
of people's lives. Because most factories were
located in urban areas, people moved from
farms to find work in the towns and cities.

Our study of the modern world concludes
with a brief look at the growth of empires.
Many empires were a result of trade
relationships that had developed centuries
earlier. European powers settled many far-off
lands. For example, Spain and Portugal
established colonies in South America and
Central America. Britain, Holland, and France
had colonies in almost every corner of the
world. All of the empires left permanent
imprints of their cultures on the peoples of
those lands, including Canada.

RENAISSANCE	1347-1350	c. 1350	1363	c. 1415	c. 1440-1450	c. 1449-1492	1492
	The Black Death reaches Europe and kills 20 million people.	The Renaissance begins. The Humanist movement is popular among the educated and wealthy.	To boost the workforce decimated by the Black Death, prisoners (Greeks, Russians, Slavs, Mongols) are allowed into Florence as slaves.	Prince Henry of Portugal starts the first school for navigators in Europe.	Gutenberg perfects his movable printing press.	Lorenzo de' Medici is one of the leading patrons of the arts in Italy, commissioning works from artists such as Leonardo da Vinci.	Christopher Columbus reaches San Salvador Island (West Indies).

REFORMATION	1453	1492	1500	1516	1517	1520	1521
	Ottoman Turks capture Constantinople and rename it Istanbul.	Spanish Jews are given the choice to convert to Christianity or leave Spain.	Ottomans have conquered Greece, Albania, Serbia, Bosnia, and Bulgaria.	Ottomans have conquered Egypt, Syria, and parts of Arabia.	Martin Luther publishes his Ninety-five Theses.	Suleiman the Magnificent becomes sultan of the Ottoman Empire (until 1566).	Martin Luther is denounced by the pope.

THE AGE OF REVOLUTIONS	1543	1609	1616	1632	1661	1665	1751
	Copernicus, a Polish astronomer, suggests the sun, not Earth, is the centre of the universe.	Galileo Galilei proves Copernicus's theory.	The Roman Catholic Church forbids anyone to teach that the sun is the centre of the universe.	Anthony van Leeuwenhoek improves the magnification of microscopes.	Louis XIV (1661-1715) takes absolute power in France.	Robert Hooke publishes Micrographia; the book includes never-before-seen closeups of insects and the human body. London is hit by a plague.	Denis Diderot begins to publish a multi-volume work titled Encyclopedia. The book is a showcase for Enlightenment thinkers.

INDUSTRY AND EMPIRE	1700s	c. 1760	1768	c. 1800	1806	1825	1829
	The slave trade helps to fuel the economies of countries in Europe.	The Agricultural Revolution and Industrial Revolution begin at about the same time in England.	Captain James Cook maps much of the Pacific Ocean for England.	Towns and cities throughout Europe are becoming overcrowded as people move from the countryside looking for work in the factories.	Britain seizes Cape of Good Hope from the Dutch.	A revolution is attempted in Russia. The first steam railway is built in Britain. Hot-air balloon rides are becoming the rage among the wealthy in France and England.	Restrictions on Roman Catholics are removed in Britain.

1497	1498	1499	1501	1519-1522	1533	1534
John Cabot lands in Newfoundland.	Vasco de Gama sails around the southern tip of Africa.	Amerigo Vespucci reaches South America.	Michelangelo completes his sculpture of *David*.	Magellan sails around the world.	Pope Clement VII refuses to declare Henry VIII's marriage to Catherine of Aragon invalid.	Jacques Cartier explores the Labrador coast and the St. Lawrence River.

1529	1534	1558	1562	1570	1572	1598	1604
The word *protestant* is used for the first time.	John Calvin, fearful of persecution because he is Protestant, leaves France and settles in Geneva, Switzerland.	Elizabeth I becomes queen of England. 10 000 books are burned in Venice because they have not been approved by the church.	Joseph Nasi helps negotiate peace between Poland and the Ottoman Empire.	Pope St. Pius IV declares Elizabeth I to be a heretic. In response, Elizabeth outlaws the Roman Catholic Church in England.	Thousands of French Protestants, called *Huguenots*, are killed in the St. Bartholomew's Day massacre in France.	Edict of Nantes grants religious freedom to the Huguenots. (In 1685, King Louis XIV revokes the Edict of Nantes.)	King James I, a Protestant, orders a new English translation of the Bible.

1756	1775	1776	1783	1789	1792	1793	1799
The Seven Years' War between France and England begins.	The American Revolution begins. American army invades Quebec and loses.	The thirteen colonies sign the Declaration of Independence.	England recognizes the independence of the United States of America. Five years later, in 1788, the United States adopts a new constitution.	George Washington becomes the first president of the United States. The French Revolution begins.	French revolutionaries abolish the monarchy. (Twelve years later, in 1804, Napoleon Bonaparte becomes emperor of France.)	The king of France, Louis XVI, is executed by revolutionaries. The Reign of Terror begins in France.	The French Revolution ends.

1830	1832	1833	1847	1850
Belgium wins its independence from Holland.	Men who pay a certain level of tax are given the right to vote in Britain.	England makes it illegal for children under the age of nine to work in textile factories.	Laws restrict working hours of women and children in textile mills to ten hours a day.	Workers in most industrial countries win the right to organize unions. Governments begin to get involved in local health and safety issues.

The Renaissance

Our Study of the Renaissance

Our study of the Renaissance includes the following topics:

- Why Study the Renaissance?
- Humanism
- A Communications Revolution
- Important People
- Travel
- In the Homes of the Rich
- Help for the Poor
- The Legacy of the Renaissance

Figure 12.1 This painting shows what Florence looked like in about 1470. At the time, Florence was surrounded by 30 000 estates owned by merchants and the nobility. These estates provided the city's population with meat, wine, vegetables, cheese, grain, and wood. When the city was first built on the banks of the Arno River, a wall (see right side) was constructed to protect the inhabitants from overland attacks. Many historians believe the Renaissance began in Florence.

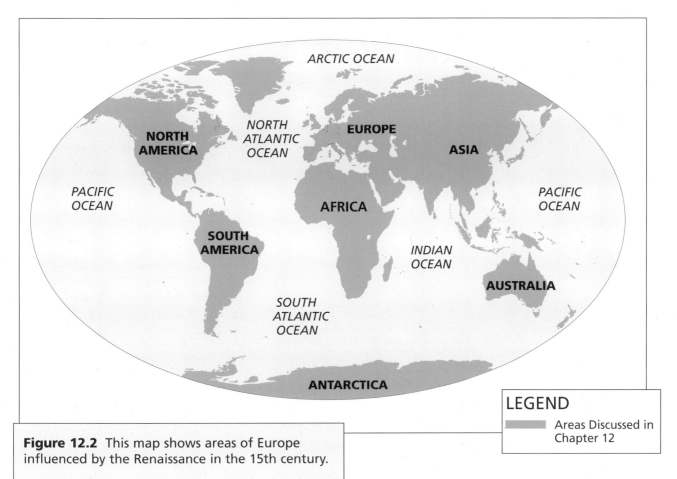

Figure 12.2 This map shows areas of Europe influenced by the Renaissance in the 15th century.

The European Renaissance (the word means "rebirth") began in what is now Italy in about 1350 CE and lasted until about 1550 CE. During this time, Italian scholars revived the literature and art of ancient Greece and Rome, which had been ignored for centuries. In the 1400s, the Renaissance spread into northwestern Europe.

The way of life for most Europeans during the Renaissance was not much different from life in the Middle Ages. Women, for example, had few rights, and the lives of peasants and the poor did not improve.

Questions to Think About

◆ What social conditions caused the Renaissance?

◆ How did life change in the Renaissance from life in the Middle Ages? How did it remain the same?

◆ What were the main achievements of the Renaissance?

◆ How has the Renaissance influenced your life today?

Figure 12.3 These paintings show how the three classes of society – lower, middle, and upper – lived in 15th-century Florence.

Why Study the Renaissance?

The Renaissance was a time of great cultural and political change in Europe. Inventions such as the compass enabled explorers to measure a ship's position and progress more accurately, making ocean travel safer. As more sailors explored the seas, they arrived at lands and came upon civilizations previously unknown to Europeans. The printing press (see page 255) increased the number of books produced. This, in turn, gave more people access to writings and the ideas of others.

Trade between port cities such as Genoa and Naples was handled by traders and merchants who had become quite wealthy. Often these people were members of large families who had great sums of money. This enabled them to dominate the costly business of trade. Together with bankers, tradespeople, and shopkeepers, they formed a middle class between the poor peasants and the wealthy nobility.

Many people from the middle class and nobility financed the construction of fine buildings and commissioned works from popular artists of the day. Florence was a major centre for art and architecture, and it remains an excellent source of historical information for this period in time. Two of the world's great artists, Leonardo da Vinci and Michelangelo, lived in Florence during the Renaissance.

Some merchants and almost all nobles had servants who did much of the work. Wealthy people then had time to spend on their own interests. One popular pursuit was reading the writings and ideas of Greek historians such as Herodotus and Roman poets such as Virgil. Many people began to ask questions about the world around them.

Renaissance Geography

During the 14th and 15th centuries, ships from Dutch, Italian, Portuguese, and Spanish cities often sailed to the Azores, Canary, Cape Verde, and Madeira islands. Ships also sailed the Bay of Biscay, the North Atlantic Ocean, and the North Sea in search of fish. Although Europeans were familiar with Europe and parts of Africa and Asia, they knew nothing of the other continents. With the exception of the Vikings (see page 240), European ships had yet to make a voyage across the Atlantic Ocean.

The age of exploration began in the late 15th century. The greatest exploits belonged to Portugal and Spain. Merchants in these countries were eager to become involved in the valuable spice trade with countries in east Asia.

The Americas are named after the Italian explorer Amerigo Vespucci. The Cabot Trail in Nova Scotia is named after another famous explorer, Giovanni Caboto (John Cabot, in English).

European Explorations, 15th and 16th Centuries

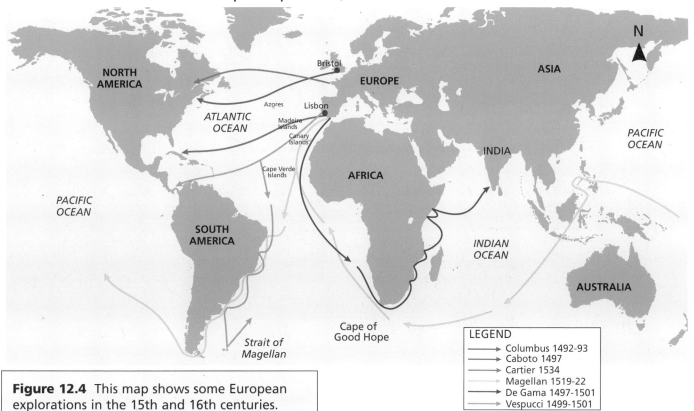

LEGEND
→ Columbus 1492-93
→ Caboto 1497
→ Cartier 1534
→ Magellan 1519-22
→ De Gama 1497-1501
→ Vespucci 1499-1501

Figure 12.4 This map shows some European explorations in the 15th and 16th centuries.

However, trade routes to these places crossed the Mediterranean Sea and were dominated by Italian merchants, mainly from Genoa and Venice. The overland portion of the voyage was costly and dangerous. The search for an alternative sea route to the East led sailors from Portugal and Spain across the Atlantic Ocean, where they found lands and peoples of whom they had no previous knowledge.

In 1492, Christopher Columbus of Genoa set sail from Palos, Spain. Queen Isabella and King Ferdinand of Spain provided Columbus with three ships, and on October 12, 1492, he landed on San Salvador Island in the area we know today as the West Indies.

In 1498, Vasco da Gama, a Portuguese navigator, with the aid of a Muslim navigator, found a route to India by sailing around the southern tip of Africa. In 1499, Amerigo Vespucci sailed from Spain to South America. Then, in 1522, Ferdinand Magellan sailed around the world.

Other countries also sponsored explorers. Giovanni Caboto of Genoa was sent out on a voyage by England in 1497. Caboto eventually landed in Newfoundland. In 1534 and 1535, Jacques Cartier of France explored the Labrador coast and the St. Lawrence River.

These voyages eventually led to great wealth for most of the countries that financed the explorations. The voyages also laid the foundations for the European empires that ruled most of the world in later centuries (see chapter 15) and expanded Europeans' knowledge of the existence, for example, of North America and South America and of the peoples living there.

Figure 12.5 This map, which was printed in 1586, shows what explorers of the Renaissance period thought North and South America looked like.

In his book, *The Prince*, the Florentine writer Niccolo Machiavelli said that a ruler must be as cunning as a fox and as fierce as a lion. He must seem to be good, but should do whatever he has to in order to gain his goals. In other words, "the end justifies the means."

Government

Florence was one of the richest city-states in what is now Italy. With a flourishing population of about 70 000, it was also one of the largest.

When Florence's government was first set up, the rulers were chosen from members of the guilds. Guild members were considered "citizens of Florence." At first, the term of office of those in power lasted only two months. This was to make it difficult for anyone to seize control of the government. At the same time, such a short term of office made it almost impossible for anyone to accomplish anything.

This type of government – control by a small group of people – is called an **oligarchy**. It had more in common with Greek and Roman forms of government than it did with the rule of kings and princes that had existed in the Middle Ages. Like absolute rule, though, only a few people make all the decisions in an oligarchy.

To vote, a person had to be a member of a guild, and only about 12 percent of Florentines were guild members. As in Greek and Roman times, women could neither vote nor hold office. Therefore, government in Florence was limited to only a few men.

In late 15th-century Florence, wealthy families were the real rulers. Since the Medici [may-DEE-chee] family was the richest of all, the Medici family was also the most politically powerful. Family members sometimes took government positions, but they preferred to use their wealth and prestige to influence state decisions without becoming directly involved.

The Medici family was a dominant force in Florence for about 300 years. The family was praised for its diplomatic skills, maintaining friendly relations with neighbouring city-states, helping to keep peace within the city of Florence, and providing generous financial support to the city's artistic community.

Figure 12.6 In this painting, Michelangelo is reading his poetry to Vittoria Colonna (seated, centre) and a group of humanists. Vittoria was born into one of Rome's noble families, and she and Michelangelo became close friends.

Humanism

From about 1300, some educated Italians developed a strong interest in ancient Greece and Rome. Like the ancient Greeks, they emphasized the power of humans to control their own lives, as opposed to the medieval belief that people were limited in this regard. For this reason they are called **humanists**. It soon became fashionable for humanists to meet to talk about Greek and Roman values, ideas, and writings. Although humanist ideas were not accepted at first, this small group eventually influenced Renaissance writing, fashion, and manners.

Humanists placed high value on the quality of human life. They believed in physical fitness, good appearance, education, and the ability to deal with people in a dignified way. They emphasized the value of learning to read, speak, and write Greek and Latin. They believed that almost everything worth knowing could be found in ancient Greek and Latin writings.

In the Middle Ages, religion and tradition had discouraged change and independent thinking. Humanists, on the other hand, placed a high value on human ability and believed people were capable of doing whatever they chose to do. Pico della Mirandola, a humanist in the

Lorenzo de' Medici and his brother, Giuliano, each fathered a son who became pope. Lorenzo's second son, Giovanni de' Medici, became Pope Leo X (1513-1521), and Giuliano's son, Giulio de' Medici, became Pope Clement VII (1523-1534). Leo X was pope when Martin Luther posted his 95 Theses criticizing the Roman Catholic Church (see page 274). Clement VIII, who was raised by Lorenzo following the murder of his father, was a weak pope and had major disagreements with political leaders of his day. In 1533, for example, he refused to declare King Henry VIII's marriage to Catherine of Aragon invalid. This led to England's split from the Roman Catholic Church (see page 278).

Medici household, summed up the humanist enthusiasm as follows: "Oh, highest and most marvellous man. To him it is granted to have whatever he chooses, to be whatever he wills."

The women of wealthy families were at the forefront of the humanist movement. Vittoria Colonna of Florence wrote many poems and letters about humanism, and she often met with the leading thinkers and artists of her day. Only men could become humanists, however, since women had no rights or freedoms.

When men like Lorenzo de' Medici set up schools for their children, they hired humanists as teachers. They wanted their children to learn and follow humanist ways and values.

Humanists travelled widely, spreading their ideas. When humanism became fashionable, humanist thinkers such as Pico della Mirandola were welcomed into the courts of European kings and nobles. Humanists also spread their ideas through the letters they wrote. The use of the printing press helped make humanist thought available to anyone who could read.

A Communications Revolution

In about 1440, Johann Gutenberg developed a new printing process – movable type.

This process involved thousands of individual pieces of wooden (and later, metal) type, which could be moved around to form words and sentences. Gutenberg did not have the finances he needed to set up a print shop, however. As a result, he took on a partner, Johann Fust. Fust was a goldsmith, who, between 1448 and 1455, provided the money that Gutenberg needed. From a small shop in the city of Mainz in what is now Germany, Gutenberg and Fust used the new movable type process to print the now-famous Gutenberg edition of the Bible. Later, when Gutenberg could not repay Fust, the two men parted company, and each continued to print books using the new technique.

Many of the first books printed were religious, such as the Bible, and were widely read. Books by Greek and Roman writers were also popular. They were translated into several languages including English, French, and Italian. Soon, works written by Renaissance writers were published. Because of the printing press, these writers had access to a much larger audience than earlier writers had.

Figure 12.7 These printers are setting type and printing books. Although movable clay type was first invented in China in the 11th century, Gutenberg invented the printing press with replaceable wooden or metal letters. Gutenberg's invention made it possible to print books at less cost and more quickly than ever before. However, books were still too expensive for most people; only the rich could afford to buy them.

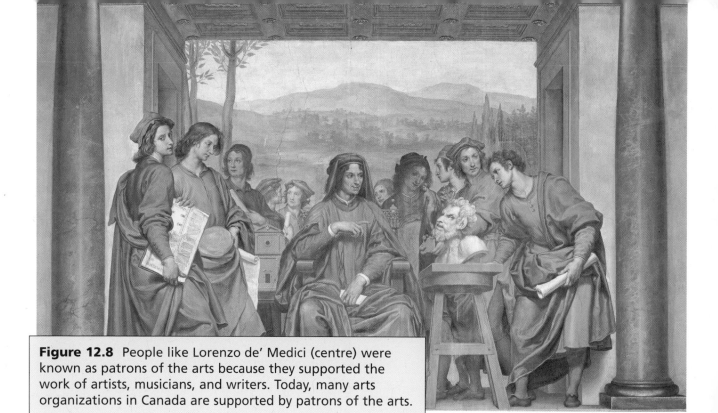

Figure 12.8 People like Lorenzo de' Medici (centre) were known as patrons of the arts because they supported the work of artists, musicians, and writers. Today, many arts organizations in Canada are supported by patrons of the arts.

Important People

Lorenzo de' Medici

Lorenzo de' Medici was a poet and a scholar. He was interested in ancient Greek philosophers such as Plato and Aristotle, and he supported many of the artists in Florence. He was also a clever politician. He realized that he would have the best chance to pursue his interests if he controlled the government of Florence.

De' Medici never became the official head of Florence's government, however. He controlled the city's affairs by influencing members of the city council. Members of the Medici family were the leading merchants and bankers of their time. Their immense wealth gave them great power and influence.

In addition to the affairs of government, de' Medici found time for many other endeavours. He managed his family's four country estates, as well as his large palace in Florence. He planted botanical gardens at his villa. He also raised cows, which he used to produce cheese for the people of Florence.

Lorenzo de' Medici is, perhaps, best remembered for the financial support he gave to philosophers, poets, sculptors, and painters. Many of the great artists of the Italian Renaissance, including Michelangelo, worked for the Medici's. Lorenzo bought and commissioned so many beautiful works of art for Florence that he was given the title "Lorenzo the Magnificent." When he died at the age of forty-three, most of Florence mourned his passing.

The Pazzi Family

The bell sounded to signal the most solemn moment of the mass. Lorenzo de' Medici and his brother, Giuliano, raised their eyes to heaven.

Suddenly, four members of the Pazzi family appeared out of nowhere with their swords drawn. The Pazzi family were wealthy merchants who rivalled the Medici's

Figure 12.9 This scene depicts one of the Pazzi brothers leaving home to join the attack on the Medici brothers. Power struggles among Florence's leading families were not uncommon.

for control of Florence. Two of the Pazzi men stabbed Giuliano nineteen times.

The two family members who had been directed to kill Lorenzo were less successful. With his sword drawn, Lorenzo forced them back and leaped over the altar rail. His friends rushed to help him, and he escaped.

The Pazzi conspiracy against the Medici family, and specifically Lorenzo, had failed. Those involved in the murder plot were caught and quickly punished. That same evening in 1478, Francesco Pazzi was hanged from one of the upper windows in the Palazzo della Signoria. The Medici family continued to prosper and to control Florence until 1737.

Figure 12.11 This image of Isabella d'Este was drawn by Leonardo da Vinci, who painted the *Mona Lisa,* one of the world's most famous paintings.

Figure 12.10 Towns and cities had a main square, called a *piazza*, where major events took place. In Florence, the Piazza della Signoria was the scene of Francesco Pazzi's execution.

Isabella d'Este

During the Renaissance, women, especially those from the upper class, were expected to marry early, often as young as fifteen years of age, and to devote their lives to their families. Some women did this and much more.

Isabella d'Este [DES-tay] was born in 1474 into the ruling family of Ferrara, located in northern Italy (see figure 12.12). At the age of only six, she was betrothed to Francesco Gonzaga, the Duke of Mantua. Isabella grew up surrounded with literature and the arts. She studied Greek and Latin, religion, and literature. She loved poetry and was a good musician. Like many people of her time, she played the lute.

Isabella married when she was sixteen and moved to her husband's estate in Mantua. Isabella's husband was a soldier, and when he was away she ruled Mantua. She even defended the city when it was attacked. She raised six children, three boys and three girls. She was interested in politics and was well-informed and influential in the political activities of the day. Today, we know of Isabella's influence through the many letters she wrote to scholars and statesmen. Two thousand of these letters still exist. They tell us a great deal about what it was like during her lifetime.

Like Lorenzo de' Medici, she became a leading patron of the arts, collecting and commissioning works from important artists such as Leonardo da Vinci. She soon had the best art collection in all the Italian city-states.

Isabella died in 1539. On her deathbed, she is reported to have said: "I am a woman, and I learned to live in a man's world."

Italy in the 15th Century

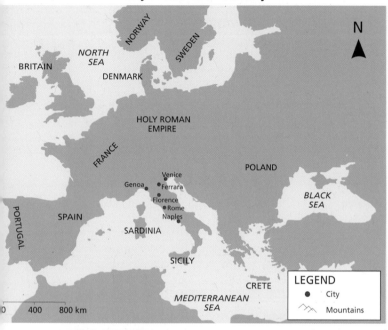

Figure 12.12 This map shows the locations of Florence, Rome, Genoa, Ferrara, and Naples in 15th-century Italy.

Slaves

The Black Death, which reached Florence in 1348, greatly reduced the number of workers, and Florence's booming economy quickly slowed down. To get the economy going again, some way had to be found to rebuild the workforce. In 1363, prisoners were allowed into the city as slaves. The slaves were brought from the East. They were mainly Greeks, Russians, Slavs, and Mongols.

Among the wealthy, the use of slaves quickly became popular. Many Florentine nobles and merchants owned at least two or three. We know this because slaves are referred to as property in legal documents and records of the time.

The Middle Class

During the Middle Ages, most Europeans were peasants, knights, nobles, or members of the church (the clergy). The peasants were members of the working class. They raised food and provided services such as taking care of livestock and cleaning houses. The nobles and knights were landowners and formed the upper class. They inherited their land, positions, and wealth from their families. The nobles were involved in government, and they provided the defence for their communities.

When trade between states increased, the number of merchants and bankers also increased. They soon formed a **middle class** between the peasants and the nobility. The middle class emphasized the importance of home and family, being good citizens, serving the state, and working hard. In time, many members of the middle class in Florence became quite rich, and these families gradually became more involved in government.

Travel

Increased trade among the major cities of Europe meant that people travelled more than ever before. Soldiers and state officials added to the traffic on the roads. Most people travelled overland on horses or on foot. The horse-drawn coach was new and not widely used.

Figure 12.13 The travellers (left) are seeking lodging from innkeepers. The man in the centre is a servant.

The Life of a Merchant

By the time a boy was in his mid teens, he was working at a full-time job.

Filippo felt good. It was May 14, 1491, his sixteenth birthday. He had just finished his first year working as a merchant for Jacopo Bianchi. Bianchi was a wealthy trader in Florence.

Filippo bought and sold goods such as salt, steel, and silk for Bianchi. These items were imported into the city. Other products, such as wool and wine, were exported to other cities in Italy and northern Europe.

It was not easy working for a trader. Despite his youth, Filippo had to make some important decisions at his job. For example, to know how much to pay for imported goods, he had to know how much he could sell the goods for in the marketplace.

Filippo also kept a record of transport and storage costs. Often, he had to convert weights and measures from the standards used elsewhere to those used in Florence, much as traders today have to convert between the metric and imperial systems of measurement. At all times, Filippo had to be prepared to tell his employer how much profit was being made.

Filippo was good at his work. He had learned to read, write, add, and subtract at school. Many Florentine boys went to schools that were run by the church or by a guild. However, few girls received an education. They were expected to marry young, have children, and then devote their lives to their families. The daughters of some of the wealthier merchants and nobles were taught at home by tutors or in convent schools.

When Filippo had completed his schooling the previous year, he planned to apprentice as a cabinetmaker. That was his father's trade, and the trade of his two older brothers. By joining the cabinetmakers' guild, Filippo could expect to make a modest, but comfortable, living.

His plans changed when Bianchi, a customer of his father, offered him a job. Working as a merchant offered Filippo greater opportunities than working as a cabinetmaker. Now, he daydreamed about becoming a trader himself someday. He would buy wheat from Sicily, wool from the nearby Tuscan countryside, cloth and other products from local artisans, and silks and spices from eastern Asia. Then, he would make money by selling these products at higher prices in the local market and to merchants in other European trading centres, such as London or Geneva.

The old Roman roads had not been maintained and were in poor condition. For years, people who needed building supplies helped themselves to the stones and earth that the Romans had used to make the roads.

Overland travel between cities was not only difficult, it was also dangerous. Wherever roads ran through forests, travellers often found themselves at the mercy of bandits. To protect themselves, merchants hired guards or travelled in large groups. If they did travel alone, they might withhold their destination from strangers by saying that they were going in a different direction from what they really were.

Journeys took a long time, and travellers usually had many overnight stays before they reached their destinations. Most arranged to stay at monasteries and private houses, although some stayed at inns.

Inns varied in size. Many were small, but in Padua, Italy, one inn was so large that it had stables for over 200 horses. The inns were often dirty and sometimes unsafe. One innkeeper became rich by murdering and robbing almost 200 of his guests over a number of years.

Figure 12.14 In this picture, a banker is counting out money for a customer. Early Italian banks were little more than benches or stalls set up in the marketplace. The word *bank* comes from the Italian word *banca,* which means "bench."

In the Homes of the Rich

Furniture was surprisingly sparse – even in the homes of the rich. These homes had plenty of space and were richly decorated with frescoes and ornate plaster, but they were not luxurious. Keeping warm in winter was a problem because houses had little insulation and were not centrally heated. All houses were damp and chilly. After dark, people used candles for light.

The activity centre of homes of the upper class was the reception hall, with tables and benches for guests to sit at. Chairs were not common pieces of furniture. Because there were few rooms, there was almost no privacy. The bed of the head of the household, with its large, heavy curtains, might be positioned near the banquet table. Family members, guests, and servants constantly passed by it. The curtains provided a bit of privacy and warmth.

Figure 12.16 Many households owned slaves, and almost all of the slaves were domestic servants.

Figure 12.15 This picture shows the bedroom of a very wealthy family.

Many Renaissance men wore bright colours together. Parti-coloured tights, which men often wore, had one leg in one colour (such as yellow) and the other leg in another colour (such as red).

What They Wore

Wealthy women wore splendid clothes, which were low cut and exposed the neck and shoulders. Dresses had wide sleeves and gold and silver embroidery. They were made of luxurious satin, silk, and velvet in rich colours. Many women wore wigs or dyed their hair blonde. They wore rouge, nail polish, and false eyelashes much the same as women do today.

Fashions were constantly changing because wealthy men and women had many beautiful fabrics and styles to choose from and the time and money to invest. Before the Renaissance, clothing styles had not changed much for several centuries. Not surprisingly, the many changes in fashion during the Renaissance shocked some people and delighted others.

Florence became a major centre for making beautiful fabrics and dresses. These fabrics and designs were sold in many other European centres. The wealthy, and those who were prepared to do without basic needs to give the appearance of wealth, cared most about fashion. Still, most people dressed in the style of the day. Those who had little money wore clothing made from less expensive and decorative fabrics.

Figure 12.17 To preserve fuel, the poor were advised to cook once a day – in the morning. Many poor people lived in one-room homes, where they cooked, ate, and slept.

Figure 12.18 Many women from poor families worked as yarn spinners. The women in this painting are members of a guild.

At Home with the Lauris

Women who did not have to work for a living devoted their lives to the family and household.

Bianca Lauri, Filippo's mother, ran her household very carefully. She had to do so since her husband, Alberto, did not earn a lot of money. It took half their income just to feed their small family of six. And that did not include buying bread! Bianca saved money by baking the bread herself from the wheat that she had the miller grind into flour.

Bianca's main duty was to make sure that her home ran smoothly. She kept the house clean, managed the household budget, kept the kitchen well stocked, and cared for the family's clothing. Bianca was proud that she did this work well. From time to time, however, she wondered what it would be like to work in a shop as Alberto did.

Many Florentine women worked at trades. In town, they worked as spinners and weavers, usually in their homes. In the country, they worked in the fields with the men. Some women also had jobs in convents, as artists and as healers. Wherever they worked, women were usually paid only half as much as men for the same work. In merchant families, women often helped run their families' businesses and looked after the household.

When the family sat down to supper, Bianca and her daughter Giuliana served the men their meal. Sometimes, Bianca grumbled that even once it would be nice if the men served the women. She knew, though, that since men had always come first, it must be right. Her parents had taught her that, as had the parish priest. Like all women, Bianca had been trained since she was a child, when her marriage had been arranged, that her duty in life was to serve her husband. No matter how rich or poor a family was, that was the way it was.

Bianca served a simple meal: bread, soup, pasta, and wine. Meat was expensive, and she served it, and desserts, only on special occasions. Rich people like Jacopo Bianchi, Filippo's employer, ate meals that were much more lavish. The wealthy were always served several courses of meat and ate small sugar cakes for dessert.

The Lauris cut their food with knives, but ate with their hands. Some wealthy people used forks, but most poor people – including the Lauris – had never seen a fork. The Lauris drank their wine from metal containers. Everyone in Florence drank wine, since the unsanitary conditions in the city made drinkable water scarce.

The Lauris lived in a single room above the shop Alberto rented. Because Alberto was a cabinetmaker, the family had more furniture than most of their neighbours. The room contained two stools, a table, a bench, a chest, and a four-poster bed for Bianca and Alberto. The children slept on sacks of straw that were thrown on the floor each evening. The room had an open fireplace, a pot and two frying pans, and little else for cooking.

Figure 12.19 City planners established standards for street grids and where buildings should be located along streets. Often, they designed the buildings. In this painting, city planners (foreground) are discussing the latest ideas.

Figure 12.20 Several homes of wealthy families still exist, and many have been made into museums. Today, people from all over the world travel to Florence to see the architecture and artwork commissioned during the Renaissance.

Urban Planning

Before the Renaissance, cities developed in a haphazard way and did not grow very quickly. When the population of Florence began to increase again after the Black Death of 1347-1350, the demand for housing and other buildings increased. The government hired **city planners** to oversee the expansion.

In Florence, many of the narrow, winding alleys were replaced by wider, straight streets. Poor areas, especially those just outside the town walls, were cleaned up. The large squares, or piazzas, were rebuilt in attractive designs. City planners had never done this kind of work before. The results of their work are still visible today with many buildings and piazzas standing as they did 600 years ago.

In 1472, Florence had 270 wool shops, 83 silk warehouses, 33 banks, 84 cabinetmaking shops, 54 stonecutters, 44 goldsmiths and jewellers, 66 druggists and grocers, 70 butchers, 8 shops that sold fowl, 62 taverns, and 55 wine shops.

Dirt, Sewage, and Sludge

The beautiful buildings in Florence could not hide the fact that cities were filthy places to live in. Garbage was constantly dumped into the streets. This garbage consisted mainly of organic matter, which, in time, broke down into a thick, oily, black sludge. Sludge was everywhere. It covered the ground and stained the walls of buildings. The unhygienic conditions created by garbage contributed to the spread of diseases such as the Black Death (see page 232). Adding to the filth, Florentines buried their dead near the city's water wells. In time, foul water found its way into the wells and polluted the water supply.

Help for the Poor

In 1457, about 30 000 people in Florence had no means of providing for themselves. These people owned no land, held no job or political office, and had almost no money. They received some help from charitable

Figure 12.21 Hospitals were often funded by money left by the wealthy when they died.

organizations. These included the hospitals, orphanages, and schools that were run by churches, monasteries, and craft guilds.

Even many of the men who had jobs were too poor to survive without aid. They received some help from their guilds, whose members all worked in the same trade. For instance, the wool guild in Florence provided pensions for the old and the sick, gave time off to its members to visit medicinal baths, and provided clothing for the needy.

Those who owned businesses, such as trading companies, had little to fall back on. For example, sometimes a crop of wheat would get wet and spoil while it was being taken to market. Sometimes the cost of producing an item was higher than the people could afford to pay. There were many ways a trader could become bankrupt. To avoid debt and ruin, traders tried to make as much profit as they could on each business deal. In this way, they could build up their savings in case of emergencies.

Figure 12.22 Once each year, the wool guild provided clothing for the poor.

Figure 12.23 Many people consider Michelangelo Buonarroti the greatest artist of all time. He worked mainly as a sculptor. He also painted and in 1508 was commissioned by the Roman Catholic Church to paint a fresco on the ceiling of the Sistine Chapel in the Vatican. He was chief architect of St. Peter's Church in Rome, and he designed fortifications to defend Florence. Michelangelo's *Pietà*, shown here, depicts Jesus and his mother, Mary.

The Arts

When most people think of the Renaissance, they think of art: Michelangelo and his famous sculpture *David*, Leonardo da Vinci and his painting *Mona Lisa,* the elaborate decorations on the facades of buildings such as the church of St. Peter in Bologna by Properzia de Rossi. The remarkable production of art at this time was made possible by the support that wealthy people and churches provided artists.

Many beautiful buildings were designed and built during the Renaissance. As merchants became wealthier, they often commissioned or bought art. The poor could not afford to live in these buildings or buy art. However, they could see the buildings, and art purchased by churches was accessible to everyone.

The art of the Renaissance is more realistic than the art of the Middle Ages. Paintings and sculptures show the artists' interest in anatomy, in Greek and Roman art, and in drawing pictures in perspective. Even when the subject matter is religious, Renaissance paintings often have a robust, three-dimensional, earthy quality.

Fun and Games

People from wealthy families had a great deal of leisure time, as the following excerpt from a 1491 letter shows:

Immediately after lunch, we began to play ball with great energy, and after having played some while, we went to see the very beautiful palace. We went down beside the palace, where they had set up a catch of lampreys [eel-like fish] and crayfish, of which we took our fill, and sent some of the lampreys to the Duke. When this fishing was over, we went on to another, where we took more than one thousand very large pike, and after taking what we needed as presents and for our own sainted stomachs, we had the rest thrown back into the water. Then we mounted and began on the spot to fly falcons along the bank. When we were through, we went on a deer hunt.

Regardless of their wealth, most people took part in fairs and processions or watched the horse races, bullfights, jousts, or other sports events held in their cities. These spectacles were often as violent as the chariot races and gladiator fights of ancient Rome (see page 158).

Figure 12.24 Soccer was a popular game with men.

Many sports reflected the violence and cruelty that were common in everyday life. One event involved a group of naked youths who ran through a stadium of deep mud. In another, a man with a shaven head was stripped to the waist and put into a cage with an angry wild cat. He was not allowed to use his hands; he could use only his teeth to kill the cat.

The Legacy of the Renaissance

Many inventions, ideas, art forms, and buildings of the Renaissance are still with us. The following are some that have influenced our world today:

- Writers began to use their own languages (e.g., French, German, Italian) instead of Latin.

- People began to question aspects of the Roman Catholic faith. This planted the seeds from which the Reformation grew. (See chapter 13.)

- Nations began to develop. People from Italy, Portugal, England, Spain, and elsewhere increasingly thought of themselves as Italian, Portuguese, English, Spaniards, and so on.

- Strong leaders and government institutions began to appear. This led, eventually, to the end of city-states and to the rise of strong, unified nations.

- Schools were no longer run solely by the church.

- The rediscovery of Greek and Latin languages allowed people to read the works of ancient philosophers, which influenced ideas.

Summary

The Renaissance began in Italy and spread throughout most of western Europe. While it arrived later in some places than in others, each country experienced a growth of ideas, discoveries, architecture, art, and businesses.

About the same time, the Aztecs in what is now Mexico and the Ming Dynasty in China flourished. Their art and technology equalled and often surpassed much that Europe had to offer.

The printing press was perhaps the most important breakthrough in the 15th century. The new interest in education had increased the demand for books. Printers were now able to meet this demand, and books appeared quickly. More people were reading, and this meant that the ideas of writers were reaching more people than had ever been possible in the past.

Portugal, Spain, and, later, England and France established colonies in North America, South America, Africa, and Asia. These were the roots of the European empires that controlled much of the world until well into the 20th century.

While there was great prosperity, many people still lived on a day-to-day, hand-to-mouth basis. They lived and died where they had been born, seldom travelling more than a few kilometres from their homes. Most often their trades were the trades of their parents, and their tools were the same as those their grandparents had used.

Connecting and Reflecting

Reflect on the impact of the changes and discoveries that took place during the Renaissance. Use the information that you have learned to describe how these changes and discoveries have affected your life today. Explain why knowing about the Renaissance is important to you *as a citizen of Canada and a citizen of the world.*

Be an Historian

Do you believe everything that you read in a history text? Do you ever wonder what information has been left out? When you study history, you are usually reading the results of what historians have researched and written. In this section, you will have the opportunity to do your own research and ask yourself the same kinds of questions that historians ask themselves. You will not be reading history; you will be doing history!

Historical research is very complicated. (see chapter 1.) It demands knowledge, skill, and patience. Historians have to:

- locate their evidence
- interpret what it means
- sort out what is true from what is probable and what is false

Read the excerpts below. When you are finished, answer the following questions:

- Where do these sources come from?
- Are they sources that you can trust?
- What do you know about the author? If you do not know anything, how can you find out?
- Does the author have knowledge, experience, or credentials that makes you willing to trust his or her work?
- As you try to understand the past, how important is chronology?

The Impact of Printing

Professor Nicholas Heems, doctor of humanities and outstanding professor of law, was tutoring a small number of privileged students in private, in his home, dictating to them an introduction to the Institutes of Justinian. By this excellent means he was able to make the whole subject of jurisprudence (law) easier for them. Some of these young people transcribed their master's lectures with great accuracy, and later showed him their notes. When he realized how much they had benefited from his coaching he judged it appropriate to use the art of printing to produce a thousand copies. I, the printer, agreeing that such a book would profit you as students of law, accepted the handwritten text from your master, and produced a large number of copies in my printing house. Here I offer the fruits of my labour to the Faculty of Law. If you like this little work, in a few months I will produce more printed texts on the same sort of subject.

(Lisa Jardine, Worldly Goods: A New History of the Renaissance. *London:* Macmillan, 1996, 311-312.)

The Joy of Reading

When evening comes, I return home and go into my study. On the threshold I strip off my muddy, sweaty, workday clothes, and put on the robes of court and palace, and in this graver dress I enter the courts of the ancients and am welcomed by them, and there I taste the food that alone is mine, and for which I was born. And there I make bold to speak to them and ask the motives of their actions, and they, in their humanity, reply to me. And for the space of four hours I forget the world, remember no vexation, fear poverty no more, tremble no more at death; I pass indeed into their world.

(John R. Hale (ed.), The Literary Works of Machiavelli. *Oxford University Press, 1961: 139.*)

The Value of Books

From my youth, even from childhood, I have always endeavoured … to acquire as many books as I could.… Books are full of the voices of the wise, full of lessons from antiquity, full of moral and legal wisdom, full of religion. Books live, they speak directly to us, and teach and instruct us, they bring us consolation. They show us things far remote from our times.… Without books, we should have almost no memory of the past, no examples to follow, no knowledge of either human or divine affairs. Were it not for books, the same tombs that consume men's bodies would likewise bury their names.…

To the best of my ability I have tried to collect the best books, rather than a multitude of books …. In this way I have brought together a collection of almost all the works of the great Greek thinkers, especially those which are rare and difficult to find.…

Wherefore, conscious that death lies ahead of me, and mindful of the weight of my years … I have given all my books, in both languages, to the most sacred temple of St. Mark in your renowned city…. My chief wish is that you, and your children and descendants, may enjoy bountiful and lasting fruit from my labours. It is also my wish to extend this benefit to others associated with you who will in future devote themselves to sound learning.

(Adapted from L. Labowsky, Besarion's Library and the Biblioteca Marciana Rome : Edizioni di storia e litteratura, 1979, p. 147-156; reprinted in D. Englander et al., Culture and Belief in Europe 1450 1600: An Anthology of Sources. Oxford: Blackwell, 1990: 149-150.)

Let the working masses and the humblest sector of the middle classes struggle for the good of the Republic. Those who are lazy in a way that does harm to the city, and who can offer no just reason for their condition, should either be forced to work or be expelled from the commune [community]. The city would thus rid itself of that most harmful part of the poorest class. If the lowest order of society earn enough food to keep them going from day to day, then they have enough.

(Matteo Palmieri, rich merchant and humanist)

An Artist's Dilemma

Domenico:

As the marbles have turned out to be excellent for me and as those that are suitable for the work at St. Peter's are easy to quarry and nearer the coast than the others, that is, at a place called Corvara; and from this place no expense for a road is involved, except over the small stretch of marsh land near the coast. But for a choice of the marbles for figures, which I need myself, the existing road will have to be widened for about two miles [3.25 kilometres] from Corvara o Seravezza and for about a mile [1.6 kilometres] of it or less an entirely new road will have to be made, that is, it must be cut into the mountains with pickaxes to where the said marbles have to be loaded. Therefore, if the Pope is only prepared to undertake what is required for his own marbles, that is, the marsh, I haven't the means to undertake the rest and I shouldn't have any marble for my own work. If he does not undertake this, I

cannot take any responsibility for the marbles for St. Peter's, as I promised the Cardinal, but if the Pope undertakes the whole of it, I can do all that I promised.

I've told you all about it in other letters. Now, you are experienced and discreet and are, I know, well disposed towards me; so I beg you to arrange the matter in your own way with the Cardinal and to reply to me quickly, so that I may reach a decision, and if nothing else eventuates, may return to Rome to what I was doing before. I could not go to Carrara, because in twenty years I shouldn't get the marbles I need, since, owing to this business, I've become an object of great hostility there and I should be compelled, if I return to Rome, to work in bronze, as we agreed.

I must inform you that the Commissioners have already made great plans in regard to this business of the marbles since they got my report, and I believe that they have already fixed the prices, the duties and the dues and that the **notaries**, and arch-notaries, the **purveyors** and sub-purveyors are already resolved to wax fat on their profits there. So think it over and do whatever you can to prevent this affair falling into their hands, because later on it would be more difficult to get anything out of them than out of Carrara. I beg you to answer me quickly as to what you think I should do, and to commend me to the Cardinal. I am here as his agent, so I will not do anything, except what you tell me, because I assume that to be his wish.

If in writing to you I haven't written as grammatically as one should, or if I've sometimes missed out the main verb, please forgive me, because I'm troubled with a ringing in my ears, which prevents my thinking as clearly as I'd like.

Your Michelangelo Sculptor in Florence (mid-March 1518)

(E. H. Ramsden (ed.). The Letters of Michelangelo, Vol.I, 1496-1534. Stanford University Press: Stanford, CA, 1963. pp. 108-109.)

The Reformation

13

Our Study of the Reformation

Our study of the Reformation includes the following topics:

- Life During the Reformation
- The Importance of Religion
- What Was the Reformation?
- The Ninety-five Theses
- The Reformation in England
- Mennonites and Hutterites
- John Calvin
- The End of the World
- The Catholic Reformation
- Witchcraft
- Discrimination Against the Jews
- The Spread of the Reformation
- The Ottoman Empire
- Suleiman the Magnificent
- Religious Freedom
- Jews, Christians, and Muslims
- The Legacy of the Reformation

The Renaissance and the Reformation marked the beginnings of the modern world. Writers began to publicly question authority. They wanted to know how the world came to be the way it was. In doing so, they helped create the kind of thinking that led to the Protestant Reformation.

The word *catholic* (without a capital C) means "universal" or "wide-ranging." For instance, someone with catholic musical tastes likes a wide variety of music. The church was catholic because it included, or hoped to include, all people of the known world. Its religion would be universal. It was Roman because it acknowledged the pope in Rome as its head.

The Reformation divided Europe and led to many religious wars between Catholics and Protestants. It also affected the world beyond Europe. In North America, for example, New England was settled by Protestant refugees from England, called **Puritans**, who were looking for a place to practice their religion

Questions to Think About

- Why did some people demand changes in the church?
- What major changes took place during this period?
- How has the Reformation influenced society today?
- Why is religion so important in so many societies?
- What role has religion played in the development of society?

13 Chapter 13

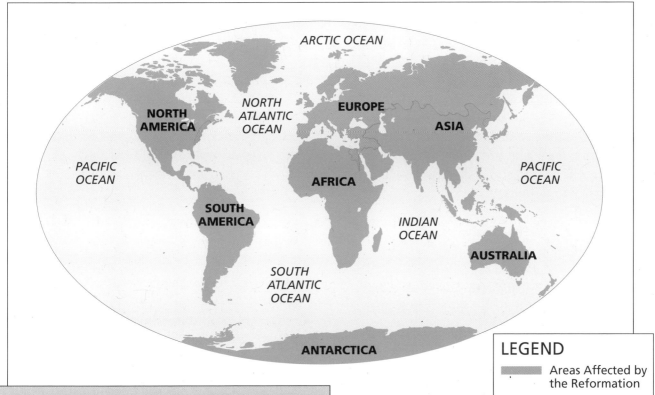

Figure 13.1 Europe and parts of Asia, Africa, and North America were affected by the Reformation.

LEGEND

▨ Areas Affected by the Reformation

freely. Roman Catholicism was brought to Quebec by French priests, nuns, and missionaries. The Reformation was also a time when missionaries, both Roman Catholic and Protestant, struggled to convert the peoples of North America, South America, and Asia to their particular form of Christianity.

Figure 13.2 John Calvin was an important thinker and writer who dedicated his life to the Reformation.

Life During the Reformation

Most Europeans in the 16th century lived and worked on the land as peasants much as they had for centuries. They rented their land or, more often, worked as labourers. Most of the time, they lived close to starvation. Meat was a luxury. People ate mainly bread, cheese, and vegetables and drank water or weak beer. Tea and coffee were still unknown in Europe, as were many of the foodstuffs we eat today.

Most people lived in huts, which were usually built of wood, mud, straw, and other easily available materials. The huts were badly lit and poorly heated. Diseases and illnesses, such as the Black Death, influenza, food poisoning, and blood poisoning from infections, were common and often fatal. Lack of sanitation, unclean water, and unhygienic living conditions contributed to illnesses.

People believed in spirits and witches to help them make sense of their world. Their holidays, celebrations, and forms of entertainment were

Very few people owned clocks or watches in the 16th century. Time was measured by the rhythms of nature. For example, most people got up at dawn and went to bed at dusk. The pace of work was controlled by the demands of the job at hand. Few people knew exactly when they had been born or exactly how old they were. Martin Luther knew that he was born on November 10 because that was St. Martin's Day and the reason his parents named him Martin. However, he was never certain that the year was 1483, since it was unusual to date years like that.

In England, years were identified in terms of who was on the throne. For instance, acts of parliament and other official documents stated "the twentieth year of Her Majesty Queen Elizabeth" instead of "1578."

often noisy and violent, as they looked for some relief from their everyday worries and fears.

The roles of both men and women remained much the same as they had been a hundred years earlier. Women were still subordinate to men. Women were not allowed to become priests or ministers, for example. Both the Roman Catholic and Protestant churches stated a woman's most important duties were to support her husband, run the household, and raise the children.

Town and City Life

While most people lived in the countryside, towns were growing in size. Towns, still small by modern standards, were surrounded by walls, with gates that were locked at night. Town authorities kept careful watch over people's comings and goings to ensure that strangers and non-residents did not settle in their towns.

Towns and cities were crowded, dirty, and noisy. People dumped both their garbage and human waste in the streets. Water was often contaminated. Streets were unpaved, and there were no sidewalks. Houses of two or three storeys were built close together, so streets – usually not more than narrow, crooked lanes – received little natural light. At night, people put

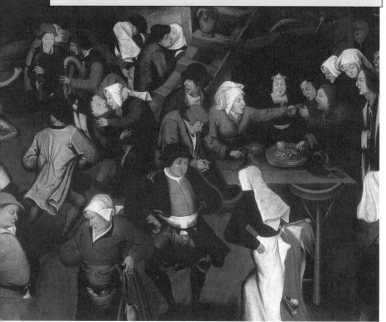

Figure 13.3 People could forget their daily worries and have a good time at holidays or at weddings such as the one shown here. In this painting by Pieter Brueghel, peasants are dancing at a wedding feast. Many Protestant reformers thought this kind of behaviour was undignified and even sinful. These reformers were encouraging people to find enjoyment in attending church and studying the Bible.

Figure 13.4 In this painting, musicians entertain guests at a French upper-class wedding in the 16th century. This picture shows a very different kind of wedding from that shown in figure 13.3.

Entertainers might perform a *masque* later in the celebration. Masques were a combination of dance, poetry, and music, often using a theme from ancient Greek mythology. Masques were very popular in Europe in the 16th and early 17th centuries, although radical Protestants disapproved of them.

towns than in the countryside. There were more things to do. It was also easier to be anonymous. In villages, everyone knew everything about everyone; in towns, it was easier to blend into the crowds. With the mixture of people, as well as the continual coming and going of traders from different regions, towns were becoming centres of new ideas and new ways of thinking.

lanterns outside their houses, but these provided very little light. Because most houses were built of wood and people used open fires for cooking and heating, fire was a constant danger. Skilled workers often ran their businesses from their homes, and certain streets were devoted to specific kinds of businesses. For example, butchers were located on one street, tailors on another, and so on.

Towns could be dangerous and violent places, especially at night. The authorities organized patrols of night watchmen, but these patrols were never very effective. As a result, most people stayed home after dark.

Market days were special. The crowds often had money to spend or goods to exchange and, therefore, attracted entertainers such as musicians, jugglers, acrobats, actors, and magicians. Pickpockets, swindlers, and other criminals also found market days profitable, as did beggars, who were licensed so that their numbers could be controlled.

Despite the problems, towns were attractive to many people. Jobs became easier to find in

Figure 13.5 Once a week, farmers came into town and set up tables with goods to sell in the market square. City workers and craftspeople also set up shop.

Figure 13.6 In the 16th century, a large minority of Protestants, called *Huguenots*, lived in France. From the 1560s to the 1590s, Roman Catholics and Huguenots fought a bitter civil war in France. The worst incident took place in 1572 when thousands of Protestants were taken by surprise and killed in the St. Bartholomew's Day massacre, depicted here. The fighting was ended in 1598 when the Edict of Nantes granted religious freedom to the Huguenots. In 1685, King Louis XIV revoked the edict. About 200 000 Huguenots fled France to settle in Holland, England, and other Protestant countries.

The Importance of Religion

Today, most Canadians believe in religious freedom and see religion as a private matter. In early 16th-century Europe, before the Reformation, the thinking was very different. Religion was not a matter of private belief but of membership in one's community.

Life in almost every community revolved around the local church. The most significant events in people's life were celebrated there, such as baptisms, marriages, and funerals. People who did not attend church services or who rejected the teachings of the church were punished with fines, imprisonment, and even death in extreme cases.

Most people believed in a heaven and a hell; life after death was a very real concern. Famine, illness, and death were a regular part of everyday life. In these circumstances, religion offered security in the present and hope for the future. People believed that what they did in their lives on Earth affected them for all eternity. They would be saved and go to heaven or be damned and go to hell.

While there were **Orthodox churches** in eastern Europe, in western Europe people followed only one form of Christianity – Roman Catholicism.

Most rulers rejected religious freedom. They believed that law and order and security depended on their subjects sharing the same beliefs and religion. People took their religion so seriously that they were prepared to kill and be killed for their beliefs. Rulers felt that religious differences would lead to civil war. Rulers also believed that their authority came from God; therefore, the church should support them. This sometimes led to power struggles between rulers and the church.

What Was the Reformation?

The Protestant Reformation began in Germany in the early 1500s. At first, it was an attempt to reform the Roman Catholic Church, hence the name *Reformation*. The word *Protestant* was first used in 1529, when a group of religious reformers issued a *protestatio* (a Latin word for a declaration of protest) describing their beliefs. The word then came to describe people who were protesting against the organization and some of the customs of the Roman Catholic Church. Protestants believed that the Roman Catholic Church was no longer following what they believed to be the true teachings of the Bible.

Protestants could not agree on how the church should be reformed. They all believed in the authority of the Bible, but they did not all agree on what the Bible meant. As a result, a number of different Protestant groups developed. Among the largest were the Lutherans, the Calvinists, the Anglicans (or Church of England), the Mennonites, and the Hutterites. Most rulers in northwestern Europe broke away from the Roman Catholic Church, and each adopted one of the Protestant faiths.

Figure 13.7 The church was usually the most prominent building in towns and villages. In addition to attending church services, people gathered at the church to celebrate festivals and holidays.

Figure 13.8 This painting shows people in the afterlife. Some are in heaven, some are in **purgatory**, and some are in hell. In the 16th century, a central question was: What did people have to do to earn God's forgiveness for their sins? Some believed they would be saved if they did good deeds during their life on Earth. Some thought that only those who truly believed in God would be saved. Still others thought that only God could decide who was going to go to heaven and who was not.

The Ninety-five Theses

On October 31, 1517, Martin Luther published a list of ninety-five statements, or **theses**, that questioned some Roman Catholic practices. From this action, the Protestant Reformation developed. By 1521, Luther had been denounced by the pope, excommunicated from the Roman Catholic Church, and declared an outlaw by the Holy Roman Emperor, Charles V. Only the protection of his own ruler, Frederick of Saxony, saved him from imprisonment, and probably from execution or murder.

To understand how the Ninety-five Theses led to the breakup of the Roman Catholic Church – and how it affects our lives even today – we need to try to find the answers to three other questions:

1. Who was Martin Luther?

2. What did Luther say in the Ninety-five Theses?

3. Why did the Ninety-five Theses have such an impact?

Who Was Martin Luther?

Martin Luther was born in 1483 in what is now Germany. When he was a teenager, his father sent him to university to become a lawyer. Luther, however, wanted to be a monk and serve the church.

From the time he entered the monastery in 1505, Luther struggled with a problem that he found almost unbearable. He was convinced he was not good enough to deserve God's forgiveness and mercy. It did not matter how many prayers he said, how many times he went to confession and performed other religious duties, how often he studied the Bible, and how carefully he followed the teachings of the church, he believed that God was angry with him.

What Did Luther Say in the Ninety-five Theses?

Luther began to think more and more about what he saw as the central question of faith: What did people have to do to earn God's forgiveness for their sins and go to heaven.

Figure 13.9 Martin Luther did more than post his Ninety-five Theses to a door. To help spread his ideas, Luther published his theses. He was one of the first people to use the printing press to help spread his message.

The Roman Catholic Church taught people to believe in God and to follow the teachings and ceremonies of the church. Luther concluded that what really mattered was that people have faith in God. It was too easy, he felt, to follow the rules and teachings of the church without really believing in them.

For centuries, the Roman Catholic Church had argued that the Bible was not always easy to understand. It was up to the church to explain its meaning. Otherwise, people would interpret it however they pleased. Luther, though, felt that many of the church's rules and teachings were wrong because they were not based on the Bible as he understood it. He was especially critical of how the church sold *indulgences* – pardons that people could buy to reduce punishment for their sins. Further, he rejected the Roman Catholic rule that priests could not be married, because he found no authority for the rule in the Bible. He, himself, married a former nun, Katherine von Bora.

According to the church, priests held a sacred position as a bridge between humans and God. It was only through priests that people could learn what God really meant. Luther believed that true believers did not need priests to speak for them – they could speak directly to God. He called this the "priesthood of all believers" and described priests as *ministers* (from a Latin word meaning to give help or be of service).

He wrote constantly in both Latin and German, producing an essay or pamphlet almost every two weeks. Although people before Luther had criticized the church, Luther's ideas reached a wider audience due to the invention of the printing press (see page 255). Before the printing press, books had been copied by hand and were few in number. Now, authorities were unable to control the spread of Luther's ideas.

At first, Pope Leo X did not take the ideas of Luther – an unknown university professor – seriously. The pope had more important problems. He was involved in political disputes with the Holy Roman Emperor and with rulers such as Francis I, the king of France. The pope was also concerned with the ongoing expansion of the Ottoman Empire (see page 286). However, as Luther's ideas spread beyond his town, the pope ordered Luther to obey the teachings of the church. Luther refused. He was a monk and had taken a vow of obedience, but no one could show him where he was wrong on the authority of the Bible.

Between 1517 and 1521, an increasingly fierce conflict developed between the pope and Luther. Because religious matters were so important, people began to take sides.

Figure 13.10 Here, we see Luther burning the papal order that condemned his ideas. When Luther received orders from Pope Leo X to obey the teachings of the church, Luther defiantly burned them in front of a crowd of his supporters. What had started as a local debate over some of the church's activities became a serious challenge to its authority.

Figure 13.11 This Protestant cartoon criticizes the sale of indulgences by portraying them as a purely monetary affair. A priest and a monk on horseback hold up a cross to attract attention and show that this is a religious occasion. The pope's authorization is mounted on a pole with four seals attached to show it is genuine. As a priest reads the announcement explaining what indulgences can do, customers buy their indulgences at the sales counter. In an age where people believed in the existence of everlasting hellfire and the certainty of divine punishment for their sins, it is easy to see why people would want to buy indulgences.

Indulgences

One of Luther's main objections was to the church's use of indulgences. Most people believed that they would go to either heaven or hell after they died. However, even those who went to heaven were punished for their sins in a place in the afterlife called *purgatory*. To lessen the punishment for sins committed during life on Earth, people could buy indulgences from the church.

Indulgences were supposed to be sold to people only when they were truly sorry for their sins. In reality, indulgences could be bought for almost anything, and pardons became an easy way for the church to raise money. The indulgences that upset Luther the most were designed to raise money to build a new cathedral in Rome. He felt that Germans were not benefitting from the sale of indulgences.

In addition, those selling the indulgences made many false claims, including that indulgences had the power to release people who were already in purgatory. Luther argued that indulgences were a waste of people's money. Moreover, he felt that people were more likely to do wrong if they believed they could avoid punishment by buying indulgences. Finally, Luther argued, the pope did not have the power to authorize indulgences because they were not based on the authority of the Bible. This last argument was the most dangerous of all. It meant that Luther was challenging the authority of the Roman Catholic Church and its leader.

Why Did the Ninety-five Theses Have Such an Impact?

In the German states, those who sided with Martin Luther resented that most of their money ended up in Rome. In addition to what they

Figure 13.12 At the Diet of Spires in 1529, Roman Catholics and Christian reformers met to discuss the powers and influence of the Roman Catholic Church. Reformers wanted countries to have the freedom to choose their religion. The word *Protestant* comes from this meeting.

spent on indulgences, ordinary people were required to give the church a tenth of their income, either in money or goods. They also had to pay fees for weddings, funerals, baptisms, and other ceremonies. Luther argued that German money should be used to help Germans, not to pay for the pope's expenses.

When ordinary people began to look deeper into the actions of those involved in church affairs, they did not see its leaders following the teachings of Christ. Instead, they saw bishops and archbishops living like nobles, with palaces and servants. Some priests even bought church positions, took the money that came with the position, then hired substitutes to do their work.

Rulers, too, began to resent the wealth and power of the church. They wanted some of the church's possessions, particularly its lands and buildings. They also wanted to make sure their own power was greater than the power of the church. Luther's criticism of the church offered these rulers a chance to achieve their goals.

Figure 13.13 Christ had emphasized poverty, charity, and virtue. What Luther's supporters saw were churches filled with gold.

The Reformation in England

In England, the Reformation began with a personal problem of King Henry VIII (1509-1547). Henry wanted a son who would succeed him as king, but with his wife, Catherine of Aragon, he had only a daughter. Henry feared that a woman would not be strong enough as a ruler to maintain law and order and control the country's powerful nobility. He asked Pope Clement VII to **annul** his marriage so that he could marry Anne Boleyn, by whom he hoped to have a son. It did not help Henry's case that Catherine was the aunt of the Holy Roman Emperor, Charles V, and she put pressure on the pope to protect her. The pope refused Henry's request.

Henry made himself the head of the Church of England and annulled his own marriage. He remained a Roman Catholic in faith, but he broke all ties with the pope. Henry closed all the Roman Catholic monasteries and convents in England: he wanted their land and property, and he feared their loyalty was to the pope rather than to him.

Henry eventually married a total of six times, but he had only two more children, a daughter and a son.

Henry was succeeded as king by his only son, Edward VI. Under the rule of Edward (1547-1553) and his advisers, the church in England became strongly Protestant. Edward died in 1553 and was succeeded by his eldest sister, Mary, the daughter of Henry and his first wife, Catherine of Aragon. Mary was a devout Roman Catholic. She restored Roman Catholicism in England, and accepted the pope's authority. During Mary's reign (1553-1558), about 270 Protestants were burned at the stake, and many prominent Protestants fled the country.

Mary died in 1558 and was succeeded by Henry VIII's daughter Elizabeth. As queen (1558-1603), Elizabeth I, a Protestant, immediately reversed Mary's Roman Catholic policies and changed the name of the Church of England to the Anglican Church. Elizabeth, who was twenty-five years old when she became queen, had seen firsthand how much

Figure 13.14 Charles V became Holy Roman Emperor in 1519, when he was only 19 years old. His vast territories in Germany, Spain, Italy, Burgundy, the Netherlands, and the Spanish colonies in Central America and South America caused him many problems. He was involved in conflict with the pope, war with France, continual opposition from German princes, and the threat of Ottoman expansion – not to mention the challenges of Protestantism. In 1556, Charles abdicated his throne and retired to a Spanish monastery where he died in 1558.

trouble religion could cause. She left Roman Catholics in peace as long as they did not oppose her new Protestant church. People could believe what they wanted provided they attended Anglican services and acted as though they accepted Anglican beliefs. This policy was known as "outward conformity."

In 1570, the pope, St. Pius IV, declared Elizabeth to be a heretic. It was the duty of all Roman Catholics to overthrow her. This decree

In 1604, Elizabeth's successor, King James I, ordered a new English translation of the Bible. In 1611, the *Authorized Version of the Bible*, sometimes also known as the *King James Version*, was published. The publication of the *King James Version* had an important influence on the development of the English language. For the next 300 years, it was the only version of the Bible that most English-speakers heard in church every Sunday. It was also the only book that many people owned and read. As a result, the *King James Version* shaped ideas on how the English language should be written.

Religious Freedom or Treason?

In Elizabethan England, many Roman Catholics risked their lives to participate in a Roman Catholic church service.

Anne was helping her family prepare for a special mass. It was to be conducted by a Jesuit priest. As a Roman Catholic, Anne admired the Jesuits. She had heard many stories about Ignatius Loyola, who had founded the Jesuits in 1540. She also knew the Jesuits had been working undercover in Protestant lands and serving as missionaries in all parts of the world.

Anne's parents had made her promise not to tell anyone of the plans. In Queen Elizabeth's England their religion was illegal, and Catholics were under suspicion.

Anne's father had already paid fines to the government because of the family's refusal to attend services in the local Anglican church. He had been questioned by the authorities several times and been threatened with imprisonment. Anne knew that the mass was much more dangerous than anything the family had ever done. The year before, in 1581, a new law declared that sheltering a Jesuit priest was an act of **treason** against the queen. Suspects could be tortured and even put to death.

The government feared the Jesuits were planning a rebellion. To Roman Catholics like Anne and her family, though, the Jesuits were special. The priests heard confession, performed mass, and helped Catholics maintain their religious beliefs at a time when they were not allowed to practice their religion freely. Anne was very excited. She was fourteen years old and would be meeting a real priest for the first time.

Despite the risks, Anne volunteered to bring the priest to their house. The priest was disguised as a merchant. Anne's task was to ride to a nearby village and guide him to the house. She had worked out a route over the fields to ensure that they would avoid government agents or patrols. To be caught would be death for the priest and, perhaps, for Anne's family.

Anne met the priest as arranged, and the journey back went smoothly. Her parents showed the priest to his room and, more important, to the priest hole. He was to hide there if government agents raided the house. The priest hole contained a bed and enough food and water to last for two days.

When it was dark, Anne and her brothers and sisters informed their Catholic neighbours of the priest's arrival. They were careful not to arouse suspicion. Everyone knew that severe punishment awaited them if they were caught.

put England's Roman Catholics in a difficult position. Should they be loyal to their pope or to their queen? Elizabeth took no chances. For the remainder of her reign, she subjected Roman Catholics to heavy fines and terms of imprisonment. She ordered the execution of Roman Catholic priests who entered England illegally to minister to those who wanted to maintain their Catholic faith.

When Elizabeth died in 1603, the Anglican Church was firmly established in England. Roman Catholics did not believe in this new church, but most did not publicly oppose it. Some extreme Protestants, called Puritans, did not think the Anglican Church was Protestant enough. In the early 1600s, many Puritans sailed to North America where they set up their own brand of Protestantism in New England. Most people in England, however, accepted the Anglican Church.

Figure 13.15 When the Roman Catholic country of Spain tried to invade Protestant England in 1588 and overthrow Elizabeth I, a combination of English warships and stormy weather helped to defeat and scatter the Spanish Armada.

Mennonites and Hutterites

Some Protestants wanted to live in communities where they could have their own way of life. They gave up private property, arguing that real peace and equality could come only when property was owned in common. They said their first loyalty was not to any government, but to God. They renounced all violence, even in self-defence, and tried to base their way of life on their strict understanding of the Bible.

These Protestants believed that people should be baptized only when they were adults and could fully understand the purpose and meaning of the ceremony. Because the followers were re-baptized, they were called *Anabaptists*. They were active in what are now Germany, the Netherlands, and Switzerland. Two groups of Anabaptists were the Mennonites and the Hutterites. Each group was named after its leader: the Mennonites after Menno Simons (1496-1561), and the Hutterites after Jakob Hutter who was burned at the stake as a heretic in 1536.

John Calvin

Some Protestants felt that Luther's criticism of the Roman Catholic Church did not go far enough. The most influential of these Protestants was John Calvin (1509-1564).

Calvin left France in 1534 because he feared persecution for his Protestant beliefs. He travelled to Switzerland and in 1541 settled in the city of Geneva.

Calvin's most distinctive belief was *predestination*. Before a person was even born, God knew his or her future. People were destined either to be saved and go to heaven or not to be saved. Destiny was in God's hands. Predestination was not a new idea. It dated back to the 5th century BCE, but Calvin gave it new emphasis. He believed that no one deserved to be saved. It was only through God's mercy that some people were saved. Only God could decide.

Calvin believed the church and government should work closely together to establish God's law. In Geneva, Switzerland, every aspect of

Figure 13.16 Anabaptists were persecuted for their beliefs. As a result, the Mennonites and the Hutterites were frequently on the move. In the 18th century, they found homes in Russia, where they were valued for their farming skills. In the 1870s, the Russian government began forcing Hutterite and Mennonite men to serve in the Russian army. Both groups decided to emigrate to North America where they found more freedom to practice their religions.

people's lives was subject to the rules of the local church. Church officials could inspect people's houses. Activities such as drinking alcohol, gambling, dancing, and playing cards were banned. Geneva became famous as a model of how Protestantism could shape a whole society.

Religious Divisions in Europe in the 17th Century

NORWAY
SWEDEN
N

SCOTLAND
NORTH SEA
DENMARK

IRELAND
ENGLAND
GERMANY

HOLY ROMAN EMPIRE

TIC
N

FRANCE
HUNGARY

ITALY

SPAIN

MEDITERRANEAN SEA

AL

LEGEND
Protestant
Catholic
Mixed

0   500   1000 km

Figure 13.17 This map shows the division of Europe into Catholic and Protestant countries at the beginning of the 17th century. Since there was a great deal of conflict between Catholics and Protestants at this time, the official religion of some countries changed often. As well, many Catholic countries had large pockets of Protestants, and vice versa. For these reasons, this map can only represent religious divisions in an approximate way.

The End of the World

The 16th century was a very troubled time in Europe. Not only were there many wars, but the wars were more destructive than ever before – due to the availability of guns and the increasing size of armies. Rapid population growth increased the chances of famine and disease.

The voyages of Christopher Columbus, Vasco da Gama, Ferdinand Magellan, and other explorers showed Europeans that the world was much bigger and more puzzling than they had thought. Astronomers, such as Copernicus, were even suggesting that the sun, not the earth, was the centre of the universe.

In these circumstances, it is perhaps not surprising that many people saw the Reformation as one more sign that their world was collapsing around them. The Bible was the most reliable book they knew, and it predicted a final battle between Christ and the anti-Christ after which God would return to Earth. Many Protestants believed that their conflict with the Roman Catholic Church was the beginning of this final battle. All the signs – war, disease, the split in the Roman Catholic Church – seemed to point that way.

Figure 13.18 This drawing is from a letter written by Christopher Columbus. He is depicting the islands he reached in the Caribbean. The castle represents Spain.

Figure 13.19 Saint Theresa of Avila was born into a wealthy noble family in Spain. During her lifetime, she founded 17 convents in Spain.

The Catholic Reformation

Many Roman Catholics agreed that their church needed reform. However, their solution was to improve the church, not to start another one. They supported new orders of nuns and monks and did all that they could to rid the church of corruption and abuse.

Some emphasized the importance of personal belief. Saint Theresa of Avila spent much of her life establishing convents in which the nuns lived poor and simple lives and dedicated themselves to prayer. Other Catholics founded more active organizations, such as the Society of Jesus (the Jesuits). Others founded hospitals, schools, orphanages, refuges for the poor and homeless, and homes for old people. Beginning in the 1530s, for example, Ursuline nuns dedicated themselves to educating young women from poor families.

Leaders in the Roman Catholic Church aimed to win back countries that had converted to Protestantism and to prevent Protestantism from spreading any further. Martin Luther's success had shown them how important it was to control the printing press. In Protestant and Roman Catholic countries alike, books were not supposed to be published without government approval. In Roman Catholic countries, no book could be published without the permission of the church; every book sold to the public had to carry a notice saying that it had been officially approved. The church began a list, called the **Index**, of books that Catholics were not allowed to read. When illegal books were found, they were publicly burned and their owners punished. In 1558, for example, Venice burned 10 000 books.

In addition, the Inquisition, a special department of the Roman Catholic Church, was enlarged and strengthened.

All such measures to stop the spread of Protestantism were second-best, however. The most effective way to halt the progress of Protestantism was to make sure people were not attracted to it in the first place. It was for this reason that the Roman Catholic Church began its reformation from within.

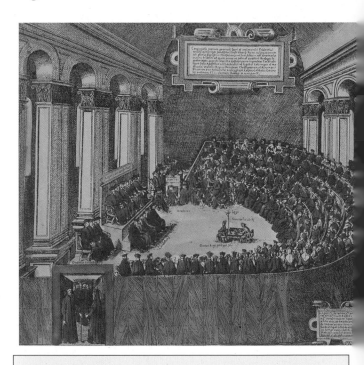

Figure 13.20 In 1545, the Council of Trent met in Trent, Italy. The gathering of the pope, bishops, and other high-ranking church officials was the first of what would be three sessions to initiate reform of the Roman Catholic Church.

Figure 13.21 Agents from the Inquisition were always on alert for any communication of non-Catholic ideas, whether in writing or in conversation. Non-Catholic ideas were considered heresy, and courts like this one quickly passed judgment.

Witchcraft

Today, we are familiar with a variety of superstitions. For example, it is considered bad luck to walk under a ladder or to break a mirror. In the Reformation period, almost everyone believed in magic and witchcraft. In a dark room lit only by a fluttering candle, with the wind howling outside, it was hard not to believe in the presence of ghosts and spirits. Like religion, magic and witchcraft helped people to understand and cope with the problems of daily life. Famine, illness, the sudden death of animals or people, the spoiling of crops – in fact, any unexpected or disastrous event – could be explained by witchcraft.

Between 1550 and 1680, perhaps as many as 100 000 people were executed as witches in Europe. Most were single women who were unpopular in their village or who acted different from the majority of people. Many accusations came from neighbours who had suffered injury or loss.

Although the persecution of so-called witches started in the 1400s, some historians think that it was made worse by the Reformation. The Reformation period produced a much greater awareness of both God and the devil – and the forces of good and evil. It was easy for people to see witches as servants of the devil and,

therefore, as evil people. Some historians believe that male doctors who felt threatened by women healers used their dominant position in society to have the "witches" destroyed without any opposition.

Once arrested, people suspected of witchcraft were questioned under torture, which helps explain why so many of those who were accused confessed even when they were innocent. Since so many believed in witchcraft, it is even possible that accused people thought that they really were witches.

Another kind of magic also led to accusations of witchcraft. This magic was performed by healers, usually women, who had extensive knowledge of traditional medicines, spells, and charms. People turned to healers to cure minor illnesses, ensure success or good luck, find lost objects, and cope with the everyday problems of life. Before the Reformation, the Roman Catholic Church usually turned a blind eye to this kind of activity. Most Protestants, however, saw magic as dangerous because it took away from God's authority.

Discrimination Against the Jews

During the Reformation, prejudice against Jews continued to grow. Roman Catholics and Protestants alike were convinced that their own particular beliefs were the only real ones. Jews and Muslims, for example, were not only wrong, but sinful. Roman Catholics and Protestants were determined to protect their religions from others.

In Europe, Jews had been discriminated against for centuries. Most Christians thought the Jewish religion was false and treated Jews as outsiders. Jews were forced to live in ghettos and to wear special clothes. Many jobs were closed to them. Jews had also been expelled from several countries. During the Reformation, more expulsions took place, especially from the German and Spanish kingdoms. In 1492, for example, Spanish Jews and Muslims were given a choice by the king of Spain: leave Spain or convert to Christianity. Even Jews who chose to convert to Christianity often found themselves under suspicion from the Inquisition.

The Spread of the Reformation

The Reformation began in western Europe, but its effects were soon felt in other parts of the world. In the 16th century, politics and religion were closely connected, and religious differences played a part in the rivalries of several western European countries.

Powerful countries such as Spain and Portugal, and later Holland, France, and England, began to establish worldwide empires, and religion had an important role. Even before the Reformation, priests and missionaries accompanied traders, explorers, and soldiers on their voyages.

As European countries developed their empires, they claimed to be acting, at least in part, for religious reasons. Each country wanted to convert the world to its particular form of Christianity. In the process, the traditions and beliefs of the indigenous peoples of the conquered territories were ignored. Their own religions and cultures were stamped out. Some peoples were forced to work for their European conquerors, usually as slaves, as happened in Spain's colonies in Central America and South America (see chapter 10).

Figure 13.22 By the late 1500s, Jesuit priests were visiting countries all around the world. Between 1542 and 1552, for example, St. Francis Xavier lived in India, the East Indies, and Japan, and died en route to China. The Jesuits wanted to spread Christianity, but they were also interested in finding out about other cultures. Much of what Europeans first learned of other parts of the world came from the letters and reports of the Jesuits. In China, Jesuits gained a special place at the emperor's court thanks to their knowledge of mathematics and science. Although they made a few converts, Christian missionaries found it difficult to persuade people outside Europe to abandon their own religions. This picture shows two Jesuits (in black robes) talking with an East Indian prince and his advisers.

Hans and the Peasants' Revolt

In this story, Hans, joins a revolt to protest the poor living conditions of peasants in Germany.

Hans was worried. He had not really wanted to join the peasants' army; he had a wife and three children to support. But the other men in his village said that if he really cared for his family he would join the army and fight.

Like most villagers, Hans could no longer support himself and his family. As a serf, he owed many duties to the lord of the village. One of those duties was working on the lord's land. Since the work usually came at the busiest times of the year, such as seeding and harvest times, he often had to neglect his own land – although, in reality, all land belonged to the lord. He was not allowed to keep everything he grew. He had to give much of the harvest to the lord as a kind of tax. He also had to pay taxes to the church. Hans might have been able to get some food by hunting and fishing, but only the lord was allowed to hunt and fish.

Hans was tired of living on only bread, cheese, vegetables, and water and weak beer – that is, when he and his family were not facing starvation. It was bad enough in the summer, but in the cold of winter it was unbearable. He and the other villagers agreed that something had to be done to improve living conditions. Since the lord ignored their petitions and insisted that they obey his rights, the villagers felt they had no choice but to fight.

Hans had hoped that Martin Luther and other Protestant reformers would support the peasants, but Luther had condemned them as rebels and mad dogs and was urging the princes to kill them.

As far as Hans could tell, the peasants' demands were reasonable. They wanted an end to the taxes that they had to pay to the clergy and the lords. They wanted the right to hunt and fish. They wanted fair treatment in the courts run by the nobles. They wanted the right to choose their own church ministers. In short, they wanted more freedom and independence.

When he joined the peasants' army just before Christmas in 1524, Hans hoped he was doing the right thing. But now there was fighting all around the district and across much of Germany. What hope did the peasants have of success? With their daggers and axes, they were no match for the trained soldiers who were armed with muskets and cannons.

Sooner or later, Hans's army was likely to be involved in battle. He was tempted to desert, but if he was found to be deserting he was certain to be executed. He worried about his family. He had not received any news from home in days. Many villages had been destroyed. Now, bandits and thieves were stealing what they could from the ravaged villages. Whatever he did, Hans faced serious problems.

Figure 13.23 Roman Catholic and Protestant princes in the various German states put aside their differences and joined forces to crush the peasant revolt. They showed no mercy to anyone they suspected of rebellion.

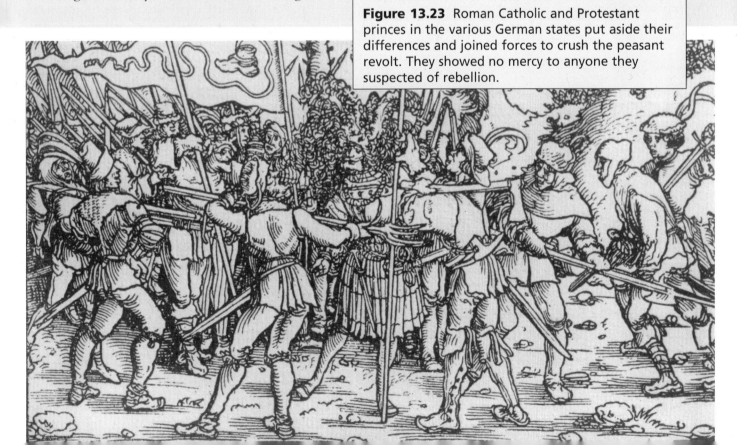

The Ottoman Empire

The Ottomans were Turkish warriors and nomads who, in the 13th century, were driven from their homeland in Central Asia by the Mongols. They settled in the semi-independent kingdom of Anatolia (modern Asia Minor). There, they found themselves in a world where warfare was almost an everyday occurrence. As battle-hardened warriors themselves, they adapted to this situation easily. In fact, aided by a series of strong and effective leaders, they quickly expanded their territory.

In some instances, their attacks were in response to attacks against them. Sometimes, they took advantage of alliance breakups and differences among the rulers of Europe. Their main motivations were to spread the Islamic faith and to control the rich trade routes that criss-crossed the Mediterranean Sea.

So great and swift was their expansion that Martin Luther and many Protestant leaders thought the Ottoman invasions were a sign that God was punishing Christians for their sins.

The Ottomans became deeply involved in European politics. In the 1530s, for example, the king of France allied with them against his rival, the Holy Roman Emperor, Charles V. In 1543, an Ottoman fleet spent the winter in the French port of Toulon. For their part, the Ottomans encouraged the Protestants in the German states to resist the Holy Roman Emperor – even offering them money to do so.

In the 1560s, the Ottomans began to experience defeat. As their forces moved farther west, they found that they were too far away from their bases to fight effectively. A succession of weak sultans further eroded the power of the Ottoman Empire. At the same time, western European governments had finally learned how to cope with Ottoman military tactics. By the end of the 16th century, the expansion of the Ottoman Empire came to an end.

Fighting, however, continued through much of the 17th century. In 1669, the Ottomans had their last major conquest, the island of Crete. They besieged Vienna unsuccessfully in 1683 and a few years later made peace with the Holy Roman Emperor.

Ottoman Empire, 1500 CE

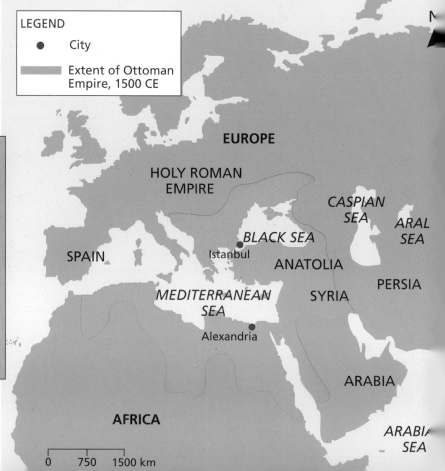

Figure 13.24 By 1350, the Ottomans ruled territory from Anatolia to Europe. In 1361, they made the Greek city of Adrianople their new capital. Their most dramatic victory came in 1453 when they captured the Byzantine capital of Constantinople, renaming it Istanbul. By 1500, they had also conquered Greece, Albania, Serbia, Bosnia, and Bulgaria. Until the late 1600s, the Ottomans continued their expansion into southeastern Europe, the areas around the Mediterranean and the Black Sea, the Middle East, and North Africa.

Figure 13.25 Osman I (1258-1324) was the founder of the Ottoman Empire.

Indian Ocean; Russia and Poland to the north; the Holy Roman Empire, Venice, and Spain in the west. No one – including the pope, the Holy Roman Emperor, and the king of Spain – could ignore Suleiman. He declared himself **caliph**, meaning "Lord of all Islam," and he saw himself as the successor of Alexander the Great and the Caesars of Rome.

As sultan, Suleiman became famous as a lawmaker. He enforced **Sharia**, or Muslim law, fairly and, where Sharia did not apply, designed new laws that treated everyone equally. He supported the arts and architecture and was, himself, a distinguished poet. Like many rulers, however, Suleiman could be cruel. In the Ottoman Empire, the eldest son of the ruler did not automatically become heir. Suleiman killed two of his own sons in order to ensure that they would not challenge his third son for the throne. Throughout his rule, he did not hesitate to kill anyone whom he thought might be a threat.

During the 19th century, the Ottomans lost much of their territory. The Ottoman Empire eventually became the modern-day republic of Turkey and lost all its territory except Istanbul and Asia Minor. The Ottoman Empire lasted over 500 years, and for much of that time it was one of the world's great powers.

Suleiman the Magnificent

Suleiman (c. 1495-1566) was sultan of the Ottoman Empire from 1520 to 1566. He was responsible for a vast expansion of the Ottoman Empire, including nearly all of southeastern Europe, the eastern Mediterranean, the Middle East, and North Africa. He made the Ottoman army and navy the most successful military force in Europe. During his rule, the Ottomans became one of the most powerful empires in Europe and Asia.

Suleiman faced many enemies: Persia in the east; Portuguese fleets in the Red Sea and

Figure 13.26 Most Muslims, and many Christians, saw Suleiman as the greatest man of his time. Christians gave him his title, "the Magnificent." Muslims called him "the Lawgiver."

Religious Freedom

Unlike in western Europe, there was very little religious persecution in the Ottoman Empire. The Ottomans saw Muslims, Jews, and Christians as similar in many ways. All three faiths worshipped one God and followed a sacred scripture, which they saw as God's word. They were all "people of the Book."

In most of their European conquests, the Ottomans made no attempt to convert people to Islam. Jews and Christians had to pay a special religious tax. However, as long as they accepted Ottoman rule, did not try to convert Muslims to other faiths or teach that Islam was wrong, and did not openly attack Islam, they were left alone to practice their own religions.

Jews, Christians, and Muslims: The Case of Joseph Nasi

Joseph Nasi was Jewish. In about 1520, he was born in Portugal where his parents had moved when Jews were expelled from Spain in 1492. Under pressure, the Nasi family converted to Christianity but secretly practiced their Jewish faith. Tired of being under constant suspicion, they moved to Antwerp (in present-day Belgium) in 1536. Antwerp was one of the few places outside the Ottoman Empire where Jews and others could worship freely. Even here, however, the Nasi family did not feel safe, and, in 1553, they moved to Istanbul.

By this time, Joseph was in his early thirties. He was well established in the family banking business and had contacts throughout Europe and the Mediterranean world. As a banker and merchant, he knew about conditions around Europe: whether harvests were going to be good or bad, which shipping routes were free from pirates, what different governments were planning, where it was safe to invest money, and so on. Europeans everywhere turned to Joseph for information about developments in the Ottoman world. Ottoman officials valued his knowledge of developments in Europe.

Not long after his arrival in Istanbul, Joseph became an important adviser to Ottoman officials and even to the sultan himself. In 1562,

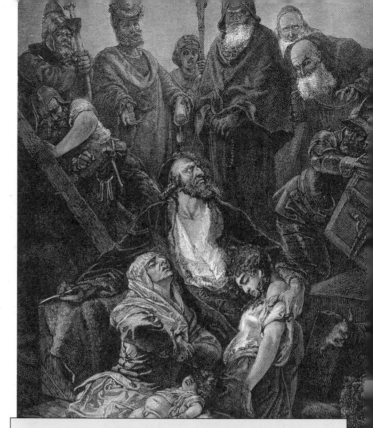

Figure 13.27 One of Joseph Nasi's goals was to find a place where Jewish refugees from Roman Catholic Europe could settle. With the approval of the sultan, Joseph tried to establish a Jewish settlement at Tiberias in Palestine. The first shipload of Jewish settlers from Italy was captured by pirates and sold into slavery. We do not know if Joseph was able to save them. Soon afterwards, the outbreak of war with Venice in 1569 ended his plans for a Jewish settlement. Joseph did, however, establish a Hebrew printing press and continued to promote Jewish culture.

he helped negotiate peace between Poland and the Ottoman Empire. In 1569, through his contacts, he was one of the first to learn about a destructive fire in Venice's main armoury. He suggested to the sultan that this might be a good time to attack Venice. As a result, Cyprus, a territory of Venice, was succesfully seized by the Ottomans.

Joseph was made the Duke of Naxos, a Greek island, by the Ottoman government. This meant that Joseph Nasi, a Jew, using a Spanish Roman Catholic as his agent, ruled the Greek Orthodox Christians of Naxos in the name of the Muslim Ottomans. Such a mixture of religions would never have been possible in western Europe.

Janissaries and Slaves

One reason for Ottoman military success was the effectiveness of their elite troops, called *Janissaries*. Originally, most Janissaries were Christian prisoners who agreed to accept Islam and fight for the sultan.

Despite their status as slaves, successful Janissaries became leading officials in the Ottoman Empire. From the sultan's point of view, this meant that he could get good advice without having to worry that his advisers had more power than he had. In Europe, rulers relied on advice from aristocrats whose wealth, pride, and power sometimes made them too independent of their king or queen. European rulers often had to worry about what they called the "over-mighty subject."

The Legacy of the Reformation

Despite the upheavals of the Reformation, much of the world we know today has its origins during this period in history:

- *Separation of church and state*
- *Different Christian religions* Today, we accept the many different Protestant churches, as well as Roman Catholicism. Until the Reformation, all Christians were members of the Roman Catholic Church.

- *Religious freedom* Today, people are free to choose the religion they wish to practice. It took many years and many wars before religious freedom became a reality, but the Reformation made it possible.

Figure 13.28 Although Janissaries were slaves, they were treated well, and their loyalty was to the sultan. Many were children from conquered Christian towns and villages. The Ottomans forced the towns and villages to hand over some of their children, no questions asked, then trained them either as palace servants or Janissaries. Taken from their birth families, these slaves saw the army as their family.

Summary

In Europe, the Reformation destroyed the unity of the Roman Catholic Church and saw the establishment of a variety of competing Protestant churches. Outside Europe, it created a wave of Christian missionary activity and emigration that had enormous impact on North America and South America and created greater contacts with Europe, Africa, and Asia. Bitter wars were waged over religion, power, or territory.

The Thirty Years' War, which lasted from 1618 to 1648, was fought for all three reasons. In the end, a peace treaty established the principle that a ruler had the right to decide the religion of his or her country, and all other rulers had to accept that decision.

Connecting and Reflecting

Reflect on the impact of the events, ideas, and changes that were generated during the Reformation. Use the information you have learned to describe how the events, ideas, and changes have affected your life today. Explain why knowing about these ideas is important to you *as a citizen of Canada and a citizen of the world.*

Be an Historian

Do you believe everything that you read in a history text? Do you ever wonder what information has been left out? When you study history, you are usually reading the results of what historians have researched and written. In this section, you will have the opportunity to do your own research and ask yourself the same kinds of questions that historians ask themselves. You will not be reading history; you will be doing history!

Historical research is very complicated. (See chapter 1.) It demands knowledge, skill, and patience. Historians have to:

- locate their evidence

- interpret what it means

- sort out what is true from what is probable and what is false

Read the excerpts below. When you are finished, answer the following questions:

- Where do these sources come from?

- Are they sources that you can trust?

- What do you know about the author? If you do not know anything, how can you find out?

- Does the author have knowledge, experience, or credentials that makes you willing to trust his or her work?

- As you try to understand the past, how important is chronology?

Luther at the Diet of Worms, 1521

Note: A *Diet* was an assembly of the rulers, princes, and leading figures of the Holy Roman Empire. In 1521 the Holy Roman Emperor, Charles V, ordered Luther to attend the Diet in the city of Worms to answer for his beliefs and to show that he was not a heretic. It was a very dramatic occasion. Luther did not know what might happen to him. He had already been excommunicated by the pope. The emperor guaranteed Luther's personal safety, but Luther's supporters feared it might be a trick and, in any case, assassins might be on the loose. The emperor and the pope were convinced that Luther was dangerous and had to be stopped. Luther was convinced that he was right. Both sides believed that God was on their side. The following sources tell what happened.

Luther's Defence

You asked me yesterday whether I wrote these books and whether I would disown them. They are all mine but, to answer your second question, whether I am willing to disown them, I must say that they are not all of the same kind. Some deal with life and faith so simply and sincerely that even my opponents respect them…. If I renounced these books I would be the only person on earth to deny the truth we all accept. A second group of books describes how the Christian world is being ruined by the supporters of the Pope. Who can deny that they speak the truth when people everywhere complain that their consciences are torn apart by the Pope's laws. If I deny these books, I will open the door to more tyranny and unholiness, and this will be all the worse since it will seem as if the Holy Roman Empire did not object. A third group of my books attacks private individuals and I admit that I may have been more bitter and personal than a monk should be, but I cannot disown these books either without opening the door to tyranny and sin…. If I am shown that I am wrong then I will be the first to throw my books into the fire. I have been reminded of the disturbances which my teachings have produced. I can only reply in the words of Our Lord: "I come not to bring peace, but a sword."…. I must walk in the footsteps of Our Lord. I say this not to put people down, but because I cannot escape my duty to the German people.

A Church Official Challenges Luther

Martin, how can you assume that you are the only one to understand the sense of Scripture? Would you put your judgment above that of so many famous men and claim that you know more than all of them? You have no right to question the holy faith, established by Christ the perfect lawgiver, proclaimed throughout the world by the apostles, sealed by the red blood of the martyrs, confirmed by the sacred councils, defined by the Church in which all our fathers believed until death and gave us as our inheritance and which both Pope and Emperor have forbidden us to discuss lest there opens up a never-ending debate. I ask you, Martin, to answer honestly and without tricks: do you or do you not renounce your books and the errors they contain?

Luther Replies

Since Your Majesty and Your Lordships want a simple reply, I will answer honestly and without tricks. Unless I am found guilty through Scripture and through plain reason, for I do not accept the authority of Popes and Church Councils, since they have contradicted each other, my conscience is captive to the Word of God. I cannot and will not renounce anything, for to go against one's conscience is neither right nor safe.

The Holy Roman Emperor Passes Judgment

I am descended from a long line of Christian emperors of this noble German nation, and of the Catholic kings of Spain, the archdukes of Austria, and the dukes of Burgundy. They were all faithful to the death to the Church of Rome and they defended the Catholic faith and the honour of God. I have resolved to follow in their steps. A single monk who goes counter to all Christianity for a thousand years must be wrong…. Not only I, but you of this noble German nation, would be forever disgraced if by our negligence not only heresy but the very suspicion of heresy were to survive. After hearing Luther's obstinate defence yesterday I regret that I have delayed proceeding against him and his false teachings for so long. I will have nothing more to do with him. He may leave under his safe conduct but without preaching or causing any disturbance. I will proceed against him as a notorious heretic….

The Emperor Outlaws Luther

This devil in the clothing of a monk has brought together ancient errors into one stinking puddle and has invented new ones…. His teaching makes for rebellion, division, war, murder, robbery, arson, and the collapse of Christendom. He lives the life of a beast. He has burned the Pope's decrees…. He does more harm to government than to the church. We have laboured with him but he says he recognizes only the authority of Scripture and he interprets this in his own way. We have given him twenty-one days, dating from April 15th…. Luther is to be treated as a convicted heretic…. We strictly order that … you shall refuse to give Martin Luther hospitality, lodging, food, or drink; neither shall anyone, by word or deed, secretly or openly, give him advice or help; wherever you meet him, you shall proceed against him; if you have enough force, you shall take him prisoner and deliver him to us; or let us know where he can be captured…. In the same way, you shall proceed against his friends, supporters, sympathizers, and followers…. We command that no one shall buy, sell, read, keep, print or cause to be printed or copied, any books written by Luther, since they are foul, harmful, and written by a notorious and stiff-necked heretic. Nor shall anyone dare to support, approve, defend, or proclaim his opinions in any way.

(Adapted from translations of sources in R. Bainton, Here I Stand: A Life of Martin Luther (1978); and Hans Hillerbrand, The Reformation: A Narrative History Related by Contemporary Observers and Participants (1989).)

14

The Age of Revolutions, 1600-1800

Introduction to the Age of Revolutions

The Scientific Revolution of the 17th century established a new way of thinking about the world. It also paved the way for the Industrial Revolution (see chapter 15). The Enlightenment of the 18th century built on the discoveries of the Scientific Revolution. These social **revolutions** led to new ways of thinking about humans, government, and society. The Scientific Revolution and the Age of Enlightenment are discussed in section A of this chapter.

In the second half of the 18th century, two important political revolutions took place. The American Revolution created the United States. The French Revolution abolished the French monarchy and led to widespread upheaval across Europe. Both revolutions resulted in new ideas about government and what it meant to be a citizen. The American Revolution and the French Revolution are discussed in section B of this chapter.

Each revolution had an enormous impact, and all helped shape the world we live in today. The revolutions:

- opened up new ways of thinking about human affairs and the natural world.

- presented a serious challenge to traditional ways of thinking (for example, in government, religion, education, and values).

- produced a new science based on experiment, which, many people thought,

The word *revolution* comes from Latin. It means "turning around," as in a wheel. Today, we use the word to describe a far-reaching change in existing thinking. In a political revolution, one form of government is overthrown and another takes its place (for example, when a **dictatorship** becomes a democracy). Similarly, an intellectual revolution results in a new way of thinking (for example, the Renaissance and the Reformation). Today, with advances in electronic technology and computers, we speak of the communications revolution.

offered the opportunity to control the natural world.

- placed new emphasis on an idea that went back to ancient times – people should have a voice in government – and they showed how this could be made a reality.

- made it possible for Europe to dominate the world in the 19th century.

In North America in 1600, most of the continent remained the territory of First Nations peoples. In Asia, India and China developed according to their own traditions, although there was increasing trade with Europe. The slave trade was doing enormous damage to some African societies, but most of Africa remained under African control.

By the middle of the 19th century, however, the revolutionary ideas that began in Europe were affecting the rest of the world.

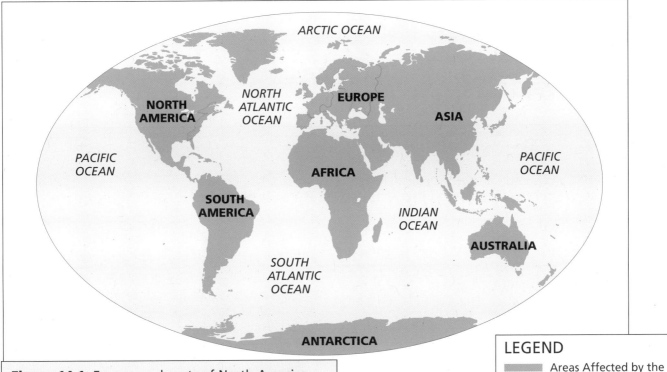

Figure 14.1 Europe and parts of North America were, initially, the most affected by the revolutions.

Questions to Think About ⟲

✦ How did the Scientific Revolution change the way people thought about and understood their world?

✦ How did the Enlightenment of the eighteenth century influence the way people thought about themselves and the world?

✦ What have been the historical influences of the American Revolution and the French Revolution?

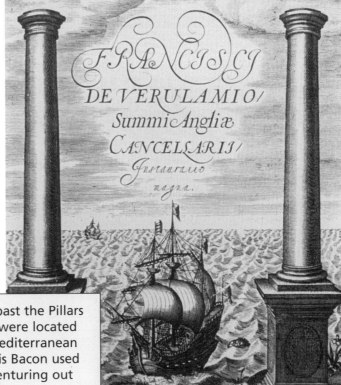

Figure 14.2 This illustration shows ships sailing out past the Pillars of Hercules. In ancient legend, the Pillars of Hercules were located at the Straits of Gibraltar at the eastern exit of the Mediterranean Sea and marked the limits of the known world. Francis Bacon used the illustration in 1620 to show that scientists were venturing out beyond the limits of the known world.

The Age of Revolutions **293**

The Scientific Revolution and the Age of Enlightenment

THE SCIENTIFIC REVOLUTION

Our Study of the Scientific Revolution

Our study of the Scientific Revolution includes the following topics:

- The Origins of the Scientific Revolution
- The Scientific Method
- Mapping the Skies
- Mapping the Natural World
- Printing
- The Microscope
- Isaac Newton
- The Impact of the Scientific Revolution

Humans have always tried to make sense of the world in which they live. For thousands of years, they explained natural events as the work of gods, spirits, or magic. In Europe during the Middle Ages, for example, science was based on the teachings of the church and the findings of Greek and Roman writers. Topics included subjects such as human anatomy and the movement of the stars and planets.

The Scientific Revolution was something very different. By the 17th century, scientists no longer relied on what earlier scientists and philosophers had written. They questioned everything. They used observation or experimentation to prove or disprove their findings.

Many people began to challenge the very idea that tradition and established authority should shape people's beliefs. Some historians believe this created a connection between Protestantism and science.

Figure 14.3 This map, produced in Germany in 1482, was based on ancient Greek maps made by Ptolemy. In Europe, maps like this weakened the authority of Greek and Roman writers such as Ptolemy because people realized the world was not shown accurately.

The Origins of the Scientific Revolution

The Scientific Revolution probably resulted from a combination of the following factors:

1. An unusual number of very talented people lived at about the same time, and, due to the invention of printing (see page 255), they read about and learned from the works of other scientists.

2. With the growth of cities and the increase in trade, merchants wanted to know as much about the world as possible. Many business people had the money to support scientists and researchers.

3. New technologies, such as the microscope and the telescope, disproved the science of the ancient world (for example, Galileo used his telescope to prove that planets revolve around the sun, not the earth).

4. European expansion into previously unknown parts of the world, especially North America and South America, revealed plants, animals, and peoples that ancient writers had not known about. These findings cast doubts on the reliability of those writers.

The manner of their fishing.

Figure 14.4 In 1585, an English artist painted a series of pictures of local scenes around Roanoke Island, North Carolina. Drawings of people, plants, and animals never seen before by Europeans further weakened the authority of ancient Greek and Roman writers and aroused people's interest in new approaches to science.

The Scientific Method

The most influential defender of the scientific method was Francis Bacon (1561-1626), an English writer and philosopher. Bacon rejected the science of earlier times. He insisted that true knowledge came from controlled experiments based on careful observations of the real world. He believed that this kind of scientific knowledge would, one day, make it possible to control nature for the benefit of the human race. Ironically, Bacon is said to have died from a chill he caught on a cold winter day conducting one of his own experiments. He had stuffed a dead chicken with snow and spent several hours outside observing whether or not the snow would help preserve the chicken.

René Descartes (1596-1650), a French philosopher and mathematician, took a different approach to science. He believed true knowledge came from a step-by-step process of reasoning. Each step followed logically from what had gone before, as in mathematics. For example, if 2 + 2 = 4, then 2 + 3 must equal 5. According to Descartes, knowledge was based on logic and careful reasoning, not on observation or experiment.

Descartes' first principle was to doubt everything. He even doubted his own existence – unless he could find evidence that he did exist. He eventually decided that since he was able to doubt his existence, he must be alive. Both church and government were troubled by the new scientists whom they saw as a threat to their authority.

Mapping the Skies

In the 16th century, most people still believed that the earth was the centre of the universe, and the stars and planets revolved around the earth. However, astronomers were finding it difficult to make this belief fit with their observations. In 1543, a Polish astronomer, Nicolaus Copernicus (1473-1543), suggested astronomy would make more sense if people accepted the idea that the sun was the centre of the universe.

Figure 14.5 In 1543, Nicholaus Copernicus published his theory that the planets moved around the sun. He said that the sun, not the earth, was the centre of the universe.

Some years later, a German astronomer, Johannes Kepler (1571-1630), using the observations of another astronomer, Tycho Brahe (1546-1601) of Denmark, determined that Copernicus's theory must be correct. He also found that the planets did not travel in perfect circles, as the Greeks said, but in elliptical orbits. His observations further weakened people's faith in the authority and reliability of ancient writers.

In 1613, an Italian scientist, Galileo Galilei (1564-1642), publicly supported the theories of Copernicus and Kepler. Galileo's position contradicted the teachings of the Roman Catholic Church. The church enforced the belief that Earth was the centre of the universe. The church feared that Galileo's ideas might weaken its authority in much the same way Martin Luther's Ninety-five Theses had a century earlier (see pages 265-266). In 1616, the Roman Catholic Church forbade anyone to teach that the sun was the centre of the universe. Galileo continued to speak out. In 1633, he was placed under house arrest and forbidden to publicize his ideas. He died in 1642. In 1992, the Roman Catholic Church reversed its condemnation of Galileo.

Despite the opposition of the church, the new findings in astronomy could not be ignored. The discoveries showed that traditional beliefs could be wrong. Observation and experiment, not ancient writers, were the most reliable ways to learn about the natural world.

Mapping the Natural World

Seventeenth-century scientists made many other scientific discoveries that showed the ancient Greek and Roman philosophers were wrong.

- They explained how light and liquids and gases behaved.
- They formulated laws of motion and of optics, which is the science that explains how light and vision work.
- They began to explore magnetism.
- They made great advances in mathematics and showed that mathematics could be used to explain and even predict many natural phenomena, such as the movement of the stars and planets and the flow of the tides.

- They discovered that the heart pumped blood around the human body.

These scientists saw themselves as explorers of a new and unknown world. They used the scientific method as a way of understanding the world.

Figure 14.6 With his telescope, Galileo saw the moons of Jupiter, sunspots, and some features of the moon's surface. Most important, perhaps, Galileo observed things that the Greeks and Romans knew nothing about.

Figure 14.7 For centuries, anatomy had been taught from the writings of the ancient Greek doctor Galen. Galen, however, had not realized that the anatomy of animals and humans was different. Andreas Vesalius, a doctor from Belgium, was a strong believer in observation and experimentation. He believed that to learn about the real world, the real world, not books, had to be studied. He gained an international reputation as a researcher and teacher, because he dissected actual human bodies and explained what he was doing while he worked. In 1543, Vesalius published a book about human anatomy that caused a sensation. In the book were illustrations that showed him dissecting human bodies and diagrams showing the human nervous system, as well as detailed sketches of bones and human organs. For most, it was the first time they had ever seen the human body in this way.

Printing

Scientists benefitted greatly from the invention of the printing press in the 1400s (see page 255). By the 17th century, improvements in print technology made possible the reproduction of accurate pictures of microscopic specimens of plants, insects, animals, and the human body. Increasing numbers of people saw things they had never seen before such as **protozoa** in water and the detailed anatomy of small insects. Printing also enabled scientists to make public the results of their research, which kept them informed of one another's work. They could re-test other scientists' experiments and build on the work of others.

The Microscope

In 1665, a British researcher, Robert Hooke (1635-1703), created a sensation with his book, *Micrographia*. In it, he presented detailed drawings of what he had seen through his microscope, including the cell structures of various materials such as cork and wood and a variety of small insects such as fleas and lice.

In Holland, Antony van Leeuwenhoek (1632-1723) improved the magnification of

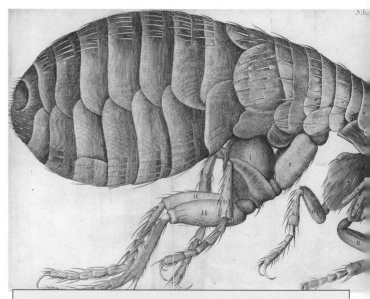

Figure 14.9 In the 17th century, everyone knew about fleas. However, no one had ever seen one in the kind of detail Robert Hooke provided in his *Micrographia*. Hooke used words as well as pictures. Not many people think of fleas as beautiful, but here is part of what Hooke said about them: "But, as for the beauty of it, the microscope manifests it to be all over adorn'd with a curiously polish'd suit of sable armour, neatly jointed, and beset with multitudes of sharp pins, shap'd almost like porcupine's quills, or bright conical steel **bodkins**; the head is on either side beautifi'd with a quick round black eye...." Pictures such as this helped people understand the discoveries of the new science.

Figure 14.8 Leeuwenhoek's microscope was more like a powerful magnifying glass than like a modern microscope. He put his specimen on the pointed spike on the left and looked through the lens in the metal plate to examine it. Historians are still not certain how Leeuwenhoek obtained the accurate results he did with such a basic instrument.

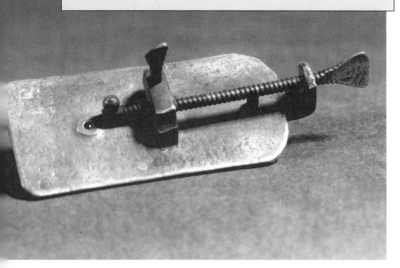

microscopes beyond anything previously known. He examined saliva, water, blood, insects, fabrics, and a variety of everyday objects such as wood and feathers. Ordinary people were amazed to learn about the existence of a world of minute creatures and structures that could not be seen with the naked eye.

Hooke, van Leeuwenhoek, and other scientists used the microscope and other precision instruments to demonstrate the powers of observation and experiment. These scientists showed how science could be used to discover new worlds. They helped to revolutionize the way people thought about the world in which they lived.

Good Times or Bad Times?

Richard has to decide whether to stay in London or move to a new land across the Atlantic Ocean.

Richard Andrews could not decide whether these were good times or bad times. On the one hand, the world seemed full of trouble. Some people were even predicting the end of the world. On the other hand, the world seemed full of promise.

Richard liked living in London, but the last several years had been full of trouble. He had lived through the violent and bloody civil wars – supporters of parliament had defeated supporters of the king in a fight to decide who should govern England. In 1649, Richard watched the beheading of King Charles I after parliament had sentenced him to death.

Richard supported parliament against the king, but parliamentary rule had not worked out. It was fairly simple to get rid of the king. It was much more difficult to decide how to replace him. Everybody seemed to have a different idea. In 1660, after more than a decade of political turmoil, King Charles's son was declared king, and the monarchy was restored. People like Richard, who had once supported parliamentary rule, remained suspect. Many still favoured government by an elected parliament rather than by a king or queen.

In 1665, London was hit by plague. Tens of thousands of people died in and around the city. Fortunately, Richard survived. His dog, though, was killed when the city authorities ordered all animals exterminated for fear they were carrying the plague.

Richard also escaped the Great Fire of 1666. The fire began in a bakery oven and quickly spread to other buildings.

Now, in 1667, England was at war with Holland. A Dutch fleet had even sailed up the River Thames and attacked English ships close to London, causing great panic in the city. At least England had captured New Amsterdam, Holland's colony in North America. Richard heard it was going to be renamed New York.

Richard thought about moving to America. It would be interesting to see a whole new world. He would also be free of the restrictions that the government placed on his religion. He was an *Independent*. He believed that each local church should be free to run its own affairs, provided that it always remained Protestant. However, the king's government insisted that everyone belong to the Church of England and attend its services.

The more Richard thought about moving to America, the more convinced he was that he should stay home. His skills as a lens grinder were needed in London, thanks to the high demand for microscopes and telescopes. He had already seen exciting miniature worlds through the new microscopes. Not so long ago, who could have imagined that a person's mouth contained little creatures invisible to the naked eye? Or that a drop of water was full of tiny creatures called *animalcules?* Or that it was possible to examine the insides of tiny insects? What would be next?

Richard did not know if the future would be better than the past, but it would be interesting.

Figure 14.10 The London fire burned for five days and destroyed over 80 churches and more than 13 000 houses.

Isaac Newton

Isaac Newton (1642-1727) was professor of mathematics at Cambridge University. Later, he was in charge of England's Royal Mint.

Newton first became well known for designing a new kind of telescope. Existing telescopes had become too large to be useful. Newton used his skills as a lens grinder to make a small, portable telescope that was more powerful than much bigger models.

He also made important contributions to mathematics. (1) He invented calculus, which is the mathematical study of moving objects. (2) He established the basis of modern theories that explain light and colour. (3) He discovered the laws of motion and the theory of gravity. (4) He explained the movement of the tides and accurately predicted the appearance of comets.

His most important contribution was to arrive at a scientific explanation of the way the universe works as a whole. He did this by using his theories of motion and gravity, observation and experiment, and his new mathematical techniques. In particular, he showed how the force of gravity and the laws of motion can be used to explain the movement of the stars and planets. In doing this, he showed that the universe could be understood, and he explained how it worked.

The Impact of the Scientific Revolution

The Scientific Revolution had many results:

- It produced vast amounts of new information about the natural world.

- It led to the development of scientific laws and principles. The success of space travel today is due, in part, to such 17th-century discoveries as the laws of motion, the movement of stars and planets, and the force of gravity.

- It led to improvements of existing technologies in industry and medicine.

- It laid the groundwork for inventions such as steam power, which became a major force in the Industrial Revolution of the 18th and 19th centuries (see chapter 15).

- It introduced a new way of understanding the world based on observation, experiment, mathematics, and scientific method.

- It changed the role of religion in society. Before the Scientific Revolution, people believed that the earth was the centre of the universe; plagues and storms were seen as signs of God's anger. The new scientists distinguished between religion and science and explained the natural world in terms of science, not religion.

Figure 14.11 Isaac Newton became one of the best-known and most admired scientists of his time. One English poet wrote: "Nature and Nature's laws lay hid in night; God said, 'Let Newton be,' and all was light."

Figure 14.12 These three men were important scientists of the Scientific Revolution: Francis Bacon (left), René Descartes (centre), Nicholaus Copernicus (right).

- It introduced the idea of progress. Scientists respected the work of the philosophers and scientists of ancient Greece and Rome, but they were looking to the future not to the past. In science, they saw a way of making sure that each new generation would be more knowledgeable and better off than the one before.

- It established the idea that nature could and should be controlled for the benefit of humans. Today, some environmentalists consider the kind of thinking that fueled the Scientific Revolution – nature is something to be controlled and exploited rather than appreciated and respected – as the beginning of environmental exploitation.

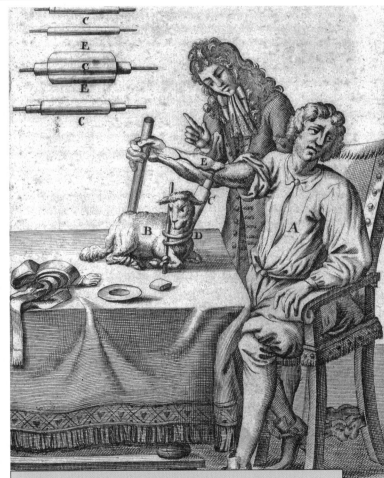

Figure 14.13 Seventeenth-century experimenters did almost anything in the name of science, including the transfusion of blood from animals to humans. Amazingly, some people survived these experiments.

THE AGE OF ENLIGHTENMENT

Our Study of the Enlightenment

Our study of the Enlightenment includes the following topics:

- What Was the Age of Enlightenment?
- What Is Enlightenment?
- The *Encyclopedia*
- Women and the Enlightenment
- Enlightenment and Government
- Absolutism
- Constitutional Monarchy
- Three Views of Government
- The Right to Vote

What Was the Age of Enlightenment?

The 18th century is often described as the Age of Reason or the Age of Enlightenment. This was the name given by the philosophers and writers of the time, especially those living in France. Many philosophers hoped to find a way to understand human nature and society using the same methods that Isaac Newton had

Figure 14.14 Events like this, showing air travel in Paris in 1783, helped people believe in the power of science and technology.

used to explain the physical world (see page 300). They believed that they could explain everything through reason and by observing and experimenting.

Figure 14.15 This painting was done in England in the 1780s. It shows a bird being revived after being subjected to a vacuum to demonstrate the importance of air.

What Is Enlightenment?

Immanuel Kant (1724-1804) was an influential German philosopher whose writings are still studied today. In 1784, Kant wrote the following description of what it meant to be enlightened:

Dare to know! Have the courage to use your own reason! That is the motto of enlightenment.

Laziness and cowardice are the reason why... it is so easy for others to act as our guardians. If I have a book that tells me what to think, a priest who acts as my conscience, a doctor who tells me what to eat, and so on, I need not think....

For enlightenment, we need only the freedom ... to use our reason at all times.... The public use of reason must always be free, and it alone can bring enlightenment.

The Encyclopedia

In 1751, a French philosopher, Denis Diderot (1713-1784), began publishing the *Encyclopedia*. Over twenty volumes, with contributions by many philosophers, were published during the next fourteen years.

The *Encyclopedia* was a way of spreading Enlightenment ideas such as freedom of thought, religious tolerance, and the scientific methods of people like Francis Bacon and Isaac Newton. The *Encyclopedia* paid particular attention to the development of trade and industry since this was how science most directly affected everyday life. The *Encyclopedia* was condemned by the French government because of its radical ideas. Nevertheless, it became one of the most successful statements of Enlightenment thinking.

Women and the Enlightenment

Enlightenment writers, who were almost all male, campaigned for freedom, equality, and human rights. Most, however, held traditional views about the place and role of women in society. They believed in a basic difference between men and women. They saw men as naturally active, rational, and independent.

Men, they said, were suited for political and public life. They saw women as passive, emotional, and submissive, suited to be wives and mothers. Enlightenment writers believed women should be treated fairly but not the same as men.

A few women became philosophers and writers. In France, Madame de Chatelet, for example, was a skilled mathematician, spoke five languages, translated the writings of Newton into French, and conducted scientific experiments. When she was banned from a men's coffeehouse, she dressed in men's clothes and was admitted. Her disguise did not fool anyone, but her courage was admired.

No woman was asked to write for the *Encyclopedia*. Its definition of *citizen* read: "This title is allowed to women, young children and servants only inasmuch as they belong to the family of a citizen; but they are not citizens." The Enlightenment was a man's world.

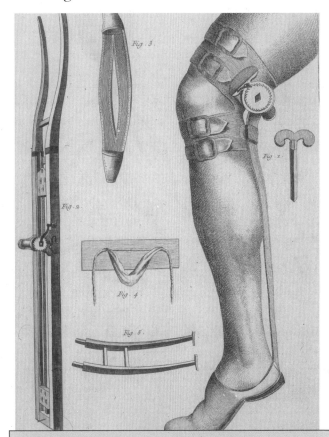

Figure 14.16 This picture, which appeared in the *Encyclopedia*, shows how to repair a torn Achilles tendon. The *Encyclopedia* devoted a lot of space to the human body and to descriptions of technology.

Enlightenment and Government

The Scientific Revolution changed the way the thinkers of the time thought about many other things. They hoped to use scientific principles and laws to build a science of government, just as Isaac Newton had used the scientific method to discover the law of gravity. Enlightenment writers believed in freedom and equality, but they did not believe in democracy as we understand it today. They felt most people were too uneducated to participate in government.

The writers believed that democracy would lead to **mob rule**, because most people were ruled by emotions, not by reason. Only people who owned property or were reasonably wealthy should have a voice in government. These people, the philosophers reasoned, would not make hasty decisions since they had something to lose if things went wrong.

Most Enlightenment thinkers did not want to overthrow kings and princes; they wanted to teach them to rule according to Enlightenment ideals. They believed that the changes they wanted, such as religious freedom, a fairer system of laws, and education, would best be brought about by the people with power.

Absolutism

Most European rulers in the 18th century held absolute power. Some believed that they were God's representatives on Earth and, therefore, their power came directly from God. They ruled by divine right: to disobey the king was to disobey God.

The theory of **absolutism** taught that the power and the authority of the king or queen held society together. If ordinary people were allowed to disobey their lawful ruler, they would end up doing whatever they pleased – and no one would be safe.

Frederick the Great was an example of what was called *enlightened* **despotism**. In this system of government, a king or queen had great power but ruled according to Enlightenment ideas. For example, schools were built, freedom of religion was allowed, and laws were more fair and humane.

Figure 14.17 Frederick the Great of Prussia was a great admirer of Voltaire, one of the most influential writers of the Enlightenment. In this illustration, Frederick is seeking the advice of Voltaire. Voltaire was also an historian, poet, playwright, and philosopher. He used his motto, *Écrasez l'infâme* ("Crush the infamous one") to campaign against injustice wherever he saw it – especially the intolerance of different religions and beliefs. Voltaire was a supporter of reason and science and often attacked the Roman Catholic Church and abuses of the law.

Constitutional Monarchy

England, unlike most other European countries of the 18th century, was governed by a constitutional monarchy. The king or queen could rule only with the agreement of an elected parliament, and the powers of the monarchy were limited by law. For example, the monarchy could not raise taxes or pass laws without the consent of parliament.

In England's first civil war of 1642-1648, parliament fought King Charles I (1600-1649) for control of the government. Parliament finally won control, and King Charles was executed in 1649. For the next eleven years, England was a **republic**; that is, the country was without a monarch or any other hereditary head of state.

In 1660, the monarchy was restored under a new king, Charles II (1630-1685). His brother, King James II (1633-1701) succeeded him. In 1688, James II was expelled after his opponents feared he wanted to rule as an absolute monarch. They also feared he wanted to restore the Roman Catholic religion, which had been banned since the reign of King Henry VIII over 125 years earlier.

The new king, William III (1650-1702), agreed to restrict the powers of the monarchy: the king or queen would rule with the agreement of parliament and could act only with parliament's approval; regular elections of government officials were guaranteed. The French Enlightenment writer Jean-Jacques Rousseau (1712-1778) observed that while the English thought they were free, they were really free only at election time. Between elections, they had to do whatever their government decided.

Three Views of Government

An English philosopher, Thomas Hobbes (1588-1679), believed that humans were greedy and violent by nature. Otherwise, he asked, why would people worry about their safety? The only reliable protection was to agree to obey an all-powerful ruler. What people gave up in personal freedom, they gained in safety and security. For Hobbes, the best government was one that had absolute power.

Another English philosopher, John Locke (1632-1702), disagreed with Hobbes. He believed that people were born with rights that could not be taken away. The two most basic rights were life and property. If government did not protect the lives and property of its people, the people had the right to overthrow it. For Locke, the best government was one that people elected and could vote out of power.

Jean-Jacques Rousseau believed that people were born good, not violent or greedy, as Hobbes said. However, they were corrupted by society, which made them jealous and suspicious of one another. For Rousseau, the best government was one that allowed people to govern themselves directly and gave them a

Figure 14.18 When Louis XIV become king of France in 1643, he was only five years old. His royal power was exercised by **regents**, since he was so young. He took full power in 1661 and ruled until his death in 1715. The reign of Louis XIV is regarded as the greatest example of absolutism. He had the Palace of Versailles, seen here, built at enormous expense and made it the centre of government. The palace was built, in part, as a display of his power and importance.

voice in all decisions, not through elected representatives but through face-to-face meetings.

The Right to Vote

Even in England, where parliament largely controlled government, the right to vote was restricted to men who owned property and paid taxes. The theory was that men who owned property were educated and would not be influenced by bribes or threats. They would vote rationally and carefully because they had property to protect. Most other people, including women, could not vote. Women were thought to be too delicate and considerate to handle the arguments and disagreements of the political world. Their role was to stay at home and be good wives and mothers.

The American Revolution and the French Revolution

THE AMERICAN REVOLUTION

Our Study of the American Revolution

Our study of the American Revolution includes the following topics:

- What Caused the American Revolution?
- What Was the American Revolution?
- The Declaration of Independence, 1776
- A New Constitution
- Who Are the People?
- The Importance of the American Revolution

What Caused the American Revolution?

From the middle of the 17th century, Britain and France had fought a series of wars. France wanted to become the most powerful country in Europe. British governments feared a powerful France would destroy Britain's trade with the rest of the world. Even worse, France might cross the English Channel and invade Britain.

Both Britain and France had colonies in North America – Britain's colonies were in New England and France had colonies in Quebec and Louisianna – and some of their wars were fought there. During the Seven Years' War (1756-1763), Britain and France fought each other in many parts of the world, including North America. At the end of the war, France, which had been defeated, handed over its North American colonies to Britain.

Figure 14.19 This cartoon by a colonial revolutionary shows the fate of a British tax collector in Boston prior to the American Revolution.

The war cost the British government money. The government felt that the colonists should help pay for the war since, in North America, it had been fought in their defence. To raise money, Britain began to tax the colonies. Angered by what they saw as British **tyranny**, the colonists refused to pay these new taxes.

The colonists argued that citizens had to agree to new taxes before they were required to pay them. Since the colonists could not vote in British elections and, therefore, were not represented in parliament, Britain had no right to tax them. Their slogan was "no taxation without representation." They insisted that before they paid taxes to Britain, they needed the approval of their own elected assemblies in

French and English Colonies, 1763

Figure 14.20 Taxation was not the only cause of the American Revolution. When Britain acquired Quebec following the Seven Years' War, the colonists no longer feared an attack by France, and became less dependent on Britain for security. When Britain banned white settlement west of the Appalachian Mountains, colonial merchants and landowners who hoped to expand westward were outraged. Anger and a sense of self-reliance helped to fuel the colonies desire for independence.

What Was the American Revolution?

In 1775, fighting broke out between English troops and a group of colonists near Boston. The fighting soon spread out of control. In 1776, the thirteen colonies signed a Declaration of Independence. In it, they accused England of treating them unjustly, and they pledged to fight until they won their independence from England.

For the next few years, neither side was strong enough to defeat the other. Then, in 1778, France, seeing a chance to get even with England, supplied the colonies with weapons, money, soldiers, and ships. In 1781, the English army was forced to surrender at Yorktown. This was a major defeat. The English government realized that it could not win the war. In 1783, England recognized the independence of the colonies. The United States of America was born.

Figure 14.21 In December 1775, an army from the thirteen colonies, led by General Montgomery, invaded Quebec hoping to get the support of the French population. Montgomery was killed in battle, and the French remained loyal to the British government that had ruled them since 1763.

the colonies, not from the parliament of far-away Britain. Britain argued that parliament represented all British subjects – even those who did not have the right to vote.

Britain's attempt to collect these new taxes led to a series of violent incidents between colonists and British troops. When the two sides could not reach an agreement, colonists threatened to form their own nation to become an independent country.

Are All Men Equal?

In this story, we learn that even free African-Americans are not treated the same as white settlers.

John King had to make a decision. Should he go to Africa, or should he stay in Nova Scotia?

Fifteen years ago, in 1776, he had been a slave in Virginia. Now here he was, a free man in Nova Scotia. Yet, he often wondered just how free he was.

When the Americans published their Declaration of Independence in 1776, they proclaimed that all men were created equal and were entitled to life, freedom, and the pursuit of happiness. John soon found out that the Declaration did not include former African slaves like him. In American law, he was not even considered a man. Slaves could not be citizens of the new United States.

When the British had offered freedom to any slave who joined their army to fight against the Americans, John jumped at the chance. He spent the next few years serving with the British army. When the Americans won the war, he accepted the British offer of land and freedom in Nova Scotia.

John and other ex-slaves who fought against the American rebels considered themselves to be Loyalists, loyal subjects of King George III. In Nova Scotia, however, he soon found out that the British treated blacks differently from whites. White Loyalists received three years of supplies and plenty of land. Black Loyalists were given only a bit of land and eighty days of supplies. They were also forced to work on the roads.

John was happy he was no longer a slave. He sometimes wondered, though, what it really meant to be free when you were still treated so unfairly. Now the British were offering Black Loyalists like him a chance to start a new life in Africa. John had been born in Virginia. What little he knew about Africa came from the few stories he had heard from old people when he was still a slave. He knew nothing about Sierra Leone, the new country in Africa where the British were going to set up a Black colony.

Despite John's fears, he was tempted to accept the British offer. About half the people he knew had decided to go, and the ships would be sailing from Halifax in a couple of months. Perhaps in Africa he could be a full citizen at last. John was going to have to make up his mind soon.

The Declaration of Independence, 1776

The Declaration of Independence was drawn up by colonists in 1776. It describes the revolutionaries' view of the purpose of government, and it explains why they felt they had a right to rebel. The following passage is from the Declaration:

*We hold these truths to be self-evident, that all men are created equal, that they are endowed by the creator with certain **inalienable rights**; that among these are life, liberty, and the pursuit of happiness; that to secure these rights governments are instituted among men, deriving their just powers from the consent of the governed; that whenever any form of government becomes destructive of these ends, it is the right of the people to alter or to abolish it, and to institute new government, laying its foundation on such principles and organizing its powers in such form, as to them shall seem more to effect their safety and happiness.*

A New Constitution

The American Revolution created a union of thirteen separate states without a strong central government. As a result, the states often disagreed on what should be done or who should do it. This led to the establishment of a national government and a state government. The national government was made responsible for things that concerned the United States as a whole, such as currency, defence, and foreign affairs. The state government was responsible for local matters, such as roads and schools.

In 1788, the United States adopted a new constitution. It created the American system of government much as it exists today: a president and congress are elected for the whole country. A Supreme Court is appointed to interpret and enforce the constitution. At the local level, each state elects its governor and legislature.

Figure 14.22 This is a drawing of the slave trade in the 1790s. An estimated 12 to 15 million Africans were sent to the Americas as slaves between 1500 and 1850. Enlightenment writers strongly opposed slavery. Historians believe that the ideals of the Enlightenment helped create the public opinion that slavery was wrong and led to the **abolition** of slavery.

Americans were guaranteed freedom of speech and religion, freedom of the press, freedom to assemble and petition the government, the right to bear arms, and the right to a fair trial. People were not subjects of a king, a queen, or an emperor; they were citizens with rights.

Figure 14.23 In 1787, George Washington addressed the attendees of the Constitutional Convention who had gathered to draw up the American Constitution. Washington was one of the leaders of the American Revolution and became the first president of the United States in 1788.

Who Are the People?

The Declaration of Independence and the American Constitution state that all men are created equal and enjoy basic rights. However, only white men who were landowners could vote. Slavery was abolished in 1865 following the American Civil War (1861-1865), and former slaves were given the right to vote in 1870. Even then, African Americans often were stopped from voting. Not until 1965, did the American government amend the constitution to prevent states from interfering with a citizen's right to vote.

Women did not gain any political rights following the American Revolution. In fact, women first voted in American federal elections in 1920, although they won the right to vote in some state elections earlier. Native Americans did not win the right to vote until 1924.

Nonetheless, the United States had gone further than any other country in determining who was a citizen and had the right to vote.

Today, in the United States, Canada, and other democratic countries, every person is entitled to citizenship rights such as the vote, equal protection under the law, and freedom of speech.

The Importance of the American Revolution

The American Revolution is important for two reasons: (1) It created the United States as an independent country. (2) It established a new idea of what it meant to be a citizen. In Europe, people were seen as subjects of their ruler. They had some basic rights, but few had any voice in government.

The American Revolution proved that government by the people was not just a theory of some Enlightenment philosophers; it could actually work in the real world. For Europeans interested in changing their system of government, the United States became a practical example of what could be done.

THE FRENCH REVOLUTION

Our Study of the French Revolution

Our study of the French Revolution includes the following topics:

- What Caused the French Revolution?
- The Revolution Deepens, 1789-1795
- War
- The Rise and Fall of Napoleon
- Transforming Society
- The Importance of the French Revolution

What Caused the French Revolution?

In 1789, France faced serious problems.

- Food was scarce and prices were high.
- The government could not pay its bills. The government wanted to tax the aristocracy, for example, but the **aristocracy** refused to pay taxes.
- Many people were dissatisfied with a government that did not represent the people. The writers of the Enlightenment had created a demand for reform. The attitudes of many powerful people would have to change if the government was to enact the reforms that were needed.

To deal with the crisis, the government called a meeting of the Estates-General. The Estates-General consisted of representatives of three estates, or classes: the church (First Estate), the aristocracy (Second Estate), and the people (Third Estate). Each estate met separately and voted as a block. The Third Estate was convinced that the First Estate and the Second Estate would join forces and outvote it 2-1.

To prevent this, the Third Estate demanded that the estates count every member's vote. When the other estates refused, the Third Estate declared itself to be a National Assembly. It, not the king or the church or the aristocracy, represented the nation. The people of Paris showed their support for the National Assembly by seizing the royal fortress of the Bastille on July 14, 1789.

Figure 14.24 This illustration depicts a cartoon of the Three Estates, showing a peasant carrying a lord and a priest on his back.

Figure 14.25 On June 20, 1789, the Third Estate was locked out of its meeting hall. In defiance, they took over the royal indoor tennis court at the Palace of Versailles. There, all but one member of the Third Estate pledged to continue to meet until a constitution had been written. This revolutionary act, referred to as the Tennis Court Oath, is considered to be the beginning of the French Revolution.

The Revolution Deepens, 1789-1795

The new National Assembly abolished the aristocracy's privileges and the whole feudal system, took control of the church and confiscated its property, and reduced the king's powers. It wrote a new constitution. Some people resisted these changes; others felt the National Assembly did not make enough changes. These two opposing responses to the reforms caused widespread upheaval and unrest throughout France.

In 1792, the revolutionaries abolished the monarchy. In 1793, they executed King Louis XVI (1754-1793) for plotting against the revolution. This action led some foreign governments to declare war on France in an attempt to stop the revolutionary ideas before they spread beyond France's borders. The revolution was now being challenged from within the country and by outside influences.

To protect the revolution, the government adopted emergency measures. Young men were **conscripted** into the army. Everyone was expected to defend the revolution and its goals. Emergency laws were enacted, and people's rights were suspended.

Those who did not support the revolution were imprisoned or executed. Thousands of people were beheaded as enemies of the revolution. This period of time, from about March 1793 to July 1794, is referred to as the "Reign of Terror."

By 1795, the French revolutionaries had turned back all foreign invaders and silenced their opponents within the country.

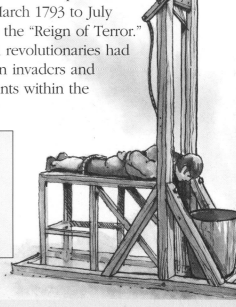

Figure 14.26 One revolutionary reform was the introduction of the guillotine to execute people who were enemies of the revolution.

An Uncertain Future: Paris in 1794

The optimism that most French people felt at the onset of the French Revolution had given way to fear, distrust, and frustration by the fourth year of the revolution.

Charlotte Lebrun had supported the revolution from the beginning. She still wore the red cap that was the sign of a revolutionary. She even approved of the execution of the king and queen in 1793, or Year I of the Revolution as it was now officially known. Her two sons had been conscripted when the government decreed that all young men must join the army. They were fighting to defend France from the invading Austrians.

Charlotte had taken part in the March of the Women to the royal palace at Versailles back in 1789. The marchers forced the king and queen to leave Versailles and move to Paris where the people could keep an eye on them. Charlotte had even taken part in the storming of City Hall, where she helped seize the cache of guns and cannons. It was best for these weapons to be in the hands of the people, not the king's government.

Now, though, the revolutionary government was ruling by terror. Charlotte liked the new regulations that kept food prices down and prevented hoarding. However, the Law of the Suspect of last September meant that anyone could be reported to the authorities as an enemy of the revolution, with no proof required. Even she had recently been investigated as a possible enemy of the revolution.

France seemed to be in a lot of trouble. Civil war had broken out in the west. Foreign armies were invading on all sides. Foreign governments had promised to restore the French monarchy.

A few weeks earlier, Charlotte's friend, Olympe de Gourges, a supporter of the revolution, had been executed as an enemy, because she opposed the execution of the king. It did not matter that she had written the sensational Declaration of the Rights of Woman in 1791, demanding that women be granted the same rights as men. She had done these things as a friend, not an enemy, of the revolution, but that had not saved her.

In any case, the men had not listened. They preached liberty and equality, but only as long as women were not included. They believed that a woman belonged in the home, looking after her husband and children. Charlotte did not know how the revolution would turn out. She hoped women would get the rights they deserved. After all, they had helped the revolution just as much as men had.

War

From 1793 to 1815, France was at war with most of Europe. Foreign governments saw the French Revolution as a threat to their power. The revolutionaries saw themselves as bringing freedom and justice to the people of Europe.

After defeating invading armies of Prussia and Austria, the French revolutionaries spread their ideas to neighbouring countries such as Belgium, Holland, and Italy. In those countries, as in others, many people supported the changes made by the revolution.

The Rise and Fall of Napoleon

In the wars, one revolutionary general had stood out. His name was Napoleon Bonaparte.

After brilliant victories in Italy, Napoleon invaded Egypt in 1798. However, his navy was destroyed by a British fleet, and his army was cut off from supplies and reinforcements. In 1801, he surrender to the British. When Napoleon returned to France, he turned to politics and became one of the leaders of the government. In 1804, he declared himself emperor of France and set out to make France the greatest power in Europe.

Figure 14.27 The revolutionaries did not intend to replace the king with an emperor. Napoleon, however, kept many of the revolutionary reforms. He made the legal system fairer and more open. He allowed religious freedom. He supported education. He believed all people had the right to make the best of their abilities, regardless of their family background.

Napoleon's Conquests

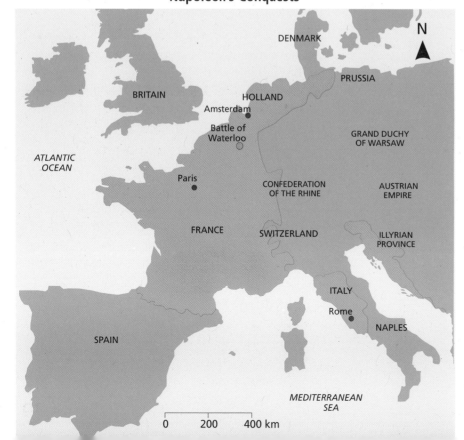

Figure 14.28 This map shows Napoleon's empire at the height of his success.

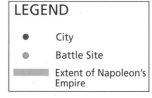

LEGEND
- City
- Battle Site
- Extent of Napoleon's Empire

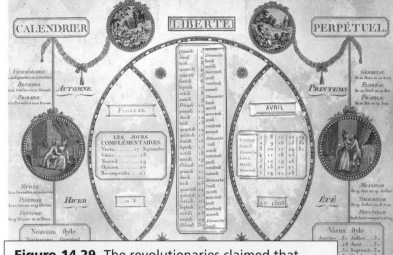

Napoleon spent most of his reign at war. While Britain was supreme at sea, Napoleon controlled the continent of Europe on land.

Napoleon's downfall began when he invaded Russia in 1812. He was unable to secure victory, and his armies suffered huge casualties. In 1815, Napoleon was defeated at the Battle of Waterloo. It was his final campaign. The British exiled him to the remote island of St. Helena in the South Atlantic Ocean where he died in 1821. With the removal of Napoleon from power, the monarchy was restored in France. The monarchy survived until 1848, when Napoleon's nephew seized power. He made himself Emperor Napoleon III in 1851.

Transforming Society

The French revolutionaries changed more than the system of government. They changed French society.

- They abolished the monarchy and created a republic.

- They enshrined human rights in the constitution.

- They sold the church's lands and, for a time, even tried to abolish Christianity.

- They ended the feudal system and abolished the aristocracy.

- They abolished traditional provinces and created a system of local governments based on new geographical divisions called *departments*. The departments were run by officials, called *prefects,* appointed by the national government in Paris. Other officials, such as mayors, were elected locally.

- They replaced traditional weights and measures with the metric system.

- They created a new revolutionary calendar – the execution of the king and queen in 1793 and the establishment of a republican government became the beginning of Year I of the Revolution.

Figure 14.29 The revolutionaries claimed that they were following the teachings of the Enlightenment. The new revolutionary calendar was based on reason rather than on tradition. The months were renamed to reflect the weather; for example, May became Floréal (blossom time). Using the metric system, each month was divided into three ten-day weeks. The five days that were left over in the year were devoted to revolutionary festivals. The days of the week were named after their numerical order.

The Importance of the French Revolution

The French Revolution affected more than France. According to one recent historian, the revolution caused the most profound crisis Europe had ever known.

Across Europe and in the Americas, reformers saw the revolution as an example for their own countries. They viewed it as a victory for the ideas of government by the people and for human rights. It showed that the ideas of the Enlightenment were not just theories but could actually work.

Opponents of the revolution saw it as nothing more than mob rule and dictatorship, especially after the Reign of Terror. To them, it showed what happened when people overthrew existing institutions and ignored the power of tradition. They argued that moderate, peaceful change was more effective than revolution.

Our modern idea of revolution comes from the French Revolution. Revolution is not just a change of government but a complete overthrow of what exists, including a total transformation of society. The French Revolution was an important step in the developing debate about the meaning and nature of citizenship and democracy.

The Legacy of the Age of Revolutions

Citizenship

Following the American Revolution and the French Revolution, citizens had some basic rights. Both revolutions established the idea that government existed to protect these rights; citizens had the right to change and, if necessary, overthrow their government if their rights were not protected. Most important, the idea that no government should exist without the agreement of its citizens was established.

By the end of the 18th century, the United States and France still restricted citizenship to white men who owned property. Throughout the 19th and 20th centuries, people around the world struggled to win the rights of citizenship, regardless of race or gender or wealth.

Democracy

Democracy means "rule by the people." Citizens have the right to collect information, discuss public policy, and speak their minds freely. They also have a right to an education as part of the democratic process.

Three main theories exist as to how citizens should have a voice in government.

1. *Enlightened despotism* What really matters is not how a government is chosen, but that it should rule in the interests of the people.

2. *Direct or participatory democracy* All citizens must be personally involved in making important decisions (ancient Greek city-states, see chapter 7).

3. *Representative democracy* People elect representatives to act on their behalf in a parliament that chooses and controls the government. Elections are held at regular intervals so that citizens can remove a government they do not like. Elections are free and fair. All citizens have an equal voice. Representative democracy is the most common type of democracy today. These democracies usually have constitutions and laws that protect the rights of citizens and restrict what governments can do.

The success of democracy depends on elections and constitutions, and on citizens living by democratic values, especially freedom of speech and respect for human rights.

The Age of Revolutions did not create democracy, but it did lay the foundations on which democracy evolved from a theory to a reality.

Nationalism

The American Revolution and the French Revolution established the idea that to be a citizen means to belong to a country (such as the United States or France). Before the revolutions, most people believed that citizenship could exist only in very small countries, such as the ancient Greek city-states (see chapter 7).

The leaders of the revolutions emphasized the idea of nationhood. To ensure the thirteen separate British colonies saw themselves as one country, they called their new country the "United" States of America. The French, similarly, emphasized that France was a nation. Both countries expected citizens to identify with and be loyal to their nation, rather than to a ruler.

France, under Napoleon, also strengthened the sense of national identity in other countries. Nationalistic feelings arose in countries that Napoleon conquered, as their people struggled to overthrow French rule.

Global Connections

- Influenced by the Scientific Revolution, explorers set out to learn everything they could about the world. For example, when Napoleon invaded Egypt in 1798 he brought almost 1000 researchers to carefully study the remains of ancient Egypt. The Rosetta Stone was their most important discovery (see page 78). Explorers drew careful maps, described in detail the new types of vegetation and wildlife they found, and described the people they met. By the middle of the 19th century, most of Africa, Australia, the interior of North America, and the Pacific region had been mapped and described.

- Inspired, in part, by the Enlightenment ideas concerning human rights and, in part, by Christian teaching, social reformers in England campaigned to end slavery. In 1807, Britain outlawed the slave trade. In 1833, slavery was abolished in all British colonies.

- The Age of Revolutions helped make it possible for Britain to become the world's most powerful country in the 19th century. As a result of winning wars with France, Britain gained possession of new colonies in South Africa, Malta, India, Singapore, and Malaysia. By establishing new naval bases in these colonies, Britain was able to expand trade and control the seas.

- Many peoples were inspired by the American and French revolutions' goal of self-government. Independence movements in Africa, Central America, South America, and Asia used the examples of the American and French revolutions to gain support for their causes.

Figure 14.30 In 1791, Toussaint l'Ouverture led a slave revolt on the French island colony of Haiti. Inspired by the ideals of the French Revolution, he believed that all people were entitled to the same human rights, regardless of race or colour. In 1801, he conquered Santo Domingo. The next year, however, he was defeated by one of Napoleon's generals. He was sent to France where he died in prison. By 1804, Napoleon recognized the independence of Haiti.

Summary

Many people saw the Scientific Revolution and the Enlightenment as an attack on religion. Others argued that certain fundamental human values, such as love and respect for other people, were more important than reason alone. Some feared that the examples of the American Revolution and French Revolution would produce chaos and lawlessness by turning the poor against the wealthy. People who were doing well often saw no reason for change.

We benefit from the application of the scientific method with almost everything we do today – from switching a light on and off, to understanding diseases, to watching television. We also benefit from fundamental values about government that were established.

Advances in science have brought us many benefits but have also caused serious environmental problems such as pollution. Most of us take many of the ideas of the Age of Revolution – for example, the importance of science, **self-government**, and human rights – for granted. It is easy to forget that they once provoked considerable opposition.

Connecting and Reflecting

Reflect on the ideas and legacies of each revolution. Use the information that you have learned to describe how each revolution has affected and shaped your daily life. Explain why knowing about these ideas and legacies is important to you *as a citizen of Canada and a citizen of the world.*

Be an Historian

Do you believe everything that you read in a history text? Do you ever wonder what information has been left out? When you study history, you are usually reading the results of what historians have researched and written. In this section, you will have the opportunity to do your own research and ask yourself the same kinds of questions that historians ask themselves. You will not be reading history; you will be doing history!

Historical research is very complicated. (See chapter 1.) It demands knowledge, skill, and patience. Historians have to:

- locate their evidence
- interpret what it means
- sort out what is true from what is probable and what is false

Read the excerpts below. When you are finished, answer the following questions:

- Where do these sources come from?
- Are they sources that you can trust?
- What do you know about the author? If you do not know anything, how can you find out?
- Does the author have knowledge, experience, or credentials that makes you willing to trust his or her work?
- As you try to understand the past, how important is chronology?

The National Assembly Explains Itself, 1790

The National Assembly, as it goes on with its work, is receiving the congratulations of the provinces, towns, and villages, expressions of the people's satisfaction and appreciation. But it also hears complaints from those who have been affected by its attacks on so many abuses and wrongs.... Some people have objected to what has been done and voiced doubt and anxiety about what we intend to do in the future. We will explain.

What has the Assembly accomplished? Despite all the upheavals, it has drafted a constitution that will protect your freedom for ever. The rights of man have been misunderstood and insulted for centuries; they have been established for all humanity by the Declaration, which will stand as a permanent battle-cry against oppressors and as a law for legislators.

The nation had lost its right to make laws and raise taxes. These rights have been restored, while the true principles of monarchy have been established....

Formerly you had the Estates-General; now you have a National Assembly, which can never be taken away from you. The three estates were necessarily opposed to each other and the privileged estates decided the laws and blocked the national will. They no longer exist. They have been replaced by the honorable title of "citizen." Citizens demanded citizen-defenders and the National Guard was created. Called together by patriotism and commanded by honour, it everywhere protects law and order and watches over the safety of each person for the benefit of everyone.

Our laws were nothing but special privileges. They have been destroyed.... A vexatious feudal system covered France; it has been eliminated, never to return....Arbitrary commands threatened the liberty of citizens; they have been eliminated.... At the same time, the National Assembly has created a new division of France, which will replace provincial selfishness with true love of our country and serve as the basis of a fair system of representation of citizens....

This, Frenchmen, is our work, or rather yours. For we are only your representatives, and you have enlightened, encouraged and supported us in our work. What a glorious time this is that we now enjoy! How honorable the heritage you will pass on to your descendants! Raised to the rank of citizens; eligible for every type of employment; enlightened watch-dogs of government when it is not in your actual hands; certain that everything will be done by you and for you; equal before the law; free to speak, write, and act; subject to no one except the common will – what conditions could be more happy? Is there a single citizen worthy of the name who dares to look backwards?.....

Some people say we have been too hasty; others that we have been too cautious. Too hasty! Does not everyone realize that it is only by destroying all abuses at the same time that we can ever be freed of them? That slow and limited reform means no reform at all? That even one abuse left untouched can be the means of restoring all the others we thought we had destroyed?

Critics say our meetings are disorderly, but so what, if our decisions are wise? We do not wish to defend every detail of our debates. They have sometimes upset us. But this disorder is the almost inevitable result of this, our first conflict between right and error.

Critics accuse us of trying to achieve an unrealistic state of perfection. It is a strange criticism and hides a poorly disguised wish to restore the abuses of the past. The National Assembly has not allowed itself to be influenced by selfishness or fear. It has had the courage, or rather the good sense, to believe that useful ideas, essential to the human race, are not destined to remain in books....

But we have done nothing for the people, claim the so-called friends of the people. But in fact the people's cause is everywhere victorious. Nothing done for the people? Does not every abuse which we have abolished bring them relief?....It is not that the people are unhappy, but rather that they are still unhappy. But not for long, this we swear.

(Adapted from J.H. Robinson, Readings in European History, *Volume 2. Boston, Ginn, 1906, 417-422.)*

The National Assembly Criticized, 1791

Unless it wishes to deny the facts, the Assembly cannot fail to recognize that, as a result of its ideas and actions, it has destroyed religion, degraded morals, encouraged vice, trampled on the rights of property, and reduced our army and navy to a worse state than they were before it began its work. It has shaken, perhaps destroyed, the basis of France's military strength. It has reduced our finances to chaos, increased the public debt and the annual deficit, and left taxes uncollected. All this is the result of the recklessness of the radically new system of government which has led people to believe they do not have to pay taxes.

The Assembly cannot deny that France's influence and reputation in Europe have disappeared; that our trade has suffered; our industry is less productive; our population has shrunk.... And that the police are more oppressive and less effective than before the Revolution....

We must avoid the debating tricks which our new law-makers always use to deceive the common people. They compare the present state of affairs in France with the most horrible dictatorship. But this a false comparison that fools and villains always use. Citizens do not want either the old or the new system of government. The Assembly must prove that, without its actions and the calamities they have produced, France would never have gained the freedom, personal safety, and security of property which are the first condition of good government. It would also have to prove that it had no choice but to do what it did, that no middle course was available to it, that the only form of government we could have was the one that the Assembly established....

(Adapted from J.H. Robinson, Readings in European History, *Volume 2. Boston: Ginn, 1906, 433-435.)*

15

Industry and Empire

Our Study of Industry and Empire

Our study of Industry and Empire includes the following topics:

- A Revolution in Agriculture
- What Was the Industrial Revolution?
- New Discoveries and Inventions
- The Nature of Work
- The Cotton Industry
- Capitalism: A New Way of Using Money
- Some Problems of Industrialization
- Trade Unions
- New Responsibilities for Governments
- Liberals and Nationalists
- Socialism
- Conservatives and Conservatism
- The Beginnings of Empire
- Nineteenth-Century Empires
- The Legacy of the Industrial Revolution

The Industrial Revolution had a tremendous influence on scientific and technological developments in 18th-century and 19th-century Europe. This chapter focuses on the Industrial Revolution, its impact, and how it shaped the modern world.

Figure 15.1 At the heart of the Industrial Revolution was the growth of factories.

Questions to Think About

- ✦ What were the causes and results of the Industrial Revolution?

- ✦ How did the Industrial Revolution change the way people lived?

- ✦ How did the Industrial Revolution change the kinds of work that people did?

- ✦ How did the Industrial Revolution affect the relationship between Europe and the rest of the world?

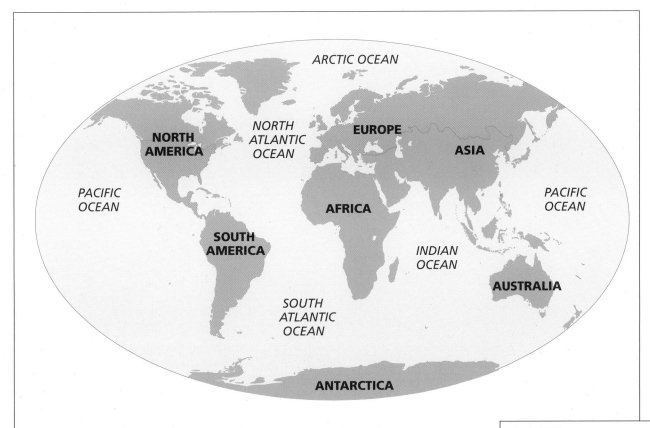

Figure 15.2 This map shows the countries most affected by the Industrial Revolution in the 18th century.

LEGEND

Areas Discussed in Chapter 15

Figure 15.3 This meeting took place in the house of inventor James Watt (1736-1819). The Lunar Society, which began in 1765, was made up of great thinkers of the Industrial Revolution who met to discuss scientific questions and how science could be applied to manufacturing, mining, transport, education, and medicine. The society got its name from the practice of meeting when the moon was full so that its light would guide the members home through otherwise unlit streets. Some other famous members of the society included Erasmus Darwin (1731-1802), the grandfather of Charles Darwin, and ceramics pioneer Josiah Wedgwood (1730-1795).

Figure 15.4 The **reaping machine** in this illustration, invented by Patrick Bell in 1826, helped revolutionize the way harvesting was done. The farmer operated the machine by guiding two horses that push the harvester forward. Blades at the bottom operated like scissors to cut the grain.

A Revolution in Agriculture

A revolution in agriculture began at about the same time as the Industrial Revolution. The revolution in agriculture made farming much more efficient and productive than in the past. For centuries, farmers living in northern climates had to kill their animals each winter because feed was not available at that time of year. The introduction of new crops, such as clover and turnips, made it possible to feed more livestock throughout the year.

Improved breeding methods ensured that only the best animals were used, thereby producing healthier sheep and cattle. New systems of crop rotation, in which crops such as barley, wheat, and clover, were grown in succeeding years, made better use of the soil. More efficient ploughs, mechanical hoes, and seed drills increased the output of food. Despite England's growing population, people could be fed more easily than ever before.

One of the most important aspects of the revolution in agriculture was the ability of farmers to grow more food than they needed for their own survival. Farmers began to sell excess food for profit. The farmers then used the profit to buy more land or equipment, or to invest in another business.

The traditional open fields, where people farmed different strips of land and made decisions collectively, were now seen as inefficient and unprofitable. Through a process called **enclosure**, landowners moved people off the land. They then enclosed the land with fences and hedges and worked it themselves, using the new, more efficient machines. Those forced off the land often moved to the towns and cities looking for work.

What Was the Industrial Revolution?

The Industrial Revolution began when work usually done by hand was replaced by power-driven machinery. The new machines changed how and where people worked. As large factories replaced small businesses and home businesses, more and more people began working outside the home. The first factories were equipped with expensive, new machines for spinning and weaving cloth and for manufacturing iron goods such as nails, pots, and tools. The products were made more quickly, more uniformly, and in greater quantities than ever before. The machines were powered by coal, water and steam, and, later, the **internal combustion engine** and electricity.

The Industrial Revolution began in England in the late 18th century. Throughout the 19th and 20th centuries, other countries throughout the world felt its influence. The factories combined new inventions and machines to speed up, standardize, and increase the production of goods such as plates and dishes, shoes, textiles, and clothing.

At the beginning of the Industrial Revolution, most urban areas were not prepared for the large number of people moving in from the countryside. In the towns and cities, the living and working conditions for most were miserable. Many workers were crowded into substandard housing. They worked long hours in factories where safety was not a concern. Many others ended up homeless.

Eventually, the Industrial Revolution provided much higher standards of living for a great number of people. It also created a very different way of life from the traditional farming societies of the past – and in the process caused much disruption.

> **Figure 15.5** The Industrial Revolution forced people to move to cities, but the city governments were unprepared to handle the growing population.

Figure 15.6 The steam engine quickly became a symbol of the Industrial Revolution.

New Discoveries and Inventions

Before the Industrial Revolution, roads were little more than dirt tracks. Long-distance land transport was by pack horse. Travel was slow, unreliable, and expensive. Wherever possible, goods were carried by riverboats and sailing ships that followed the sea coasts.

Hard-surface roads were first built in the 1700s, usually by private contractors who charged tolls to those who used the roads. Rivers were straightened and deepened, and canals were built to make the transportation of large cargoes cheap and dependable.

One of the most important discoveries of the Industrial Revolution was the use of steam power. Using steam as power depended on finding a material that could stand up to the pounding produced by steam engines. That material was iron. Iron made it possible to build boilers and fireboxes that could withstand heat and pressure without bursting or melting. Iron also made it possible to build pistons and cylinders that fitted together and withstood the wear and tear of constant motion. Iron was obtained by refining iron ore with **coke**, a product that came from coal. England possessed large and accessible deposits of both coal and iron ore, which is one reason the Industrial Revolution began there.

In industry, factories used machines powered by steam to mass-produce goods that had previously been made by hand. Transportation was also revolutionized by the steam engine. On land, steam-powered trains could carry both people and goods over long distances at relatively low cost. On water, steamships greatly decreased the time it took to travel from one place to another.

Steam power also made it possible to build factories close together, since they no longer had to be located near sources of waterpower such as rivers or waterfalls. The factories attracted large numbers of workers, who were also customers for the products being made – clothing, furniture, footwear, pots and pans, screws and nails, pins and needles, tools, and all kinds of everyday objects. In turn, these workers needed somewhere to live, which created a huge demand for housing.

The Nature of Work

Before the Industrial Revolution, work was often loosely organized. People followed the rhythms of nature. In an agricultural setting, people could, to a large degree, work at their own speed. Farm workers might know that a certain field had to be ploughed by the end of the day, for example, but it was up to them to decide how quickly they worked.

With the Industrial Revolution, the new machines determined the speed of work. Workers had fixed hours and followed the schedules of the factory – not the rhythms of nature. Critics of industrialization said that rather than the machines serving people, people were becoming slaves of the machine.

The production of many handmade crafts, such as shoemaking and barrel-making, was largely replaced by machines. At the same time, new skilled workers, such as mechanics and factory supervisors, were needed. Most manual jobs were broken down into small tasks, with each worker performing the same task repeatedly. For the factory owners, this helped to lower costs and increase productivity. For the workers, jobs became boring and repetitive.

Factory owners needed to make a profit if they were to stay in business. To keep the prices of their products lower than those of their competitors, they had to pay their workers as little as possible. In contrast, factory workers needed to make enough money to live on, and they wanted to improve their working conditions. Fulfilling these demands would cut into the profits of employers.

Figure 15.7 Robert Owen (1771-1858) was a factory owner in Scotland who believed the well-being of his employees was more important than remaining competitive with other factory owners. He built houses for his workers and charged them low rent. He paid his workers a decent wage and even kept them on the payroll when business was slow. To the surprise of most, his factory continued to make a profit.

Owen established a school at his factory and made his workers enroll their children there. At the school, teachers encouraged children to learn through activity and through models and pictures that they made. In this picture, Owen is showing his school to visitors.

Owen's factory attracted much attention but, despite his success, his ideas did not catch on. In the 1820s, Owen moved to the United States. There, he established model villages where people worked together in a spirit of co-operation.

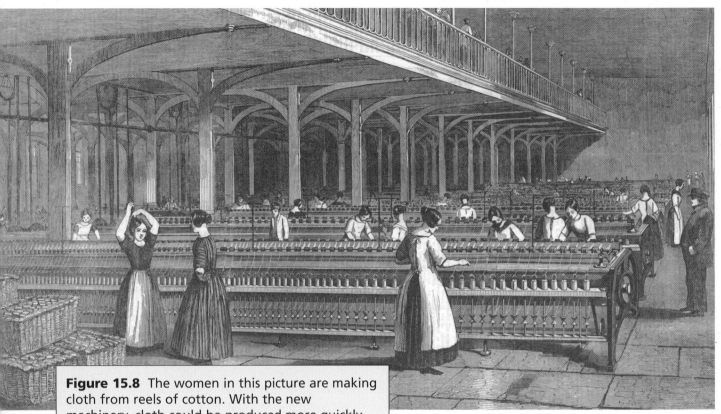

Figure 15.8 The women in this picture are making cloth from reels of cotton. With the new machinery, cloth could be produced more quickly than with the handspun method. Factory workers had to put up with the noise, smells, dust, and heat produced by the machines. Factory owners preferred to employ young women in jobs like this. Women had the skills needed, were thought to be less likely to rebel against the harsh working conditions, and could be paid less than adult men. Note that the supervisor is male.

The Cotton Industry

The first industry to be affected by the Industrial Revolution was the cotton industry. Cotton cloth was inexpensive to produce, easy to wash, and could be produced in many colours and patterns. Spinning cotton from raw material was a slow process when done by hand, but the 18th century saw the steady development of new and better spinning machines. England had a ready source of raw cotton from its colonies in North America and India, and its growing population provided a good market for cotton products. England also sold cotton goods to its colonies in the West Indies, India, Canada, Australia, South Africa, and elsewhere. By the 1780s, spinning machines were powered by steam produced by burning coal. People no longer produced cotton cloth at home.

The growth of the cotton industry had many effects. With the large number of new factories, there was need for better transportation to bring in the raw cotton and ship out the finished goods. Steamships and railroads were especially efficient. Manufacturers realized they needed financial services such as banks. Other industries – shipbuilding, railroad building, railroad locomotive and wagon building, and engineering, for example – soon began to develop.

Figure 15.9 This painting of an iron foundry shows the terrible conditions most men worked in.

Living in the City

This is the story of one family whose lives were drastically changed by the Industrial Revolution.

A banging on the door let Jane Robertson know that it was 5 o'clock in the morning. It was time to get up and wake her husband and three children. None of them owned a watch or a clock. For that matter, none of them could tell the time. When they had lived in the countryside, their lives were shaped by nature, not by clocks. They arose at daybreak, went to bed at dusk, and ate when they were hungry.

In the city, everything was different. The factory machines paid no attention to nature. Everything was run by the clock. The neighbour banged on the door once more. Just as Jane crawled out of bed, the factory sounded its warning siren.

The whole family had to be at work by six. Jane and her children worked on the spinning machines. Her husband was a stoker. His job was shovelling coal into the furnace that produced the steam that the factory used for power. The Robertsons had been working in the factory for two years – ever since they had left their village.

Living outside of the city had never been easy. However, the Robertson's use of the **common land** had allowed them to keep a few pigs for food. They always had firewood for cooking and warmth and even earned enough income for an occasional luxury such as store-bought candy or a silk scarf. When the common land was converted into private farms, the family was forced to leave and find work in the city.

None of the Robertsons liked living in the crowded, dirty, and expensive city. They had to work six days a week, from early morning until at least six at night – longer if the factory was busy. By the time they finished work, they were all too tired to do anything more than eat and sleep.

If they broke any of the factory rules, they could be fined, and the children could be strapped. If they complained, they could be fired. As bad as it was working in the factory, they knew they were lucky. Plenty of unemployed people would be only too happy to have their jobs.

Jane and her husband did not want their children working in the factory. Without the children's wages, though, they could not afford to buy enough food. What choice did they have?

The Robertsons lived in a dirty, rundown one-room house. They did not have fuel for heating or cooking, water for washing or drinking, or lighting to see in the dark. They could not afford meat or milk very often. They usually ate bread and cheese with, perhaps, some cheap beer to drink.

While life in the country had been difficult, at least the Robertsons had been able to breathe fresh air and have some independence. Here in the city, they were barely able to survive. The goods in the shops were too expensive. They could not afford new clothes and, without water or soap, it was impossible to clean the ones they had.

No one in the family could read, but Jane had been told that the newspapers were describing the times they were living in as the Age of Progress. As far as Jane could see, her family's only progress was downwards.

Figure 15.10 This drawing of a street scene in 19th-century London is by Gustave Doré (1832-1883), a French artist. Critics accused him of concentrating on scenes of poverty and distress. Few people, however, could deny that scenes like this actually existed in London and other European cities. Governments were unprepared to handle the growing population.

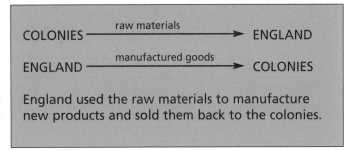

England used the raw materials to manufacture new products and sold them back to the colonies.

Capitalism: A New Way of Using Money

The Industrial Revolution was, in part, a result of *capitalism*. In a capitalist system, people invest their money in businesses. The money invested is used to pay for the expenses of these businesses. Expenses can include employees' salaries, rent for work space, the costs of buying and repairing equipment, and the cost of obtaining materials needed to make products. Investors expect to share in the companies' profits.

If a company does not make a profit, people will look elsewhere for a company in which to invest. Capitalism, then, is based not only on private ownership and profit, but also on competition. Companies that become more profitable attract even more investors.

By the 16th century, capitalism was becoming a reality in western Europe. Traders were finding both raw materials and markets for their products around the world. In the process, they were making large profits for the people who financed them.

Rich people began to look for ways to use their money to make more money. Investing – in new industries such as canal and railroad building, cotton and textile manufacture, coal mining, and iron production – was one way to do this. Some landowners made fortunes when their lands were found to hold rich deposits of coal, iron, and other minerals that were in demand during the Industrial Revolution. Without the money of investors, the new industries would have found it much more difficult to get started.

Figure 15.11 Capitalism made some people, such as factory owners, very wealthy. For most people, however, capitalism represented poor health, terrible working conditions, and substandard housing. This 1843 illustration, which shows "death knocking on the door," was inspired by a British government report on the horrific state of workers in coal mines.

Figure 15.12 This picture of a child pulling a wagon of coal in a mine appeared in an official British report on child labour in 1842. In 1833, England made it illegal for children under the age of nine to work in textile factories. Children between the ages of nine and 13 could not work more than 48 hours a week. Teenagers between 13 and 18 could not work for more than 69 hours a week. In 1842, it became illegal in England for children under ten years of age to work underground in coal mines. In 1847, laws restricted the working hours of women and children in textile mills to ten hours a day. Little was done to restrict the working hours of male workers, however. Women and children were thought to need special protection, but men were expected to look after themselves.

Some Problems of Industrialization

In many of the new industries, working conditions were extremely bad. Most factories were noisy and dirty. Hours were long, pay was low, and safety standards were non-existent. Workers had few, if any, rights. They were subject to harsh and, sometimes, brutal discipline. These harsh conditions applied to men, women, and even to young children.

Figure 15.13 In 1842, the same year this illustration was published, it became illegal for women to work underground in coal mines.

By the middle of the 19th century, both working and living conditions slowly started to improve. Concerned individuals and some governments became involved in setting standards. These standards controlled the employment of children, limited the number of hours that could be worked, and improved safety standards in mines and factories.

Figure 15.14 These miners are secretly meeting to discuss their working conditions. For most of the 19th century, unions consisted of workers such as carpenters, mechanics, or locomotive engineers – people whose jobs demanded special training and skills. Most unskilled employees did not belong to unions. Unlike skilled workers, they could be easily replaced if they were fired.

Trade Unions

Trade unions are organizations formed by workers to lobby for better wages and working conditions. At the start of the Industrial Revolution, trade unions were illegal. The factory owners had the power and the rights to do as they wished with their property. These rights were more important than the rights of the individual workers.

By about 1850, however, after much struggle, workers in most industrial countries had won the right to organize unions. In many countries, though, it remained illegal to go on **strike**. By negotiating with factory owners, unions were able to gain some of their demands. In time, unions in different industries began to

co-operate with one another and formed a united labour movement. Their slogan was: "Workers of the world unite; you have nothing to lose but your chains."

One consequence of the Industrial Revolution was the creation of the working class. The needs and interests of these people were different from factory owners and other wealthy people. The priorities of the unions were to protect the rights of workers, to limit working hours, and to improve working conditions.

Today, we take trade unions for granted. We accept as basic human rights such things as a minimum wage, limitation of working hours, the right to join a union, the right to strike, and the right to a safe work environment.

New Responsibilities for Governments

The rapid growth of cities brought on by the Industrial Revolution created many problems:

- pollution from the factories

- inadequate sanitation, public health, housing, and transportation

- widespread occurrences of infectious diseases such as tuberculosis, cholera, and pneumonia

- poverty created by low wages

- crime

At first, governments did not know how to respond to the problems. Around 1850, governments started to get involved in local issues. Police forces were organized to prevent and control crime. Health and safety laws and regulations were passed to protect the public. Schools were built and attendance became compulsory. Hospitals were built. Sewage and garbage disposal systems were created. Governments provided clean water, operated public transport, and built parks and other recreational facilities. They delivered the mail. This growing power of government was, partly, responsible for the creation of working-class political parties. The working class was determined to have a voice in government decisions.

With the onset of the Industrial Revolution, a debate began that continues today: What should be the powers and responsibilities of government? What should be done by private businesses? What should people do for themselves?

Figure 15.15 By the 1830s, public concern at the quality of London's water supply was growing. In 1831 and 1832, the city suffered its first cholera outbreaks, although at the time the connection between the disease and a contaminated water supply was not realized.

Figure 15.16 Sewers were deepened in London in the 1840s in a move to control water-borne diseases.

Liberals and Nationalists

As described in chapter 14, the Enlightenment, together with the American Revolution and the French Revolution, created a growing demand for self-government and basic human rights. The idea that citizens are entitled to basic rights – including the right to choose who governs them and a voice in government decisions – became increasingly popular. People who accepted this idea were known as **liberals**, from the Latin word *libertas*, meaning liberty.

Governments could not stop the spread of liberal ideas. Between 1820 and 1850, liberal reformers throughout Europe struggled to win the right to vote and to be governed by elected parliaments.

- In 1820, revolutions occurred in Spain and some Italian states.

- In 1825, there was an attempted revolution in Russia.

- In the 1820s, Greece fought a long war to win its independence from the Ottoman Empire.

- In 1830, there were revolutions in France, Holland, Russia, and Poland. In South America, Spain's former colonies won their independence.

- Many smaller rebellions occurred across Europe.

- Rebellions occurred in Lower Canada (Quebec) and Upper Canada (Ontario) in 1837 when colonists attempted to establish a government that would be responsible to the people.

Figure 15.17 Nationalists were often imprisoned because of their views. This illustration shows the leader of the Irish Nationalist Movement, Daniel O'Connell (1775-1847), just after his release from prison in September 1844.

Many rebellions and revolutions were nationalist as well as liberal. Inspired by the example of the French Revolution, nationalists believed that each nation should have its own government and become an independent country.

In Europe, the combined pressures from liberals and nationals peaked in 1848, a year now known as "the year of revolutions." Every country except Britain, Belgium, and Russia faced some kind of revolution. All were fought in the name of self-government and national independence.

The revolutionaries were defeated because they did not have the military forces to resist the armies that remained loyal to their countries' rulers. They also did not have widespread backing from the people. Liberal and nationalist ideas were popular with students, teachers, journalists, and middle-class professionals but were largely unknown to the peasants, who still formed the majority of the population. The peasants were more interested in issues that concerned them directly – land ownership, rents, and protection from landlords.

Nonetheless, 1848 was an important year in the evolution of liberal and nationalist ideas.

Figure 15.18 During the 1800s, people became more vocal in their demands for better wages and working conditions. They also began to demand more rights. Among the demands from this political crowd, which gathered in 1819, was **universal suffrage.**

As momentum for social and political changes grew, rulers realized they could not ignore the demands for reform. In 1870, both Germany and Italy became united countries. By the 1890s, most countries had some kind of elected parliament, even though the powers of these parliaments were sometimes very limited.

Liberal and nationalist ideas spread beyond Europe. In Asia and Africa, people began to ask why they could not be independent and govern themselves.

Figure 15.19 In Lower Canada, the French population was largely excluded from government. In 1834, the Patriotes, a party led by Louis Joseph Papineau, sent to Britain a list of demands for change. Among the demands, called the Ninety-Two Resolutions, were that the legislative council be elected and that the members of the executive council be chosen by the assembly. In early 1837, Britain responded by refusing to consider the demands for reform of the legislative and executive councils. In late fall, violent clashes broke out between British troops and Patriote forces. By the middle of December the Papineau rebellion had been crushed.

Figure 15.20 While socialists agreed on some general principles, they disagreed on how the principles of socialism could become reality. Some socialists believed that changes could be achieved only by revolution. Others agreed that socialism could be achieved peacefully once workers won the right to vote.

Socialism

Socialism was another idea that took hold during the Industrial Revolution. There are many different kinds of socialism. In the 19th century, **socialists** spent as much time arguing among themselves as they did with their opponents. They did, however, agree on four principles.

1. Socialists rejected capitalism's emphasis on competition and profit. Capitalists believed that to make a profit and stay ahead of competitors, factory owners had to keep wages as low as possible and get the maximum amount of work out of their workers. Socialists opposed the way workers were treated as though they were machines rather than humans.

2. Socialists said factories and other businesses should be owned by society as a whole, not by private owners. In this way, industry would work for the good of everyone, not just for factory owners; products would be made because they were useful and necessary, not because the products would make a profit for someone. Once businesses were owned and operated by society as a whole, socialists argued, it would be possible to plan the economy so that industry would produce only what society needed.

3. Socialists believed that working-class people could only become poorer and rich people richer in a capitalist society. They wanted to see a society where everyone was more or less equal.

4. Socialists said that in a democracy the working people should control the government since they formed the largest segment of the population. Workers would then vote for the party that best served their interests – the socialist party. Until then, socialists wanted to correct the injustices of capitalism and improve workers' lives by, for example, negotiating for improved wages and working conditions.

Some opponents of socialism argued that a socialist government would have too much power. Some said that socialism was contrary to human nature; private property, competition, and profit making motivated people. Others said that only a capitalist society would produce the goods that people wanted. Moreover, the opponents argued, there was nothing wrong with capitalism that could not be corrected.

By 1850, socialism was still an idea, not a political movement. By the end of the 19th century, however, socialist parties were active in all industrialized countries. Socialist ideas had become part of the continuing debate about how best to respond to the changes introduced by the Industrial Revolution.

Conservatives and Conservatism

Some people were alarmed by the Industrial Revolution. In their opinion, too many changes were occurring too fast. The result, as they saw it, was chaos and disorder. Kings and queens were being overthrown. The church was being stripped of its land and property. The aristocracy was losing power and influence.

People who wanted to conserve as much of the past as possible were called **conservatives**. They were suspicious of change. Unlike liberals and socialists, conservatives did not believe "progress" was always desirable. Something as complex as human society could not be easily changed. Historical traditions and values mattered.

Some conservatives were driven by fear and self-interest. Many aristocrats, for example, were afraid of losing their privileged place in society. Rich property owners worried that they might lose their property. Church officials were alarmed by the prospect that the church would lose influence. For instance, many liberals and socialists wanted to abolish church schools and replace them with non-religious schools controlled by elected officials.

Other conservatives were genuinely concerned that society was changing for the worse. They believed that competition created societies where a few people were successful, but most people were resentful and dissatisfied.

Conservatives were equally disturbed by socialism. Socialists spoke of the victory of the working class. They attacked all forms of privilege and inequality. Many spoke of abolishing private property altogether. Socialists wanted radical changes in society, including votes for all adults, public ownership of industry, and free education for all children. Conservatives thought these kinds of changes were dangerous.

Figure 15.21 The growth of factories destroyed the livelihoods of hundreds of thousands of workers in the cottage industries. In an effort to regain their way of life, many banded together and formed the Luddites. In groups, they broke into factories and destroyed the machines. They always left behind a handwritten sign that attributed the destruction to General Ludd, their fictitious leader.

By the middle of the 19th century, conservatives in many countries had organized themselves into political parties ready to oppose liberalism and socialism. In politics, as in so many areas of life, the Industrial Revolution helped lay the foundation for the kind of politics we see today – liberals, conservatives, and socialists debating about how society should be organized.

British Empire in 1850

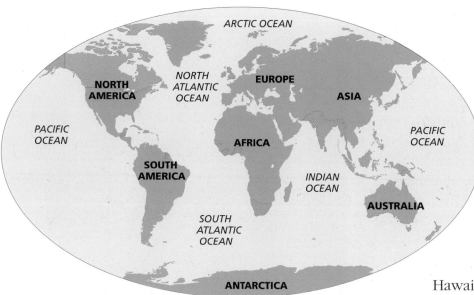

Figure 15.22 This map shows the extent of the British empire around 1850.

The Beginnings of Empire

The peoples in China, India, Central America, South America, and the societies of Ghana, Mali, and the Middle East were, at different times, among the most advanced in the world in the arts, sciences, technology, and their standard of living.

From the Middle Ages onwards, European travellers and explorers brought back reports of the sophisticated ways of life they found in other lands. The crusaders reported on the achievements of Muslim societies in the Middle East. When Marco Polo returned to Venice in 1295 after spending years in China, his descriptions of his experiences made Europeans aware of the richness of Chinese culture. Europeans wanted some of the goods.

Some European countries – especially Spain, Portugal, Britain, France, and Holland – began to establish world empires long before the onset of the Industrial Revolution.

In the 16th and 17th centuries, for example, Spain and Portugal took possession of Central America and South America. Spain also conquered the Philippines, and Portugal established small colonies of Goa in India, and Macao in China. Similarly, Britain, Holland, and France established colonies in North America and in the East Indies and West Indies. Europeans were impressed by the gold that Spanish explorers such as Cortés and Pizarro brought back from Central America and South America. Jesuit missionaries wrote letters and reports describing the advanced societies they visited in India, Japan, and China.

Beginning in 1768, the English sailor James Cook (1728-1779) mapped much of the Pacific before he was killed in Hawaii in 1779. At the same time, the French sailor Louis de Bougainville (1729-1811) explored and mapped the islands of the Pacific Ocean. In Russia, land-based explorers travelled east across Siberia. In the United States and Canada, explorers ventured west across the Great Plains and the Rockies to the Pacific Coast. In Africa and Australia, too, explorers headed inland.

From the 17th century to the 19th century, Europe extended its influence throughout the world. Europeans began to take an increased interest in the world. There were several reasons for this.

1. *Exploration* The Industrial Revolution led to major improvements in shipbuilding, gunnery, and such navigational aids as the compass. These gave Europeans the power to explore and largely control the world's oceans.

2. *Self-interest* Europeans began to see nature as something they could control and use to their benefit. Many Europeans viewed the rest of the world as something they could use for their own advantage.

3. *Economics* Countries such as France, England, and Holland were always looking for new sources of

sugar, spices, tobacco, fish, and furs. To develop and protect their sources, they established colonies, naval bases, and trading posts around the world.

4. *Workforce* To find a workforce large enough for the new **plantations** located in the Caribbean and the Americas, the European powers forced millions of Africans into slavery. It was not long before the trans-Atlantic slave trade became an important source of wealth for countries such as Spain, Holland, Portugal, and England, as well as for England's North American colonies.

For manufacturers to make a profit, they had to find new markets for all the goods they were producing. Gradually, the manufacturers, supported by their governments, began selling their products to countries around the globe. Many small, local manufacturers, unable to compete with mass-produced, inexpensive goods, were driven out of business. Some countries, like India, became increasingly dependent on European producers to supply goods. When the people in these countries later rebelled against the economic dominance of Europe, European governments used their superior power to protect their trade.

Figure 15.23 Captain James Cook raised the Union Jack on an Australian beach. On most ocean expeditions in the 18th century, many crew members died from malnutrition. James Cook took many precautions to ensure the well being of his crews. To prevent scurvy, a disease caused by a lack of vitamin C, for example, he and his crew ate carrot marmalade and sauerkraut. During his second voyage, which lasted from 1772 to 1775, only one crew member died.

Figure 15.24 In this illustration, slaves at a plantation in the Caribbean are processing sugar cane before it is loaded onto a ship. The sugar is being exported to Europe.

Nineteenth-Century Empires

During the 19th century, Europe's population grew from 190 million to 423 million people. A rise in birth rates and decrease in death rates were the result of improvements made to the supply and quality of food and new medical knowledge and medicines. Approximately 40 million Europeans left Europe in the 19th century. Most moved to the United States, but many went to British colonies in Canada, Australia, New Zealand, and South Africa, and some to countries in South America. This migration was one of the largest movements of people in human history. It helped to establish links between the new lands where the emigrants settled and the European countries from which they came.

Sometimes, European governments seized land elsewhere in the world, not because they wanted it but to protect territory that they already had. For example, Britain had seized the Cape of Good Hope at the tip of South Africa from the Dutch in 1806. To protect its new colony, Britain had to expand northward into South Africa and then beyond. Britain also possessed many islands and coastal settlements around the world, because these lands were good naval bases and protected Britain's important trade routes. Britain controlled Gibraltar, Malta, and Cyprus in the Mediterranean Sea, for example; the Cape of Good Hope in South Africa; Sri Lanka and India in the Indian Ocean; the Suez Canal and Aden; Singapore, Malaya, Hong Kong, and a series of Pacific islands.

To rule a world-wide empire was a sign that a country was a great power. Europeans saw themselves as bringing what they called "civilization" to the rest of the world. They believed that they were the most advanced societies in the history of the world, and that

Dates of South and Central American Independence

N

MEXICO 1821

UNITED PROVINCES OF CENTRAL AMERICA 1823-1838

VENEZUELA 1830

NEW GRANADA 1831

ECUADOR 1830

PERU 1829

BRAZIL 1822

PACIFIC OCEAN

BOLIVIA 1825

PARAGUAY 1811

ARGENTINA 1810

URUGUAY 1828

CHILE 1818

ATLANTIC OCEAN

0   800   1600 km

Figure 15.25 By the 1820s, Central America and South America had rejected Spanish and Portuguese rule and created the independent countries we know today.

they were superior to all other races. In their eyes, their global dominance was proof of their superiority. At best, they saw their superiority as giving them the right to rule other peoples for their own good. At worst, they believed they were entitled to exploit and oppress those they dominated.

By the mid-1800s, Britain ruled Australia, New Zealand, most of the West Indies, much of India, areas of Africa, and islands and coastal territories around the world. France had taken possession of much of North Africa and was penetrating into other parts of that continent.

The Legacy of the Industrial Revolution

Benefits of the Industrial Revolution:

- higher standard of living for more people than ever before in history
- unprecedented improvements in medicine and health care
- highly effective and efficient means of communication and transportation
- technological inventions that improved people's everyday lives (for example, safe running water, adequate sewage disposal, electricity, air conditioning, heating)
- convenience items (for example, ready-to-wear clothing)

Problems of the Industrial Revolution:

- a widening gap between wealthy countries and poor countries
- pollution
- widespread use of non-renewable resources such as coal

Figure 15.26 This textile picture was made in 1834. In it, the artist predicts that in the year 2000 people will travel by steam carriage and will fly by balloons and wings that attach to the body.

Summary

The Industrial Revolution that began in Britain in the late 18th century went on to change the shape of the whole world. It laid the foundation for the scientific and technological developments that we now take for granted. Equally important, the Industrial Revolution created a new way of thinking about the world – progress was seen as desirable and change as inevitable.

By the end of the 19th century, the Industrial Revolution made Britain, France, and Germany the most powerful countries in the world, both economically and militarily. The Europeans had used new sciences and technologies to establish world-wide empires based on the possession of colonies, control of trade with other countries, and superior military power.

The Industrial Revolution continues today. While coal-based steam power drove the Industrial Revolution in the 19th century, the revolution is now being driven with oil, electricity, and nuclear power. The question for the 21st century is: Will there be enough power and resources to support a continuing, world-wide Industrial Revolution?

Connecting and Reflecting

Reflect on the ideas and inventions of the Industrial Revolution. Use the information that you have learned to explain how the Industrial Revolution and building of empires has influenced your life *as a citizen of Canada and a citizen of the world.*

Be a Historian

The Industrial Revolution led directly to the kind of education you are now receiving. Before the Industrial Revolution, parents chose whether or not to send their children to school. Schools were operated by either churches or private teachers who charged fees. As the Industrial Revolution spread, more and more governments realized the importance of education. Industrial workers needed to be able to read, write, and do basic arithmetic. Equally important, workers needed good work habits; for example, doing what tasks they were told to do, working according to schedules fixed by clock-time, and carrying out tasks reliably. When working-class people won the right to vote, governments wanted to ensure the people understood what they were voting for.

As explained in chapter 1, schools were expected to teach citizenship. Liberals, socialists, and other reformers also wanted schools to teach children to think for themselves and to understand democratic ideas and values. By the end of the 19th century, governments in most countries saw education as one of their responsibilities.

Do you believe everything that you read in a history text? Do you ever wonder what information has been left out? When you study history, you are usually reading the results of what historians have researched and written. In this section, you will have the opportunity to do your own research and ask yourself the same kinds of questions that historians ask themselves. You will not be reading history; you will be doing history!

Historical research is very complicated. (See chapter 1.) It demands knowledge, skill, and patience. Historians have to:

- locate their evidence

- interpret what it means

- sort out what is true from what is probable and what is false

Read the excerpts below. When you are finished, answer the following questions:

- Where do these sources come from?

- Are they sources that you can trust?

- What do you know about the author? If you do not know anything, how can you find out?

- Does the author have knowledge, experience, or credentials that makes you willing to trust his or her work?

- As you try to understand the past, how important is chronology?

Education for Work

There is considerable use in children being somehow or other constantly employed at least twelve hours a day, whether they earn their living or not; for by this means we hope that the rising generation will be so habituated to constant employment that it would at length prove agreeable and entertaining to them.
(William Temple, English writer, 1770s)

Education for Society

Education is the same for man and beast. It can be reduced to two principles: to learn to endure injustice and to learn to endure boredom. How do we break in a horse? Left to itself, a horse strolls, trots, gallops, walks, but does so as it chooses, when it wishes. We teach the horse to move as we wish, against its own desires and instincts. That is the injustice. We make the horse do it for two hours or more. There is the boredom. It is just the same when we make a child learn Latin or Greek or French. The value or usefulness of it is not the point. The aim is that the child learns to obey another person…. Education is a matter of learning the weariness of concentrating one's attention on the matter in hand.
(Abbé Galiani, French philosopher, 1780s)

Educating Citizens

I know no safe depository of the ultimate powers of the society but the people themselves; and if we think them not enlightened enough to exercise their control with a wholesome discretion, the remedy is not to take it from them, but to inform their discretion by education. This is the true corrective of constitutional power.

(Thomas Jefferson (1820), a leader of the American Revolution and President of the United States from 1801 to 1809.)

National Education

I have indeed two great measures at heart, without which no republic can maintain itself in strength: 1. That of general education, to enable every man to judge for himself what will secure or endanger his freedom. 2. To divide every county into hundreds, of such size that all the children of each will be within reach of a central school in it.

(Thomas Jefferson, 1810)

Public instruction is an obligation of society towards its citizens. It would be pointless to declare that all men possess equal rights, and for the laws to respect the first principle of eternal justice, if the inequalities in men's intellectual powers prevented them from enjoying their rights to the fullest extent.

(Condorcet (1791). Condorcet was a French Enlightenment philosopher and supporter of the French Revolution. He was arrested as a suspected enemy of the revolution during the Reign of Terror and died in prison in 1794.)

Education and Progress

Although I do not, with some enthusiasts, believe that the human condition will ever advance to such a state of perfection as that there shall no longer be pain or vice in the world, yet I believe it susceptible of much improvement, and most of all in matters of government and religion; and that the diffusion of knowledge among the people is to be the instrument by which it is to be effected.

(Thomas Jefferson, 1816)

By the successive discovery of all kinds of truth, civilized nations have freed themselves from barbarism and for all the evils that arise from ignorance and prejudice. By the discovery of new truths, the human race will continue its progress towards perfection…. It is therefore a duty of society to promote the discovery of new truths as the only way to advance the human race to the degree of perfection and of happiness that nature permits us…. So far, only a very small number of people receive an education that lets then develop their natural abilities….Nothing can compensate for this lack of basic education. It alone can teach the habits of method and the variety of knowledge that people need if they are to reach the highest level of development possible for them…. It is important therefore to create a system of public instruction that allows no talent to go unnoticed, but gives it all the help previously available only to the rich.

(Condorcet, 1791)

The Power of Education

No one, it may now be supposed, is so defective in knowledge as to imagine that it is a different human nature, which by its own power forms itself into a child of ignorance, of poverty, and of habits leading to crime and to punishment … or that it is a different human nature which constitutes the societies of the Jews, of Friends, of all the various religious denominations which have existed or now exist. No! Human nature, save the minute differences which are ever found in all the compounds of creation, is one and the same in all; it is without exception universally plastic, and by judicious training, the infants of any one class in the world may be readily formed into men of any other class….

It follows that every state, to be well governed, ought to direct its chief attention to the formation of character; and that the best governed state will be that which shall possess the best national system of education.

Under the guidance of minds competent to its direction, a national system of training and education may be formed to become the most safe, easy, effectual, and economical instrument of government that can be devised. And it may be made to possess a power equal to the accomplishment of the most grand and beneficial purposes.

(Robert Owen (1813). Owen was a British industrialist who believed that workers should be treated fairly.)

Conclusion

You have finally reached the end of your textbook! Now it is time for you to think about everything you have learned and pull together, or connect, all of the societies that you have been reading about. Below, and in the pages that follow, you will find the timeline from each chapter. A globe icon beside each timeline reminds you of where in the world the events on the timeline took place. When timelines are put together in this way, you should be able to "see" a more complete picture of world history.

THE EARLY PEOPLES	2 500 000 BCE– 1 200 000 BCE	1 000 000 BCE– 700 000 BCE	250 000 BCE	100 000 BCE	40 000 BCE– 13 000 BCE	13 000 BCE– 10 000 BCE	8000 BCE
	Beginning of Paleolithic Age (Old Stone Age). Homo habilis, our first direct human ancestor, appears in East Africa. First use of tools made from stone. Homo erectus, a new human species, appears in Africa. 2 000 000 BCE Ice Age begins.	Humans begin to move from Africa to Europe and Asia. 700 000 BCE Fire is used for the first time.	Homo sapiens humans appear. Neanderthals appear in Europe. Humans extract ochre, a type of iron ore, from the earth and use it as paint or dye.	Cro-Magnons appear in North Africa, Europe, and Asia.	Humans move from Asia, first to North America and then to South America. 20 000 BCE Humans are making musical instruments.	Humans are painting on cave walls at Lascaux, France. End of the last Ice Age. End of Paleolithic Age and beginning of Mesolithic Age (Middle Stone Age).	End of Mesolithic Age and beginning of Neolithic Age (New Stone Age). Humans begin to domesticate animals and cultivate plants. 6000 BCE Jericho, thought to be the world's first town, has a population of about 2000.

MESOPOTAMIA	c. 8500 BCE	c. 7000 BCE	c. 5000 BCE	c. 4300 BCE	c. 3300 BCE	c. 3250 BCE	c. 3000 BCE
	People are farming in the Middle East.	People begin to settle in the valley between the Tigris and Euphrates rivers in an area called Mesopotamia.	A group of people called the Sumerians begin to settle in southern Mesopotamia.	The Sumerians have established several city-states including Ur, Lagash, Kish, Nippur, and Uruk.	Sumerians develop a format of writing based on pictographs.	Sumerians are using the wheel for pottery-making and transportation.	Doctors and veterinarians are practicing medicine.

EGYPT	c. 5500 BCE	c. 4000 BCE	c. 3300 BCE	c. 3100 BCE	c. 2700 BCE	2558 BCE– 2532 BCE	c. 2500 BCE
	People began to settle in permanent villages along the Nile River.	First evidence of medical treatments.	First appearance of hieroglyphics.	King Menes unites Upper Egypt and Lower Egypt.	Great Step Pyramid is built at Saqqara.	Khafre, credited with building second largest pyramid in Giza, rules.	The Sphinx is built.

5000 BCE	3500 BCE	2500 BCE	1500 BCE	1 CE	600 CE
Before 6000 BCE South American Indians are growing corn. 5000 BCE People in Mexico are gathering wild potatoes. 5000 BCE Surgery is being practiced.	End of Neolithic Age. Beginning of Bronze Age. The first systems of writing are developed in Mesopotamia.	The building of Stonehenge begins in southern England.	Beginning of Iron Age.	The statues on Easter Island are carved.	Nazca lines are made in Peru.

c. 2760 BCE	2324 BCE	c. 1800 BCE	c. 1770 BCE	c. 760 BCE	c. 550 BCE
Sumerians begin to combine copper and tin to make bronze.	The Akkadians, led by Sargon the Great, take control of many Sumerian cities.	Babylonians move into Mesopotamia.	The Code of Hammurabi, a set of 282 laws, is created.	Assyrians invade Mesopotamia.	Persians invade Mesopotamia.

c. 2000 BCE-1700 BCE	c. 1800 BCE	c. 1650 BCE	c. 1550 BCE	c. 1400 BCE	c. 1361 BCE	c. 1300 BCE	332 BCE
Egyptians begin to write down descriptions of medical knowledge.	Hebrews move from the Arabian Desert to Egypt.	End of pyramid-building era.	Use of term *pharaoh* begins.	Queen Hatshepsut, the best-known female pharaoh, begins her rule.	King Tukankhamen, the boy king, begins his rule.	Hebrews begin to settle in Canaan (the area between Egypt and Mesopotamia).	Alexander the Great conquers Egypt.

THE INDUS VALLEY				c. 2600 BCE
				Evidence people have a system of writing by the time they moved into the Indus Valley.
				Indus Valley people settle along the Indus River and River Riva and establish several cities, including Mohenjo-Daro and Harappa.
				Cities have well-planned and well-made drainage and sewage systems.

CHINA	c. 5000 BCE	c. 4000 BCE		2737 BCE
	Silk production begins.	Neolithic farmers settle near Huang Ho River.		According to legend, Chinese emperor Shen Nung discovers tea.

GREECE & ROME	c. 1200 BCE	c. 1100 BCE	1000 BCE	776 BCE	753 BCE	c. 750 BCE	c. 600 BCE
	Trojan War begins.	Mycenaean society collapses.	Latins move into Italian peninsula and settle in villages.	The first Olympic games takes place in Greece.	City of Rome is founded.	City of Pompeii is founded.	Etruscans capture Rome.

	270 BCE	241 BCE	146 BCE	73 BCE	44 BCE	31 BCE	27 BCE
	Romans conquer all of Italian peninsula.	Rome defeats Carthage. Twenty years later, in 221 BCE, Hannibal begins his march on Rome. In 202 BCE, Hannibal is defeated.	Rome begins conquests of Greece and Asia Minor.	Slave revolt, led by Spartacus, threatens Rome.	End of Roman Republic. Julius Caesar is assassinated.	Roman armies conquer the Greek Kingdom of Egypt.	Caesar Augustus becomes the first emperor of Rome. Latin literature flourishes.

c. 2000 BCE	c. 1900 BCE	c. 1500 BCE		c. 1000 BCE		c. 600 BCE	c. 567 BCE
Indus Valley people teach Chinese how to cultivate rice.	Indus society in decline. Semi-nomadic Indo-Aryans begin moving into Indus Valley.	Indo-Aryans begin to settle on farms to raise cattle and dominate the river valley.		Indo-Aryan domination of Indus Valley ends.		A new society that practices Hinduism emerges in India.	Buddha (Siddhartha Gautama), founder of Buddhism, is born.

1766 BCE	1027 BCE			551 BCE	c. 500 BCE	221 BCE
Beginning of the Shang dynasty. Chinese develop a form of writing using drawings called *pictographs*.	The Shang dynasty is overthrown.			Confucius, founder of Confucianism, is born.	Metal coins are invented.	Qin Shi Huang Di unifies China. All existing walls throughout the Chinese kingdom are joined together and form the Great Wall.

509 BCE	490 BCE	431 BCE	399 BCE	c. 385 BCE	359 BCE	331 BCE	312 BCE
Roman Republic established. Nine years later, in 500 BCE, the Latins overthrow the Etruscans.	Persian wars begin when Persia invades Greece.	The Peloponnesian War between Athens and Sparta begins (lasts until 404 BCE).	Socrates is put to death in Athens.	Plato opens his school in the Academy at Athens.	Philip, king of Macedonia, attacks Greece.	Alexander the Great conquers Persia and declares himself king of Persia.	First highways and aqueducts are built in Roman Empire.

c. 3 BCE	79 CE	180 CE	313 CE	c. 395 CE	410 CE	476 CE
Jesus Christ is born.	Mount Vesuvius erupts and buries the city of Pompeii.	Height of the Roman Empire.	Christianity is officially accepted in Rome.	Roman Empire is officially divided into eastern and western sections.	Visigoths destroy Rome.	The Western Roman Empire ends and is divided into several small kingdoms.

ANCIENT GHANA AND MALI

	c. 400 CE	c. 1000	c. 1200
	Ancient Ghana is the most powerful kingdom in West Africa. Traders start to use camels instead of horses and oxen to cross the Sahara Desert.	Kumbi-Saleh, the largest city in ancient Ghana, has a population of between 15 000 and 30 000 people. Al-Bakri, a Moorish geographer, uses the accounts of others who have travelled to Africa to write about ancient Ghana.	Ancient Ghana can no longer sustain an economy based on agriculture. The kingdom of Mali takes over the gold mines to the south of Ghana and overtakes a weakened Ghana.

MAYA, AZTECS, AND INCAS

c. 2600 BCE	300 CE-900 CE	c. 500-1500	c. 1224	1325	1424	1430
Maya settle in Mexico and Central America.	Mayan culture at peak. Farmers are growing several vegetables including corn, beans, squash, tomatoes, pumpkins, sweet potatoes. Maya have a writing system of about 800 hieroglyphs.	Chimu live in northern Peru.	Maya abandon Chichén Itzá.	Aztecs begin to build the city of Tenochtitlán.	Aztec Empire begins.	Inca Empire begins.

THE MIDDLE AGES

570 CE	711	800	c. 1000	1066	1095	1192
Muhammad, messenger of Islam, is born.	Tariq ibn Ziyad defeats the Visigoths and sets up a Muslim state in Spain.	Charlemagne is crowned emperor of the Romans, or Holy Roman Emperor. The Vikings begin to look for new lands throughout Europe.	Leif Eriksson journeys along northeastern coast of North America.	William the Conqueror, from Normandy, France, invades England. Twenty years later, he takes the first census.	The First Crusade begins (and lasts until 1099).	Saladin and Richard the Lionhearted negotiate a resolution allowing Christians a safe passage to Jerusalem.

1312		c. 1324	c. 1330	c. 1400
Mansa Musa begins his reign in Mali.		Mansa Musa, the king of Mali, leaves on a *Hajj*. His generosity to lands he visits on his pilgrimage becomes legendary.	Architectural styles begin to change due to the designs by an architect who Mansa Musa brought back from Eygpt.	The Portuguese arrive in ancient Mali and overtake the kingdom.

1492	1493	1519	1521	1527	1532	1572
Columbus arrives in the Americas.	Topa Inca dies.	Spaniards arrive in Aztec Empire.	Cortés conquers and destroys Tenochtitlán and the Aztecs.	Civil war breaks out across Inca Empire.	Pizarro conquers the Incas.	Spaniards captured last Inca stronghold and kill Tupa Amaru, the last emperor of the Incas.

1212	1215	c. 1200	1279	1431	1453	1480
Almost 30 000 French and German children join a crusade to the holy lands to fight the Muslims.	King John I of England agrees to the demands in Magna Carta.	Genghis Khan rules the largest empire the world has ever known.	Kublai Khan is emperor of China.	Jeanne D'Arc (born 1412) is burned at the stake.	Fall of Constantinople, capital of Eastern Roman Empire.	Russian army, led by Ivan the Great, forces the Mongols to withdraw from Russia.

RENAISSANCE	1347-1350	c. 1350	1363	c. 1415	c. 1440-1450	c. 1449-1492	1492
	The Black Death reaches Europe and kills 20 million people.	The Renaissance begins. The Humanist movement is popular among the educated and wealthy.	To boost the workforce decimated by the Black Death, prisoners (Greeks, Russians, Slavs, Mongols) are allowed into Florence as slaves.	Prince Henry of Portugal starts the first school for navigators in Europe.	Gutenberg perfects his movable printing press.	Lorenzo de' Medici is one of the leading patrons of the arts in Italy, commissioning works from artists such as Leonardo da Vinci.	Christopher Columbus reaches San Salvador Island (West Indies).

REFORMATION	1453	1492	1500	1516	1517	1520	1521
	Ottoman Turks capture Constantinople and rename it Istanbul.	Spanish Jews are given the choice to convert to Christianity or leave Spain.	Ottomans have conquered Greece, Albania, Serbia, Bosnia, and Bulgaria.	Ottomans have conquered Egypt, Syria, and parts of Arabia.	Martin Luther publishes his Ninety-five Theses.	Suleiman the Magnificent becomes sultan of the Ottoman Empire (until 1566).	Martin Luther is denounced by the pope.

THE AGE OF REVOLUTIONS	1543	1609	1616	1632	1661	1665	1751
	Copernicus, a Polish astronomer, suggests the sun, not Earth, is the centre of the universe.	Galileo Galilei proves Copernicus's theory.	The Roman Catholic Church forbids anyone to teach that the sun is the centre of the universe.	Anthony van Leeuwenhoek improves the magnification of microscopes.	Louis XIV (1661-1715) takes absolute power in France.	Robert Hooke publishes *Micrographia*; the book includes never-before-seen closeups of insects and the human body. London is hit by a plague.	Denis Diderot begins to publish a multi-volume work titled *Encyclopedia*. The book is a showcase for Enlightenment thinkers.

INDUSTRY AND EMPIRE	1700s	c. 1760	1768	c. 1800	1806	1825	1829
	The slave trade helps to fuel the economies of countries in Europe.	The Agricultural Revolution and Industrial Revolution begin at about the same time in England.	Captain James Cook maps much of the Pacific Ocean for England.	Towns and cities throughout Europe are becoming overcrowded as people move from the countryside looking for work in the factories.	Britain seizes Cape of Good Hope from the Dutch.	A revolution is attempted in Russia. The first steam railway is built in Britain. Hot-air balloon rides are becoming the rage among the wealthy in France and England.	Restrictions on Roman Catholics are removed in Britain.

1497	1498	1499	1501	1519-1522	1533	1534
John Cabot lands in Newfoundland.	Vasco de Gama sails around the southern tip of Africa.	Amerigo Vespucci reaches South America.	Michelangelo completes his sculpture of *David*.	Magellan sails around the world.	Pope Clement VII refuses to declare Henry VIII's marriage to Catherine of Aragon invalid.	Jacques Cartier explores the Labrador coast and the St. Lawrence River.

1529	1534	1558	1562	1570	1572	1598	1604
The word *protestant* is used for the first time.	John Calvin, fearful of persecution because he is Protestant, leaves France and settles in Geneva, Switzerland.	Elizabeth I becomes queen of England. 10 000 books are burned in Venice because they have not been approved by the church.	Joseph Nasi helps negotiate peace between Poland and the Ottoman Empire.	Pope St. Pius IV declares Elizabeth I to be a heretic. In response, Elizabeth outlaws the Roman Catholic Church in England.	Thousands of French Protestants, called *Huguenots*, are killed in the St. Bartholomew's Day massacre in France.	Edict of Nantes grants religious freedom to the Huguenots. (In 1685, King Louis XIV revokes the Edict of Nantes.)	King James I, a Protestant, orders a new English translation of the Bible.

1756	1775	1776	1783	1789	1792	1793	1799
The Seven Years' War between France and England begins.	The American Revolution begins. American army invades Quebec and loses.	The thirteen colonies sign the Declaration of Independence.	England recognizes the independence of the United States of America. Five years later, in 1788, the United States adopts a new constitution.	George Washington becomes the first president of the United States. The French Revolution begins.	French revolutionaries abolish the monarchy. (Twelve years later, in 1804, Napoleon Bonaparte becomes emperor of France.)	The king of France, Louis XVI, is executed by revolutionaries. The Reign of Terror begins in France.	The French Revolution ends.

1830	1832	1833	1847	1850
Belgium wins its independence from Holland.	Men who pay a certain level of tax are given the right to vote in Britain.	England makes it illegal for children under the age of nine to work in textile factories.	Laws restrict working hours of women and children in textile mills to ten hours a day.	Workers in most industrial countries win the right to organize unions. Governments begin to get involved in local health and safety issues.

Glossary

abbesses Women who head communities of nuns.

abolition Cancellation of a law or rule.

absolution Church declaration of forgiveness of sins.

absolutism Rule by a monarch who seemingly has total power, such as Louis XIV of France.

acacia Type of tree or shrub. Many varieties of acacia have thorns. Acacia trees in Africa are useful for building shelters. The trees can grow in dry climates, because their roots go far into the ground.

adobe Sun-dried brick made from clay and straw.

agave Tropical American plant with thick fleshy leaves and tall flower stalks; sometimes called the *century plant*. Some agave plants are used to make soap, sisal (fibre), and alcoholic drinks.

alabaster Smooth, white, translucent stone that lets light shine through. Egyptians often used it in statues and buildings.

annul To end or cancel something, such as a marriage.

apprenticeship First stage in medieval guild system; period when a person begins to learn a craft or trade.

aqueduct Channel made of stone for carrying water to towns and cities. Sometimes, aqueducts ran high above ground on a series of great arches; sometimes they ran underground.

archaeologist Scientist who studies, describes, and interprets artifacts. Archaeologists carefully excavate (dig up) artifacts and other materials, documenting everything they find at the site and recording the exact location where each item was found. Later, archaeologists analyze the information in laboratories and write reports of their findings.

aristocracy Rule by a few people who inherit power; rule by the nobility.

artifacts Anything made by humans; for example, tools, pottery, or fabric. Archaeologists study artifacts to help them determine how peoples from the past lived.

atrium Central court of an ancient Roman house. The atrium was the social and religious centre of the home.

Augustus Roman adjective that means "majestic" or "dignified." This title was given to Octavius/Octavian, the grandnephew of Julius Caesar, and was used by all the Roman emperors who followed him.

autobiography Story of a person's life, written by that person.

berserkers In the 1st and 2nd centuries CE, the name for Norse or Viking warriors who fought fiercely. Today, *berserk* means someone in a wild fury.

Black Death Name given to the two types of plague that periodically killed millions of people in Europe and Asia. Bubonic plague was a bacterial infection causing painful swelling of areas in the armpit and groin. The pneumonic variety of plague affected the lungs. These epidemics reappeared at intervals for several centuries.

bodkin Large, blunt needle with a large eye, used to pierce cloth and draw tape or ribbon through cloth.

brazier Pan or stand (usually made of metal) for holding lighted coals and used for heating or cooking.

Buddhism Religion and philosophy founded by Siddhartha Gautama (known as the Buddha).

burgess 1 Citizen who represents the people and makes laws for them on a local council. **2** Member of parliament for a borough in Britain.

burgher 1 Town official. **2** Citizen, especially from the middle class, of a borough or town that has a charter from the local lord giving the town independence.

calabash Tree that produces large gourds; calabash also refers to the gourd.

caliph Title given to the chief ruler of a Muslim state. A caliph is chief of both government and religion.

calpulli 1 Cluster of homes and land jointly owned by an Aztec family. **2** Group of Aztec families descended from the same ancestor.

canopic jars Stone or ceramic containers used by Egyptians for burying the organs removed during mummification. This practice started about 2566 BCE and ended by about 570 BCE.

caravan Group of merchants or religious pilgrims that travels across Asian or North African deserts. People travel together for safety. By the 4th century CE, caravans used camels for transportation.

cartouche Long oval outline representing a coil of rope folded and tied at the end and enclosing part of the royal title of the pharaoh, written in a hieroglyph. It was intended for protection and cartouches found with mummies were also intended for protection. Tourists today can have their names written in a cartouche of gold or silver, but originally cartouches were only for royalty.

caste Social class. A caste system ranks people according to their occupation, family, or wealth.

cataract Large and steep waterfall, such as Niagara Falls or Victoria Falls.

cenote Very deep, water-filled, limestone cave, regarded as sacred by the Maya. The word *cenote* comes from the Maya word, *dzonot*.

census In ancient Rome, a census was a registration of citizens only, usually for tax purposes. The officials in charge were called *censors*. The modern meaning for *census* is an official count of the population of a country. We have a different meaning for *censor* today.

centurion Army officer in charge of a century (a Roman army unit of 60-80 men).

Christianity Religion based on the teachings of Jesus Christ; includes Roman Catholic, Protestant, and Orthodox church groups.

chuño Flour prepared from dried potatoes by the Incas.

circus Stadium in which chariot races were held. The track was oval-shaped. In ancient Rome, the biggest stadium was the Circus Maximus.

citadel High part of an ancient city, usually having a castle or fortress on top. People came to the citadel for safety during war. There are citadels in Quebec City and Halifax.

citizen In ancient times, a citizen was a male member of a particular city-state or society. Today, the term refers to all members of a nation.

city planners (also called *urban planners*) Refers to people who establish rules and map out possible districts for cities. The profession was begun during the Renaissance.

city-state Independent city and the surrounding area, with its own laws and government.

civil wars War between people of the same country, such as the American Civil War, or the Civil War in England, where royalists fought the people who supported parliament. Members of a family may be on opposite sides in a civil war.

coca leaf Leaf from a South American shrub; the Incas sometimes used the coca leaf as medicine.

cochineal Scarlet insects that live on cacti in Mexico; red dye is made from dried bodies of the female insect.

codices Plural of *codex*, an ancient manuscript in book form.

coke Concentrated carbon, a by-product of coal, that burns at high heat and is used for smelting iron to make steel.

colony Territory that another country (home country) claims to own. The home country has control of the colony's economy and its politics. Colonies often provided resources that the home country did not have. Canada was once a colony of Great Britain.

commodity Something of value that can be traded, especially a food crop or a raw material such as gold, salt, or wood.

common land Open land that was shared in common among all the people living on a manor during the Middle Ages. Common land was usually used as shared pasture.

compurgation System of justice used during the Middle Ages. A person accused of a crime could be cleared of wrongdoing if a number of people supported the oath of the accused that he/she was innocent. Compurgation was an alternative to trial by ordeal.

compurgators Those who supported the oath of the accused; character witnesses.

Confucianism Chinese philosophy and religion based on the teachings of Confucius.

conscript To order people to serve in an army in times of war. Canada had conscription in World War I.

conservatives People who resist great changes in politics and want to conserve as much of the past as they can. People in power are often conservative, because they think they will lose their privileges if there are political changes.

cowrie shells Small sea creature of the Indian Ocean; belongs to the same animal group as snails, slugs, and limpets. Some societies, such as China, used cowrie shells as money.

creationist Person who believes the theory that the universe and everything in it were specially created by divine guidance and are not the result of accident or evolution. This theory is called *creationism*.

culture Society's way of life, including its material culture (the things it makes), knowledge, values, institutions, and practices or ways of doing things. Culture is often identified by the art, religion, literature, music, and other creations of a society.

cuneiform Describes certain types of writing in wedge-shaped strokes that were pressed into a substance such as clay. The writing was usually done with a sharpened reed. Examples have been found in the remains of ancient civilizations in Mesopotamia.

deity God or divine being. The Romans used the Latin word *deus* to describe a god.

demesne Land held under the feudal system and worked by the owner to provide for his own household; usually the land adjacent to a manor house and kept by the lord for his own use.

democracy Means "rule by the people" and is usually said to have been invented by Athenians, but Athenian democracy did not include all people. Only male citizens of Athens were eligible to participate in Athenian government. Modern democracies usually allow all adult citizens to vote.

despotism Rule by a person or government that has absolute political control.

dictatorship Rule by a person who has absolute control on every area of life; often a dictator has suppressed a democratic government.

disciples Followers, or pupils; from the Latin word *discipuli*, which means "pupils."

divine right Belief that the ruler of a country has been chosen by God or, in ancient societies, gods. Many medieval kings and queens believed that they ruled by divine right and answered only to God.

dowry Property or money brought by a bride to her husband at the time of marriage.

dynasty Succession of rulers from one family with an ancestor in common. The ancient Chinese and the Egyptians were often ruled by dynasties.

embalm To treat a dead body with drugs and chemicals to keep it from decaying. Embalming preserved some bodies for centuries.

enclosure Fencing or enclosing of common lands during the Industrial Revolution. Common lands that were once used by all the people in the area became privately owned. Enclosure made it difficult for tenant farmers to find enough pasture for their animals, forcing most to move to the cities.

epic Long story of the adventures and achievements of an heroic person; for example, *The Epic of Gilgamesh*. As an adjective, *epic* means grand, heroic, and huge.

evidence Material (artifacts, written documents) that supports an argument. In history, evidence is usually taken from primary sources.

evolution 1 Theory that the earth and its lifeforms evolved over a period of time. **2** Any process of gradual change from a simple to a more complex form.

excommunication Sentence by which the Christian Church expels a person from the church and forbids any priest to give the person communion or any of the sacraments. Excommunication was a very serious punishment during the Middle Ages and Renaissance, because life revolved around the church. Excommunication was sometimes used to punish someone for writing or speaking against church practices (as in the Reformation) or to punish a ruler who disobeyed the pope's rulings.

famine Period of time when there is a severe scarcity of food in a particular area. Famines happened frequently in early societies that were unable to store extra food for years when crops were poor.

feldspar Group of very common minerals (the most common on Earth); most are colourless or pink. One use of feldspar is in the making of porcelain.

feudalism Medieval system of landholding in Europe based on the relationship between a lord and his superiors (often the king was at the top) and on duties and services to each other. All members of the system had some rights. Feudalism had its roots in the Roman Empire.

filial piety Great respect for one's parents and elders. This was part of the teachings of Confucius. Early Romans also cared for and obeyed their elders.

Forum Open space in the centre of Rome where markets, law courts, and political meetings were held. All Roman cities and towns had a forum.

garderobe Toilet in a castle. During medieval times, people sometimes hung expensive clothing in the garderobe to keep moths away.

gens In ancient Rome, a clan or related families who used the same name.

glazed faience *Faience* refers to decorated and glazed earthenware and porcelain; glazed faience is covered with opaque coloured glaze.

globalization Process of opening businesses worldwide rather than just in one country. Connects countries through business, politics, and culture.

glyph Symbol used for a word or sound in some written languages.

grid Network of regularly spaced lines, crossing each other at right angles, such as those on a sheet of graph paper; horizontal and vertical lines on a map used to help locate places.

griot Oral historian, poet, and storyteller in West Africa whose main job is to keep track of the tribe or village history. A position of griot is usually inherited.

groundnut Another name for peanut.

habeas corpus Writ or court order to determine if someone can be kept in prison before being charged with anything. It is an important part of the British tradition of law, because it means that people cannot be thrown into prison and kept there without a legal reason. *Habeas corpus* means "thou shalt have the body (in court)."

Hajj Pilgrimage to the Sacred Mosque at Mecca undertaken in the 12th month of the Muslim year. It is one of the sacred religious duties of Islam.

Hebrew Member of a Semitic group of people who lived in ancient Palestine and descended from Abraham, Isaac, and Jacob; an Israelite; a Jew. The offical language of Israel.

helots Spartan slaves who were bound to the land. *Helot* originally meant "captive," and helots had no legal rights. They greatly outnumbered the Spartans, and Spartans constantly had to put down slave revolts. Any helot attempt to escape was punished by death. A fixed proportion of the food helots raised fed Spartan citizens; without the helots, Spartans would not have been able to survive.

hieratic Cursive form of writing developed from hieroglyphs but simpler to learn and faster to write; always written from right to left. Originally, the script was used for everyday business. Later, the script was used by priests.

hieroglyphs Any of approximately 6000 characters of the ancient Egyptian writing system.

Hinduism Major religion of India. Hindus worship many deities, and their religion emphasizes the sacredness of all forms of life. The caste system is part of the Hindu religion.

humanists Philosophers who believe that humans should be responsible for solving their own problems, rather than expecting a divine being to do it for them. Many Renaissance thinkers were humanists.

hunters and gatherers People whose way of life is based on hunting wild animals and gathering wild plants and berries for food. Hunter-gatherers do not usually raise or grow their own food.

Ice Ages Times when regions of the earth were covered with glaciers. The most recent ice age to affect North America began to recede about 10 000 years ago.

inalienable rights Refers to rights that cannot be transferred or taken away.

Index Official list of books or sections of books prohibited by the Roman Catholic church. Members of the church were forbidden to read the books, because they were deemed morally undesirable or questioned church beliefs and practices.

indigenous "Native to" or "belonging to a certain area." Indigenous people are the original people of a region. First Nations people in Canada and Aborigines in Australia are indigenous. Plants can also be indigenous to a region.

internal combustion engine Engine powered by the explosion of gases or vapour with air in a cylinder. Our modern cars developed from this invention.

irrigate System of channels or streams passing through land, often with a sprinkler; used to supply water to farmlands.

Islam Religion established through the prophet Muhammad. Followers of Islam are called *Muslims*. May also be referred to as the Muslim religion.

jizyah Poll (per person) tax imposed by Islamic law on non-Muslim subjects in Muslim countries. When the Moors ruled in Spain, they imposed this tax on Christians and Jews. Historians comment that this was more humane than execution or torture.

joust Part of a medieval tournament where knights and men-at-arms fought on horseback with lances, at fairly close quarters. Jousts provided entertainment and gave knights an opportunity to practice their skills.

Judaism One of the world's major religions; followers of Judaism are called *Jews*.

karma In both Hinduism and Buddhism, the sum of a person's actions – especially intentional actions – in life. Karma is one way humans can attain union with the Supreme Being; determines a person's future in reincarnation.

kiln Oven for baking bricks or for firing pottery. Important clay tablets were baked in kilns so that the tablets would be preserved.

kohl Called *mesdemet*. Black paste made of water and powdered lead and applied around the eyes to make them look larger, to serve as a natural disinfectant, and to protect the eyes from the sun; may also have had religious symbolism. Kohl pencils were developed in Egypt during the Middle Kingdom.

kola (also spelled *cola*) Tree that grows in West Africa and produces nuts and seeds for a variety of uses. Cola drinks are flavoured with cola seeds.

land bridge Land that appears when sea levels fall, creating a way to travel across an area that was once under water. Scientists think that there was once a land bridge between Asia and Alaska, across what is now the Bering Strait.

legionnaire Soldier in the largest division of the Roman army. Each *legion* had its own standard, a silver eagle, which was carried into battle.

liberals People whose political views make them favour individual rights and freedoms, and free trade.

madder Climbing plant with rough stems and small yellowish flowers. Aztecs made reddish-purple dye from the roots.

Mandate of Heaven Belief that early Chinese rulers had been chosen by a god or gods; form of divine right.

manor In the feudal system, the house and estate given to a lord or knight in exchange for certain duties including providing troops for war.

mausoleum Huge and magnificent tomb for an important person, usually a king. Named after King Mausolus, a 4th-century BCE king of Halicarnassus (in what is now Turkey) who had an unusually splendid tomb. Qin Shi Huang Di, a Chinese emperor, also has an impressive mausoleum.

megalith Very large stone, especially one that is part of an ancient monument such as Stonehenge.

mêlée In medieval times, a battle fought hand-to-hand at close quarters. Now we use the word to mean a muddle or a lot of turmoil.

middle class Although the term is used in this textbook to describe social order in many of the societies, the middle class as we know it did not develop until the late Middle Ages. The middle class consisted of townspeople between the peasants and the nobility on the social scale.

millet Cereal grass usually grown in warm countries. Plants yield many fine grains about the size of sesame seeds.

milpa Method used by the Maya to clear land; trees and shrubs were cut down and burned. Neolithic farmers also used this method to clear land. This method, now called *slash and burn*, is still used in many parts of the world but is considered wasteful and harmful to the environment.

mob rule Situation where mobs of people take control, and decide what the rules will be in the situation, how the rules will be enforced, and who will suffer.

monsoon Wind that blows at certain times of the year in the Indian Ocean and southern Asia.

Moors Originally, natives of Mauretania, a region of North Africa now called Morocco and Algeria. Name was later applied to Muslim people of mixed Arab and Berber ancestry who conquered Spain during the 8th century CE.

mosaic Picture made of small cubes of stone or glass, cemented to a flat surface. The cubes were called *tessarae*. Romans had mosaics on walls, floors, and pool bottoms.

mummy Body of a human or animal that has been preserved with salt and spices, and wrapped in cloth (Egyptian style). Some mummies in South America were dried by exposure to sun or air.

myrrh Gum resin from trees similar to pine or spruce. Commonly used for perfume, medicine, and incense in the Middle East. The word comes from Sumer.

nationalists People committed to their country and who often put the interests of their country ahead of everything else. If the country is a colony, nationalists work for an independent country. *Nationalism* is loyalty and devotion to one's country and people.

nation-state Large group of people who are associated with each other because they may share common ancestors, history, language, and culture. They usually live in a particular area, sometimes called a *state*. France is a nation-state.

natron Natural compound found in Egypt and used for mummification. It was similar to baking soda and was also used by the Egyptians as soap and toothpaste.

nirvana In the Buddhist religion, nirvana is the state in which a person has reached freedom from suffering. The term is also used in Hinduism to describe the time when the soul is released from the body.

nomadic Way of life where people move from place to place to find pasture for their herds.

notary Person who has the authority to draw up and certify some types of legal documents.

Ñuchu plant Plant with bright red flowers found in Peru. Flowers give a pale red dye, which is used in dying wool.

obsidian Volcanic glass; a black stone formed when lava from a volcano cools. Obsidian was chipped to make an edge and then used for knives and spears by the Egyptians and the Aztecs.

oligarchy Government by the few, particularly if they govern for their own interests.

ophthalmology Study of the diseases of the eye. Egyptians seem to have had frequent eye infections, perhaps due to parasites and blowing sand. Many people who worked on the pyramids had eye injuries, and doctors were assigned to these workers to deal with the injuries.

Orthodox churches Group of churches that separated from the Western Christian church (headed by the pope in Rome) around the 11th century CE. Their leader was the patriarch in Constantinople (now Istanbul). The national churches of countries such as Russia, Greece, and Rumania are Orthodox churches.

pedagogue (originally spelled *paedagogus*) A man, often a Greek slave, who took Roman children to and from school and supervised their behaviour. Later, pedagogue was used to mean teacher.

pharaoh Title of ancient Egyptian rulers. A pharaoh was also considered a god (or goddess). The title, which originated during the New Kingdom, was *per-aa*, meaning "great house," and referred to the ruler's palace.

phoenix Mythical bird with magnificent plumage.

piazza Public square or marketplace, originally in an Italian town.

pictograph Pictorial symbol or sign that represents a word or a group of words.

pilgrimage Journey to a specific location taken for religious or sentimental reasons.

plantation Estate or large farm on which a cash crop such as cotton, tea, tobacco, or coffee is grown. Originally, plantation work was done by slaves. The term is commonly used in former British colonies and in the American South.

pope The title of the bishop of Rome who is the head of the Roman Catholic Church.

portcullis Strong gate made of wooden or iron bars and suspended by chains over the entrance to a castle. Vertical grooves down the side allowed the portcullis to slide into place very quickly.

praetor Important elected Roman government official. The word was later used to mean a judge or even a governor of a Roman province.

propaganda Organized program of publicity and information intended to persuade people to support a particular policy or government program. Propaganda gives only one side of an issue and may not be truthful.

protozoa Very small animal organism, usually microscopic in size.

purgatory Belief of the Roman Catholic Church. Place of temporary suffering or spiritual cleansing for the souls of those Christians who have died in God's grace.

Puritans Group of English Protestants who disagreed with the practices of the Church of England. Puritans wanted to get rid of all ceremonies and practices not specifically mentioned in the scriptures. They were most prominent in the late 16th and early 17th centuries CE; many moved to the Thirteen Colonies (now the United States). The word *puritan*, without a capital P, means any person who practices extreme strictness in religion and morals.

purveyor Businessperson who sells goods.

pyramid Four-sided stone structure used for religious ceremonies or as a tomb for important people. Egyptian pyramids had pointed tops; Sumerian and Central American pyramids had flat tops.

quetzal 1 Name given to several kinds of brightly coloured birds found in Central and South America. **2** The basic money unit of Guatemala.

quinine Bitter-tasting drug made from cinchona bark; used as a remedy for malaria and added to tonic water. Cinchona is a South American evergreen tree or shrub of the madder family.

quorum Number of people who must be present at a meeting to make the decisions at the meeting valid.

Quran Holy Book of Islam; also spelled Qur'an and Koran.

rabbi Jewish religious leader and teacher.

reaping machine Machine that harvests crops.

regent Person or group of people chosen to rule a kingdom or country on behalf of the ruler, who is unable to rule because of absence, illness, or age. Most regents rule because the king or queen is too young to do the job.

reincarnation Belief of Buddhists and some other East Indian religions that the soul can be reborn in a new body – either human of animal.

republic State where the political power is held by the people, and government positions are filled by representatives elected by the people.

revolution Huge change in the way that people think or the way that certain things are done. A revolution can involve radical changes in government, or it can be a complete change in something such as technology; for example, the communications revolution.

sacraments Religious ceremonies that give special spiritual grace or spiritual benefits to the people participating. In Christianity, a sacrament may be a ceremony such as baptism, marriage, or communion.

sagas Old Norse stories that tell of great deeds of heroes or of the history of families; form of oral history.

sarcophagus Refers to the outer stone container that held one or more Egyptian coffins. The coffin and sarcophagus were intended to protect the body but actually led to the deterioration of the body. *Sarcophagus* means "flesh-eating."

savannah Open, grassy plain with few or no trees in a tropical or subtropical region.

scribe Person whose job is to write for someone else. In ancient times, few people could read and write, so scribes were hired to write letters and documents for others.

seal Engraved stamp of metal or other hard material used to make an impression on wax or paper. Included figures of animals or symbols of deities. Some seals may have been used as bottle stoppers.

self-government The right of a group of people, especially members of a colony, to form and control their own government.

selion Narrow strip of land between two furrows, used in the feudal system to divide an open field among a number of tenants who were usually serfs.

serape Shawl or blanket worn as a cloak, especially in Mexico and Central America.

serf Person who is not allowed to leave the land on which he or she works, without permission of the manor lord.

shaduf Irrigation tool made of a long wooden pole with a pail (or other water container) at one end and a weight at the other. It was used to take water from a river or canal to water crops.

shaman Medicine man or priest believed to have the ability to influence spirits for good or evil.

Sharia Name of the Islamic code of religious law. It is based on the Quran and the traditional sayings of Muhammad.

Silk Road Name given, about 100 years ago, to the ancient caravan route used by traders going to China (and India) to bring silk and other exotic trade goods back to the West. The Silk Road traditionally began in Xian and ended in the Eastern Mediterranean. The route was begun in Roman times and covered some 6400 kilometres. It was also the route used to spread Christianity to the East.

sistra (sing. *sistrum*) Rattling musical instruments of ancient Egypt. They were usually played by women, except when the pharaoh was making offerings to the goddess Hathor.

socialists People who support a political and economic theory that says the community as a whole should own and control land, resources, and business of the area.

sorghum Cereal grass similar to maize; grown in Africa and southern India. Guinea corn is a variety of sorghum. Often used as animal feed and is also made into syrup.

steatite Type of soapstone or talc; easy to carve.

stela Upright slab or pillar of stone that usually has a commemorative inscription or sculptured design on it. Stelae often serve as gravestones.

stola Long dress worn by women in ancient Rome. It was belted at the waist and could be plain or decorated with embroidery. Women often wore a cloak called a *palla* over the stola.

strike Refusal of a group of employees to work until a particular work-related grievance has been remedied.

stylus Sharp, pointed reed or stick used for making marks in clay or wax tablets. The stylus was used for writing in Mesopotamia, Greece, and Rome.

Talmud Book of Jewish law.

terra cotta Unglazed earthenware (usually reddish-brown but can be other colours) used as an ornamental building material or in flowerpots.

theses (sing. *thesis*) Propositions or statements that have yet to be proved. Martin Luther produced 95 theses that questioned the practices of the Roman Catholic Church.

toga virilis White woollen robe worn by Roman citizens. The toga was a large circular piece of cloth and had to be folded in a special way. The *toga virilis* was the toga young boys put on to signify that they had reached adulthood.

totem **1** Emblem, badge, or symbol. **2** (In North America) The emblem or symbol of First Nations family; often a plant or an animal, such as the bear or the turtle.

treason Serious crime by a citizen who breaks the oath of allegiance (loyalty) to the ruler or the government of the citizen's country. Treason may take the form of plotting or trying to overthrow the government or killing the ruler.

trepanning Operating on a person by drilling a hole in the skull, often to relieve pressure on the brain. Several ancient cultures seem to have used this procedure.

tribune **1** Someone who was elected to represent the interests of the common people of ancient Rome. **2** Rank in the Roman army.

tundra Vast Arctic region that is nearly level; usually treeless and marshy.

tyranny Rule by an absolute ruler who has no concern for the rights or welfare of the people.

unguent Soft substance such as a perfumed oil, used as an ointment.

universal suffrage Suffrage is the right to vote. In early days, only certain people could vote, so others campaigned for "universal" suffrage, or votes for all adults of a country. Most industrialized countries have universal suffrage.

untouchables Hindus who do not belong to an hereditary caste. Untouchables do such jobs as street cleaning, and members of higher castes are not supposed to touch them.

urban planning See *city planning*.

urbanization Process of developing more cities in rural areas. Countries such as Canada have more and more people moving to cities.

Vedas Most-ancient Hindu scriptures.

vizier Pharaoh's chief minister; he was in charge of almost all areas of government and reported directly to the pharaoh. The vizier was responsible for building the pharaoh's pyramid.

wu In early Chinese society, this was a name given to a sorcerer – a person claiming magic powers.

zebu Humped ox found in India, East Asia, and Africa. The zebu is suited to hot, damp climates, because it secretes an oily, smelly substance that repels ticks and other insects. The zebu is regarded as sacred by Hindus.

Index

Illustration Credits

1.2 © Parks Canada/A. Cornellier/H.07.70.06.09 (224); 1.3 The New York Public Library/Art Resource, NY; 1.4 © The Manitoba Museum; 1.5 The Waterways Trust/British Waterways Archive; 1.6 #93.049P/3147 N [Christmas Cheer, ca. 1912] The United Church of Canada/Victoria University Archives, Toronto; 1.7 National Gallery of Canada, Ottawa; 1.8 Victoria & Albert Museum, London/Art Resource, NY; 1.10 © Canadian Museum of Civilization, photo Harry Foster, 1977, no.77-26; 1.11 Robert Barrow; 1.12 © Francis G. Mayer/CORBIS; 1.13 © Angelo Cavalli/SuperStock; 1.14 With permission of the Department of Canadian Heritage; 1.15 Raymond Wiest; 1.18 W.S.A. Beal.

2.2 Sid Kroker; 2.9 © Bettmann/CORBIS; 2.12 © Stephanie Maze/CORBIS; 2.14 © Peter Johnson/CORBIS; 2.17 © Adam Woolfitt/CORBIS; 2.18 Joan & Bob Hambly; 2.19 © Charles & Josette Lenars/CORBIS; 2.20 Réunion des Musées Nationaux/Art Resource, NY; pp. 46-47 (lamp) Réunion des Musées Nationaux/Art Resource, NY; (harpoons) Giraudon/Art Resource, NY; (flute) Réunion des Musées Nationaux/Art Resource, NY; (bracelet) akg-images/ Herbert Kraft; 2.21 Kenneth Garrett/National Geographic Society Image Collection; 2.22 © Chris Lisle/CORBIS.

3.1 © British Museum/HIP/Art Resource, NY; 3.3 © British Museum/ HIP/Art Resource, NY; 3.6 Erich Lessing/Art Resource, NY; 3.8 Left: Courtesy of the Trustees of the British Museum, Right: Erich Lessing/Art Resource, NY; 3.10-3.11 Erich Lessing/Art Resource, NY; 3.15-3.17 Erich Lessing/Art Resource, NY; 3.18 Scala/Art Resource, NY; 3.19 Erich Lessing/Art Resource, NY; 3.20 akg-images.

4.1 akg-images/Dr. E. Strouhal; 4.3 © Roger Wood/CORBIS; 4.4 Gary Evans; 4.5 akg-images/Andrea Jemolo; 4.6 © Kurt Scholz/ SuperStock; 4.7 Giraudon/Art Resource, NY; 4.8 Werner Forman/Art Resource, NY; 4.9-4.10 Erich Lessing/Art Resource, NY; 4.11 © Explorer Paris/SuperStock; 4.13 Réunion des Musées Nationaux, Paris; 4.16 © Sandro Vannini/CORBIS; 4.17 Scala/Art Resource, NY; 4.18 Gary Evans; 4.20 Egyptian National Museum, Cairo, Egypt/Bridgeman Art Library; 4.21-4.22 Photography by Egyptian Expedition, The Metropolitan Museum of Art.

5.2 Copyright J.M. Kenoyer, Courtesy Dept. of Archaeology and Museums, Govt. of Pakistan; 5.5 Bridgeman Art Library; 5.6 © Galen Rowell/CORBIS; 5.7 Bridgeman Art Library; 5.8 Copyright J.M. Kenoyer, Courtesy Dept. of Archaeology and Museums, Govt. of Pakistan; 5.9 © Angelo Hornak/CORBIS; 5.10 Liverpool Museum, Merseyside, UK/Bridgeman Art Library; 5.11 Copyright J.M. Kenoyer, Courtesy Dept. of Archaeology and Museums, Govt. of Pakistan; 5.12 National Museum of India, New Delhi, India/Bridgeman Art Library; 5.13 Scala/Art Resource, NY; 5.14 National Museum of India, New Delhi, India/ Bridgeman Art Library; 5.15 Scala/Art Resource, NY; 5.16 © Brian A. Vikander/CORBIS; 5.17 National Museum of India, New Delhi, India/ Bridgeman Art Library.

6.1 © Keren Su/CORBIS; 6.3 Lowell Georgia/National Geographic Society Image Collection; 6.5 O. Louis Mazzatenta/National Geographic Society Image Collection; 6.6 © Royal Ontario Museum/ CORBIS; 6.8 Réunion des Musées Nationaux/Art Resource, NY; 6.14 © Asian Art & Archaeology, Inc./CORBIS; 6.16 O. Louis Mazzatenta/ National Geographic Society Image Collection; 6.18-6.19 O. Louis Mazzatenta/National Geographic Society Image Collection; 6.20 © Dean Conger/CORBIS; 6.21 akg-images/Laurent Lecat; 6.22 O. Louis Mazzatenta/National Geographic Society Image Collection; 6.24 © SuperStock, Inc./SuperStock; 6.25 Werner Forman/Art Resource, NY; 6.26 akg-images.

7.1 akg-images; 7.4 akg-images; 7.6 akg-images/Peter Connolly; 7.7 The Granger Collection, New York; 7.8 © Bettmann/CORBIS; 7.9 Courtesy of the Trustees of the British Museum; 7.10 Scala/Art Resource, NY; 7.11 akg-images/Peter Connolly; 7.13 akg-images; 7.14 Erich Lessing/Art Resource, NY; 7.15 With permission of the Royal Ontario Museum © ROM; 7.16 akg-images; 7.17 akg-images/Andrea Baguzzi; 7.18 Réunion des Musées Nationaux/Art Resource, NY; 7.19 Scala/Art Resource, NY; 7.20 Martin Von Wagner Museum der Universität Wirzburg, Photo: K. Oehrlein; 7.22 © Araldo de Luca/CORBIS; 7.23 Réunion des Musées Nationaux/Art Resource, NY; 7.24 Erich Lessing/Art Resource, NY.

8.2 akg-images; 8.3 Alinari/Art Resource, NY; 8.4 Scala/Art Resource, NY; 8.5 akg-images; 8.7 akg-images; 8.8 Alinari/Art Resource, NY; 8.9 © Bettmann/CORBIS; 8.11 The Granger Collection, New York; 8.13 Erich Lessing/Art Resource, NY; 8.14 © Bettmann/CORBIS; 8.15-8.16 Scala/Art Resource, NY; 8.18 akg-images; 8.19 Vanni/Art Resource, NY; 8.20 Scala/Art Resource, NY; 8.21 Bridgeman Art Library; 8.22 © Patrick Ward/CORBIS; 8.23 © Archivo Iconografico, S.A./CORBIS; 8.24 Scala/Art Resource, NY; 8.25 © Gérard Degeorge/ CORBIS; 8.27 The Granger Collection, New York; 8.28 By Permission of the British Library; 8.29 © Francesco Venturi/CORBIS; 8.31 akg-images; 8.32 Archives Charmet/Bridgeman Art Library; 8.33 akg-images; 8.34 Erich Lessing/Art Resource, NY.

9.4 © Yann Arthus-Bertrand/CORBIS; 9.5 © Nik Wheeler/CORBIS; 9.6 Courtesy of the Trustees of the British Museum; 9.9 © Nik Wheeler/ CORBIS; 9.10 © Robert van der Hilst/CORBIS; 9.11 © Nik Wheeler/ CORBIS; 9.12 © British Library/HIP/Art Resource, NY; 9.13 The Stapleton Collection, UK/Bridgeman Art Library; 9.15 Bibliothèque Nationale, Paris.

10.1 Top left: Robert Harding World Imagery/Getty Images, Top right: © Dave Bartruff/CORBIS, Bottom: Photographer's Choice/ Getty Images; 10.4 Lonely Planet Images/Getty Images; p. 200 (Quetzal bird) © Anthony Merceica/ SuperStock; 10.6 Peabody Museum, Harvard University, Photo 50-63-20/018487 T738; 10.11 © Charles & Josette Lenars/CORBIS; 10.12 Bridgeman Art Library; 10.14 The Granger Collection, New York; 10.15 Image # 326597 American Museum of Natural History Library; 10.16-10.17 The Granger Collection, New York; 10.19 Scala/Art Resource, NY; 10.20 akg-images; 10.22 Library of Congress, Washington, D.C., USA/ Bridgeman Art Library; 10.23 The Granger Collection, New York; 10.24 © Holton Collection/SuperStock; 10.25-10.26 The Granger Collection, New York; 10.27 © Charles & Josette Lenars/CORBIS; 10.28 Top: © Galen Rowell/CORBIS, Bottom: © Michael Freeman/ CORBIS; 10.29 © Steve Vidler/SuperStock.

11.6 © Austrian Archives/CORBIS; 11.7 Bridgeman Art Library; 11.10 The Pierpoint Morgan Library/Art Resource, NY; 11.11 Bridgeman Art Library; 11.12 Scala/Art Resource, NY; 11.13 © Bettmann/ CORBIS; 11.16 Bibliothèque Nationale, Paris; 11.17 © Bettmann/ CORBIS; 11.18 Scala/Art Resource, NY; 11.19 The Granger Collection, New York; 11.20 Snark/Art Resource, NY; 11.21 Giraudon/Art Resource, NY; 11.22 Scala/Art Resource, NY; 11.23 Masters and Fellows of Trinity College, Cambridge; 11.26-11.27 Scala/Art Resource, NY; 11.28 Réunion des Musées Nationaux/Art Resource, NY; 11.34 © The Stapleton Collection/CORBIS; 11.35 The Granger Collection, New York.

12.1 Scala/Art Resource, NY; 12.3 Left and centre: Réunion des Musées Nationaux/Art Resource, NY, Right: Giraudon/Art Resource, NY; 12.5 Bildarchiv Preussischer Kulturbesitz/Art Resource, NY; 12.6 Scala/Art Resource, NY; 12.7 Giraudon/Art Resource, NY; 12.8-12.11 Scala/Art Resource, NY; 12.13-12.14 Scala/Art Resource, NY; 12.15 Erich Lessing/Art Resource, NY; 12.16 Scala/Art Resource, NY; 12.17 Bridgeman Art Library; 12.18-12.19 Scala/Art Resource, NY; 12.20 Erich Lessing/Art Resource, NY; 12.21-12.22 Scala/Art Resource, NY; 12.23 The Granger Collection, New York; 12.24 Scala/Art Resource, NY.

13.2 Snark/Art Resource, NY; 13.3 © Sotheby's/akg-images; 13.4 Réunion des Musées Nationaux/Art Resource, NY; 13.5 Scala/Art Resource, NY; 13.6 akg-images; 13.7 Bridgeman Art Library; 13.8 Mauro Magliani/SuperStock; 13.9 Foto Marburg/Art Resource, NY; 13.10 Bridgeman Art Library; 13.11 Art Resource, NY; 13.12 Victoria & Albert Museum, London, UK/Bridgeman Art Library 13.13 Scala/Art Resource, NY; 13.14 The Stapleton Collection/Bridgeman Art Library; 13.15 akg-images; 13.16 Foto Marburg/Art Resource, NY; 13.18 akg-images; 13.19 Erich Lessing/Art Resource, NY; 13.20-13.21 akg-images; 13.22 © The Trustees of the Chester Beatty Library, Dublin; 13.23 Foto Marburg/Art Resource, NY; 13.25 The Stapleton Collection, UK/Bridgeman Art Library; 13.26 British Museum/Bridgeman Art Library; 13.27 The Granger Collection, New York; 13.28 Giraudon/ Bridgeman Art Library.

14.2 Image Select/Art Resource, NY; 14.3 Erich Lessing/Art Resource, NY; 14.4 © British Museum/HIP/Art Resource, NY; 14.5 © Stefano Bianchetti/CORBIS; 14.6 © akg-images/Johann Brandste; 14.7 The Wellcome Trust Medical Photographic Library; 14.8 © Ann Ronan Picture Library/HIP/Art Resource, NY; 14.9 © The Royal Society; 14.10-14.11 akg-images; 14.12 Left: © Sotheby's/akg-images, Centre: Erich Lessing/Art Resource, NY, Right: © Archivo Iconografico, S.A./CORBIS; 14.13 The Wellcome Trust Medical Photographic Library; 14.14 The Granger Collection, New York; 14.15 Art Resource, NY; 14.16-14.17 akg-images; 14.18 Réunion des Musées Nationaux/Art Resource, NY; 14.19 Art Resource, NY; 14.21 © Francis G. Mayer/CORBIS; 14.22 akg-images; 14.23 Art Resource, NY; 14.24 Musée de la Ville de Paris, Musée Carnavalet, Paris, France/Bridgeman Art Library; 14.25 Réunion des Musées Nationaux/Art Resource, NY; 14.27 Réunion des Musées Nationaux/Art Resource, NY; 14.29 Snark/Art Resource, NY; 14.30 © British Library/HIP/Art Resource, NY.

15.1 The Granger Collection, New York; 15.3 © Science Museum Library/Science and Society Picture Library; 15.4 © Science Museum Pictorial/Science and Society Picture Library; 15.5 akg-images; 15.6 The Granger Collection, New York; 15.7 The Stapleton Collection/Bridgeman Art Library; 15.8 Time Life Pictures/Getty Images; 15.9 akg-images; 15.10 Getty Images; 15.11 The Granger Collection, New York; 15.12 Getty Images; 15.13-15.14 The Granger Collection, New York; 15.15 © Science Museum Pictorial/Science and Society Picture Library; 15.16-15.17 The Granger Collection, New York; 15.18 © Guildhall Library, London/HIP/Art Resource, NY; 15.19 © Leonard de Selva/CORBIS; 15.20 Snark/Art Resource, NY; 15.21 Time Life Pictures/Getty Images; 15.23 Getty Images; 15.24 © CORBIS; 15.25 © Science Museum Pictorial/Science and Society Picture Library.